THE MOST DANGEROUS BRANCH

THE MOST DANGEROUS BRANCH

Inside the Supreme Court
in the Age of Trump

David A. Kaplan

B\D\W\Y
BROADWAY BOOKS
NEW YORK

Library of Congress Cataloging-in-Publication Data
Names: Kaplan, David A.
Title: The most dangerous branch : inside the Supreme Court in the age of Trump /
    David A. Kaplan.
Description: New York : Crown, 2018. | Includes bibliographical references and
    index.
Identifiers: LCCN 2018004533 | ISBN 9781524759902 (hardback) |
    ISBN 9781524759919 (paperback) | ISBN 9781524759926 (ebook)
Subjects: LCSH: Judicial corruption—United States. | Judicial ethics—United
    States. | Political questions and judicial power—United States. | United States.
    Supreme Court—Officials and employees | Constitutional law—United States. |
    BISAC: POLITICAL SCIENCE / Government / Judicial Branch. | LAW /
    Courts. | LAW / Constitutional.
Classification: LCC KF8779 .K37 2018 | DDC 347.73/26—dc23
LC record available at https://lccn.loc.gov/2018004533

Printed in the United States of America

Book design by Andrea Lau

9 8 7 6 5 4 3 2 1

First Paperback Edition

In memory of my grandfather, Adolph Fox (1887–1980)

"Whoever attentively considers the different departments of power must perceive that in a government in which they are separated from each other, the judiciary . . . will always be the least dangerous to the political rights of the Constitution. . . . The Executive not only dispenses the honors, but holds the sword. The legislature not only commands the purse, but prescribes the rules. . . . The judiciary may truly be said to have neither force nor will, but merely judgment."

—*Alexander Hamilton, Federalist No. 78 (1788)*

"If you have five votes here, you can do anything."

—*Justice William J. Brennan Jr.*
(many times, typically while brandishing
a wide wry smile and the fingers
on his left hand)

CONTENTS

PART II
CASES

THE END OF THE WORLD AS THEY KNEW IT

June 27, 2018, Washington trembled.

on before noon, after the U.S. Supreme Court issued its last two
of the 2017–18 term, Justice Anthony M. Kennedy arose from
h, turned away from the audience, and left as always through
te exit in the back of the great courtroom. After three decades,
be the last time he did so. He walked down the hallway to his
ent chambers, reviewed the one-page letter he had considered
all year, and then proceeded with his bodyguards to a wait-
/ that would take him two miles down Constitution Avenue
val Office. Kennedy apprised the other justices of what he was
nly minutes before he headed out the door. Almost nobody at the
House knew he was coming.

ere, Kennedy was hurriedly escorted through a side entrance,
n a little-used corridor, and brought to the upstairs residence, the
ter not to be seen by the press elsewhere in the building. The presi-
ent, Donald Trump, had just been informed that a justice was on his
vay to see him. Kennedy's name wasn't on the morning schedule and
Trump had only surmised it was him, given the rumors about Ken-

nedy's remaining time on the Court. No student of the Court, let alone American history, Trump could not have known how unusual it was for a justice to show up unannounced—and to do what Kennedy was about to do. Yet such a stunt was altogether Kennedyesque. Other justices declared they were retiring by having a law clerk deliver a letter to the White House. The matter-of-fact David H. Souter sent in his retirement by fax. With Kennedy, there was little wonder that he didn't arrive in an ermine-trimmed cloak.

Kennedy, 81, brought with him the letter, which he handed to Trump. "My dear Mr. President," Kennedy wrote. "Please permit me by this letter to express my profound gratitude for having had the privilege to seek in each case how best to know, interpret, and defend the Constitution and the laws that must always conform to its mandates and promises." He modestly left out that in a lot of those cases he was the key vote. Sometimes he was with the four liberal justices; often he was with the four most conservative justices.

He wrote the 2015 ruling that made same-sex marriage a constitu-tional right, and he had been the Court's voice for gay rights for a gen-eration. He voted to uphold *Roe v. Wade*, the 1973 decision that blocked states from banning abortion. In the last decade alone, he with the liberals more than 50 times to make a narrow majority also was the vote that broadened gun rights under the Second ment, gutted the Voting Rights Act of 1965, and cut back on ca finance limits. As the swing justice, truly in the middle, Kenne tively *was* the Court. His power had nothing to do with the wi his views or his skill at attracting allies—only that he lucked o the fulcrum.

The president recognized he was getting the opportunity to the Court—and to push it decisively to the right. His nomina Neil M. Gorsuch the year before, to succeed Justice Antonin Scali ted nothing: It was mostly a one-for-one ideological swap of cons tives. Kennedy's departure represented something else entirely. Replac him with a diehard conservative meant 5-to-4 decisions that occasional tilted left—like preserving abortion rights, creating gay rights, allowing affirmative action, restricting capital punishment, and maintaining the authority of federal agencies like the EPA and the SEC—could go in the opposite direction. For movement conservatives, mostly Republicans, reversing *Roe* had been the great grail. For nearly half a century, one justice after another—Sandra Day O'Connor, David Souter, Anthony Kennedy—had foiled the Republican presidents who appointed them, by failing to abandon *Roe*. That now seemed within reach. For liberals, it was the end of the world as they knew it at the Supreme Court.

Trump and Kennedy made small talk for half an hour. The president asked if Kennedy "had certain people" that he "had great respect for" who "potentially could take his seat"—"a very hard seat to fill," as Trump subsequently described it. Given that two of Kennedy's former law clerks were strong contenders to replace him, Kennedy was understandably noncommittal.

That evening, the president could hardly contain his glee at the opportunity Kennedy had handed him: a second Court appointment in his first 18 months in office; another trophy to flaunt to his base; the chance to turn the Court into the most radical in modern history. Kennedy's retirement, one commentator wrote, was "the most consequential event in American jurisprudence at least since *Bush v. Gore* in 2000 and probably since *Roe*." At a rally in North Dakota, Trump described Kennedy as "a very special guy" and praised his "great legacy"—even though Kennedy's jurisprudence, on such matters as abortion, was frequently anathema to the extremist views of Trump's supporters. But the most important part of Kennedy's legacy, of course, was that he chose to skip town for good while Trump was in office, and to do so before the midterm elections that might end GOP control of the Senate. For, as Trump had explained at the rally, only he'd name a justice who wouldn't "erase your borders, throw open the jailhouse doors and destroy your freedoms"—and a justice who could serve "40 years, 45 years!" He apparently believed his nominee might be barely 40, or might live to 100. Chanting "USA! USA!" the crowd of 6,000 went wild.

The stakes were indeed high. For decades now, the Court has been central in American life. It is the nine justices who decide so many of the controversial issues of our time. More than Congress, sometimes more than the president, it is the Court that holds sway. That was why so many voters in the 2016 Trump-Clinton election made their choice based on whom they thought their candidate would appoint to the Court—as if the Court was just another political prize. Is that really how democracy was supposed to work? Kennedy's retirement—and the storm that followed it—underscored just how distorted the Court's role had become. The sky may actually be falling this time. But part of the reason is that we've come to accept the enrobed justices as our own Jedi High Council: *Help us, Obi-Wan, you're our only hope.* They are not.

The abasement of the current Court will likely culminate with the confirmation of Brett M. Kavanaugh, a 53-year-old devoted conservative, to replace Kennedy, giving the right flank of the Court resolute control. But the judicial revolution began more than two years earlier, when Justice Antonin Scalia died, unexpectedly and mysteriously, on a hunting vacation in Texas. That's where the tale of today's Supreme Court—the Trump Court—begins.

DEATH AT THE RANCH

If you're going to die, the Cíbolo Creek Ranch in West Texas is a bucolic place to do it. So it was on Saturday, February 13, 2016, for 79-year-old Antonin Scalia, the 103rd justice of the U.S. Supreme Court.

Silhouetted by the Chinati Range of the high Chihuahuan Desert, far from the din of Dallas, the 30,000-acre luxury resort is an oasis of tranquility. In this strange land of the Big Bend, the skies are vast, the people are few, and the rush of tumbleweed is ever-present. Native American legend has it that this is where the Great Spirit deposited any leftover rocks after He created Earth. The sun-baked Big Bend is "where the rainbows wait for the rain," according to Mexican cowboy poetry.

Cíbolo Creek Ranch itself has room for only 36 guests at a time. They stay in a compound of restored adobe forts that date to the pioneer days of 1857. For roughly $400 a night, guests can hike, bike, stargaze, and enjoy such signature Texas cuisine as Squab Jalisco Style in the antique-filled dining hall. Mick Jagger and Julia Roberts have visited. Parts of "No Country for Old Men" and "There Will Be Blood" were filmed there. *Vogue* did a photo spread. But many guests really come to hunt on remote areas of the property. There are elk, deer, pheasant, chukar, and white-winged doves. Scalia came to hunt blue quail, bringing along his new double-barreled shotgun.

He was a serious gun aficionado. Not only had he written the majority opinion in *District of Columbia v. Heller*—the Supreme Court's watershed 2008 ruling declaring for the first time that the Second Amendment protected an individual's right to bear arms, which he regarded as among his finest decisions. Scalia, the doctrinaire Reagan-appointed conservative, had also taught Justice Elena Kagan, the Obama-appointed liberal, how to shoot. When Kagan made the usual informal courtesy calls to senators after she was nominated, she was asked her views on the Second Amendment more than on any other topic. She declined to answer, as any nominee would have. Senators then asked if she'd ever gone hunting or even held a gun. She replied she had not; after all, she grew up on Manhattan's Upper West Side, where, as she put it, "that's not really what you do." Finally, after the umpteenth time she was asked the question, she responded in one meeting, "You know, Senator, if you were to invite me hunting, I would really love to go." Describing the episode three years later, Kagan said a "look of abject horror passed over his face." She beat a graceful retreat. "But I'll tell you what," she said. "If I am lucky enough to be confirmed, I will ask Justice Scalia to take me hunting."

Once on the Court, Kagan quickly sought Scalia out and told him, "This is the only promise I made during my entire confirmation proceedings, so you have to help me fulfill it." She said Scalia found the whole thing "hilarious—a total crackup." And he did take her hunting several times—usually for birds, but on a three-day summer trip to Wyoming, Kagan proudly recalled, "I shot myself a deer!" (Still, becoming an occasional hunter did not make her interpret the Second Amendment sympathetically—although she wasn't on the Court when *Heller* was decided. On one of her first trips with Scalia, to rural Virginia, another hunter asked her—after she had bagged two pheasants—if she was having a good time. "Oh, yes!" she said. The hunter wanted to know if she thought the experience would change her views on the Second Amendment. "Oh, no!" she said.)

Though Scalia grew up in the wilds of Elmhurst, Queens, he traced his love of hunting to his childhood there. "My uncle Frank had a large vegetable garden," he reminisced in 2013, "and my grandfather would sit on the back porch of this bungalow . . . and would wait for the rabbits to come to him. *Boom!* He would shoot them there." On his subway ride to private high school in Manhattan, Scalia carried a rifle for drill practice. At the Supreme Court, the centerpiece of his personal office was the mounted head of a Rocky Mountain buck he shot in 2003 from 460 yards away. "Meet Leroy!" he would tell visitors (though he never explained the origin of the name).

Scalia's visit to Cíbolo Creek was set up by his longtime friend C. Allen Foster, a trial lawyer in Washington, D.C. The two had been hunting buddies for 30 years. The ranch was owned by John Poindexter, a Houston-born multimillionaire, conservationist, and decorated Vietnam veteran. Scalia, Foster and 34 others arrived at the ranch at noon on Friday—all as Poindexter's personal guests for the weekend. Scalia's only expense was airfare—a Southwest flight from Washington to Houston and his share of a small chartered prop plane to Cíbolo's private airstrip. On the way, he was in fine spirits, reading Court briefs and listening to Mozart on headphones. On the 737 to Texas, Scalia—seated on the aisle with a 6-feet-8, 300-pound traveler between him and Foster—reached over to Foster and cracked, "Look, it's King Kong!"

Foster and Poindexter were prominent names in the world of hunting, part of the leadership of the International Order of St. Hubertus, a hunting fraternity founded in the 17th century by the Hapsburg count Franz Anton von Sporck. With nearly 900 members worldwide, the fraternity's motto, without any apparent irony, was *Deum Diligite Animalia Diligentes* ("Honoring God by Honoring His Creatures"). Scalia had turned down the chance to be a knight of the order, perhaps due to cost. It wasn't expensive to join, but members were expected to participate in several annual activities that could cost thousands of dollars apiece. As Scalia liked to say, it's tough to raise nine children on a government worker's salary. Despite not being a member, Scalia's connection to the Order of St. Hubertus generated media interest. An investigative piece by the *Washington Post* 11 days after his death detailed that "Scalia spent his last hours with members of this secretive society of elite

hunters." The article was in keeping with other breathless coverage of his
demise—the kind more readily expected on the death of a head of state.

At the ranch, Scalia and Foster and a few other guests took in a full
afternoon in the field. "Don't call me Justice Scalia," he told the others.
"I'm 'Nino.'" Although he'd never hunted blue quail, he held court on
the best way to bag one as they drove along in a Humvee. His compan-
ions seemed to know the routine: He talked, they listened, everybody
laughed. Scalia loved to be the center of attention, but he also understood himself. He'd been raised an only child—and that, he sometimes
explained to friends, was "why I am the way I am." It was a marvelous
day, and Scalia did bag a bird.

At dinner, the group enjoyed medallions of beef, as well as conversation that stretched into the night. For most of the evening, Scalia chatted with Poindexter's 37-year-old girlfriend, Veronika Liskova, about
families, religion, the history of the Hagia Sophia in Istanbul, and the
quietude of St. Peter's Basilica at sunrise. At 9, Scalia got up—he was
first to leave—saying he was exhausted after a long week. "I don't want
to offend anyone, but I want to go to bed so I'm fresh for activities tomorrow," he told Foster, as he headed off to the EL PRESIDENTE suite by
the lake. "I'll see you in the morning."

WHEN SCALIA DIDN'T SHOW FOR BREAKFAST, they figured he was sleep-
ing in. In time, Foster knocked on his door. When nobody answered, he
assumed Scalia was in the shower. By midday, though, Foster and Poindexter grew worried and decided to enter the suite through an unlocked
patio entrance. They found Scalia lying on his back in bed, wearing
pajamas, his head on three pillows, his arms at his sides, with the sheets
up to his chin—in ghostly "perfect repose," as Poindexter described
the scene. Foster said he dreaded approaching the bed. "It was obvious
he was dead," he recalled. To be sure, he checked Scalia's pulse. There
wasn't one.

Poindexter called the physician on duty at the local hospital to ask if there might be some medical condition under which a person with no pulse and no body temperature could still be alive. "No" was the answer.

For a moment, Foster, a dedicated conservative who appreciated Scalia's pugnacious, abiding influence on constitutional law, thought about what his death would mean. "God save our country," he said to himself. But he and Poindexter had more immediate issues to deal with. "What the fuck do we do now?" Foster asked. They decided Poindexter would handle law enforcement, and Foster would call Scalia's family back in Virginia. Then began a sequence of screw-ups that would have been funny under other circumstances. The U.S. Marshals Service in Washington was responsible for security when the justices traveled. Scalia had opted to have no bodyguards with him, and the marshal whose number Foster had been given when the trip began didn't answer. So Poindexter called the marshals' outposts in San Antonio, Fort Stockton, and El Paso. He got only answering services. When he tried the main office in Washington, without mentioning a justice had just died, the duty officer said he'd pass along the message to his superiors.

Next, Poindexter contacted the county sheriff, Danny Dominguez, and decided to disclose the identity of the deceased, hoping—wrongly—that the information wouldn't leak out before Scalia's family was notified. The sheriff, who had been in office 19 years, insisted jurisdiction resided with him, no matter who had died, and said he was coming to the ranch. Meanwhile, the White House—which had already learned Scalia had died and that Foster was with him—texted Foster to ask how President Barack Obama might best reach John Scalia, one of the justice's sons.

An hour and a half later, Dominguez arrived and was escorted to the suite. Foster again informed the sheriff who had died: "Antonin Scalia of the Supreme Court."

"Now—what's his name again?" the sheriff asked.

"Antonin Scalia," Foster replied.

"Who is he?"

"He's a justice of the United States Supreme Court."

"Is that in Texas?"

"No, no, no—it's in Washington, D.C."

"How do you spell his name?"

"S-C-A-L-I-A."

The sheriff wrote the name on the palm of his hand.

Dominguez called a mortician in nearby Presidio, which was why a hearse showed up so swiftly. When it departed before dusk, TV crews already camped out near the ranch entrance incorrectly assumed it was carrying Scalia. But because Foster had talked with Scalia's family and made other arrangements with the Sunset Funeral Home in El Paso, the hearse was empty. Another guest at the ranch got a local priest to administer last rites for Scalia, a devout Roman Catholic. When the diocese of El Paso found out Scalia had died, it offered to find the bishop and send him, but the family said a priest would be fine. At midnight, in a convoy of law enforcement vehicles, Scalia's body finally was taken away. The next day, the body was flown home to Virginia.

In their written report, county officials quickly concluded that there was nothing suspicious about the death of "Antonio" Scalia. The physician for the Court informed officials that Scalia, a smoker, had suffered from a range of medical conditions—including coronary heart disease, obesity, hypertension, and diabetes—that put him at risk for sudden death. (Recent presidents have routinely disclosed their medical records, though there's no legal requirement they do so. Justices do not, but some have announced surgeries and hospitalizations.) Scalia had just seen the physician in Washington for a shoulder injury. The Marshals Service had the view that even a trip like the one Scalia took to Cíbolo presented peril, but he had chosen to go. Shortly before leaving—first to Singapore and Hong Kong, then to Texas—Scalia had run into Justice Anthony Kennedy at the Court. "Nino, you have to take care of yourself," Kennedy urged him.

"Tony," Scalia replied, "this is my last big trip."

The FBI declined to investigate the death, and at the request of the Scalia family, no autopsy was conducted. Even so, the conspiracy industry quickly went to work. In addition to speculation about the involvement of the Order of St. Hubertus—"shrouded in mystery" and "founded by the Bohemian Grove as a feeder group for the real Illuminati," as two widely trafficked websites argued—one theory had it that President Obama was behind the death and that a pillow found covering Scalia's eyes was evidence of the plot. "My friends, it's Saturday night, and this is an emergency transmission," began paranoiac troll Alex Jones, the purveyor of infowars.com. "The question is, was Anthony [*sic*] Scalia murdered? . . . This is the season of treason. This is the time of betrayal." Donald Trump, who would become the Republican presidential nominee in a few months, joined in. "It's a horrible topic," he told radio host Michael Savage, "but they say they found a pillow on his face, which is a pretty unusual place to find a pillow. I can't give you an answer."

By the end of the week, Scalia's body lay in repose in the Great Hall of the Supreme Court—the cavernous, marble-columned main corridor, with doors at its east end opening into the actual Court chamber. His chair on the bench where he served for 30 years was draped in black wool crepe—a custom for honoring the death of a sitting justice dating to Chief Justice Salmon P. Chase in 1873. Scalia's death in office was only the third at the Court in 62 years. The flags on the front plaza of the Court flew at half staff for a month. President Obama and his wife Michelle came to pay their respects; Vice President Joe Biden attended the memorial service.

The president's decision not to go to that service created the kind of partisan frenzy for which Washington had become notorious. "I wonder if President Obama would have attended the funeral of Justice Scalia if it were held in a Mosque?" tweeted Trump—who didn't attend the funeral either. Few D.C. pundits bothered to point out that presidents since World War II haven't normally attended the funerals of justices. But such was the tempest over Scalia's death.

His death set off a political brawl that would last 14 months—coloring the campaigns of both presidential candidates; emboldening already obstructionist Republican senators who refused even to meet with President Obama's eventual nominee, thus exposing Democrats as inferior at the game of blocking Court nominees; and unnerving a sitting justice, Ruth Bader Ginsburg, who openly condemned a possible Trump presidency, which in turn infuriated the chief justice, who at least in public was a model of discretion. When the brawl ended, an unabashed

conservative named Neil Gorsuch was on the Court—leaving its liberal wing thoroughly dejected. Scalia had died a full 11 months before Obama's presidency was to end. The four liberal justices believed
they would soon be joined by a decisive fifth appointed by Obama (or
a Democratic successor), giving them control of the Court for the first
time in 50 years. That assumption blew up when Senate Republicans
denied Obama's nominee, federal appellate judge Merrick Garland, a
hearing—and Trump then won the presidency in November 2016.

That election made clear how central the Supreme Court has become
in American politics. Exit polls showed that 70 percent of voters believed that Court appointments were either "the most important factor"
or "an important factor" in determining their vote. That percentage had
jumped by more than a third since Obama's first win in 2008. Among
Trump voters alone, 27 percent said the Court was "the most important
factor"; 19 percent of Clinton supporters said the same. One could argue
that Trump won the presidency because of the importance voters placed
on the Court.

But the stakes were higher than a single seat on the Court. They were
greater than what would happen on any single issue like abortion or
gay rights or campaign finance. The reaction to Scalia's death exposed a
little-acknowledged orthodoxy about the Court's role. The justices have
become supremely triumphalist: They do because they can. Such dominion is now so assumed that scarcely anyone in civic life challenges it.
Not Democrats or liberals, not Republicans or conservatives.

As much as any occupant of the White House or any paralyzed session of Congress, it is that orthodoxy that imperils self-governance. Democracy is legitimate not just because of some vague Athenian ideal, but
because the ideas that come out of its competitive rough-and-tumble
best represent the will of the people. That is better than so often leaving
it up to nine unaccountable judges.

LESS THAN AN HOUR AFTER the news from Cíbolo Creek hit the wires,
the majority leader of the Senate, Republican Mitch McConnell, an-

nounced he would preempt consideration of *any* Obama nominee to replace Scalia. Franklin Roosevelt in 1937 had tried to pack the Court by adding to it more seats that he would then get to fill. McConnell was now trying to unpack it, by leaving unfilled a vacancy during the remaining term of a Democratic president. Because the Senate needed to confirm any nomination, the nine-member Court would have to function at less than full strength for at least a year. McConnell's stance was totally consistent with the pledge he made early on in Obama's tenure to subvert him at all costs.

In spite of strained efforts to create a convincing historical analogy, there was no precedent for leaving a Court seat open that long. In February 1988, Anthony Kennedy was confirmed by a Democratic Senate during the last year of Ronald Reagan's presidency. And if Mitt Romney, instead of Barack Obama, had won the White House in 2012, it was unthinkable that McConnell would now be holding up a Court nomination in the twilight of a Republican administration. But Republicans had won control of the Senate in 2014, and most other GOP senators closed ranks behind McConnell, saying they wouldn't meet with an Obama nominee. Conservative advocacy groups, especially those focused on constitutional litigation, also inveighed against filling the Scalia seat. A month later, when Obama nominated Garland—a widely lauded centrist whom Obama picked specifically to overcome the objections of conservatives—Republicans held their ground.

Twelve years earlier, it was Scalia himself who had advised of the dangers of a Court that wasn't at full strength. He had been spelling out why he refused to recuse himself in a case involving his now-and-then duck-hunting partner Vice President Dick Cheney. The fact of only "eight justices," Scalia wrote at the time, raised "the possibility that, by reason of a tie vote, [the Court] will find itself unable to resolve the significant legal issue presented." (If the justices are tied, the ruling of the lower court stands.) Even one vacancy, he said, "impairs the functioning of the Court." Unintentionally, Scalia had presaged why leaving his own seat vacant was unwise.

More important, though, than the GOP's conduct was the bipartisan, if inadvertent, consensus on what the vacancy meant. The

Court—rather than Congress or the president—would be the branch of government that resolved a range of political issues. From same-sex marriage to voting rights, from immigration to the environment, the website for Hillary Clinton's campaign stated the 2016 election "really will decide the future of the Court—and, as a result, the future of the country." (She later amended that belief, predicting Trump appointments to the Court would "threaten the future of our planet.") Trump warned that if Clinton won and nominated justices, "our country is going to be Venezuela" and would adopt "socialism." The usually less excitable front page of the *New York Times* joined the chorus: "Court Nominee Could Reshape American Life."

A Trump administration or a Clinton administration would of course produce different policies. The outcomes—whether on border security, climate change, entitlements or the tax code—were consequential. But Trump and Clinton themselves, as well as academics and editorialists, agreed the next president's choices for the Court could reverberate for a generation. The candidates' thinking reflected the Court's place in American society. And with Scalia's seat now opening up, no single vacancy in modern times had been more freighted.

Without Scalia, the Court was evenly divided between justices appointed by Democratic presidents and justices appointed by Republican presidents. All four of the "Republican" justices—John G. Roberts Jr. (the chief justice) and Samuel A. Alito Jr., both appointed by George W. Bush; Clarence Thomas, appointed by George H.W. Bush; and Anthony Kennedy, appointed by Ronald Reagan—were ideologically to the right of their "Democratic" counterparts. All the "Democratic" justices— Ruth Bader Ginsburg and Stephen G. Breyer, both appointed by Bill Clinton; and Sonia Sotomayor and Elena Kagan, both appointed by Barack Obama—were to the left.

In the prior decade, the Court had been split 5–4 or 4–5 (depending on one's perspective) on an array of high-profile issues: gun control (the *Heller* case in 2008), campaign spending limits (*Citizens United* in 2010), voting rights (*Shelby County* in 2013), and same-sex marriage (*Obergefell* in 2015). On abortion, all the way back to *Roe v. Wade* (in 1973), the justices have clashed for 45 years. In each case, the Court had decided, first, to use its broad discretion to get involved at all in the constitutional issues, and second, to countermand what elected legislative majorities had enacted. By interjecting themselves into issues that the two elected branches of government were confronting—and rendering those branches largely impotent—the justices had been upping the ante for each future seat on the Court.

If a Democratic president were to name Scalia's successor—shifting the balance of power on the Court to frustrated liberals—that new justice could help to overturn rulings that had expanded gun owners' rights and limited the reach of voting rights laws. Conversely, a Republican president's nominee would likely maintain the status quo in favor of conservatives. And if a liberal justice retired during a Republican president's term, the conservatives would be in position to strike down major decisions on such social policy as abortion and same-sex marriage, thereby returning those issues to the states.

Such calculus by conservatives was more than morbid conjecture. Justice Ginsburg, a liberal, was then 83. Justice Breyer, another liberal, was 77. Based on life-expectancy data, there was a good chance a justice would die during the next presidential term and an even better chance that two would die over the course of two terms extending into early 2025. Justice Kennedy, the relative centrist—and the swing vote on so many key cases—was 80 and also in play. And of course that didn't even take into account that most justices choose to retire rather than depart the Court in a pine box. (The age of the justices is a peculiar by-product of life tenure. At the time of the 2016 election, five of the eight justices were 65 or over. In Congress, less than a third of the 535 members were in that age group. In the White House, only a quarter of the presidents in history had left office when they were 65 or over.)

If a Republican president like Donald Trump were nominating politically conservative justices, the Court could become a five- or six-justice conservative juggernaut. But in a more far-reaching sense, the new Court could become such a president's greatest legacy, rippling far beyond his administration—the instrument for accomplishing the long-standing conservative dream of curtailing the powers of the federal government. Except, of course, the reach of the Supreme Court itself.

IN OUR CONSTITUTIONAL SYSTEM, the justices are regarded as deities, announcing from on high the supreme law of the land. And while they disagree about desired results, liberals and conservatives are indistinguishable in their view about that primacy. Asked about the premise of this book—that the Court, in case after big case, acts when it should not—a liberal justice and a conservative each gave the same answer: "I half-agree with you!"*

Distrustful of popular will when it's inconvenient, liberal and conservative litigants rush to the Court to prosecute constitutional grievances or to claim perceived rights that eluded them in Congress (or in state legislatures). When the Court anoints itself as arbiter, the winning side exalts the justices' courage. The losers holler about "an imperial judiciary" who are just politicians in fine robes. What exactly is the difference between "making the law" and "interpreting the law"? It's merely about whether you like the way the justices voted in today's case. We all favor "judicial restraint" and oppose "judicial activism"—except, naturally, when we don't, in which case we just call them by the opposite label. "Judicial restraint"—and its cousin, "strict construction" of the Constitution— are the chameleons of American law, instantly able to change philosophical color when expediency requires. "Judicial activism" is what the other guy does. But in truth, everybody's an activist now.

---

* To be sure, *liberal* and *conservative* are simplified, reductionist labels. A binary liberal-conservative axis doesn't exist in every case. Nor does every justice vote every time in an ideologically consistent way, or in a way that suggests partisan leaning. But in describing the Court, the labels remain useful. Just as liberals in the elected branches tend to champion minorities, gun control, regulation of campaigns, federal power, and the rights of criminal defendants, so do liberal justices. And just as elected conservatives back broader police discretion, gun rights, unlimited campaign spending, property rights, smaller government, and the autonomy of states, so do conservative justices. It's also worth keeping in mind that the current liberal justices fall well short of the brand established in the glory days of the 1950s and '60s when Earl Warren was chief justice— just as today's conservatives bear little resemblance to those of that era.

Scalia made a career out of preaching "originalism" and "textualism," kindred creeds that he helped make respectable among conservative judges. Originalism piously maintains that the words of the Constitution can and must be interpreted as its Framers understood the words. Textualism means an exclusive focus on the words themselves—their "plain meaning," as they were understood at the time—to the exclusion of the words' context and purpose, history and tradition, as well as of the consequences of competing interpretations. Textualism trivializes the possibility of fair inferences; it sees trees but no forest.

Originalism and textualism sound reasonable enough, until one realizes the Framers deliberately chose extraordinarily elastic terms in numerous clauses of the Constitution. Think about the vagueness of such terms as "due process of law" and "equal protection," as opposed to the specific directive that the president must have "attained to the age of 35 years." In a 1918 case, long before literalism became fashionable, Justice Oliver Wendell Holmes Jr. noted: "A word is not a crystal, transparent and unchanged. It is the skin of a living thought, and may vary greatly in color and content according to the circumstances and the time in which it is used." Alexander Bickel, the great constitutional scholar at Yale, later pointed out that while the Constitution (and statutes) dealt only in "abstract and dimly foreseen problems," courts had to reckon with "the flesh and blood of an actual case." One could even argue that an originalist mindset *requires* that the meaning of those intentionally abstract, skeletal phrases be worked out by succeeding generations.

Nowhere in the Constitution's seven articles and 27 amendments does it state, "Thou shall interpret me based on what judges think the Framers believed." How, for instance, can one reconcile *Brown v. Board of Education* with originalism? *Brown* has been a touchstone of constitutional law since it was decided in 1954. Nobody seriously contends that its invalidation of segregated schools was illegitimate, but on the other hand, nobody seriously believes the drafters of the Fourteenth Amendment contemplated such a constitutional result. The justification for any theory of how to interpret the Constitution necessarily must come from outside the text. The words will not apply themselves.

In fact, originalism and textualism are just another means of interpretation. And because they favor a status quo forever fixed in the 18th century, they tend to favor the "haves" of that time—and to disfavor all others, including minorities and unpopular litigants. Conservatives, usually committed to preserving that fossilized status quo, conveniently gravitate toward originalism. Justices, like most of us, tend to find what they're looking for, which is why most justices appointed to the Court in recent years have cast predictable votes—in line with what their presidential patrons hoped for. That's not because justices are political sycophants—they're merely human. The task of any jurist is to put aside personal and political predilections, and base decisions on neutral legal principles. While most jurists at least try to do so, they don't always succeed. No method of interpretation miraculously removes human judgment from the equation. "The Constitution is merely words—deathless words, but words," Bickel wrote. "And the future will not be ruled; it can only possibly be persuaded."

It didn't aid the originalist-textualist cause that the Ninth Amendment provides that the "enumeration in the Constitution, of certain rights, shall not be construed to deny or disparage others retained by the people." The plain *words* of the Ninth Amendment thus can be read as an invitation to future generations to identify "certain rights" not enumerated in the Constitution but still "retained by the people"—things like terminating a pregnancy or marrying someone of the same sex. Scalia and his apostles loved to claim that originalism and textualism rein in judges who might otherwise be tempted to insert their own partisan preferences into rulings. But the notion that determining the right outcome to a case before the Supreme Court—and cases frequently reach the Court precisely because of disagreement among lower courts—can be reduced to searching a dictionary or mechanically implementing a command belies the very concept of *judging*. Constitutional clauses aren't lines of computer code. Judges aren't bots; they don't have it that easy. The quest for rigid rules of interpretation is a fool's errand, rendered hopeless by the Constitution itself. As the legal scholar Andrew Koppelman observed, echoing Sartre, "Constitutional interpreters are condemned to be free."

Originalism and textualism themselves cannot avoid subjectivity. Different Framers had different views on the same issues. Different clauses pull in conflicting directions. The words of the Fourteenth Amendment protect both equality and liberty. If one always favored the latter, the former vanished—and vice versa. Even the canons of stare decisis—respect for prior rulings (called "precedent" by lawyers)—may suggest different outcomes based on changed factual circumstances since an initial ruling. A justice is invariably presented with choices. For example, few thought the First Amendment's "Congress shall make no law abridging" freedom of expression meant that obscenity statutes or the entirety of libel law were hence unconstitutional.

The best jurists, as Breyer has described them, chose neither the "willful" nor the "wooden" approach, but rather "an attitude that hesitates to rely upon any single theory or grand view of law, of interpretation, or of the Constitution." It is a style and an ethos that has been embraced along the way, in differing degrees, by many legendary justices, including Holmes and Louis D. Brandeis in the early 20th century, and Felix Frankfurter and John Marshall Harlan II in the mid-20th century. More recently, Lewis F. Powell Jr., Sandra Day O'Connor and David Souter espoused no overarching method, yet they generally displayed deference to other branches, as well as a lot of common sense. There is a reason Breyer has a photo of Holmes in his chambers. The Holmes approach was incremental, pragmatic, distinctly undogmatic. It favored prosaic "on the one hand, on the other hand" analysis over loud policy pronouncements. In this view, constitutional law should develop gradually—building on earlier rulings, watching how lower courts responded, respecting legislative enactments.

Scalia's ideological opponents pointed out his methodological flaws. They talked instead of a "living" Constitution that needed to reflect changing times—a country of 325 million rather than 4 million people, with a global rather than a rural economy, dominated by technologies and industries unknown in the 18th century. That dynamic approach means asking a different set of questions: What is the broader goal of a constitutional clause? How should text be evaluated within the context of the overall document? What's happened in society since a particular clause was written? Should amending the Constitution—a nearly impossible task—be the only way to clarify its meaning?

Justice William J. Brennan Jr., the Court's liberal lion from 1956 to 1990, was the paragon of the living Constitution. But the problem with such adaptive thinking is it can amount to nothing more than what five justices say it is, seemingly unconstrained by anything that can be tethered to the Constitution. "If you have five votes here, you can do anything," Brennan so often liked to say, with a wide smile and holding up all the fingers on his left hand. Scalia recognized as much about Brennan's Rule of Five, which is why he claimed to depersonalize the act of judging. His counter: "The only good Constitution is a dead Constitution. . . . It's not a living document—it's dead, dead, dead."

TODAY, LIBERALS AND CONSERVATIVES ALIKE blithely rely on the Court to settle society's toughest issues—at the expense of the two branches of government that are designed to be democratic. Why fight out politically charged questions in an election—the results of which can be overturned in the next one—when a victory in the Supreme Court can cement an outcome for a lifetime? Why try persuading millions of citizens to endorse a position when all you need is five of nine appointed justices? When demonstrators convene outside the Court, they surely miss the irony that they're marching right past the Capitol across the street.

The corrosive result is twofold: an arrogant Court and an enfeebled Congress that rarely is willing to tackle the toughest issues. Each feeds on the other. The justices often step in because they believe the members of Congress—elected by the people though they may be—act like fools or, like cowards, fail to act. Happy to stay off the battlefield, Congress seldom raises a peep, other than to crowd the cameras during occasional Senate confirmation hearings on a new justice. The result is dwindling public faith in both institutions.

It's all a bit of a charade, producing a Court that's short on humility—convinced of its own superiority in settling what the law is, seemingly oblivious to the possibility that its legitimacy takes a hit. "A gift to America," Sotomayor in 2010 called the Court's role. Her claim was at once ordinary and remarkable. Roberts was even more direct, uncharacteristically so in an extrajudicial setting. "If [the people] don't like what we're doing," he said during the same C-SPAN program, "it's more or less just too bad." Alito went so far as to say the Court's work was "objective."

For much of its history, the Court stayed almost entirely out of the affairs of Congress. Before the 20th century, the justices declared federal laws unconstitutional only five times. By midcentury, they were doing so at a rate of about one a term. And by the 1990s, the Court was throwing out three or four federal laws each term. The numbers didn't suddenly go up because legislation had been written with less care—or because the justices had become wiser.

The triumphalism of the Court—its eagerness to be in the vortex of political disputes, its wholesale lack of deference to other constitutional actors—explains in part the cynical uses to which it has been subjected by presidents and senators. That cynicism, masquerading as "fidelity to the rule of law," is understandable. But the Court's drop in standing among the public in recent decades—the reason opinion surveys and mainstream commentary have so often reflected an attitude that the justices are partisans-in-robes—is a mostly self-inflicted wound. Forget the robes—maybe the job should come with tights and a cape. That reflects not a liberal or conservative sentiment, but a growing conviction that the Court has squandered its institutional capital. It is altogether possible to be politically liberal and to oppose an aggressive Court. It is entirely consistent to be politically conservative and to oppose an aggressive Court. Political ends do not justify judicial means.

Of course, the Court must issue unwelcome rulings. By its very nature, it's a countermajoritarian institution, a bulwark against the momentary passions of the political majority. A central "paradox" of American constitutionalism, as one scholar put it, is that "to preserve democracy, we must limit democracy." Majorities, by definition, aren't disposed to look out for the interests of the unpopular. The First Amendment's guarantee of free expression envisions the need to protect repugnant views—there's no need to safeguard favored ones. Few stepped up to defend the speech of, say, anarchists after World War I, Communists during McCarthyism, or white nationalists in the current age. Thus it falls to the Supreme Court to vindicate those individual freedoms. Apart from a presidential tweet here or a demagogic governor there, the Court doesn't raise much lasting political fuss when it forbids Congress to criminalize flag-burning or to outlaw animations of child pornography.

In the same vein, the constitutional rights of criminal suspects— set out, for example, in the Fourth Amendment's bar of "unreasonable searches and seizures," the Fifth Amendment's prohibition of self-incrimination, and the Sixth Amendment's guarantee of a right to a fair trial—require vigilance by the Court. Indeed, legislative incursions or prosecutorial excesses in matters of criminal procedure could fairly be seen as direct attacks on the role of the judiciary. In short, in the name of root constitutional principles, the Court at times must act in counterpoise to Congress, the president, and the states. As Justice Hugo Black wrote in 1940: "Courts stand against any winds that blow, as havens of refuge for those who might otherwise suffer because they are helpless, weak, outnumbered, or because they are non-conforming victims of prejudice and public excitement."

But these are identifiable areas in which other government actors may be inclined to overstep their bounds and in which specific commands of the Constitution—or its very structure in creating a separation of powers in the national government—apply a brake. They are not normal, they are not routine. Breyer liked to say in various talks, "The job is to decide. We decide." But "*Should* we decide?" must precede "We decide." Or as Brandeis remarked decades ago, "The most important thing we do is not doing." Thwarting abuses by the other branches isn't the same as acting as a political referee or counterforce to them. As a general proposition, respect for the will of the people and their representatives—misguided as that will can be—confers great legitimacy. Alongside the courage to act must come the courage *not* to do so.

Many of the justices, much of the time, will tell you they're not about usurping power. After all, they say, more than half of their opinions over the years have been unanimous. But that begs the question of *when* it's correct to intervene—unanimity doesn't prove legitimacy. More significant, it ignores that it's the divisive cases that typically matter most. Though the Court would have us believe it's a mere bystander awaiting appeals that magically appear on its docket, the justices have virtually total control over which cases they hear. Too many times the Court intervenes purely because it can. Worse, it does so along a polarized divide. The interference may be well intentioned, but it is no less pernicious.

Under Chief Justice Roberts, we have a Supreme Court of blue chambers and red chambers. It wasn't always that way. In the past, justices sometimes disappointed the presidents who appointed them—think of Dwight D. Eisenhower lamenting his pick of Earl Warren to be chief justice in 1953, or George H.W. Bush regretting selecting David Souter in 1990. Now, thanks to better vetting, nominees turn out to act on the bench about the way their presidential appointers expect. Obama got what he wanted with Kagan and Sotomayor. So, too, in the great majority of votes, did George W. Bush with Roberts and Alito, and Bill Clinton with Ginsburg and Breyer.

When the votes of justices in controversial cases can be predicted at the outset, constitutional law simply becomes partisan politics by another name. If you usually know beforehand how justices will come out—and if it's a function of the political party of the president who appointed them—what's the point of having a Court? Did we really establish a system of self-government in which those life-tenured judges decide so much social policy?

Acrid confirmation hearings have demonstrated that awareness. They're just the scorched-earth preliminaries over how a newly composed Court will interpret the Constitution. Not so long ago, nominees to the Court were confirmed easily. In the 1980s, Scalia and Kennedy received no negative votes in the Senate; in the 1990s, Ginsburg and Breyer received only three and nine, respectively. By contrast, the last five nominees—Alito, Sotomayor, Kagan, Gorsuch and Kavanaugh—averaged 39 nays; in the last three of these roll calls combined, only five Republicans and four Democrats broke ranks. If the Court is now seen as just another electoral prize rather than a locus of principle, the confirmation votes made complete sense. "We need more Republicans in 2018 and must ALWAYS hold the Supreme Court!" Trump tweeted as the midterm elections approached.

There is a conservative "bloc" of justices, appointed by Republicans, and there is a liberal "bloc," appointed by Democrats. When journalists write about a justice, they routinely include the party of the president who appointed the justice—as if members of the Court were little different than stand-ins at the Department of Agriculture. The tendency toward viewing judges as political proxies only accelerated during the early months of the Trump presidency. When part of Trump's travel ban on certain foreigners was temporarily halted by one federal judge, then another, Trump and his supporters bellowed that the judges were simply card-carrying members of the anti-Trump "resistance." Those critics weren't random lightweights from the blogosphere, but respectable members of the legal academy. Trump himself dismissed judges as "so-called."

For most of U.S. history, constitutional law aspired to be based on "immutable principles protecting our liberties," as a prominent commentator described it. The Court was the only branch of the national government expected to explain its actions, not merely decree. The Court didn't always succeed, but the public fairly believed that the justices—unlike legislators and the president—at least aimed to apply principle, above the commotion of politics. But principle, as the commentator wrote, has now "morphed into rule by whichever faction happens to have a one-vote majority on the Supreme Court." Not surprisingly, public confidence in the Court, according to national opinion polls, has steadily declined in the age of the Roberts Court.

The chief justice recognized the problem, even if he seemed blind to the possibility the Court was complicit. "When you have a sharply political, divisive hearing process, it increases the danger that whoever comes out of it will be viewed in those terms," Roberts told a law school audience just 10 days before Scalia died. "If Democrats and Republicans have been fighting so fiercely about whether you're going to be confirmed, it's natural for some members of the public to think, well, you must be identified in a particular way as a result of that process." Did he truly expect otherwise, when the Court's own rulings increasingly made it appear to be just another political forum, dressing up the politics with legalese? It sounds nice to say, as Roberts did in 2006 after his first term on the Court, that "it's a high priority to keep any kind of partisan divide out of the judiciary." But that only works if the justices themselves resist the urge to interfere in the political domain. Too often, they have not—and even less so on his watch.

A month before the Constitution was ratified in 1788, Alexander Hamilton explained the source of the new Court's authority. The other branches—and the people—would obey the Court because of its prestige. Rulings would be based "neither on force nor will, but merely judgment," he wrote in Federalist No. 78. The Court lacked infantry and warships. It had no source of revenue except what Congress gave it. By Hamilton's reckoning, whereas the president "holds the sword" and Congress "commands the purse," the U.S. Supreme Court would be "the least dangerous branch."

That's no longer so. Of course it is the president who can initiate nuclear war and commit troops in faraway lands. Congress can pass laws that cater to donors and other special interests. But the steady institutional self-aggrandizement by the justices in recent decades is more insidious, more potentially destructive of American values in the long term. How is it that the third branch of government—consisting of nine unelected principals, a small staff, and a budget of $97 million (.000024 of the federal budget)—has become the most dangerous branch, all the more in the age of Trump? This book is the story of how that happened— and what it means for America.

PART I

CHARACTERS

CHAPTER I

THE MARBLE TEMPLE

NINE MORNINGS AFTER ANTONIN SCALIA DIED AT CÍBOLO CREEK, the justices resumed work without their beloved, blustery colleague. The rich traditions of the Court continued unabated. After the justices all shook hands in the small robing room across the hallway from the back of the courtroom, they lined up to await the gavel of the marshal. The assembled throng grew silent, then arose. "Oyez! Oyez! Oyez!" the marshal chanted at the stroke of 10, as always. The eight justices emerged from behind the tall crimson velvet drapes and somberly took their upholstered swivel chairs on the bench. "All persons having business before the Honorable, the Supreme Court of the United States, are admonished to draw near and give their attention, for the Court is now sitting," the marshal continued. "God save the United States and this Honorable Court!"

It's an opening worthy of "Hail to the Chief," the introductory anthem for the leader of another branch of the federal government. It's all carefully choreographed. The justices don't merely walk in, and they're not already seated when Court begins. From different curtains, they materialize in unison, in three groups based on where they sit. As institutional stagecraft goes, the Court puts on quite a show.

At the corner of East Capitol and First in Washington, D.C., across the street and a world away from the workaday Congress, resides the Court. Its proximity to Congress serves as a reminder of the looming power of the third branch of government. Built on the site of a prison for captured Confederates—the prison held Mary Surratt, Samuel Mudd and others arrested after Abraham Lincoln's assassination—the Court is the closest thing we have to a secular shrine. When its cornerstone was laid in 1932, amid the Great Depression, Charles Evans Hughes, the chief justice, proclaimed, "The Republic endures and this is the symbol of its faith." The Court is the most powerful in the history of the world.

In the old days (before heightened security screening), you entered by first walking up 44 broad majestic steps and then passing through two 6^1/$_2$-ton sliding bronze doors centered behind columns of the front portico. High above the entrance, engraved across the facade, are the words EQUAL JUSTICE UNDER LAW. Inside, at the end of the Great Hall on the main floor, the courtroom is as magnificent a setting as exists in American government, a testament to the splendor of Italian and Spanish marble. The Oval Office at the White House is relatively small, decorated with furniture arranged on a human scale. By contrast, the gold-trimmed Supreme Chamber is a tableau of grandiosity—82 feet long by 91 feet wide, flanked by massive windows and 24 columns, with richly colored coffers in the four-story-high ceiling. It's no wonder that for decades they had a problem with echoes during oral arguments.

Above the columns are friezes depicting such historic lawgivers as Moses, Confucius and the Prophet Muhammad. On the elevated Honduran mahogany bench, the chief sits in the middle, with the eight associate justices alternating by seniority on both sides. (The most senior justice sits to the chief's immediate right, the next most senior justice sits to the chief's immediate left, and so forth.) Since 1972, the bench has formed a crescent so that justices can better see each other. Overlooking the bench is a stately clock with Roman numerals. The gates to side corridors are in sparkling bronze latticework. Each justice gets a pewter mug of water and a porcelain spittoon that now serves as a wastebasket.

The lawyers sit at tables in front of the bench. When it's their turn to argue, they stand at a lectern in the center, barely nine feet from the bench, closer than at other courts. A red light on the lectern signals when time runs out. Ordinarily each side gets 30 minutes to make its case beyond the extensive briefs it has already submitted. Most presentations consist not of speeches but of the interruptions by justices and a lawyer's responses to their questions. Counsel tables have white-goose-quill pens at the ready. They're "gifts to you," advises the Court's *Guide for Counsel*, "a souvenir of your having argued before the highest Court in the land."

A more important suggestion: "If you are in doubt about the name of a justice who is addressing you, it is better to use 'Your Honor' rather than mistakenly address the justice by another justice's name." A luckless lawyer who does get a justice's name wrong might get needled by a justice—or rebuked by the chief. Once, when William H. Rehnquist, John Roberts's predecessor as chief justice from 1986 to 2005, was addressed as the mere "Justice Rehnquist," he leaned forward from the bench, wagged his finger, and snarled, "I am the *chief* justice!" Rehnquist, who had been an associate justice, even went so far as to ask the clerk of the Court to formally instruct lawyers about his proper title. The clerk also has cough drops at the ready, as well as sewing kits, hearing aids, and a spare necktie for the hapless counsel who spills his coffee right before going on stage.

Everything about the place signifies that "something different is going on here than what goes on in the Capitol Building or in the White House," Roberts has said. Visitors to the Supreme Court instinctively whisper. Among the other rules during arguments: No arms extending out to other seats. No visible tattoos. And if you're wearing a headdress, beware the chief justice noticing, then sending a guard over. That's what happened in 2002 when Rehnquist saw a 24-year-old Indian-American woman with an orange scarf covering part of her head. He sent over a security guard, who asked, "Is that for religious purposes?"

"No, bad-hair day," she replied, quite humiliated. She was told to remove the scarf. The case the justices were hearing at the time concerned the First Amendment, not that they were aware of the irony.

The solemnity of the courtroom is broken only by an occasional protester in the audience, or perhaps by the bounce of a basketball in the gym that's right above the courtroom—the real "highest court in the land," as everybody calls it. (A sign in the gym warns against playing when they're hearing cases below. The sign supposedly dates to when Justice Byron R. White, recused from a case in the early 1980s, went upstairs to shoot hoops. The noise so irritated Justice Sandra Day O'Connor that she had a note delivered to the ballplayer: "You're fired." Amused, White wrote back, "Please inform Sandy that she cannot fire me. I have life tenure." O'Connor has said she has no memory of the episode, but "it's such a good story—you should keep telling it.")

Someone once remarked that if the gods had an office, it would look like the Supreme Chamber. By any other name in our constitutional system, the justices are a priesthood, with all the trappings. They certainly dress the part—that's why they wear the black robes, a practice dating to the estimable John Marshall, chief justice in the early 19th century. "I'm sure we could do our work without the robes," Scalia acknowledged in an interview, but they "impart the significance of what goes on here." The justices wear them even at such nonjudicial events as the State of the Union by the president in the Capitol. For Rehnquist, austere black was not enough. He started wearing his robes with four personally designed gold stripes festooned on each sleeve, inspired by the Lord Chancellor in Gilbert and Sullivan's "Iolanthe." (Roberts abandoned the self-congratulatory practice.)

THE JUSTICES ALSO LIKE THEIR extravagant travel. After the Court adjourns for its long summer recess, they visit the old cities of Europe and other exotic destinations—including Shanghai, the Austrian Alps, the Riviera, the North Island of New Zealand, and the Bay of Naples—where they lecture and participate in "educational" programs. To get to such locales, the justices sometimes board a private jet helpfully provided by foundations or wealthy individuals—"friends of the Court" indeed. Such munificence doesn't customarily show up on the justices' federal disclosure forms, which raises questions about compliance, as well as hauteur on the part of jurists who are supposed to be purer than Caesar's wife. It can be hard to live in D.C. on a roughly $250,000 annual salary (a bit more for the chief justice)—and most of the justices chafe at the limitations, even those who built up a nest egg before taking the bench. They are abundantly aware they could be making plenty more in the private practice of law—and some of those who became judges relatively young especially feel the pinch.

When they do fly commercial, airports have been a recurring gripe. In 1972, Justice William O. Douglas wrote memo after internal memo about the hassles of parking in the "Congressmen and Diplomats" lot at Washington National, since bureaucrats strictly construed "Congressmen and Diplomats" not to include "Supreme Court justices." And woe to the airport officials who didn't appreciate who was passing through. On the way to a hunting trip in Montana, Scalia threw a fit at the check-in counter about whether his rifles were properly packaged. Once officials realized who Scalia was, they relented. To his credit, Scalia apologized to them for "losing it."

But even when the justices travel in style, there can be squabbles. Some years back, Stephen Breyer flew privately to Paris for a speaking engagement. Like other justices, he sometimes stayed at the U.S. Embassy. For the first night, he and his wife got the best suite, because he was the highest-ranking American dignitary in town. But Anthony Kennedy, more senior on the Court, arrived the next day—and nobody had told the Breyers. They were forced to move to lesser quarters and were less than thrilled. For some reason, it was Kennedy who was more annoyed at the whole thing, even though he and Breyer were close. At the event for which they were both in town, Kennedy gave his remarks first. Breyer was next, speaking in fluent French, at which point Kennedy murmured to another guest, "He thinks he knows French, but I don't think anybody understands a single word he's saying!" (These days, Breyer is learning Spanish.)

The justices prefer to appear above it all. That's why Ruth Bader Ginsburg was upbraided in the summer of 2016 for giving interviews that questioned the temperament of presidential candidate Donald Trump. Two justices, astounded, privately suggested she knock it off. To Roberts, Ginsburg's comments were exactly the kind of entanglement in politics he implored his colleagues to avoid. Trump's election made eluding the tar pits that much harder. The president's repeated attacks on the integrity of federal judges, starting with those who issued immigration rulings overturning his executive orders, just dragged the judges further in—making them seem to some no different than any other governmental officials.

When justices keep their distance, it's easier for them to make the case they are different. That is why none ever tweet. That's also why they've never permitted TV cameras in the courtroom—visitors aren't allowed to take still photos, even when the Court's not in session. Congress likely could force the Court to televise oral arguments, but it has never taken on the justices on that issue. We're well into the 21st century, but the only visual representations of what happens in the courtroom remain the quaint color sketches that publications and TV have used for decades. Courtroom sketches go back to the Salem Witch Trials in the 1690s, but one might have thought their utility had waned.

Most of the justices believe TV would diminish public understanding of their work more than enhance it. They like to say that sound bites offered up by Rachel Maddow and Sean Hannity could distort the meaning of a case. That might be true, but no more so than would an article on Page 1 of the *Washington Post*. A few justices cited a 2016 survey that showed 13 percent of Americans believed Judge Judy was on the Supreme Court, though that would seem to cut in favor of, not against, televised proceedings. Roberts has been candid enough to admit his view that "our job is not to educate the public" but only to decide cases. He insisted that cameras would inhibit justices in their questioning of lawyers during argument. "We might end up talking like they do in Congress—'with all due deference to my good friend from wherever,'" he told a college audience in 2017, taking a shot at the branch of government that many justices particularly scorn. But hubris better explains why the Court doesn't allow TV. Appearing before the House Appropri-ations Committee in 2007, Kennedy justified the exclusion of cameras this way: "We teach, by having no cameras, that we are different."

The justices do make one technological exception—for audio record-ings of oral arguments. Before 2010, and back to 1955, the audio was normally available only at the beginning of the following term. Since 2010, the Court has agreed to release audio at the end of each week, as opposed to live-streaming them as many courts do. But that wasn't a major concession. Audio from a case argued a few days ago isn't likely ever to make it onto the evening news. In 2012, the justices did agree to same-*day* release of audio in the first Obamacare case. The Republican National Committee promptly released an ad that doctored the audio to exaggerate the halting performance by the government lawyer defending Obamacare. Several justices cited the RNC ad as Exhibit A why record-ings of Court proceedings were best kept under wraps for a while. (Still, the Court has continued to allow same-day release of audio in certain high-profile appeals, most recently in a Trump travel ban case.)

The law clerks who serve the justices—usually four per chambers—might in theory be a weak link in the Court's tight control over in-formation. But the clerks treat their bosses as demigods. For one year, those top 36 recent law school graduates do research, draft opinions, act as sounding boards—and in return get a lifelong ticket to blue-chip law firm partnerships, corporate titles, teaching posts, and judgeships. Apart from having to work long nights and weekends, the first stipula-tion, spelled out in an internal code of conduct, is that clerks keep their mouths shut. Clerks who breach the vow of *omertà*, even years later, are forever ostracized within the cult of the Court. The bond between clerk and justice, and among clerks, is close and lasting—about the only way to break it is to be a talker.

Early on in each term of the Court—which runs from the first Mon-day in October to late June—the chief justice holds a rare all-hands meeting with clerks to educate them about the ways of the media. "They're always trying to get something," Roberts told them one year. And just as the mere "flutter of a butterfly's wing" can cause a typhoon on the other side of the world, even a "seemingly inconsequential" comment from a clerk to a family member can have "unintended consequences." (Roberts cares deeply about institutional decorum, so perhaps it was surprising he didn't suggest that clerks curb extracurricular activities. Several years into his tenure, one of his clerks had an affair with an Alito clerk. Both clerks were married at the time. It was the dish of the building—and new clerks still hear about it. If nothing else, the affair and the gossip were a reminder that the place was made up of real people.)

The Court's obsession with confidentiality, even in a town that seldom honors it, makes sense. If the justices think their deliberations might become an open book someday, the internal dynamics could change. Yet other institutions in government and out—the White House and Congress, the FBI and the CIA, corporate boardrooms and baseball dugouts—carry on even when confronted with inevitable leaks. Why would the Court be any different? Perhaps because secrecy speaks to the specialness of the justices, even if they are altogether keen themselves to learn what was going on behind the scenes, say, at the White House while the Scalia seat was being filled. "Who do you hear it will be?" asked one of the justices shortly after Trump's inauguration. Apparently, leaks are okay, as long as they're from other branches of government.

Unlike presidents, senators and CEOs, justices rarely deign to do on-the-record interviews with the press. Now and then, they descend from Olympus—like when it's time for the book tour to peddle a memoir. Most are also willing to speak before ideologically friendly audiences, though some justices don't want C-SPAN invited. But otherwise, they prefer to stay hidden, particularly the more media-shy—in other words, all of them other than Ginsburg, Breyer and Sonia Sotomayor. When the justices go for a walk around the Court, passersby rarely know who they are. Kennedy told of taking a stroll nearby when tourists asked if he could step out of the way so they could take a better photo of the building.

FOR ITS FIRST 145 YEARS, the Court lacked its own home. It initially met in New York City, before moving to Philadelphia and finally to Washington. The justices convened in the basement of the Capitol, in private homes, in taverns, and in the Old Senate Chamber—moving to the current site only during FDR's first term. Chief Justice William Howard Taft was the force behind the Supreme Court building for two decades, dating to his time as president. The Court, he declared, deserved a building "of dignity and importance." Taft liked being chief more than being president, after all. The acclaimed architect Cass Gilbert—who also designed Manhattan's Woolworth Building, the tallest in the world early in the 20th century—intended the Court to be a neoclassical marvel that would harmonize with the nearby Capitol but also stand alone.

Critics disparaged the Court building as "the marble palace"—which set a world record at the time for marble content. When the doors opened in 1935, several justices refused to leave the Capitol to move in. Louis Brandeis, according to his law clerk Dean Acheson, concluded that the new building would only increase the pomposity of its occupants. Brandeis "found more than symbolic importance in having the Supreme Court midway between the Senate and the House, almost directly under the dome of the Capitol, accessible to the main flow of life through the old building." Justice Harlan Fiske Stone, in a 1935 letter to his sons, complained that "the place is almost bombastically pretentious" and "wholly inappropriate for a quiet group of old boys such as the Supreme Court." One of the justices supposedly quipped that they all ought to ceremoniously enter it riding on elephants. Decades later, when Rehnquist joined the Court, his wife, more complimentarily, called it "the greatest show on earth."

Eventually, the justices took to their new home very nicely, apart from the occasional grievance about clanking pipes and fickle phones. "If you view it as something of a temple of justice," Roberts has immodestly explained, "I think that's something entirely appropriate." And Kennedy liked to ask rhetorically, "Why is it that we have an elegant, astonishingly beautiful, imposing, impressive structure?" He said, "It's to remind *us* that we have an important function."

In any organization where a senior colleague departs, those left behind jockey for better digs. The Court's no different. When there's a vacancy, the remaining eight sometimes play musical chambers, based

on seniority. But when Scalia died, everybody stayed put. Ginsburg preferred to be far from the front of the building (prime real estate for
protesters). Breyer loved the view of the Capitol from his window. Sotomayor kept the lone upper-floor office, even though it was farther away
from the courtroom and the other justices. It offered more space for her
personality, as well as room to add a full kitchen (to help manage her
diabetes) and to display innumerable mementos (there she is in a photo,
throwing out the first pitch at Yankee Stadium!). Neil Gorsuch moved
into Scalia's chambers, though those who knew him said if Kennedy
were to step down, Gorsuch would prefer his former boss's more com-
modious chambers; Gorsuch had clerked for Kennedy. (In a gesture to
Scalia's family and as a totem of his philosophical allegiance with Scalia,
Gorsuch allowed Leroy, the mounted head of the 900-pound elk Scalia
had shot, to remain. Scalia's widow didn't want it. Nor did his children.
Gorsuch did insist on moving Leroy out of his personal office; now he
stares down at the clerks in their work space.)

As the justices returned to the bench after Scalia's memorial service,
Roberts tried to comfort his colleagues. Despite Scalia's written fusil-
lades against their respective intelligences, the other justices adored him.
For all his ideological fury, he was everybody's favorite conversational-
ist. As long as it wasn't at oral argument, which he often hogged, it was
Scalia you wanted in the room for fun.

This was the first time any of the justices had been on the bench
without Scalia. He'd had the longest tenure among them. Roberts, from
his center seat on the bench, with Scalia's empty chair on his direct right,
hit Nino's biographical high notes—proud Italian-American roots, vale-
dictorian at Georgetown, honors at Harvard Law School—and then
paid a more personal tribute. "We remember his incisive intellect, his
agile wit, and his captivating prose," the chief justice said, even though
Scalia at times had drawn on all three to skewer Roberts over an opinion
with which he disagreed. The prior year, for example, Roberts had voted
to uphold Obamacare for a second time; Scalia, in dissent, deemed Roberts's reasoning to be "interpretive jiggery-pokery," "quite absurd," and
best of all, "pure applesauce." That was long ago. "We cannot forget

his irrepressible spirit," the chief continued. Scalia "was our man for all seasons—and we shall miss him beyond measure."

"Our man for all seasons" was a reference to Sir Thomas More. Scalia's desk at the Court included a portrait of More, the British martyr (and a patron saint of lawyers) executed in 1535 for refusing to recognize Henry VIII as head of the brand-new Church of England. Often alone in acerbic dissent on social issues that came before the Court, Scalia fancied himself a martyr of sorts, too. When Roberts went on to say that while Scalia had written 282 majority opinions as a justice, "he also was known, on occasion, to dissent," the courtroom erupted in laughter.

THE SENTIMENTALITY CONCLUDED and the chief turned to "the business of the Court," which comprised arguments in several cases. The most significant, *Utah v. Strieff,* concerned search-and-seizure under the Fourth Amendment, a case that would have drawn the close attention of Antonin Scalia. Edward Strieff had been arrested in Salt Lake City after he left a house under surveillance for narcotics activity. Police had no special suspicion about Strieff. He just happened to have left the residence in question. A detective discovered Strieff had an outstanding warrant for a traffic infraction. Based on that infraction, police arrested him, searched him, and found a Baggie of methamphetamine paraphernalia. The constitutional issue: Given that the initial stop was unlawful, did the drugs have to be suppressed as evidence, or was the outstanding warrant enough to justify the search? In the courtroom that morning, the justices clearly disagreed.

"What stops us from becoming a police state?" Sotomayor asked. Could not the police just "stand on the corner" and "stop every person, ask them for identification," and "if a warrant comes up," search them?

She and Elena Kagan pointed out that in Ferguson, Missouri—where policing tactics had recently come to symbolize racial tensions nationwide—roughly 80 percent of residents had outstanding traffic warrants. "I was surprised beyond measure by how many people have arrest warrants outstanding, and particularly in the kinds of areas in which these stops typically tend to take place," Kagan said.

The numbers didn't bother Roberts. Referring to statistics in Florida, he told Kagan, "I was surprised how low they were—323,000 is a big number, but that's [in] the entire state of Florida." He also pointed out that if police didn't check for warrants after the stop but before approaching the car, it was possible that "an officer walks up to the car and they're shot." So the chief justice added, "seems to me not wanting to get shot's a pretty good reason" to check for a warrant—which still didn't explain why a full search was justified if, say, a suspect had only run a red light earlier and failed to show up for a court date. The argument reminded each of the justices that although the divisive Scalia was gone, deep rifts on the Court remained. It also underscored how much was at stake in nominating a replacement for Scalia.

Four months later, in deciding against Strieff and carving out another exception to the exclusionary rule under the Fourth Amendment, the Court confirmed the ideological fissures. With Breyer breaking with the liberals, the justices ruled 5–3 that the police officer "was at most negligent." Writing for the majority, Clarence Thomas rejected the notion that the unlawful stop "was part of any systemic or recurrent police misconduct." The pre-existing arrest, he said, was entirely legitimate—and "a critical intervening circumstance that is wholly independent of the illegal stop."

In a searing dissent—different from other rulings in which she tended to give law enforcement the benefit of the doubt—Sotomayor picked up where she had left off at oral argument. Dismissing the majority's sanguinity about police motivations, she accused her colleagues of indifference, or willful blindness, to the enduring consequences of Fourth Amendment violations. "Do not be soothed by the [majority] opinion's technical language," she wrote. "This case allows the police to stop you on the street, demand your identification, and check it for outstanding traffic warrants—even if you are doing nothing wrong."

The result was that "everyone, white and black, guilty and innocent," comes to believe "that you are not a citizen of a democracy but the subject of a carceral state, just waiting to be cataloged."

The last seven paragraphs of her dissent were a rallying cry. "It is no secret that people of color are disproportionate victims of this type of scrutiny," she wrote, perhaps obliquely addressing Justice Thomas, the Court's lone African American and author of the Court's opinion. Citing W.E.B. Du Bois, James Baldwin and Ta-Nehisi Coates, Sotomayor continued, "For generations, black and brown parents have given their children 'the talk'—instructing them never to run down the street; always keep your hands where they can be seen; do not even think of talking back to a stranger—all out of fear of how an officer with a gun will react."

And then, in sentences that could have been delivered from a soapbox, Sotomayor, the Court's first Hispanic, concluded: "We must not pretend that the countless people who are routinely targeted by police are 'isolated.' They are the canaries in the coal mine whose deaths, civil and literal, warn us that no one can breathe in this atmosphere. They are the ones who recognize that unlawful police stops corrode our civil liberties and threaten all our lives. Until their voices matter too, our justice system will continue to be anything but."

The contrast in outlook between Sotomayor and Thomas—as it had been in the courtroom between Sotomayor and Roberts—was both jurisprudential and personal. Based on their backgrounds and demonstrated political beliefs earlier in their careers, nobody could be surprised that Sotomayor on the one hand, or Thomas and Roberts on the other, came out where they did. But if constitutional law is really that idiosyncratic—if we are less "a government of laws" than "a government of men" (and women)—then who the justices are makes all the difference. Though they share elite educational backgrounds and all but one were on the bench when they were elevated, the justices have different voices, orientations and foibles that unavoidably shape how they go about their jobs.

Ultimately, the Court's unchecked, unchallenged power rests with nine individuals. By every inside account, each of the current justices is collegial and diligent. Each means well. All of which has nothing to do with the problem of the Court. The justices are independent "in the fullest sense of the word"—as "Brutus," Alexander Hamilton's

pseudonymous constitutional adversary, put it in 1788. "They are independent of the people, of the legislature, and of every power under
heaven." They have the best government job in the world: no boss, no
compulsory retirement, not a lot of output required, brilliant staff, a fabulous pension—and a shortened calendar. When John Roberts worked
in the Reagan White House, Congress was considering a proposal to
lighten the load of the justices. He scoffed. "While some of the tales of
woe emanating from the Court are enough to bring tears to the eyes,"
he wrote in a 1983 memo, "it is true that only Supreme Court justices
and schoolchildren are expected to and do take the entire summer off."
(The current caseload is roughly half of what it was when he wrote that
memo. He spends much of the summer on a tiny island off the midcoast
of Maine.)

    With Scalia gone, Roberts and his colleagues wondered who would
be next to get the gig—but also who would first be subjected to the
inane confirmation process of the Senate.

CHAPTER 2

NO. 9

In the packed East Room of the White House, before a live prime-time TV audience on January 31, 2017, Donald Trump announced his nominee to succeed Justice Antonin Scalia, whose seat by now had been vacant for nearly a year. By then, most of those in the Supreme Court chattering class, as well as much of Washington itself, already knew Neil Gorsuch would be named to fill out the Court's bench.

All day long, the cable channels had suggested the administration was trying to create an event worthy of "The Apprentice," the TV reality show that Trump hosted for 14 years. In that plan, Gorsuch and the other finalist for the nomination—Thomas Hardiman, a federal appeals court judge in Pittsburgh—would both appear with the president at the podium when Trump declared his choice. In fact, that alleged plan was nonsense—it was never under consideration. "Do they really think we're that clever?" Trump asked an aide. But the White House left the story uncontradicted, believing it would build the TV audience. Hardiman had been informed earlier that day by the White House counsel that he wasn't Trump's pick. With a CNN crew in hot pursuit, Hardiman hit the road to visit a colleague in Altoona—which coincidentally was on the way to Washington. He later claimed his trip wasn't part of any ruse; it was only to seek counsel from a fellow judge. Hardiman returned home, and the rest of the announcement went off smoothly, apart from such presidential syntactic gems about Gorsuch as "brilliance being assured, I studied every aspect of his life."

Earlier, Gorsuch, a federal appellate judge in Denver, had played along with efforts to conceal his whereabouts in Colorado. Trump called him a full 24 hours before the announcement to offer him the Court spot and to emphasize the need for secrecy. Two White House lawyers, James Burnham and Mike McGinley, flew out to retrieve him. When they drove by Gorsuch's house in Boulder, they saw it had been staked out by the press. Gorsuch then hatched an escape route from his back door to the house of a neighbor, who took him to a nearby Starbucks parking lot, from which the Trump posse whisked him and his wife Marie Louise away to the local airport. To avoid Gorsuch being spotted on a commercial flight, the White House dispatched a small military jet from Andrews Air Force Base, outside Washington, to meet them. To stay hidden in D.C., he and his wife slept at the home of a White House lawyer. Before the grand finale, Trump sequestered Gorsuch upstairs in the Lincoln Bedroom.

Gorsuch portrayed himself as a man of the West who loved to ski, fish and ride a horse—and had sterling pedigree as well: Columbia, Harvard Law and Oxford. At 38, after being nominated by George W. Bush, he had been confirmed for the federal appeals court in 2006 without a single senator objecting. But while he had impressive credentials, only a naïf believed he was chosen for his credentials alone. Gorsuch had two requisite attributes for the Trump administration: relative youth and consistent, ardent conservatism. At 49, he was the youngest nominee since Clarence Thomas, who was 43 when he took his seat in 1991. Gorsuch was seven years younger than Elena Kagan, the youngest justice, and 34 years younger than Ruth Bader Ginsburg, the oldest. Given that most justices took life tenure to heart, staying on the job long past Social Security age, Gorsuch would likely be a Court fixture until 2045 or beyond.

And although his ideology was infused with a crisp writing style and by what one colleague called "preternatural equanimity"—Scalia had had the former but never the latter—it barely camouflaged a world-view that had been expressed as far back as Gorsuch's undergraduate days at Columbia. Writing in various student publications, he had said "self-proclaimed progressives" were "a vigilante squad," and he mocked "diversity" as "that cherished buzzword." In one op-ed titled "Fed Up," he labeled efforts to make the university's fraternity system coed "heavy-handed moralism."

During his decade on the appellate bench, he frequently was far to the right, despite occasional libertarian streaks in the areas of free speech and police misconduct. At times, Gorsuch showed a droll sensibility. In a 2016 dissent questioning how it could be that an unruly 13-year-old was charged with a misdemeanor, he wrote: "If a seventh grader starts trading fake burps for laughs in gym class, what's a teacher to do? Order extra laps? Detention? . . . Maybe that's too old school. Maybe today you call a police officer. . . . My colleagues suggest the law permits exactly this option and they offer 94 pages explaining why they think that's so. Respectfully, I remain unpersuaded."

But that kind of view was atypical for him. He had supported inter-pretations of the Commerce Clause of the Constitution that gave states, rather than the federal government, more latitude to regulate business; endorsed religious expression in public spaces; and most important, challenged the discretion of federal agencies to fill in the gaps left by congressional statutes that were intentionally general or unintentionally impenetrable. On that last point, concerning what in administrative law was called "*Chevron* deference" (after a 1984 Supreme Court case involv-ing the oil company), even Scalia usually disagreed.

Chevron deference meant that courts had to follow an agency's inter-pretation of an ambiguously worded statute, as long as the interpretation was reasonable. Though arcane, the rule has long been a prime target of critics who believe the federal government had run amok. Trump's team in the White House, especially chief strategist Stephen Bannon while he was there, had made "deconstructing the administrative state" a prior-ity, even if the phrase didn't make the president's Twitter feed. Whether it was about EPA rules on clean air, safety restrictions in the workplace, consumer-oriented directives about the Internet, limitations on financial markets, or volumes of other regulations, many conservatives thought bureaucrats interfered with free markets and acted far beyond what the Constitution contemplated.

If *Chevron* could be undercut, the structure of American government dating to the New Deal might be undone with it. That was the great dream for Bannon, as well as for Don McGahn, the chief lawyer for Trump's presidential bid (and then White House counsel). More than *Roe v. Wade*, it was *Chevron* that sophisticates in the conservative legal movement most wanted the Court to overrule. Although *Roe*, for many conservatives, was a moral issue that involved human life, *Chevron* in their view did more damage to the country at large because it undergirded a runaway federal regime. If you wanted to be named to the Court by Trump, hostility toward *Chevron* was an unspoken litmus test. (The critique of *Chevron* didn't necessarily hold together. In a *Chevron*-less world, power would merely shift from federal agencies to federal courts.)

In late August 2016—a month before Gorsuch's name appeared on a list of potential Trump nominees to succeed Scalia—Gorsuch just happened to write a lower-court opinion lacerating *Chevron*. "Executive bureaucracies" could "swallow huge amounts of core judicial and legislative power, and concentrate federal power in a way that seems more than a little difficult to square with the Constitution," he said. "Maybe the time has come to face the behemoth." In the interim, Gorsuch had written something that Bannon and McGahn noticed and loved.

Later, when Gorsuch became a finalist for the Court, his opinion on *Chevron* deference proved decisive in clinching the nomination. Trump didn't read the opinion, but his advisers did—and they told the president it was the reason to choose Gorsuch. The circumstances were highly unusual. Gorsuch had stated his views in a concurrence to his *own* opinion—essentially agreeing with himself. The views weren't necessary to resolve the dispute, and neither of the other judges hearing the appeal agreed with them. But it was a way for Gorsuch to call attention to himself, and it worked.

Earlier in the year, in a speech eulogizing Scalia, Gorsuch had warned of a bureaucracy that "poses a grave threat to our values of personal liberty." And yet, one had to wonder, if Congress passed laws that delegated authority (and funding) to agencies to write and administer complicated regulations on a day-to-day basis, was it so obvious that federal judges knew how to do it better? Conservatives had the habit of claiming that bureaucracies "robbed Americans of their democratic prerogatives." But it was the democratically elected legislature that had established the bureaucracies. Did congressional irresponsibility—if that's what it was—constitute a violation of the Constitution that demanded the Supreme Court to intervene?

Congress could surely be a challenging branch of government in which to get anything done. It was slow and disorderly, riven with divisions. Bills were often drafted badly. Now and again, the justices made no secret of their disdain. "Who wrote this statute?" Justice Samuel Alito asked at an oral argument in 2017. "Someone who takes pleasure in pulling wings off of flies?" (Alito has such strong dislike of Congress that, by his own admission, whenever he nears the Senate office buildings, he crosses to the other side of the street to avoid them.) But congressional ineptitude is hardly a basis for the Court to step into the breach.

Gorsuch apparently believed differently. The end of *Chevron* deference, he wrote in his 2016 ruling, would mean "very little would change—except perhaps the most important things." Indeed. The implications for federal authority, if not loud and immediate, would be profound. By Court decree, the authority of such agencies as the SEC, the FCC, the EPA, and OSHA might be gutted. That was no song of praise to judicial deference or constitutional moderation. Unlike Scalia—who sometimes acknowledged respect for elected officials—Gorsuch seemed fully willing to overturn the canons of self-rule.

In Gorsuch's mind, second-guessing the other, coequal branches of government was an entirely legitimate role for the judiciary. In another 2016 case, this one involving the Medicare-benefits maze, he eagerly took on the modern regulatory state. Congress had delegated far too much legislative power to executive agencies, which he said often were arbitrary and capricious. "The government itself—the very 'expert' agency responsible for promulgating the 'law' no less—seems unable to keep pace with its own frenetic lawmaking," Gorsuch wrote. "A world [James] Madison worried about long ago, a world in which the laws are 'so voluminous they cannot be read' and constitutional norms of due process, fair notice, and even the separation of powers seem very much at stake."

Gorsuch appeared to be advocating a reformation in the balance of power between Congress and the federal courts. That would make him anything but a measured minimalist. His views placed him in the orbit of Thomas, who had written that *Chevron* deference "wrests" from judges "the ultimate interpretative authority to 'say what the law is.'" That fabled phrase dates to 1803, penned by Chief Justice Marshall in *Marbury v. Madison*, the progenitor of American constitutional law. That case established that it was the Court that had the last word on what the Constitution meant. (At least that's what the justices came to claim by the time they heard the big desegregation cases of the 20th century. And that has been accepted wisdom since.) Ever the radical, Thomas was saying *Chevron* deference flouted *Marbury*. (Once on the Court, Gorsuch began agitating against *Chevron*. In March 2018, he and Thomas wrote a dissent criticizing the Court for "pass[ing] up another opportunity to remedy precisely the accumulation" of federal power "that the Framers warned against."

Reasonable people could differ on whether Gorsuch had said enough to indicate a bedrock philosophy about society and a judge's place in it. Reasonable people might disagree as well on the soundness of those views. But the views could scarcely be called "mainstream"—consistent with well-established norms about law and society—which all Democrats and most Republicans said was essential in a nominee. And though Gorsuch avoided the harshness that routinely characterized Scalia's opinions, or on occasion those of Thomas and Alito, Gorsuch's instincts on the merits of social and political issues also weren't much different from theirs. It wasn't happenstance that, despite having clerked for Kennedy, Gorsuch's closest friend on the Court before he was confirmed had been Alito, who was nearly two decades older, but whom Gorsuch saw as an ideological ally. They had gotten to know each other at conferences sponsored by conservative legal groups.

MISSING FROM GORSUCH'S RECORD WAS any explicit view about abortion or indication how he would vote in a case that sought to overturn *Roe v. Wade*, which in 1973 created a limited constitutional right to abortion. Conservatives and especially white evangelicals were pivotal in Donald Trump's victory. Surveys showed they voted for him in large part because he vowed to name justices opposed to *Roe*. For myriad social activists on both sides of the aisle, *Roe* alone had long been the standard by which the Court was judged. It was a political fact that presidents, particularly Republicans, chose justices based on a *Roe* calculus. The effect on the Court's stature was acutely harmful, though the justices brought that on themselves.

Back in 2006, Gorsuch published *The Future of Assisted Suicide and Euthanasia,* based on his doctoral dissertation at Oxford. The book neatly steered clear of abortion, but it wasn't hard to surmise his thinking. Acknowledging that the public increasingly accepted assisted suicide and euthanasia, he articulated a contrary conviction. "Personal autonomy" theory—he might just as easily have called it a woman's "right to choose"—was all well and good, but for Gorsuch "the inviolability of human life" took precedence. It was a compelling, moving, honorable argument "premised on the idea that all human beings are intrinsically valuable and the intentional taking of human life by private persons is always wrong." (By discussing only "private persons," he didn't have to address sanctioned forms of killing like capital punishment and war.)

In the book, Gorsuch mentioned "the inviolability of human life" 41 times. Could the words be invoked to subvert *Roe*? The Court's 7-to-2 decision rested on whether a fetus was viable. The government's right to regulate abortions expanded as a pregnancy went on. Prior to viability, the mother's "right to privacy"—and to an abortion—won out. But if "inviolability," rather than viability, were the standard, and a fetus were considered "human life," then *Roe* wouldn't merely be wrong in permitting some pre-viability abortions. It would mean that *all* abortions were *un*constitutional. The operating principle would be "equal protection of the laws" under the Fourteenth Amendment. Using that standard, fetuses couldn't be treated any differently than infants—all the more because fetuses, like the disabled and the terminally ill, are a marginalized class of individuals who cannot protect themselves. The only exception to the Gorsuch view that "the intentional taking of human life by private persons is always wrong" would be where such strong countervailing principles as self-defense from mortal harm were involved.

Although the right to life described in his book wasn't proof Gorsuch believed abortion violated the Constitution, it would be ludicrous to imagine that somebody who wrote that book had no view at all about *Roe.* The book—the very decision to publish it—also suggested calculation on Gorsuch's part. He understood exquisitely well that, should he ever be considered for the Supreme Court, the book would be noticed. In a nuanced disquisition on assisted suicide and euthanasia—issues that had receded from vehement public debate—he had provided a proxy for a novel, extreme way to think about abortion. Once on the Court, would he follow his ruminations to their logical conclusion? Without ever discussing abortion per se, he had sent a signal to a future conservative president like Trump.

Gorsuch had one other, little-noticed attribute that appealed to Trump's advisers. In his time on the bench in Denver, Gorsuch had shown an inclination to write more dissents and more separate opinions in cases in which he agreed with his court's underlying decision. That willingness to stand alone suggested he might become an especially assertive justice. Unbridled by the constraints of being on a lower court, the theory went, he'd feel far freer to revisit settled legal issues. Whereas most justices believed they were duty-bound to adhere to precedents of the Court—in the name of stability and predictability—a true believer might conclude that setting aside prior wrongs was an act of conscience. The conservative legal movement, of which Scalia had been a leader since his time as a law professor in the late 1970s, relished the idea of intellectual infidels on the Court.

Trump knew exactly what he was getting with Gorsuch. During the presidential campaign, he continually said the "ideal" Court nominee "would be Scalia reincarnated." In fact, some analyses of how Gorsuch might vote—based on imperfect models—had him to the right of Scalia as well as Alito, approaching the extremism of Thomas. The idea that Gorsuch was mainstream should have been comical to anyone paying attention.

Yet that canard seeped into even the respectable press. The day after Gorsuch's nomination, the chief legal correspondent for CBS News suggested that "mainstream" signified "simply things you might tend to agree with." It's true that what's conventional can shift over time. For example, nobody in the field of constitutional law argues anymore that the Fourteenth Amendment's guarantee of equal protection doesn't prohibit discrimination against women. But "mainstream" is more than an empty vessel into which partisans can pour their preferred views. Words have definitions. Language matters—as Gorsuch unfailingly would tell you.

Gorsuch also gave the impression he was belligerent toward that allegedly homogeneous cabal known as "liberals." It was an animus that betrayed the evenhandedness that he regularly professed was the task of federal judges to embrace. In 2005, a year before becoming an appellate judge, Gorsuch published a revealing article titled "Liberals 'n' Lawsuits," deriding litigation aimed at protecting individual rights. "American liberals have become addicted to the courtroom, relying on judges and lawyers rather than elected leaders and the ballot box, as the primary means of effecting their social agenda," he wrote in the conservative *National Review*. "This overweening addiction to the courtroom as the place to debate social policy is bad for the country and bad for the judiciary. In the legislative arena, especially when the country is closely divided, compromises tend to be the rule [of] the day. But when judges rule this or that policy unconstitutional, there's little room for compromise: One side must win, the other must lose."

All smart, sturdy points. But why did Gorsuch see this as a liberal phenomenon? His piece mentioned "liberals" eight times and "conservatives" not once. Weren't conservatives likewise "addicted to the courtroom," "relying on judges and lawyers" to try to overturn legislative "compromises" that had been reached by "elected leaders" on such tempestuous matters as voting rights and gun control? The Supreme Court had yet to issue its momentous conservative rulings on those two issues, but the lawsuits were already underway. And was it not a conservative majority of the Court that determined the outcome of the disputed 2000 presidential election, which under both federal statute and the Constitution was left to Congress (and states) alone to sort out?

Gorsuch addressed none of these contradictions in his article, raising the question whether his take on a judge's putative role was hypocritical. If you're an apolitical, detached arbiter who strives to decide cases based on neutral principles, you don't want to sound precisely like the partisan politicians whom an independent judiciary most wants to differentiate itself from. (Gorsuch disavowed the article in his confirmation hearings.)

IN THE SPRING OF 2016, in the midst of the primaries, McGahn decided he had to treat the Court as a campaign topic. The key issue: Whom might Trump, if elected, nominate as a justice? It was one thing to speechify on the evils of the lawless liberals on the Court, bloviate about judicial activism, and cite Nino Scalia as your favorite justice. It was quite another to get into actual names. But Scalia had just died, and Republicans had committed to keeping his seat vacant until after Inauguration Day. McGahn realized that Trump—possessing no law degree, lacking any curiosity about constitutional law, and having a muddled record of comments on issues like abortion—might need to offer more than other Republican candidates, to allay conservative doubts.

McGahn, a Beltway insider and a former chair of the Federal Election Commission, was a character by any estimation. Not long before, in his late 40s, he had been the part-time shaggy lead guitarist for Scott's New Band, which, according to its promotional materials, played weddings, funerals, "fraternity keggers," "VIP soirees," and "co-ed naked whatevers." His first encounter with Trump in late 2014 left him bemused more than anything else. Trump had yet to declare his candidacy, and he and his staff wanted advice about election law. McGahn met with them on the 26th floor of Trump Tower in Manhattan. The first thing he saw when he entered the conference room were walls of Trump images: photographs, paintings, magazine covers. Trump, Trump, Trump: McGahn couldn't get the scene out of his mind.

When he later joined the campaign, McGahn insisted on being in charge of judicial nominations, subject to Trump's final say. The candidate agreed. But though McGahn was among the best election law experts in the country, he wasn't versed in constitutional law generally. Nor did he participate in the Great Mentioner parlor game of identifying who might be obvious candidates for the Court. So he assigned the task of finding names to Leonard Leo, a leader of the Federalist Society—an influential conservative legal group heavily funded by wealthy business-people like Charles and David Koch, as well as companies like Google. Kellyanne Conway, a top Trump adviser, had donated, with her husband, major sums to the group.

Founded in 1982 during the Reagan administration, "FedSoc" at first sought to counter the perceived liberal hegemony at American law schools. When he was a law professor at the University of Chicago, before becoming a lower-court judge, Scalia was the faculty adviser for the local FedSoc chapter; Robert Bork, subsequently an unsuccessful Reagan nominee to the Court, was the adviser at Yale. The organization provided a platform for debate and eventually advocacy about state sovereignty, property rights, the Second Amendment, and campaign finance regulation. In time, according to the *Washington Monthly*, the Federalist Society became "the best-organized, best-funded, and most effective legal network operating in this country."

Leo was a veteran of the Court confirmation battles over John Roberts in 2005 and Sam Alito in 2006, leading a conservative coalition to get them appointed. Having spoken at FedSoc events about campaign finance, McGahn knew Leo and suggested he have lunch with Trump at McGahn's law firm in downtown D.C. "Be ready with some names of nominees," he told Leo. After sandwiches, they got down to business. There was one other person present at the half-hour meeting, Trump's confidant on legal matters: Jeff Sessions, the Republican senator from Alabama who would become Trump's attorney general. Trump, whose attention span seemed no longer than the time it took to tap out a tweet, was atypically focused on the question of process, as well as on what he regarded as the appalling failures by his two immediate Republican predecessors to appoint truly conservative justices. He appreciated what constitutional life tenure meant: Federal judges were the only presidential appointees to whom he could not say "You're fired!"—his signature line to contestants on "The Apprentice."

"Was [David] Souter as bad as people say?" Trump asked. "Is Roberts just as bad?"

"Yes. Not yet," one of the participants told him.

"Then how did both get nominated?"

Trump was adamant he wouldn't make the blunder that Republicans accused George H.W. Bush of in selecting Souter, or George W. Bush in selecting Roberts. Indeed, while Souter often did vote with the liberal wing during his 19 years on the Court—skewing left far more than Roberts has thus far—Trump's venom at the meeting was greater for Roberts because of the chief justice's role in 2012 in upholding the Affordable Care Act (otherwise known as Obamacare). "I think he just made it up!" Trump said of Roberts's determining vote in the 5-to-4 ruling that found Obamacare to be constitutional.

Although Sessions was deepest in the weeds about the Court's work, it was Trump who got the politics. At the urging of Mitch McConnell, the Senate majority leader, Trump wanted to assemble and release a list of 12 prospective Court nominees, and presented the idea to Leo.

"That's interesting, but why?" Leo asked.

"Nobody knows me in this area and people want to know what I'd do," Trump replied. "I want judges who will interpret the law, not make it up. I want judges who are respected. And I want them to be strong—*not weak.*"

"You want to create a Supreme Court brand," Leo said. "That's good."

How Trump managed the Court vacancy, as a candidate and later as president, turned out to be one of his shrewdest political decisions. The praise—and vilification—received by his ultimate nominee confirmed that strategic staffing of the Court alone could make a presidential legacy, despite any other failings. But for an instant, Leo wondered about the risks of a list of nominees. Once liberal advocacy groups "unleashed the hounds," as a Republican tactician put it, would contenders

NO. 9   51

wither if they were in the crosshairs for months? But Leo bought into Trump's idea, quickly mentioning eight names to Trump, based on the "Supremes farm team" that FedSoc informally kept for discussions with senators and the media. That list was soon expanded to 11—which didn't include Gorsuch's name; given the press of time, Leo couldn't actually come up with a 12th name to satisfy Trump's request for a dozen.

In May, the campaign released what it called the "much-anticipated" list to the public. Four months later, the group grew to 21, in part to include the names of more women and minorities. Most of the 21 contenders were sitting judges, whose opinions offered some sense of disposition and style. Some made the list solely to accommodate a particular Republican senator or governor, but had no real shot at the Court, mostly because they were too old. Trump committed to picking his first justice from the list, which now included Gorsuch's name. Democrats assailed the list as pandering to GOP fanatics, but in truth it represented wise planning. Bill Clinton had picked Ruth Bader Ginsburg at the last minute. George H.W. Bush did the same with Souter. The former worked out to the president's satisfaction; the latter did not. Trump's public list lessened the possibility of a rushed decision should he get the chance to name a justice.

One of the tall tales about Court seats is that candidates don't run for them. "It's like being struck by lightning" goes the stock phrase from aspirants. Gorsuch tried to position himself to be hit—in his selection of speaking venues, in his choice of topics, in the network he kept. When he didn't make the original Trump list of 11, he was miffed as well as mystified about where he might have gone wrong.

Gorsuch hadn't made the list partly because he hadn't been fully vetted by the judge-pickers. He had a big body of work to be reviewed—roughly 2,700 cases. But more important, he wasn't a luminary in conservative circles in the way that Antonin Scalia or John Roberts had been. That was particularly surprising in light of Gorsuch's aptitude for attaching himself to political and business aristocracy. And like Merrick Garland, Obama's unsuccessful nominee, Gorsuch was a leading "feeder" for the Supreme Court—a judge who regularly sent clerks on for the highest clerkships in the land. It didn't help that Gorsuch lived far away, in Colorado. Six of the most recent seven justices had been creatures of either Washington or Manhattan.

A curious thing about Trump's final list was who wasn't on it. The most conspicuous omission: Brett Kavanaugh, then a 51-year-old judge on the federal appeals court in Washington (called the D.C. Circuit)— who happened to be one of Gorsuch's co-clerks for Kennedy during the 1993–94 Court term and was also a top feeder. Kavanaugh and Gorsuch had even attended Jesuit Catholic high school together, in suburban D.C., where Gorsuch lived when his mother Anne Gorsuch was EPA administrator under President Reagan. And like Gorsuch, Kavanaugh had been critical of *Chevron*. Kavanaugh was talented, plenty young, well liked, and known as an analytical engine for the right—with conservative street cred that included principal authorship of the 1998 Starr report to Congress on Bill Clinton (and Monica Lewinsky), as well as five years as a senior assistant to President George W. Bush. McGahn, whom Kavanaugh had sworn in at the Federal Election Commission, thought the world of him.

The conventional wisdom for Kavanaugh's exclusion was that anti-Washington Trump had meant it when he said he wanted to reach beyond the elitist Northeast corridor that had produced most recent justices, most of whom Trump didn't like. "Guilt by association," one of his aides called it. Kavanaugh attended Yale Law School, came to D.C. in 1993, and never left. But there was a hyperpartisan aspect to it among some of the individuals advising Trump. In 2011, Kavanaugh was on a three-judge panel that heard one of the many legal challenges filed nationwide to Obamacare. Though Kavanaugh dissented from the ruling that upheld the law, he did so solely on the basis of jurisdiction. His 65-page dissent, running twice as long as the majority opinion, concluded the case could be brought only after the law took effect, which wasn't until three years later. That was because of an 1867 statute that denied court jurisdiction over any pre-enforcement lawsuit involving tax collection. Because Obamacare imposed a tax penalty on most Americans who didn't have health insurance, Kavanaugh reasoned, the lawsuit was premature. So he expressed no view on its substance.

Though his dissent was sensible, some movement conservatives called him a prevaricating milquetoast who lacked guts—a Roberts-in-waiting. If Kavanaugh was a real conservative, they said, he would have struck down Obamacare on constitutional grounds when he had the opening. Another first-rate conservative-leaning federal judge not on the list was Jeffrey Sutton. He was downright untouchable because he had voted to actually uphold not only Obamacare but also same-sex marriage laws, both on the basis of established Supreme Court doctrine. Trump had exceptional bile for Sutton, whom he labeled as "spineless."

That kind of result-driven appraisal was how a lot of otherwise intelligent people, left and right, thought about constitutional law. And for some of those advising Trump—especially those without a law degree or who were consumed with satisfying a legally unsophisticated political base—Kavanaugh's dissent was enough to extinguish his chances, at least for the first Court vacancy. With the passage of time, especially if Kennedy could be induced to retire with an assurance that Kavanaugh would succeed him, Kavanaugh might yet be nominated, particularly if McGahn, a supporter, was still in the administration. It might even be a virtue that Kavanaugh hadn't been in the running for the Scalia seat— that way, Trump had never specifically rejected him. Such was a scenario mapped out by those who were unhappy Kavanaugh hadn't made the list of 21. (In November 2017, Trump added five names to the list, including those of Kavanaugh and Amy Coney Barrett, newly appointed to the federal appeals court in Chicago. At her confirmation hearings for the lower court, Barrett, a 46-year-old Notre Dame law professor, had endeared herself to religious conservatives by pushing back against Dianne Feinstein, a Democratic senator who questioned whether her Roman Catholic faith was compatible with judicial independence.)

Eight days after the election, in his Manhattan offices, Trump gathered with Leo, Bannon, Conway, Reince Priebus (who would become, fleetingly, White House chief of staff), and Sessions. With McGahn on the phone, the group winnowed the list of 21 to six, based primarily on the contenders' professional histories, any personal red flags, and initial 45-minute interviews by Leo. Each of the six came to Washington for further screening. They were Gorsuch; Hardiman; federal appellate judges Steve Colloton, William Pryor and Diane Sykes; and federal trial judge Amul Thapar from Kentucky.

Trump's judge-pickers made three tactical judgments. First, they would be interested not only in documentary evidence of the contenders' views but in the extent to which the contenders might downplay what a paper trail or videotape showed. Notwithstanding the propensities of the president-elect, it was a judicial candidate's inability, or unwillingness, to own his or her record that was most likely to be disqualifying. Other presidents sought "stealth" nominees, with opaque paper trails. That had helped Souter, Kennedy, O'Connor and even Roberts get nominated. McGahn wanted anything but stealth.

Second, McGahn craftily asked each contender, "If not *you*, then who?" That question might bear two kinds of fruit: a sense of each's professional standing, as well as insight into character. You wanted someone who wanted the job, but not desperately. Back in 2005, when Justice O'Connor retired, overt eagerness had helped sink the prospects of Mike Luttig, then a federal judge in Virginia. Even with his towering ability, his thirst to be on the Court turned off George W. Bush, who nominated Roberts instead. Disillusioned, Luttig left the bench 10 months later to become general counsel for Boeing. (Long after he left, his old friends around D.C. wanted one thing to be known: Luttig had largely stopped talking to them, as well as to conservative justices with whom he'd been close, which included Roberts. It was Luttig's way, they assumed, of trying to dissociate himself from what caused so much pain. In the world of Court nominations, such was the wreckage of ambition unfulfilled.)

Third, the judge-pickers wanted to keep even the whittled-down list flexible, which may have been why press reports varied about which candidates were still in the running. Colloton and Sykes dropped off, while Raymond Kethledge, another federal judge from the Midwest, came on. So did the always entertaining Don Willett, a justice on the Texas Supreme Court, whom the state legislature had designated "Tweeter Laureate" for his thousands of Twitter entries on subjects ranging from

Austin barbecue to his young daughter Genevieve's handshake with Scalia. Willett made the list despite his earlier tweets taunting Trump. "We'll rebuild the Death Star," read one tweet, complete with an image of the Empire's ultimate weapon. "And the rebels will pay for it." The tweet was signed "Darth Trump." Another tweet, posted the day in 2015 Trump declared his candidacy, even included a "haiku" that asked, "Who would the Donald name as a justice? The mind reels." As it turned out, some of Trump's judge-pickers hadn't seen the tweets. That can happen when many cooks are stirring the pot. (Trump eventually put Willett on the federal appeals court based in New Orleans in late 2017.)

Even when the list got down to a few names, Trump's team didn't want to be hemmed in. A few advisers recalled that back in 1990, when Justice William Brennan retired, Ken Starr was the overwhelming favorite to succeed him. Starr was the U.S. solicitor general. He'd been persuaded by the White House a year earlier to give up lifetime tenure on the D.C. Circuit, with a promise that as SG he'd be on the short list for the Supreme Court. So sure was White House counsel Boyden Gray that his preference for Starr would prevail that his office had vetted no backups. The day after the Brennan announcement, President George H.W. Bush made clear at a private breakfast that he wanted to name someone promptly because he didn't "want the press and the Democrats to tell me whom to nominate."

But at a White House meeting soon thereafter to finalize a choice, Attorney General Dick Thornburgh said he'd walk out to the North Lawn and resign on camera if Starr were nominated. That was how much Thornburgh detested Starr personally due to Starr's infighting at the Justice Department. "Untrustworthy," Thornburgh called him. Two days later, influenced by his chief of staff, John Sununu, and a Republican senator from New Hampshire, Warren Rudman, Bush nominated David Souter, an obscure federal appellate judge—after only a perfunctory interview, in which the subject of the Court never even arose. Once Souter was on the Court, conservatives saw him as a turncoat and the process that produced his selection as a catastrophe. Bush himself regarded his appointment of Souter as a major mistake. "When everyone assumes all along it's going to be a certain individual, you wind up getting a Souter," according to one of Trump's aides. "Don't close doors until you have to—or else you'll be stuck holding the bag."

Over the next two months—with forceful opinions from Vice President–elect Mike Pence, after he couldn't advance Willett's prospects—three finalists emerged: Gorsuch, Hardiman and Pryor. Each had gone through a one-on-one "SDR" interview with McGahn, who asked a slew of personal and financial questions designed to avoid embarrassing revelations later on; "SDR" meant "sex, drugs and rock 'n' roll." Because the interviews were done at McGahn's law firm—where litigators might well recognize prominent federal judges—the administration did what it could to keep the finalists from being noticed. Though Gorsuch was staying at the Liaison Hotel just 500 feet away, his White House shepherd used his own car to pick Gorsuch up and deposit him at the side entrance to the law firm, where he was quickly taken upstairs. "This is ridiculous," Gorsuch told the staffer, James Burnham. "Couldn't we just have walked?"

On January 14, 2017, Gorsuch, Hardiman and Pryor met individually for half an hour with Trump and McGahn at Trump Tower. In each of the meetings, overlooking Central Park, Trump made sure to point to the public skating rink below that 30 years earlier he had rebuilt to much acclaim (and at city expense). At McConnell's behest, Trump later met Thapar in D.C. A former U.S. attorney for eastern Kentucky and the son of Indian immigrants, Thapar was 47 and only a trial judge, but McConnell had been his political sponsor for years. While Thapar wasn't a serious contender for the Scalia seat, he provided an ethnically and ideologically intriguing Court possibility down the road, especially if in the interim he were elevated to a federal appeals court, where he would have more responsibility. (He was in fact soon promoted, in May 2017, to the appeals court covering the mid-Atlantic, becoming Trump's second judicial appointment after Gorsuch.)

A hit on the FedSoc lecture circuit and a wit in his judicial opinions, Thapar was effective at getting publicity. Whether it was good or bad depended on whom you asked. In 2014, he made news by sentencing an 84-year-old Catholic nun to 35 months in prison for breaking into a nuclear weapons facility in Oak Ridge, Tennessee, and splashing human blood on a building that stockpiled weapons-grade uranium. Less controversially, in 2016 he drew raves for an opinion that managed to mention Exodus, Mr. Spock, Pappy Van Winkle rare bourbon, Hunter Thompson, Mark Twain, and "Sherlock or Oliver Wendell—either Holmes will do here." Thapar was so eager to curry favor that he invited Trump to attend his swearing-in ceremony for the appeals court in Kentucky. Trump declined.

The president loved to turn decision-making into a game. His penchant for sowing chaos vexed many of his close advisers. So did his shallow grasp of details and inability to appreciate that was a problem. As with many issues, his staff came to accept that Trump—though obviously an obligatory nuisance in the process—was best managed by indulging him on small-bore stuff. And as the Gorsuch selection played out, Trump's relative lack of involvement—in contrast to how other presidents handled Court selections—worked to his benefit, even if accidentally. By leaving the process in competent hands—denying himself the pleasure of tweets of the moment—he ended up with a concrete accomplishment.

Trump went back and forth on the three finalists. He had hit it off with Hardiman, as had everyone in the vetting process: Hardiman was that personable. Plus, he had a humble background that would play well in a public relations campaign. He was the first person in his family to attend college (Notre Dame), and he drove a cab to help pay for law school at Georgetown. It also didn't hurt that Hardiman came recommended by a fellow appeals court judge, Maryanne Trump Barry, who happened to be Trump's sister. Pryor impressed because the president-elect learned that the judge for years was emphatically conservative on core issues. As Alabama attorney general, for example, Pryor in 1997 had called *Roe v. Wade* "the worst abomination of constitutional law in our history." And several months before George W. Bush was elected president, Pryor had finished a speech with an admonition for the candidate: "Please, God, no more Souters!"

Pryor began the process in the lead back in November, with Hardiman right behind. But in the end, Gorsuch won out comfortably. He wasn't weighed down by Pryor's bomb-throwing, which McGahn worried could cost Pryor support from centrist Republican senators like Susan Collins of Maine and Lisa Murkowski of Alaska. And Gorsuch's intellectual candlepower seemed to exceed Hardiman's. Gorsuch was, as one Trump adviser described it, a less irascible "mini-Scalia" who "might quickly become almost as good." And unlike both Hardiman and Pryor, Gorsuch wasn't yet eligible for AARP membership. Although he was still a less familiar name in Trump's circle, he performed flawlessly in vetting. When asked by Trump, McGahn endorsed Gorsuch. None of the other advisers disagreed.

Gorsuch's stock also rose when McGahn asked contenders who would be their first choice as a runner-up. Many named Gorsuch. "It was such a clear gap between him and everyone else on the list," one finalist later said. And in naming Gorsuch, another contender's answer on McGahn's question actually boosted his own future prospects. Kethledge was so generous, so effusive in praising Gorsuch—he kept going for almost five minutes—that both McGahn and Pence thought he would be a strong candidate for a subsequent Court vacancy. In their minds, Hardiman, too, remained a credible possibility, but it was Kethledge who emerged from the vetting process as the biggest surprise.

The contenders, as well as Trump's advisers, understood the significance of filling the Scalia seat, and they all knew that substance ought to govern the new president's decision. Trump seemed to embrace that view. But there was another key aspect for him. Appearances mattered a lot for a showman who built glitzy high-rise buildings and ran beauty pageants. Trump said generals should look like generals. A secretary of state ought to look like a seasoned diplomat. And who could forget that during a campaign debate, he had pointed to one of his opponents, Carly Fiorina, and said, "Look at that face! Would anyone vote for *that*?" With a square jaw that connoted strength and a head of silver hair that connoted wisdom, Trump told an adviser, Gorsuch sure "looked the part" of a justice—"right out of central casting." Gorsuch would even be the tallest member of the current Court.

Nobody could be surprised by the script that followed.

CHAPTER 3

CONFIRMATION WORLD

DEMOCRATS REACTED TO THE NOMINATION OF NEIL GORSUCH WITH justifiable rage. Their wrath was based on how Republicans a year earlier had treated President Obama's nomination of Merrick Garland, the chief judge of the D.C. Circuit. Democrats believed Republicans had misled them.

In the past, GOP senators had cited Garland as the kind of nominee they hoped Obama would choose. Most of the justices themselves admired Garland, hiring more clerks from his chambers than from those of any other lower-court judge. (At the time Obama nominated him, only Alito and Thomas hadn't picked a Garland clerk.) John Roberts had Garland to thank for an early career break. After Harvard Law, Garland clerked for the distinguished Henry Friendly of the federal appeals court in Manhattan. Roberts succeeded Garland the following year. Garland liked to say he had no clue how he won a Friendly clerkship, but he knew "how Roberts got his"; Friendly had asked Garland to find out who was the smartest student at Harvard. Although Garland was considered more politically moderate than Obama's two earlier Court nominees,

Sonia Sotomayor and Elena Kagan, and although Garland, at 63, would be an unusually old nominee—which would presumably mean fewer years on the Court—the GOP blockaded Garland's nomination from the moment he was named in March 2016.

· The Supreme Court had long been one of Obama's special interests. He had taught constitutional law at the University of Chicago from 1992 until his election to the U.S. Senate in 2004. Before that, he was a celebrated law student at Harvard, becoming the first African-American president of the *Harvard Law Review*. Despite his progressive leanings in the political sphere—whether about voting rights or health care or abortion—his cadences about the Court's role were more nuanced. Democrats and Republicans alike "often asked the courts to overturn democratic decisions . . . they didn't like," he wrote in his 2006 political manifesto *The Audacity of Hope*. "I wondered if, in our reliance on the courts to vindicate not only our rights but also our values, progressives had lost too much faith in democracy." That view was probably influenced by the facts on the ground. The 21st-century Court hasn't often vindicated liberal values—and hadn't for decades, since the Warren Court in the 1960s and the early years of the Court under Chief Justice Warren E. Burger in the 1970s. Liberals could no longer count on the justices. But Obama's writing also evidenced his philosophical unease with judicial overreach at the expense of democratic institutions.

Obama had chosen both his early Court nominees—Sotomayor in 2009 and Kagan in 2010—for a constellation of reasons. Nobody confused either nominee with a diffident moderate, but Obama also wasn't demanding allegiance to a fire-breathing liberal agenda for the Court. Though he came to see vividly in his presidency how maddening democracy could be, Obama believed it—rather than litigation—offered the best hope for justice. "We are confident in the fundamental soundness of the Founders' blueprints and the democratic house that resulted," he wrote in *The Audacity of Hope*. "Conservative or liberal, we are all constitutionalists."

At his core, Obama preferred politics over law. That much was clear before he left Harvard. As editor of the law review, he was virtually guaranteed a clerkship at the Court, the most coveted apprenticeship in American law. "We knew Barack well," recalled Professor Laurence Tribe, one of his Harvard mentors. "A few of us spoke to [Justice] Bill Brennan and it was clear he would've been assured a clerkship" after first working for a lower-court judge. Many of Obama's professors (though not Tribe) urged him to take that traditional career path and defer his plans to return to Chicago to get right into the thick of things. Obama resisted the clerkship detour, writing a remarkable letter to Brennan in the middle of his last year at Harvard.

After recounting how Brennan's life had helped him decide to attend the law school—despite "harboring considerable doubts about leaving my grassroots work"—and after lauding the justice's "unwavering commitment to the 'little guy,' the underdog, and the less fortunate," Obama explained he wouldn't be applying for a job with Brennan. "For a variety of professional reasons," he wrote, "I have decided not to clerk." His alternative tack turned out rather well.

Obama's preference for politics over law extended to his view about what a life on the Court itself might be like. Press pundits, together with the lawyers on his own White House staff, liked to speculate whether Obama might want to be on the Court someday—maybe President Hillary Clinton would appoint him. He was only in his 50s. And it wasn't unimaginable: William Howard Taft had gone from the White House to the Court. But Obama professed little interest. Life as a justice would be "too monastic," "too removed," he told friends. By contrast, Roberts loved the isolation. Obama doubted he would even be suited to practicing law. After Kathy Ruemmler, his White House counsel from 2011 to 2014, returned to private practice, he asked her, "What is it you actually *do*?"

Given the political realities in early 2016, Obama intended Garland as a compromise choice. Garland had been a finalist once before, for the seat that went to Kagan in 2010, and several members of Obama's inner circle had championed him. (The two other finalists for that seat were judges on federal appeals courts: Diane Wood in Chicago and Sidney Thomas in Montana. The idea of a second Justice Thomas—but this one liberal—amused White House staffers no end, as did the idea of Rhode Island senator Sheldon Whitehouse on the Supreme Court, though he never made it to the final short list.) But Obama was steadfast in holding Garland back, as he put it to an aide, "for a play I can run later"—perhaps if Republicans won back the Senate.

Garland had never been an electrifying option. Even in 2009, when Sotomayor was nominated, White House counsel Greg Craig had suggested the president also consider Garland. But there was no interview, and Garland was upset not to make it to the final cut. "I had hoped to meet the president," he confessed to a friend. Although Obama himself was deliberate by nature, he saw in Garland someone whose judicial circumspection might unduly hamper his impact on the Court. In that way, and not in a good way, Garland reminded Obama and some of his advisers of Breyer.

Yet because Obama in 2010 had said Garland represented a fine fallback, one might have expected his initial selection in 2016 to be a slam-dunk. It didn't work out like that. Though the process was not as messy as when the Clinton administration took 86 days to arrive at Ruth Bader Ginsburg's door, picking Garland took a lot longer than anybody in the White House expected. Part of the problem was that Scalia had died, inconveniently. Most justices who exit do so by choice, in June, at the end of a Court term. So the White House was caught off guard in February, and its BREAK GLASS list—what staff lawyers called the names to give the president should a justice die suddenly—wasn't fresh. Several lower-court judges who in 2014 were considered too green for a Court seat had ripened by 2016 and now were possibilities. But the list hadn't been updated to show it.

More important, the administration just wasn't as organized as it had been. More staffers, including nonlawyers, were involved in the selection process and more names kept getting tossed in. "Brainstorming," they dubbed it in internal memos. That's how the name of Nevada governor Brian Sandoval, a Republican, came up—and then was leaked. Oops, he wasn't interested. "It was noisy and non-linear," remembered one senior aide. "The last minute is always a dangerous time to be doing stuff—especially a Court vacancy." The administration of George H.W. Bush was reminded of that lesson many times over, when the nominee they had hastily picked—David Souter—kept ruling the "wrong" way. At the end of the day, Obama still chose Garland, but it took a month to get there.

Had it not been for political considerations, the president's first choice this time likely would have been Paul Watford—an African-American federal appellate judge in Southern California, who had been a federal prosecutor and a Ginsburg clerk. Crucially, he was only 48. His interview with Obama in early March 2016 went especially well. Watford showed up at the Oval Office with his foot in a boot, having recently torn his Achilles tendon. He and Obama spent part of their 45 minutes talking about how the president had given up basketball because he feared the same injury. The two hit it off so nicely that when Watford mentioned his wife Sherry had come along on the trip from California, Obama asked where she was. Watford said she was down the block at the Ritz-Carlton, whereupon the president sent word over that she should come by the White House to say hello. And she did.

Back in June 2014, amid increased conjecture that Ginsburg might retire—to free up a seat before the midterm elections that November that might flip the Senate from Democratic to GOP control—Watford's name had already been on a BREAK GLASS list of 10. While the list nominally included Garland's name, his age precluded him from real consideration. Unless the president felt politically compelled to fill Ginsburg's seat with another woman, Watford looked ideal. (The likeliest woman would have been Patricia Millett, a 50-year-old judge on the D.C. Circuit.) By the time Scalia died and Obama had a third Court vacancy to fill, Watford had gained nearly four years of experience on the federal bench, making him an attractive African-American contender.

In addition to Watford and Garland, Obama interviewed two others: Sri Srinivasan and Ketanji Brown Jackson, both federal judges in Washington whose nominations would have been demographic milestones. Srinivasan, 49, would've been the first Indian-American justice; Jackson, 45, the first African-American woman on the Court. Obama liked them, but favored Watford over the two: Among other things, Srinivasan had done little public interest law, and Jackson was only a trial judge. With Republicans in control of the Senate, however, Obama picked Garland because he thought they would find him harder to obstruct.

As unhappy as Garland had been in 2009 when he wasn't interviewed, or in 2010 when he was a runner-up, he was even more frustrated when he was finally nominated and then stonewalled by Republicans. It was almost too much to bear that, when he went to bed the night before Election Day, he assumed Hillary Clinton would win and that he might be confirmed in the remaining months of the Obama administration; 24 hours later, after Trump had won, Garland realized his chance at becoming a justice was over. "He has a very good life and he's a mature human being," said a friend who saw him soon thereafter. "But there was real, real, disappointment."

At the Court, reactions to Trump's election varied. Even in the chambers of conservative justices, clerks worried about whom Trump might nominate, notwithstanding his list of 21. They knew that at least Garland was competent. In the chambers of the liberals, on the morning after the election, some clerks were sobbing. One said Trump's election was "the apocalypse." Ginsburg counseled clerks: "We'll try again in four years."

PLAYING POLITICAL GAMES WITH JUDICIAL nominations was nothing new. Since 1968, usually near the end of a president's term, the party in control of the Senate has regularly allowed dozens of nominations to lower federal courts to die out. Two nominations stood out. In January 1992, a year before losing reelection, George H.W. Bush nominated Roberts, then 37, to the D.C. Circuit; at the time, Roberts was a top appellate lawyer at the Justice Department. Anticipating victory in the coming presidential election, Democrats refused to hold hearings. (In limbo for eight months, Roberts liked to tell golfing chums that he deserved gimme putts just for his suffering, even though he was famed for protesting any mulligans given others after the first tee.) And in

June 1999, 17 months before Bill Clinton left office, Republicans let the nomination of 39-year-old Elena Kagan to the D.C. Circuit linger and lapse; she was serving as a White House domestic policy adviser. The seat on the appeals court was filled four years later—by Roberts, who was confirmed by unanimous Senate consent.

Thus, when it came to judicial nominations, neither Democrats nor Republicans could claim innocence—a pox on both their houses. Even so, Republicans had crossed the Rubicon with the position they took on Garland—a nominee for the highest court, for which linger-and-lapse treatment had never been attempted. It was true, as Republicans were quick to bleat, that a generation earlier Joe Biden, then the Democratic head of the Senate Judiciary Committee, had intimated doing the same thing. If a Court vacancy occurred in the last five months of George H.W. Bush's term, Biden declared in 1992, the Senate "should seriously consider not scheduling confirmation hearings" until "after the political campaign season is over."

But the parallel went only so far. For one thing, there was no vacancy to fill—Biden was prattling about a hypothetical. Nor was he the majority leader. Furthermore, his proscription was offered little more than four months before a presidential election, whereas Scalia died nearly nine months before the 2016 election. Finally, Biden proposed a delay only until after the election, not—as McConnell demanded—until Inauguration Day. Biden was explicit that his intention was not "to save a seat on the court in the hopes that a Democrat will be permitted to fill it"—only a judgment that hearings during the campaign season would generate "partisan bickering and political posturing." In short, the 2016 Republican invocation of a "Biden Rule" was vastly overstated.

McConnell's decision to block Obama's selection of Garland was a gambit, given the disarray in the 2016 Republican presidential contest. McConnell also had to worry the public would see it as obstinacy that went too far. But the judgment panned out. For 293 days, until the nomination expired when Congress ended its session, Senate Republicans remained unified in refusing to consider Garland. It was the longest instance of obstruction on a Supreme Court nominee in American history. Previously, only three nominations had languished more than

100 days: Louis Brandeis, confirmed in 1916 after 125 days; Potter Stewart, confirmed in 1959 after 108; and Robert Bork, rejected in 1987 after 114. The last nominee who in effect was ignored altogether was William Micou, a former postmaster of Augusta, Georgia, in 1853; Millard Fillmore somehow thought he could get Micou onto the Court three weeks before the end of his term.

The GOP's defense gave even sophistry a bad name. McConnell's rationalization, deplorably though predictably unchallenged by his GOP colleagues, that "the American people should have a voice in the selection of their next Supreme Court justice" was fatuous. The idea—in March 2016—that voters in the November 2012 presidential election had no "voice in the selection of their next Supreme Court justice" because that voice properly rested with voters in the November 2016 election made no sense and bulldozed norms that reached far back into U.S. history. Presidents were elected to four-year terms and were presumptively entitled to nominate justices of their choice, as long as the nominees met a baseline of competence and possessed views that were sufficiently reasonable. The GOP wasn't just flouting that tradition, it was threatening to upend an article of national faith—that divided government can work. Carried to its logical extreme, under McConnell's rule, Court vacancies might be left unfilled whenever the president and the Senate majority were of different parties.

Although McConnell said the rule had limited application because the presidential election was nine months away, nothing would prevent his reasoning from applying a year or two or three earlier. That's exactly what some partisans had in mind. As the election grew near in 2016— and polls indicated Hillary Clinton would probably win—several Republicans and conservative think tanks floated the idea that the Court vacancy could be kept open indefinitely, at a minimum until 2020, when the Republicans would next have the chance to take the "Scalia seat" they apparently believed belonged to them. "If Hillary Clinton becomes president," said Republican senator Richard Burr, "I am going to do everything I can to make sure, four years from now, we still got an opening on the Supreme Court." His GOP colleague, Senator John

McCain, agreed. And Republican senator Ted Cruz offered a learned perspective. "There is certainly long historical precedent for a Supreme Court with fewer justices," he said. Wouldn't you know it? That analysis changed after Hillary Clinton lost.

In his incessant ode to the "voice" of "the American people," McConnell was attempting to express a noble first principle. But his only operating precept was the application of raw power: The ends justify the means. Nevertheless, Democrats weren't able to capitalize. Unlike when Sotomayor became the first Hispanic justice and Kagan the fourth woman, liberal advocacy groups weren't especially roused by Garland. While Clinton brought up the Court vacancy during the campaign, she was lackluster, and Republicans never really had to defend their indefensible position. Then Trump won the White House and the GOP retained control of the Senate. McConnell's realpolitik had paid off.

When Gorsuch was nominated, Republicans hailed his record—and promptly demanded speedy consideration by the Senate. They were either devoid of shame or convinced, with good reason, that the American public lacked a memory. Gorsuch was entitled to "an up-or-down vote," McConnell counseled, "just like the Senate treated the four first-term nominees of Presidents Clinton and Obama." There wasn't any mention of second-term nominations like Garland's. Democrats couldn't believe McConnell's capacity for chutzpah. An assortment of conservative groups decried the possibility of Democratic "obstructionism," warning that it would be met with a multimillion-dollar ad campaign in states that Trump won in 2016 and where Democratic senators faced reelection two years later.

IN RARE MOMENTS OF REFLECTION, many Republicans rued that Supreme Court confirmation battles had become so polarized, but they quickly added it was the Democrats who were just reaping what they had sown. Hadn't Democrats started it three decades earlier when they engineered the defeat of Robert Bork's nomination in 1987? Then a judge on the D.C. Circuit, Bork was a hero to constitutional conserva-tives. He was already a renowned antitrust scholar at Yale and a senior Justice Department official in two GOP administrations (including as executioner in President Richard M. Nixon's "Saturday Night Massa-cre," in which, as the No. 3 at Justice, Bork had fired the first Watergate special prosecutor after the attorney general and deputy attorney general refused to do so). But Bork rose to become the tribune of constitutional originalism, inspiring Scalia, Alito, Thomas, and a generation of judges; the Federalist Society, which he helped found, features a video of his 2013 memorial service on its website (right below JOB OPENINGS and AMAZON BOOKSTORE).

Bork argued that American judges were captives of "a liberal elite" that had seized unto itself the authority to determine national policy on social issues. Whether on abortion or a larger right to privacy—or, most jarringly, racial equality—he said the judicial "intelligentsia" was imposing its own morals on the country in a way the Constitution never imagined. And to the extent he wasn't just quarreling about which branch of government got to do the imposing, what "morals" did Bork himself favor? In an infamous 1963 article, denouncing pending civil rights legislation, he wrote that requiring whites to serve blacks at private establishments was "a principle of unsurpassed ugliness." He never could escape that line—much as he tried to ascribe it to a libertarian world-view and to the times.

When Ronald Reagan picked Bork for the Court, it took less than an hour for Edward Kennedy, the liberal Democratic stalwart, to take to the Senate floor about the nominee's "extremist view of the Constitu-tion." "Robert Bork's America," he warned, "is a land in which women would be forced into back-alley abortions; blacks would sit at segregated lunch counters; rogue police could break down citizens' doors in mid-night raids; schoolchildren could not be taught about evolution; writers and artists could be censored at the whim of the government; and the doors of the federal courts would be shut on the fingers of millions of citizens for whom the judiciary is, and is often the only, protector of the individual rights that are the heart of our democracy." And that was just one sentence in what was a tour de force of both strategic brilliance and shabby demagogy.

It was also monumentally hypocritical, given that Kennedy 20 years earlier had stressed that any consideration of judicial philosophy, rather than credentials, was out of bounds. Back then, it was Southern segregationists going after Thurgood Marshall, who would become the first African-American justice. Other Democrats started forming what they called a "phalanx" in opposition to Bork. Democratic senators from the conservative South, responding to black electoral strength, opposed him. "Out of the mainstream" was their refrain. Gregory Peck narrated ads that shredded the nominee.

Bork never recovered, though he did little to help himself in his televised testimony before the Senate Judiciary Committee. He committed a cardinal sin in Supreme Court confirmation hearings: being candid, if a bit imperious, too. Asked by a solicitous senator why he wanted the job, Bork did not give the conventional answer about public service or doing justice, but instead said it would be "an intellectual feast." Nearing the end of his epic five days of testimony, Senator Arlen Specter, a moderate Republican who hadn't yet indicated which way he would vote, tried to coax Bork into yielding nonessential ground. Was not the supposed allure of "original intent" belied by the reality that judges applying it sometimes reached different conclusions? "Senator," Bork offered, "you're making a very powerful argument from a very strong tradition." But Bork wouldn't stand down, adding, "What I'm saying also comes from a very strong tradition."

Bork's performance was a dazzling display of transparency and doctrinal mastery—and "a suicide mission," according to more than one observer. He was just so unrepentantly reactionary that confirming him became politically untenable. Along mostly party lines, he was voted down 58–42. It was only the 11th time that the full Senate had rejected a nominee—and only the fourth since 1895. The residue of that defeat endured. "To bork," meaning to keep someone out of public office "by systematically defaming or vilifying them," entered not just the lexicon, but the *Oxford English Dictionary*. While that's part of what happened to

Bork, it's only part of it. Fundamentally, he was spurned on the merits. One can agree or disagree on those merits—maybe you think original- ism is the best interpretive tool in constitutional law, maybe you think it's a crock—but it's an argument about merits nonetheless, based on a nominee's defiantly expressed views.

And that's how it should be—the Senate's job in the Court-filling process is to provide "advice and consent." The Senate is a political body, and it defies credulity to suggest its role in approving justices for life ten- ure would be *apolitical*. Many Democrats and Republicans since Bork have tried to turn the confirmation process solely into an inquiry on whether the nominee is "qualified." But that ignores the Senate's legiti- mately exercised responsibility.

EVER AFTER, BORK'S DEFEAT HAS BEEN CITED, incorrectly so, as the epitome of confirmation dysfunction. Yes, he wasn't treated fairly by Kennedy and some other senators, but the brief for Bork conveniently overlooked that he was nominated precisely because he *was* out of the ideological mainstream. In his writings and speeches, he pretty much had been running for the job—as a rebel who would break the "lib- eral elite" of its ways. Reagan had been glad to land a judge who had impeccable credentials—they were a bonus, but they weren't the point. Rather, Bork was selected because of the likelihood he'd vote the right way—most prominently, to overturn *Roe*, a ruling he had long cited as the zenith of judicial encroachment.

It used to be that credentials were more the point. In 1932, when Oliver Wendell Holmes Jr. retired, President Herbert Hoover nomi- nated Benjamin Cardozo, widely thought to be the finest judge in the country. Hoover was a Republican; Cardozo, a Democrat. "Seldom, if ever, in the history of the Court has an appointment been so univer- sally commended," the *New York Times* reported on its front page. More than four decades later, in 1975, President Gerald Ford named John Paul Stevens, a federal appellate judge in Chicago (to replace William O. Douglas). Though not venerated in the way Cardozo had been, Stevens was respected. He was chosen primarily because Ford and particularly his attorney general, Edward Levi, in the aftermath of Watergate and Nixon's resignation, wanted a nominee who would be seen as adept, nonideological and ethical. (Levi had made up a list of 18 possible nominees he "thought worthy of consideration"—Scalia, then an assistant U.S. attorney general, only 39, was on the list; other names circulating in a White House personnel memo from Ford's "special assistant to the president for women" included a little-known 45-year-old trial judge in Arizona named Sandra Day O'Connor.)

To some degree, many presidents—including Thomas Jefferson, Abraham Lincoln and Theodore Roosevelt—looked for Court candidates who were politically in sync with their administrations. But that's very different from seeking to remake constitutional law in a way that's antithetical to long-held conventions. It was true that FDR picked several nominees because he thought that once on the Court they would uphold New Deal legislation, but even such a vote on a closely split Court would hardly be out of the mainstream. And Earl Warren and William Brennan—President Eisenhower's two best-known nominees—were based on politics rather than perceived qualifications, but they, too, held no retrograde views.

Bork was another matter—a model of extremism. When presidents based nominations principally on a forecast of how the nominees would come out on a few highly publicized issues, it would be naïve for the Senate to weigh only whether the nominee had a splendid résumé. But as much as the Bork confirmation hearings exaggerated his character, the hyperbole was rooted in well-founded concern over his extremism, the attribute for which Reagan had chosen him. Though Republicans carped about how Democrats debased the confirmation process by abusing Bork, it was clear that Republicans had teed him up as a target when they nominated him. Bork himself acknowledged that it was fair game to assess more than his CV. "I think it is also clear that you can judge a candidate's judicial philosophy," he told a senator as he began his testimony.

The year before, Scalia's nomination might have provoked a comparable confrontation, but four things worked in his favor: He had far less of an incendiary paper trail; his personal charm took the edge off his dogmatism, helping him dodge Democratic parries; Democrats mistook his affability for moderation; and Democrats opted to focus on preventing William Rehnquist from being promoted to chief justice. (Reagan had nominated Rehnquist to succeed the retiring Warren Burger.) Even though Scalia refused to answer what he thought about *Marbury v. Madison*, the 1803 ruling that served as a pillar of the Court's authority, he was confirmed 98–0. And Anthony Kennedy—the Reagan nominee who eventually got the seat Bork was denied—was confirmed 97–0.

Until Bork, contentious confirmation hearings were rare. Before 1925, nominees didn't even appear before a Senate committee. Having them answer questions was thought to demean the office. Not until 1955—the year after the Court ruled in *Brown v. Board of Education*—did a nominee address judicial philosophy, and that was only after some segregationist Southern senators demanded it. A few nominees were grilled over their finances, or supposed lack of expertise or patriotism. Yet even as hearings became part of the process of picking a justice, they were largely decorous, pro forma affairs. In 1962, Byron White, the deputy U.S. attorney general—and former rushing leader in the National Football League—was questioned for 11 minutes, and confirmed by the Senate eight days after President John F. Kennedy nominated him. A few years before Bork, O'Connor had to wait only 33 days after Reagan selected her to replace Potter Stewart, becoming the first woman on the Court.

IF THWARTING GARLAND WAS DELAYED Republican payback for Bork, it was also more proof of how broken the Court confirmation process had become. In the constant tit-for-tat of Washington, Republicans and Democrats have certainly contributed to the pathology. The principle of retaliation isn't a particularly sustainable way to govern, but in the short term the combatants seemed to have little choice. Neither presidents nor senators were likely to disarm unilaterally, lest they reward adversaries for misbehavior. But the Court itself may have been at fault, too. When the justices claim for themselves the power to resolve one intractable matter after another—the kind that a legislature was designed for—the justices raise the temperature of the battles over who will succeed them. Politicians react the way politicians sometimes do: They strut, they pander, they pervert. But the justices invited the problem.

In the post-Bork era, mainly because of him, confirmation hearings became a farce. All nominees now apparently took to heart what a 26-year-old Justice Department lawyer had written in an internal memo in 1981 to prepare O'Connor for her hearings—advice that Bork a few years later had audaciously ignored. "Avoid giving specific responses to any direct questions on legal issues likely to come before the Court," the memo stated, probably recognizing that just about any legal issue could come before the Court. The young author of the memo? John Roberts.

In his analysis, hearings on nominees weren't so much about senators scrutinizing their method of reasoning, capacity for contemplation, or what made them tick. Instead, they were to allow senators to put on a show for TV. They often talked longer than the nominees, who merrily got away with saying as little as possible. Most senators were terrible interrogators to begin with and were too vain to admit it. Were the senators wiser, they would hire professional cross-examiners to conduct the questioning—as, for instance, the Senate select committee on Iran-Contra had recruited litigator Arthur Liman. Nominees were coached during relentless practice sessions—"murder boards"—not to be forthcoming, even if they were disposed to be. If asked about puppies, say that you know everything there is to know about beagles and bloodhounds, but that kittens, too, are terrific. Nice weather we're having, isn't it? Be noncommittal—it could rain tomorrow.

Do a Nexis search after 1987 of "Kabuki" and "confirmation hearings," and you get a pile of hits, which discuss "ritualized productions" and "stylized gestures" that are "full of sound and fury" and ultimately "signify almost nothing." If asked about a hot-button constitutional topic, nominees had a go-to response: "I can't say because that issue might come before the Court"—which begged the question of why that necessarily made it improper to offer an opinion. If nominees were versed in constitutional law, wouldn't one expect them at least to have pondered the issues and competing methods of interpretation, even without reaching a final view?

At his 1991 hearings, Clarence Thomas took the MO to new depths. Patrick Leahy, a Democrat, asked if during law school he had ever discussed *Roe v. Wade* (the Court had issued that vigorously debated abortion ruling during Thomas's second year at Yale). Thomas testified he had not. "My schedule was such that I went to classes and generally went to work and went home," he said.

The senator was incredulous: "I'm sure you are not suggesting that there wasn't any discussion at any time of *Roe v. Wade*?"

"Senator, I cannot remember personally engaging in those discussions."

It might have occurred to senators that this very response might be disqualifying. Even if not demonstrably false, did the country really want a justice so incurious that in law school he never engaged in discussions about the most challenging legal issues of the day? And just why is it self-evident that having a view on a past ruling such as *Roe*—or expressing that view—makes one unfit to sit in judgment on a future analogous case?

In 1995, one legal scholar called Thomas's substantive testimony "a national laughingstock." She criticized Ginsburg for staging a "pincer movement" in 1993 to deflect almost anything: If a question was about a specific legal issue, Ginsburg couldn't answer, lest she might appear biased should the issue reach the Court; but if asked a hypothetical, Ginsburg couldn't possibly answer something so abstract. There you go: There weren't any answers. The scholar nicely described how confirmation hearings had degenerated into a "vapid and hollow" "repetition of platitudes." "When the Senate ceases to engage nominees in meaningful discussion of legal issues, the confirmation process takes on an air of vacuity, and the Senate becomes incapable of either properly evaluating nominees or appropriately educating the public," she wrote in a law review.

Professor Elena Kagan of the University of Chicago was the disapproving scholar. Fifteen years later, she appeared at her own confirmation hearings. Naturally, she walked her comments back. "In some measure," she tap-danced, "I got a bit of the balance off. I skewed it too much toward saying that answering is appropriate when it would, you know, provide some kind of hints." And so Kagan testified exactly opposite to how she had counseled 15 years earlier. The lesson for nominees to the Court: Don't be thoughtful. Skip attempts at complexity. You'd be better off being wheeled into the hearings comatose. Keep talking about intelligence and integrity. In Confirmation World, a track record—the dreaded "paper trail"—is a detriment. Mystery is the goal.

The shock was that every senator allowed Ginsburg and Kagan—and every other recent nominee, including Gorsuch—to evade discussion of specific cases, except maybe those like *Brown v. Board of Education*, which any Constitution-fearing, confirmation-yearning nominee hallowed. Yes, it might look bad to say in advance how you probably would vote on a future case or to comment on a controversial past case—if it seemed like you were making a campaign promise. But if you had thought through an issue and perhaps written on the subject, you would only be acknowledging you have an active mind. And you would add the caveat that you couldn't be certain now what the law might be later. Nor would you know every fact in a future case, appreciating that every case is different.

The point is that committing to a legal principle doesn't mean you're biased. And even if it did mean that, then if today you voted to overrule *Roe v. Wade* or declare the death penalty unconstitutional, why were you not thereby prejudiced every time those issues came up again? Since nobody suggests that justices have to recuse themselves in those cases—when the justices have committed to a position—why is merely discussing the cases unethical at confirmation hearings?

The ruling about which nominees were most often queried of course was *Roe*. But there was a better case, strategically, to ask about: *Bush v. Gore* in 2000, the worst example of Court recklessness since *Dred Scott* in 1857. The facts of *Bush v. Gore* would never be replicated, and by its own command, it didn't even have the weight of precedent. So nominees couldn't use the standard excuse for clamming up. By engaging every nominee since 2000 on the 5-to-4 ruling in *Bush v. Gore*, senators might have opened a window on how nominees thought about the Court's role. And tellingly, it's a good bet that few nominees would have challenged the Court's supposed right to intervene.

CHAPTER 4

DEPLOYING THE WARHEAD

APART FROM EXPRESSING THEIR IRE OVER A "STOLEN SEAT" ON THE Court, Democrats had to make a tactical call when Gorsuch was nominated. With only 48 of 100 votes in the Senate—and no realistic way to prevent his confirmation in an ordinary vote—should they pursue a filibuster or save their powder for a subsequent Trump nominee? Whatever Gorsuch's views on the bench turned out to be, and regardless of how it came to pass that Trump got to nominate him, in most cases Gorsuch wouldn't alter the basic ideological equilibrium of the Court: four liberals, four conservatives, and Kennedy in the middle. But the retirement of Kennedy or Ginsburg or Breyer—the three eldest justices—would allow Trump to nominate a justice who could transform the Court.

Deriving from a Dutch word for "pirate," the filibuster is a venerable parliamentary device in the Senate that distinguishes the Senate from the House of Representatives. Designed to forge consensus—to curb an untrammeled majority—the American filibuster dates to the early 19th century. Whereas in the House a simple majority has full control, in the Senate, since 1975, it took a three-fifths majority—60 votes—to bring a bill or nomination to the floor. That means an aggrieved,

motivated minority of senators could block a president's pick for the
Court. In the old days, that entailed speaking on the Senate floor inter-
minably to stall or prevent a vote from being taken—like when Jimmy
Stewart, playing an idealistic freshman senator, talked nonstop for 23
hours and 16 minutes in the 1939 classic "Mr. Smith Goes to Washington." In recent administrations, the party out of power has threatened
to use the filibuster for nominees both to the lower federal courts and to
the Supreme Court. The party in power predictably railed about abusing
Senate rules and failing to respect majority rule.

In 2005, with the GOP in control of both the White House and
the Senate, Democrats had prevented votes on three of George W.
Bush's lower-court nominations. The Democrats had done similarly a
few years earlier in Bush's presidency—most notoriously, according to
Republicans, in the case of Miguel Estrada, a 39-year-old Honduran
immigrant who moved to the United States as a teenager and became
a gifted litigator. In each instance, Democrats said Bush's choice was a
conservative zealot.

Fed up, Republican leaders warned they might try to get rid of the
filibuster for Court nominations. The president lent his support. "Every
judicial nominee deserves a prompt hearing and an up-or-down vote,"
Bush declared in a speech. Paradoxically, it took only a simple Senate
majority—51 votes—to dispose of the requirement for a supermajority
of 60 votes to break a filibuster. The GOP's ultimatum came to be called
"the nuclear option," a metaphor that reflected how much internecine
Senate warfare had mushroomed. Barack Obama, then a senator, said
as much in *The Audacity of Hope*. "I remember muffling a laugh the first
time I heard the term 'nuclear option,'" he wrote. "It seemed to perfectly
capture the loss of perspective that had come to characterize judicial
confirmations." He came to learn, though, that Republicans were not to
be underestimated.

After months of posturing, a handful of moderate Democrats, together with their Republican counterparts, reached a compromise in
2005 that averted a showdown over the filibuster. The deal was that it
would be deployed only "under extraordinary circumstances." What did
that mean? One senator helpfully explained, "We'll define it when we

see it." But the nuclear option was now part of the political arsenal on Capitol Hill.

Skirmishes over judicial nominations continued for the rest of the Bush presidency and escalated when Obama took office. And it was the Democrats who first deployed the weapon. In late 2013, facing Republican intransigence on lower-court nominations, Democratic senators—now in the majority—finally pulled the trigger. Nominees for lower federal courts would need only 51 votes for confirmation. But the Democrats had ceded the principle, and their exception for the Supreme Court wouldn't last. There was a far better argument to preserve the filibuster for all judicial appointments than, say, for mere legislation. Whereas the latter could be repealed, the former were irreversible (short of impeachment). In relinquishing any high ground over the tempering value of filibusters, Democrats had breached a line that the Republicans eight years earlier had only threatened to. The genie was out of the bottle. The only real imperative now seemed to be which party was in power.

With Republicans in control of the Senate come 2017, the Democrats were in no position to condemn them for fully weaponizing the nuclear option for Gorsuch. What was sauce for the goose was sauce for the gander. The Senate had become a schoolyard—they started it! With Trump egging him on, Mitch McConnell, the Senate majority leader, said Republicans were willing to do whatever was necessary to get Gorsuch confirmed, including doing away with the filibuster for all judicial nominations.

Democrats had a predicament. And especially when it came to judicial nominations, they weren't very good at resolving them. "Republicans have subscribed to the Capone school of politics," wrote a columnist for the *New York Times*. When Democrats "pull a knife," Republicans "pull a gun." After Republicans did so, Democrats still shilly-shallied about which knife to go with. "I was taught that two wrongs don't make a right," explained Heidi Heitkamp, a Democratic senator facing reelection in 2018 in North Dakota, which went for Trump overwhelmingly in the presidential race.

The parties' political tactics were asymmetric. Democrats had long shown they didn't know what to do about it. In power in Congress for much of the prior 50 years, and philosophically committed to the idea that government can function effectively, they were inept at being an opposition party. In the arena of judicial nominations, they had demonstrated that by failing to muster significant resistance to John Roberts and Sam Alito in 2005; 40 of 44 Democrats (along with one Republican and one Independent) voted against Alito, but they were unable to sustain a filibuster. (In 1991, Thomas, too, faced a Democratic bloc, but 11 of 57 Democrats voted for him, and there wasn't even the threat of a filibuster.)

In sharp contrast, when Obama nominated Garland in 2016, Republicans hung together in denying him even a hearing. It's possible that if the roles were reversed Democrats might have behaved identically. Maybe they would have ruthlessly obstructed any Court nomination by a Republican president in his last year in office. But there's little evidence they had the same stomach for death matches, and plenty of evidence they did not. Polling in the 2016 presidential race didn't help to motivate the Democrats either. Conservative voters cared a lot more than liberals about the Court. If somebody voted for a candidate primarily because of the Court, it was more often than not a Trump supporter. Those who voted for Trump said his predigested list of 21 Court contenders made a big difference; for those voters, the excesses of rulings on abortion and gay marriage were sufficient cause to turn to Trump.

On Gorsuch, Democrats faced several questions. Were they better off concentrating on other legislative battles—saving Obamacare, funding infrastructure, mitigating Trump's immigration orders? If they wanted to go after Gorsuch, should they do so based on the individual merits of his rulings or on his supposed illegitimacy? The former might be difficult, given his intellectual command. The latter allowed for easy, principled consistency. Because it was Garland's rightful seat, the Democrats could say they'd oppose any nominee not named Merrick Garland—even the second coming of Oliver Wendell Holmes Jr. (though he would've had age issues). And if the Democrats were going to engage fully, would they opt for a filibuster and dare the GOP to dispense with it altogether? Republicans could cite what the Democrats had done in 2013 as justification, but Republicans would have to realize that someday they no longer would hold the gavel and would then be on its receiving end. As you sow, so shall you reap.

Each side seemed to be locked in an inescapable logic. Republicans, in addition to wanting Gorsuch safely ensconced in Scalia's seat, felt they were free to punish Democrats for partially eliminating the filibuster a few years earlier, even though Republicans likely would have done the same thing under the circumstances. Most Democrats, even though they assumed Gorsuch would be confirmed, believed they had to make Republicans pay a price for it. Voting to end the filibuster was that price. It wasn't that such an outcome was perfect—only that the alternative was worse. It was just another chapter in the sorry Bork-to-Garland saga. If you don't inflict a penalty on the other side, they'll just walk all over you again. In time, the theory goes, both sides might come to see how bad behavior—in this instance, ignoring time-honored Senate norms— was suboptimal and how in the long run the costs were too high on both sides. That's the theory. In the meantime, at the very least, you threaten the threatener, fight fire with fire.

TRUE TO FORM, when the four days of Gorsuch hearings began in March 2017, the Democrats were befuddled. They just weren't as talented at confirmation politics as the Republicans. Perhaps it was of a piece with how presidents of the respective parties looked at the process. The last two Democratic presidents, Obama and Clinton, were Ivy-trained lawyers and former professors of constitutional law. For them, the selection of judges was supposed to be somewhat nuanced, like the doctrine the judges would be applying. It didn't totally work out that way, but those presidents understood what the ideal was, even if they succumbed to politics in the end. By contrast, every Republican president since 1980 has had a background in something other than law. For them, courts have been just another way to implement partisan policies.

Much as Democratic senators wanted to retaliate against Republicans for obstructing Garland, they couldn't execute the game plan. At the hearings, they would mention the ghost of Garland, ask an actual

question about it, and after getting a nonresponse, move on to something utterly different. Despite 20 hours in the dock, Gorsuch barely
had to break a sweat, perhaps devoting more deliberation to when again
to pay adoring tribute to his wife. (He wasn't two minutes into his opening statement before turning around, smiling at her, referring to her
"giving heart," telling her he loved her "so much," and then offering her
a hearty handshake that became a big hug.) Consider this early exchange
between the nominee and Patrick Leahy, the senior Democratic member
of the Judiciary Committee:

"Do you think [Garland] was treated fairly by this committee—yes
or no?" Leahy asked, under the bright TV lights of Room 216 of the
Hart Office Building.

"Senator," replied Gorsuch, "I can't get involved in politics. There are
judicial canons that prevent me from doing that, and I think it would
be very imprudent of judges to start commenting on political disputes."

And that was it. Leahy was off to another question on his list, apparently not paying much attention to Gorsuch's palpably laughable
answer. The Q-and-A was not so much a probing exploration of the
witness's ideas as a performance for the cameras: talking points from
the senators, met with pablum posing as humility from the nominee. It
wasn't exactly Otto Preminger's "Advise & Consent."

Gorsuch's canned responses were the product of punishing mock
hearings, where Don McGahn, Leonard Leo and others pelted him with
possible questions and allowed him to test answers. The nominee duly
regurgitated every banality prescribed by his handlers: He would always
"do all in my power to be a faithful servant of the Constitution and
laws of this great nation"; he would dispense justice to "poor and rich"
alike; even presidents were not "above the law"; and precedent deserves
respect. In the chronicles of American law, few would-be judges have
ever indicated otherwise. When Leahy inquired about Garland, Gorsuch essentially went on autopilot, the chief challenge being not to appear overly rehearsed.

But couldn't Leahy have pressed Gorsuch on just which "judicial
canons" supposedly proscribed him from talking about what happened
to Garland—all the more since Gorsuch in a 2002 op-ed wrote how

"grossly mistreated" Garland had been when nominated to the D.C. Circuit in 1995? (Garland had waited 18 months before being confirmed for that lower court.) Or perhaps Leahy might have pointed out how Gorsuch's refusal to discuss Garland was particularly disingenuous because Gorsuch, on the very night Trump nominated him, had called Garland "out of respect." The call was private, yet somehow it was leaked—and was repeatedly mentioned at the hearings. Garland wasn't the source, which doesn't leave a lot of other possibilities.

Other Democratic senators, after putting in a few words of their own about Garland, tried to pick apart some of Gorsuch's rulings that seemed more doctrinaire than contemplative. He had displayed admirable care in cases dealing with privacy rights and criminal defendants, but these were exceptions. One case stood out, and collectively, more than an hour was spent on it—his lone dissent in 2016 in what became known as "the case of the frozen trucker." The facts were straightforward and cruel: Late one winter night, with the temperature below zero, a trucker was stranded on the side of Interstate 88 in Illinois. The brakes on the trailer he was pulling had stopped working. He called his company for assistance. The dispatcher told him he had two options: wait for help, or continue to his destination even with defective brakes. The heater was broken in the cab of the truck. After three hours, with his feet numb and his breath short, the trucker opted for a third choice that preserved his own life and kept the roads safe. He unhitched his cab from the trailer and drove to a gas station for help. Less than a week later, the trucker was fired for disobeying orders and abandoning his rig.

A federal statute dating to the Reagan administration barred companies from firing employees who "refuse to operate" a vehicle because of safety concerns. Every other judge who considered the case, along with the U.S. Department of Labor, found that the trucker was protected by that law. Gorsuch disagreed. "The trucker in this case wasn't fired for *refusing* to operate his vehicle," Gorsuch wrote. "The trucker was fired only after he . . . chose instead to *operate* his vehicle in a manner he thought wise but his employer did not. And there's simply no law anyone has pointed us to giving employees the right to operate their vehicles in ways their employers forbid."

"Maybe someday Congress will adorn our federal statute books with such a law," the judge needlessly added. "But it isn't there yet. And it isn't our job to write one." It was one of several passages in a beautifully written dissent that, depending on your perspective, was either clever or snide, or both.

To support his cold-blooded interpretation, Gorsuch obligingly provided an *Oxford English Dictionary* definition of *operate*: "to cause or actuate the working of." This was Gorsuch trying to show off what a master of textualism he was—a judge after Scalia's own heart. But the other two judges on the case ridiculed Gorsuch's selectivity and instead found a different dictionary definition: "to control the functioning of." That definition, wrote the other judges, "clearly encompasses activities other than driving." For that reason, Gorsuch's conclusion "that a truck driver is 'operating' his truck when he refuses to drive it but not when he refuses to remain in control of it while awaiting its repair, is curious." And in a gibe at the notion that textualism slays subjectivity, the other judges then suggested Gorsuch had "concluded Congress used the word 'operate' in the statute when it really meant 'drive.' " Portraying Gorsuch as a judicial activist, they wrote, "We are more comfortable limiting our review to the language Congress actually used."

Democratic senators could have used those dueling opinions to show that at best Gorsuch oversimplified the difficulty of interpreting statutes—or at worst he was a fraud, who was no judicial minimalist and who simply didn't have much respect for legislators. Or they might have invoked a favorite example of Justice Breyer's, which he used in a 2003 case: " 'No vehicles in the park' does not refer to baby strollers or even to tanks used as part of a war memorial."

It was one thing for Gorsuch to acknowledge that judges could reasonably differ on a statute's meaning, but quite another to insinuate that whoever wrote the law was a nitwit and that the judge's role was only to follow the text as nitwitly drawn. What happened to "putting on a robe" as a reminder of "it's time to lose our egos," as he had put it during his opening statement? Gorsuch had spent much of his career belittling Congress and the unchecked discretion that courts, employing *Chevron* deference, gave to federal agencies. But senators instead used the case of the frozen trucker only to paint Gorsuch as an enemy "of the little guy." That was as overly facile as Gorsuch's opinion.

Moreover, it would be hard to justify voting against Gorsuch based on one ill-considered opinion, even if he compounded the mistake by attempting in his testimony to score sympathy points. "This is one of those [decisions] you take home at night," he said. And why was that? If, as he told his inquisitors, "my job is to apply the law that you write," and he did so faithfully, then he ought to sleep like a baby for honoring his institutional role in the legal system. Any sleeplessness should plague the legislative nitwits instead. Or was Gorsuch now conflating sound judging with rational outcomes? No senator bothered to pursue such inconsistencies. Gorsuch was testifying during an especially crazy week of the Trump presidency—the inquiry into Russian meddling in the 2016 election was intensifying, and the House was failing in another attempt to repeal Obamacare—but one might have thought Democratic senators would be more on their game in a pivotal confirmation feud.

There was one other particularly startling moment during the hearings. On the third day, as Gorsuch was still testifying, right across the street, his potential colleagues on the Court issued a unanimous ruling that humiliated him briefly—which senators quickly noted. In a special-education case from Colorado, Chief Justice Roberts, writing for the Court, found that the Individuals with Disabilities Education Act required school districts to provide substantial benefits to students. Roberts rejected a lower-court test of "merely more than de minimis." The author of that weaker standard, in an earlier case involving an autistic student, was Neil Gorsuch. Senators immediately confronted him in real time about the Court's rebuke.

It may be, as he tried to explain to senators, that he had thought he was only applying precedent. But he could not hide his irritation at the Court's slapdown. During a recess, as soon as he entered the anteroom to the hearings, he said so. He was both dumbfounded and livid that the justices would release an opinion in the middle of his testimony that made him look bad. The justices had settled on the opinion the prior week—could the chief behind closed doors not have delayed the ruling? Rulings are routinely put off, for example, to fine-tune language. Better yet, to avoid someone someday possibly accusing him of playing confirmation politics with the date of an opinion, could not Roberts have planned further ahead so the ruling wasn't close to being final at the time of Gorsuch's hearings—which were announced a month in advance?

Such machinations were not beyond the tactical capabilities of the chief justice, according to Gorsuch's supporters. The grievance of course assumed Roberts even knew that Gorsuch had authored the weaker standard. The chief didn't, and in fact was chagrined about the timing of the Court's ruling. Besides, the chief liked Gorsuch and thought his treatment by the Judiciary Committee was an abomination.

In the hive mind of the Trump White House, Roberts's decision to release the opinion when he did was another reminder that the chief justice was a faux conservative, disloyal to the Republican cause. Why would Roberts have embarrassed Gorsuch so plainly? The administration, as well as a few of Gorsuch's former clerks, believed it wasn't malevolence, just the chief making the nominee dance a bit. The more skeptical in Gorsuch's camp also wondered if Roberts might have felt slighted that Gorsuch chose not to follow Roberts's confirmation script from 2005, in effect showing him up. Whereas the chief had indicated his approval of a range of uncontroversial Court rulings, Gorsuch yielded nothing, insisting that doing so would mean prejudging subsequent appeals.

Gorsuch and the chief justice would be serving together on the Court, potentially for decades. Ideologically, they would likely be allies more than foes. So it made sense for them to get along. But even after he was confirmed, Gorsuch remained rankled.

FOR THEIR PART, REPUBLICAN SENATORS had little interest in exploring the nominee's rulings, his views on the role of precedent, or his larger judicial philosophy. Instead, those senators preferred oh-so-folksy diversions on subjects that ranged from pet goats (including "Nibbles," his favorite) and fly-fishing (with Scalia, no less) to mutton-busting (where children at rodeos try to ride sheep) to whether Gorsuch would rather fight 100 duck-size horses or a single horse-size duck. Any connection between those animal exploits and constitutional law wasn't apparent. The highlight among the digressions was Senator Ben Sasse's inquiry about Gorsuch's bladder. "How in the world is Gorsuch able to go so many hours at a time without peeing?"

The judge declined to answer.

Nor was it a shocker that Democratic grumbles about the frozen trucker or the special-education case or Gorsuch's unctuous demeanor or his refusal to castigate Trump's broadside against federal judges fell on deaf GOP ears. Gorsuch held his own, even if he wasn't the natural that Roberts had been in his confirmation hearings. Nor had Gorsuch come across as unaffected or funny, the way Kagan had in 2010. Each time Gorsuch said he'd be "delighted" to answer a question, it was clear he wasn't. About the only upside to the entire exercise was seeing a future Supreme Court justice grovel for the last time in his professional life.

Along straight party lines, the Judiciary Committee voted 11–9 to send Gorsuch's name to the full Senate. Democrats followed through with—surprise!—a filibuster, even if they still couldn't agree on why they were mounting it. For pure theater and C-SPAN addicts, one Democrat (and Ironman triathlete), Jeff Merkley of Oregon, held forth on the Senate floor overnight for $15^1/_2$ hours, accusing the GOP of trying "to take control of the federal judiciary." Republicans then followed through with the nuclear option, high-fiving each other after they turned the missile keys. The filibuster as applied to Court nominations was dead. Each side bewailed what the other was doing and what that presaged for the Senate.

McConnell—who for a year denied Merrick Garland a hearing— said Democrats were "hurtling toward the abyss" and "trying to take the Senate with them." Not so, answered the Democratic leader, Chuck Schumer. "When history weighs what happened," he said, "the responsibility for changing the rules will fall on the Republicans," conveniently forgetting it was his party that four years earlier went nuclear for lower-court judges. A few senators mourned what they themselves were doing. Anybody who thought going nuclear was good for the Senate, John McCain, a Republican, said, was a "stupid idiot." McCain then voted to go nuclear.

Another Republican, Lindsey Graham, accidentally offered the smartest observation, seeming to recognize that polarization begets polarization. "Every Senate seat now becomes a referendum on the Supreme Court," he said, before he, too, voted in lockstep with all other Republicans to get rid of the filibuster for Court nominations. That would probably mean the most ideologically oriented senators would have the most to say about whom a president nominated, which would produce more extremist nominees. That new reality, Graham said, "is going to haunt the Senate." More to the point, it would haunt the Court—confirming that, as far as the other two branches of government were concerned, its nine seats were little more than political spoils.

The Court largely had itself to blame for that. By stepping into so many issues, it raised the stakes of appointments. Presidents and senators reacted logically. Now, the Senate had changed the rules to allow more radical justices to be appointed—which in turn might produce a more aggressive Court, which in turn put that much more pressure on presidents and senators to seek extremist justices.

Ending the protracted battle over Scalia's seat, on April 7, 2017, the full Senate confirmed Gorsuch as the 113th justice. The vote was 54–45—the closest margin of approval since Clarence Thomas's nomination in 1991—with three Democrats in purple states voting with the GOP to confirm. Three days later, Gorsuch was sworn in. It was a rare triumph for the nascent Trump administration, and the president lapped it up. Appointing a justice is "the most important thing a president of the United States does," he said. "And I got it done in the first 100 days!" But with everything else going on—the American bombing of a Syrian airfield, continuing questions about Russian interference with the presidential election, Republican turmoil over legislative priorities— the country seemed to shrug. Gorsuch's confirmation didn't make it onto many front pages. Neither the media, nor much of the electorate, seemed to appreciate the significance.

Many months later, as the first anniversary of Trump's election neared, McConnell took note during a joint press conference with the president. Whatever else Trump had failed to accomplish on immigration, health care or energy policy, McConnell proclaimed that "the single most significant thing this president has done to change America is the appointment of Neil Gorsuch to the Supreme Court." Conservatives who found Trump otherwise distasteful consoled themselves that they had the perfect justice; they circulated an online meme of the nation under water but with the floating road sign BUT GORSUCH.

Trump almost snatched defeat before the victory. Like other Court nominees, Gorsuch had participated in a days-long dog-and-pony show on Capitol Hill, meeting with many senators for private conversations ahead of confirmation hearings. After one such meeting, Senator Richard Blumenthal, a Democrat, announced that Gorsuch had told him that Trump's attacks on the federal judiciary were "disheartening" and "demoralizing." Gorsuch's words were carefully chosen, discussed with handlers in advance. His aim wasn't tactical, as if to distance himself from the president and perhaps appeal to a few Democrats. Rather, he simply found Trump's attacks offensive. And he had begun to chafe at the entire appointments process. Being pawed over by vetters, being attacked in the press, being holed up many days in a suite in the Eisenhower Executive Office Building adjacent to the White House (what he called his "North Korean holding pen")—the whole thing was demeaning.

The president read of Gorsuch's comments and erupted—tweeting that Blumenthal had misrepresented Gorsuch's words, but then privately bellowing to aides that Gorsuch wasn't being "loyal." Gorsuch's handlers from the White House were told that Trump was talking about pulling the nomination. They advised Gorsuch so, as they continued to make the rounds on Capitol Hill. According to one account, Trump that evening whined to friends that he should have nominated Rudy Giuliani, the former mayor of New York City, even though Giuliani wasn't on Trump's list of 21.

Gorsuch was peeved. "Could you walk back what you said to Blumenthal?" asked Kelly Ayotte, the former Republican senator from New

Hampshire, who was Gorsuch's sherpa on the Hill. Much as he wanted to be a justice, he refused. Instead, he said, if the pressure continued, "I'll get on a plane and fly home to Colorado tonight." Later, he joked that if he withdrew his name, he could "write a book and make millions."

But like other momentary presidential explosions, this one passed. Trump stopped his threats, and Gorsuch ceased his. It didn't hurt Gorsuch's standing with the president that Gorsuch a few weeks later sent him a gushing handwritten note. "Your address to Congress was magnificent!" Gorsuch wrote of Trump's first address to a joint session of Congress. "And you were so kind to recognize Mrs. Scalia [the justice's widow Maureen] . . . and mention me. My teenage daughters were cheering the TV!" The note came so long after Trump's threats that it seemed unlikely Gorsuch was sucking up. He just was feeling good that a crisis was over, and he was given to fulsome thank-yous to those who wound up doing right by him.

At the Court, the conservative justices were mostly pleased they got what looked like a reliable, intelligent comrade. Considering who had nominated Gorsuch, they had worried they might get someone lacking in threshold credentials who might vote with them, but would tarnish the Court's image. But the chief was in a tougher position receiving Gorsuch, not Garland, as his newest colleague. Not only did he know Garland from their time together on the D.C. Circuit—and respect his craftsmanship—but Garland also was the reason Roberts got his clerkship with Judge Henry Friendly. More than Alito and Thomas and Kennedy, Roberts recognized what the Court was losing without Garland.

Gorsuch became the latest player in a long narrative about the Court's role in society. Even though he was replacing the conservative Scalia, the institution inevitably would change. It wouldn't be just a new arrangement of the lockers in the robing room or a different seating chart on the bench. When there are only nine people in the cast, personal dynamics count. Rapport matters. Trust forms. One of Gorsuch's mentors, Byron White, often had said that each time a new justice arrived, "it's a new Court."

It surely was after Gorsuch got there, marking an end to the perverse calm of the 2016–17 term. That relative lack of drama was a by-product of the political impasse that Scalia's death had triggered. The eight-justice Court had taken fewer big cases, and the cases it did take sometimes were decided 4–4, which under Court practice upheld the lower-court ruling but without setting any precedent. Opinions that did get written produced narrower rulings, more consensus, more caution. But those attributes weren't the result of newfound wisdom—only that there wasn't a fifth vote to go big and decide more controversial cases. While it took only four votes for the Court to agree to hear a case—one fewer than a majority of the full Court—the justices were reluctant to do so if it looked like an eight-member Court would be split. With Gorsuch on board, the Court could resume its triumphal march. As the term ended, the justices agreed, in a flurry of orders for the fall of 2017, to hear potential blockbusters on partisan gerrymandering, presidential authority, the power of public unions, and whether freedom of religion permitted discrimination against same-sex couples. The presence of Gorsuch was the difference why. An even more assertive docket was likely after Kennedy retired in 2018 and the conservatives solidified their majority.

IN HIS INITIAL MONTHS ON THE COURT, Gorsuch bonded only with Thomas—whose chambers were next to his, and who alone joined Gorsuch's first dissent in late June 2017. Although the case was minor, concerning the procedure for federal workers filing discrimination claims, the White House noticed. "So far, Gorsuch has a perfect record being with Clarence Thomas!" one of Trump's advisers told a colleague that day. In most of the cases in which he participated in his first months, Gorsuch and his new best friend composed what could be called the Tea Party fringe of the Court, of which not even Alito seemed a part. Several officials in the administration were so happy that they mused about Gorsuch as a future chief justice if their fondest wish ever came true and Roberts left prematurely.

Gorsuch was with Thomas not only in head count, but also when

Thomas filed a concurring opinion to stake out an outlier position unnecessary to resolve a specific appeal. (Concurrences allow justices to agree with the outcome in a case but not the reasoning the majority used to reach it.) Gorsuch did precisely what a true minimalist jurist should avoid—setting broad rules in the manner of legislators. A real conservative on the bench takes individual disputes as they come, allowing "the law" to work itself out measuredly, in dialogue with lower courts and at times with Congress as well. Gorsuch wanted none of that. Said one clerk, "He came here instantly willing to burn down the house to do what he was sure was right."

Although a handful of early opinions—on President Trump's travel ban, on carrying concealed guns in public, and especially on an Arkansas statute involving gay rights—didn't set Gorsuch in ideological stone, the only question seemed to be whether he would turn out to be even more conservative than Thomas or, for that matter, Scalia. Gorsuch was like an eight-year-old in a counterrevolutionary candy store. So many lower court rulings to overturn, so many errors of his colleagues to point out: unfair Second Amendment restrictions here, wrongheaded rights for gays and lesbians there! Soon, he was enlightening Ginsburg on how to interpret statutes. She and six other justices had found a reasonable way to reconcile a procedural flaw in a minor law. Bad judging, Gorsuch declared: "If a statute needs repair, there's a constitutionally prescribed way to do it. It's called legislation." A few days later, it was Roberts who apparently needed instruction, this time on the proper way to write opinions. They should be based on "general principles," not "ad hoc improvisations," Gorsuch explained in a freedom of religion case.

In early 2018, Gorsuch and Ginsburg were back at it. In a highly technical case on jurisdiction, a Gorsuch dissent went on about G.K. Chesterton's "fence," using the metaphor to argue that "we've wandered so far from the idea of a federal government of limited and enumerated powers that we've begun to lose sight of what it looked like in the first place." In her majority opinion, Ginsburg didn't conceal her contempt, 11 times taking on Gorsuch's "mighty strivings" and "absurdities."

Gorsuch's aggressiveness didn't much resemble the modest approach he had described before the Senate. Nor did his votes seem consistent with his repeated confirmation homily about there being "no such thing as a Republican judge or Democratic judge." In fact, his views seemed nicely aligned with the 21st-century GOP party line. Life tenure can do that to a person.

His own clerks delicately asked if he really wanted to be a pacesetter from the opening gun. "Are you sure you should be doing that?" asked one. "Will the chief be mad?" asked another. The second question was particularly astute, for the Gorsuch-Roberts relationship was already rocky. Gorsuch had not forgotten the Court ruling he believed embarrassed him during his confirmation hearings. It didn't help either that Gorsuch got grief at the very outset of his arrival at the Court. Roberts had suggested he attend the regular justices-only conference, which was taking place three days after he was sworn in. Gorsuch declined because he had yet to get up to speed on cases that would be discussed, and he needed to catch his breath after enduring the confirmation process. "Do you realize what I've just been put through?" he told another justice. He also had a long-standing date to take one of his daughters on a college visit.

Roberts was exasperated. He thought Gorsuch was disrespecting the Court by declining the invitation to "the conference," as it was called. To Roberts's detractors—in Gorsuch's camp and in other chambers—this was an example of the chief acting "chief-y." Roberts had no authority to order Gorsuch to be anywhere, but he was trying anyway. Since Gorsuch couldn't participate in cases until he made sure he had no conflicts of interests, attending would be a pointless exercise. But the chief was worried about the Court's image—about the new guy not being engaged and the press then having sport with it (which the press dutifully did). That concern for the Court, his critics alleged, was really more concern for his own image as chief. The critics loved to titter about how Roberts tried to choreograph any photo-op in which he appeared. Two rules: No photographs from behind him—that would highlight his bald spot. And never place too many tall people near the chief—it made him look smaller. (At a "class photo" shoot of the justices and clerks in the spring of 2017, two tall Thomas clerks had to move far away from the chief.) It was a close question whether the titters revealed more about the chief or the critics.

The chief also was displeased when Gorsuch disclosed he wouldn't be part of the "cert pool," which most justices had long used to reduce the burden of reviewing which cases to hear. Roberts thought the pool, which his chambers administered, made the Court more efficient. Although in recent terms the Court heard only 70 or so cases annually, it had to choose from among the 6,000 to 8,000 petitions that sought review of lower-court decisions. Losing parties had to file a "writ of certiorari" that demonstrated an important issue was in play. If at least four of the nine justices thought the issues weighty, the Court "granted cert." Otherwise, it "denied cert" and the lower-court ruling stood.

Going through thousands of petitions takes time, and none of the current justices other than Alito wanted to invest it. Instead, they assigned their clerks to the cert pool, which dates to the 1970s. Each petition was analyzed by a single clerk, who made a recommendation to grant or deny review. Justices then decided. Because each chambers no longer had to peruse every petition, the pool made life as a justice, and as a clerk, a lot easier. The pool also operated to make the docket even smaller, since a clerk who recommended a denial got in less trouble than one who granted cert that later turned out to be unwise. The problem with the system was that it invested vast discretion in newbie lawyers. Like Alito, Gorsuch wanted to read all the petitions himself. If his decision was meant to have any import, it was to signal independence, not to goad the chief. But around the courthouse, clerks saw it as accomplishing both ends.

An insignificant criminal case in late June 2017 offered a glimpse of the Gorsuch-Roberts byplay. An inmate in central Texas named Marcus Hicks claimed he had been wrongly sentenced to 20 years. Seven justices agreed. Without hearing argument and without issuing an opinion, the justices summarily returned the case to a lower court to reconsider the sentence. Roberts, joined by Thomas, dissented, saying the law was more complicated and the Court had acted rashly. It was a dissent—the chief lost. Gorsuch was part of the majority—and won.

But he still wrote a lone *concurrence* to scold his colleagues on both sides that the Court hadn't done enough and that Hicks was automatically entitled to a lesser sentence.

Roberts couldn't let that go. In his two-paragraph dissent, he twice referred to the misguided views of "my colleague" rather than "Justice Gorsuch." The use of "my colleague" didn't prove there was friction, but it was an odd, suggestive usage, and there's no more meticulous writer on the Court than Roberts. Only once before in his 12 years as chief had he referred to another justice that way, and in that case he was referring to Justice Breyer when he was a lower-court judge. In the last of his digs, Roberts mocked Gorsuch for claiming, as Roberts put it, that the case "is a no-brainer." Other than to Hicks, the case didn't amount even to small potatoes. But for Gorsuch and Roberts, on the last day of the term, it was a chance to have at each other.

For their part, the dispirited liberal justices hardly could miss Gorsuch's ways, both in substance and in attitude. New justices normally tread lightly, like rookies on a sports team. They observe how others do the job, soaking up the indigenous culture. "I was frightened to death for the first years," Breyer once told an interviewer. "I was afraid I might inadvertently write something harmful." How new justices behave—how much they adhere to the Court's seniority-based norms, quite apart from how they vote—can affect what colleagues think of them. It doesn't go over well to claim to be the smartest person in the room when everybody else in the room does, too—and they've been there a lot longer than you.

Once he started going to the justices' conference, which meets once or twice a week when the Court is in session, Gorsuch did fine. The conference takes place in a sanctum sanctorum—the large white-oak-paneled room within the chief's chambers, lined with hundreds of volumes of Court decisions on built-in bookcases. Only the nine justices attend. Clerks and staff aren't even allowed through the heavy unmarked double doors. As secret a meeting as any in American government, the conference is highly formal, with each justice sitting in an assigned seat based on seniority, each speaking and voting (on cert petitions and actual appeals) by seniority as well. All discussions are preceded by the ritual 36 handshakes, every justice with each of the others. It is the job of the most junior justice, now Gorsuch, to answer knocks on the outer door and to handle other mundane chores. Gorsuch was personally congenial and ably fetched coffee.

But in 12 weeks, he had shown himself to be a destabilizing upstart who was in an ideological hurry, taking over parts of some oral arguments and brimming with smarty-pants self-confidence that approached condescension. On the bench, eyes rolled. Off the bench, the other justices thought No. 9 was getting too big for his britches. It wasn't that they shunned him—only that they were disinclined to welcome him with the open arms that greeted most new arrivals. That didn't mean a change in voting outcomes—only that Gorsuch's opportunity for engaging his colleagues, which might help in close cases, would be limited. Scalia, his idol, knew this well. While personable, his unceasing jabs at Kennedy and O'Connor in his opinions hindered his ability to talk things out with them, in the conference or in chambers. Scalia was a fine hunting buddy, but many of the justices didn't want any part of him at work. He had unquestioned influence at the Court, but it was despite his manner. The early question about Gorsuch was whether he was following that example.

No case was too small for Gorsuch to opine on, even when most of the other justices did not. "Dude, pick your spots!" suggested a law professor who had clerked for Kennedy. Some of the clerks in other chambers took an instant aversion to the mien of the new justice. Late in the term, a retinue of clerks took him out for lunch and found him still in gosh-golly-gee Senate confirmation mode. "He kept telling us how he liked to watch the sun set over the mountains," according to one of the clerks. Even when it came to the humdrum, Gorsuch didn't quite fit in. All the justices have their own official Court photo. It's like a yearbook portrait: you're smiling and coiffed, the lighting's perfect. Gorsuch's is so blurred it's unusable. He wouldn't sit long enough for the photographer—too much bother. The wisecrack around the building was that Gorsuch had succeeded in unifying the Court: Just about everybody other than Thomas couldn't stand him most of the time.

"I respect all of my colleagues and genuinely like most of them," Ginsburg told an audience at Columbia University in February 2018.

Hmm, given her expressed affection at different times for Roberts, Kennedy, Breyer, Sotomayor and Kagan, that reduced the other possibilities.

However, the liberal justices, just like liberal advocacy groups, were still figuring the Court seat to worry about was Kennedy's. The Gorsuch-for-Scalia swap seemed to mean little in terms of case outcomes, whereas in a Trump administration, a Kennedy retirement might result in resolute conservative control. The justices themselves had been speculating about whether AMK, as insiders referred to him, would retire in June, at the end of the 2016–17 term. Enjoying the attention, Kennedy divulged nothing; "Sphinx-like," a colleague called him. Ginsburg was left to ask clerks around the building if they'd heard anything.

But the liberals quickly came to see the reality that Gorsuch's presence drove home. The point wasn't that his votes were meaningfully worse than Scalia's. It was that Gorsuch was 30 years younger and raring to go. Days after the term ended, the new justice rode atop a '59 Cadillac convertible in a Fourth of July parade back in Colorado like a returning political hero, shaking hands and complimenting kids in cowboy hats. By contrast, Breyer used the holiday to recite the Declaration of Independence, without fanfare, under an American flag, to a small group of residents in the New Hampshire village where he summered.

What's more, Gorsuch's seat was now presumably lost to the liberals for a generation. With the theft of that seat, the liberal wing of the Court had missed its best opportunity since the late 1960s to have a working majority, with five justices appointed by a Democratic president. Liberal advocacy groups abandoned plans to initiate lawsuits that might someday lead to a Court ruling dismantling loathed decisions like *Heller* and *Citizens United*—just as conservative groups now started maneuvering on the best way to challenge rulings like *Roe* and *Chevron*. Gorsuch was a reminder of what could have been, for one side, and what was surely to come, for the other. Elections have consequences.

BYRON WHITE'S LINE ABOUT A "new Court" each time a justice arrived had an obvious corollary: It's a big adjustment for the new justice. When

Thomas was confirmed in 1991, White advised him, "Well, Clarence, in your first five years you wonder how you got here. After that, you wonder how *your colleagues* got here."

How the current justices got there is a story of politics and circumstance, guile and chance. What they all shared was a view of the Court's ascendancy in American government.

CHAPTER 5

THE INSTITUTIONALIST AND THE NOTORIOUS

In barely a decade on the Court, John Roberts had made a name for himself. Arriving at 50, he was then the youngest person on the Court and the youngest chief justice since John Marshall was appointed at 45 in 1801. Only the 17th chief in American history—compared with 44 presidents—he was known as a consummate legal mind; a virtuoso with a pen, lucid and wry; and at least most of the time, a thoughtful administrator. The last quality was especially important in a small organization made up of outsize egos. The chief had continued his predecessor's policy in the conference that nobody spoke a second time until everybody had a chance to speak once. But, unlike his predecessor, Roberts gave his colleagues more leeway when it was their turn—five minutes or so—before he nudged them to wrap it up. His method made for a more harmonious conference.

Roberts also had the right touch as an ambassador of the law. He was chief justice of the United States, not "chief justice of the Supreme Court." In the spring of 2017, after giving a heartfelt commencement address at his son's boarding school that quoted Socrates and Bob Dylan, Roberts handed out signed pocket copies of the Constitution. The teenagers were actually impressed. He also could do shtick—and be very quick. On tours of his chambers, he liked to point out the 19th-century sofa on which John Quincy Adams had died after suffering a stroke at the Capitol. (The sofa made it to the Court in 1935.) Asked once what Court policy he thought most needed changing, he replied: "The odd historical quirk that the chief justice only gets one vote."

Despite an apparent inability to exhibit an innocuous midwestern smile—his boyish round face seemed to have a perpetual smirk—the other justices regarded him as a cordial colleague and an able custodian of the Court's independence. He loved the Court and treasured his role in trying to keep its reputation secure. Always dressed in a pressed suit, tailored to fit immaculately over his athletic build, Roberts was all business all the time, except maybe for wanting to talk some Notre Dame football at the lunches most justices attended in their second-floor dining room when the Court was in session. (In his study, on a shelf right below bobbleheads of himself and Abraham Lincoln, Roberts kept a football signed by the Fighting Irish coach.) So wedded was he to the suit-and-tie uniform that dinner guests at his suburban house were often amused that his concession to informality was to roll up the sleeves of his dress shirt and put on an apron.

For all his administrative dexterity, some of his colleagues found him to be somewhat vain—from the day they were officially welcomed. That initial source of irritation was the investiture ceremony in the courtroom, in which a new justice is formally installed. It's just a show and takes under 10 minutes, but with dignitaries and family there, it's a big deal. The new justice, seated at ground level in a chair once used by Chief Justice Marshall, facing his colleagues, hears some nice words and then ascends the bench. At Neil Gorsuch's investiture, attended by President Trump and the first lady, Roberts recognized Gorsuch as "the 101st associate justice of the Supreme Court of the United States." Well, that was true enough, just as Roberts in 2010 had welcomed Elena Kagan as "the 100th associate justice."

But that wasn't how it had been done before at the tradition-bound Court. In 2009, Sonia Sotomayor was the "111th justice," and in 2006

Samuel Alito was the "110th justice"—without the "associate" modifier. Gorsuch should've been the 113th, and Kagan should've been the 112th. Somehow, Roberts had changed the script by subtracting 12 from the total—which was the number of chief justices who hadn't previously served as an associate justice. (Five of the 17 chiefs overall had been on the Court earlier.) Now, there would be one running tally for "associate justice" and another for "chief," which served to make the latter rank all the more exclusive. The chief justice was often referred to as "first among equals," for he had little control over his colleagues. Separating the tallies reminded them he was still first. At least Rehnquist only added fancy stripes to his robes.

Few of the guests at the Gorsuch investiture—senators, White House staff, former Gorsuch clerks, Republican royalty from prior administrations—even noticed the switcheroo. Afterward, they were too busy bruiting about whether Anthony Kennedy would retire at the end of the term. But the new justice noticed, just as Kagan had. Other justices noticed as well. They each remembered what number they were, in the way that every president knew which domino he was in the great historical line dating to 1789. Why would the chief justice, a student of history who revered the Court's own, do this? *Why was he messing with my number?* (In Roberts's defense, court staffers say they, not the chief, made the renumbering change—to eliminate confusion over double-counting of the five chiefs who had previously been associate justices. But for those justices who cared, the defense rang hollow.)

Piddling issues of protocol seem to matter a lot more in a small institution in which the members have no boss, cannot be fired, and often work together for decades at a time. Everybody strives to get along, but little things can get them exercised. When the justices' private conference room was renovated in 2008, the large table in the middle was rotated 90 degrees, from an east-west to a north-south axis. Justices Sandra Day O'Connor, David Souter, and Anthony Kennedy supervised the committee that made the move. But "the rearrangement of the furniture" was done "without consulting all the other justices," John Paul Stevens groused in his memoir. He then devoted two more pages to discussing "the subtle and unfortunate impact," including on acoustics, proximity to mobile carts containing files, and free space for autographing stacks of photographs of the entire Court.

The chief's pride in his primus inter pares status reflected not only love of the institution but a competitive streak. Anyone who made it to the Court had to have that trait. When he was a child, he never lost a spelling bee. But for all his grace, Roberts took competitiveness to another level. One time he was out for lunch with a group of clerks and entertained them with baseball talk. The clerks listened intently. When the subject of Chicago came up. Roberts expounded on the sociological significance of Wrigley Field, home of the Cubbies, not getting lights until the 1990s. The phrase he used was the "middle of" that decade. A clerk said, no, the chief was wrong—the date was earlier.

That was too much for Roberts. "I'll bet you a dollar that it's closer to 1995 than 1985," he countered.

They did a Google phone search, and sure enough the clerk was right: The answer was 1988. Roberts didn't have any money with him, so he had to borrow a dollar from a member of his security detail to pay off the wager. But he kept chewing it over. Later, back at the Court, Roberts thanked the clerks for lunch, but as he started to walk off to his study, he announced that he'd erred in not narrowing the spread. "I should've bet on a date closer to the one you did," he told the victorious clerk. The chief justice couldn't get over losing to a law clerk.

As much as luck played a role in getting selected for the Court, for most of Roberts's career he seemed destined for it. Constitutionally—in both senses—his blend of professional excellence and personal composure made him an obvious choice for any Republican president. About the only establishment credential he lacked was prominent public service—like Earl Warren's time as governor of California from 1943 to 1954, or John Marshall's as secretary of state from 1800 to 1801. And even that weakness was an advantage, because he couldn't be tarred as a political toady.

But Roberts was still deeply conservative politically, and it drove him nuts when other conservatives questioned it. For his entire career before becoming a judge, apart from intermittent stretches at a big law firm, he had been a loyal Washington servant of the Republican Party. A year out of Harvard Law School, he had clerked for William Rehnquist, then a Nixon-appointed associate justice, who became his mentor. Roberts went on to work in the Reagan administration, first as a special assistant to the attorney general and then in the White House; in both jobs, he helped screen candidates for the lower federal courts.

Later, under President George H.W. Bush, he was the No. 2 lawyer in the Justice Department's solicitor general's office, which is responsible for representing the federal government before the Court. During the Florida recount after the 2000 presidential election, Roberts played a quiet but important part in urging an appeal to the Supreme Court; he also advised Republican Florida governor Jeb Bush and the Republican state legislature on how Florida's electoral votes could be awarded to Bush's brother even if Democratic candidate Al Gore won a recount. A few years earlier, the Clinton White House had considered Roberts, then in private practice, as a possibility to argue before the Court on behalf of Clinton in the sexual harassment lawsuit brought by Paula Jones. Roberts had been vetted by a 36-year-old staff lawyer in the White House named Elena Kagan. Roberts's artistry as an appellate advocate—the best of his time, arguing 39 times before the Court—led his admirers to say that the G in John G. Roberts Jr. stands for God. ("Glover," actually.)

So, when he noticed during the 2016 presidential campaign that various Republican candidates—most often Trump and Ted Cruz, a senator from Texas and another former Rehnquist clerk—were regularly trashing him, he reacted. The chief's ostensible offense had been to cast the decisive vote in 2012 when the Court, 5–4, upheld the Affordable Care Act. Roberts was "an absolute disaster," Trump said during a GOP debate. "He gave us Obamacare. It might as well be called RobertsCare!" Another time, Trump claimed Roberts had voted as he did "because he wanted to be popular inside the Beltway." Come summer, the chief finally had enough. After hearing his name booed during the Republican convention, in a remarkable moment he confided his indignation to a

friend. "I've been a reliable conservative," he protested. "Don't they realize I'm part of them?" Roberts believed he had done as much to curtail
the powers of the federal government as any recent justice.

Though it was Trump and Cruz who spewed the vitriol, other, calmer
conservatives had similarly lost faith in Roberts. On their scorecard, he
had cast correct votes on such matters as gun control and voting rights,
but his Obamacare ruling rendered him a traitor to the cause. Roberts's
own view was that his vote in the Obamacare case had been rational,
reasonable and necessary to keep the Court out of the upcoming 2012
presidential campaign. In his estimation, it wasn't supposed to matter
that he thought the legislation represented sausage-making at its worst.
Eventually, Roberts began saying that if both Republican and Democrat
politicians were attacking him, he must be doing something right.

One might suppose the chief justice of the United States wouldn't especially care what craven political candidates said about him. He serves
for life. They'll be gone from the scene while he's likely still center-seat
at the marble temple for years to come. But that wasn't always the side
Roberts displayed privately, in contrast to his buttoned-up, buttoned-
down demeanor at the Court. The chief also had not forgotten that
nearly two dozen Democrats had voted against his confirmation. The
justices are human, after all.

Every recent Court era takes the name of the chief who reigns—like
the Warren Court—but not every chief manages to leave a mark. From
1969 to 1986, for example, Warren Burger was the 15th chief justice, but
it was the "Burger Court" in name only. With his thick white mane and
sonorous voice, he looked and sounded the part better than he played
it. He was better known not for his opinions but for the way Justice
Thurgood Marshall derisively greeted him around the building with
"What's shakin', Chiefy baby?" Rather, Bill Rehnquist on the right and
Bill Brennan on the left overshadowed Burger, and typically led their
respective factions.

Burger's colleagues on both sides detested his self-regard, which was
second only to his dithering. Among a chief's responsibilities is to run
the conference. Burger was awful at it. Justice Harry A. Blackmun, his

colleague for most of his tenure as chief—and a friend from boyhood—kept notes of his running annoyance. "The conference today was like a bunch of cackling hens all speaking at once," he wrote, blaming Burger for being unable to "control" the conference. "Spoiled children reaction at times." It was even worse than in the days of Associate Justice Felix Frankfurter, a former law professor who could pontificate for 50 minutes at a time—which, as his irked listeners pointed out, was exactly as long as his lectures at Harvard. Rehnquist, who replaced Burger, made it a point to run a no-nonsense conference. So did Roberts.

The conference these days is an administrative session rather than a place to hash out ideas. The opportunity for cackling hens has long since passed. In the day-to-day routine of the Court, the other justices appreciated Roberts's skills at separating work from play. At their private luncheons, for example, there was a rule against shoptalk—better to confine disagreements to whether "Breaking Bad" or "Game of Thrones" was more entertaining. Justices' birthdays were always celebrated, with the chief contributing the wine; Scalia once brought the main course: a "Bambi" he had bagged himself. Even so, no amount of collegiality could mask the underlying rifts within the Court over constitutional issues.

Roberts had craved to be a justice his whole adult life. But even when he got the job, there was no guarantee his vote would be important. When he took the bench, the Court was split between four justices tilting to the left and four justices tilting to the right, with Kennedy as the fulcrum. When Scalia died in 2016, much of Roberts's power hung in the balance, dependent on who filled the seat. If Merrick Garland were confirmed as the new justice, Roberts and the conservatives might be in the wilderness for the rest of his tenure as chief. If Trump won the White House and made the next appointment, the Court would remain in relative equipoise, and Roberts would lose no ground. But a Republican presidency held the possibility of more appointments, and a conservative monolith that could rule well into the 21st century. Indeed, if Trump were able to appoint several conservatives—say, in place of Kennedy and Ginsburg—then Roberts would become the new swing vote. It would indisputably be the Roberts Court. So, while Roberts was no fan of Trump, the chief understood that a Trump pick was far more likely to result in the chief retaining influence.

In public at least, Roberts liked to call himself judicially modest, a sideline actor in the larger scheme of government. "I feel like I'm holding the reins of a horse," he told a visitor to his chambers in early 2017, but added, "I dare not pull on them too hard because I might discover they're not attached to anything." At his confirmation hearings in 2005, he offered his everlasting analogy of a justice to an umpire who merely calls balls and strikes. "Umpires don't make the rules—they apply them," he told senators, in a comparison he'd earlier used to great effect in his interview with President Bush. "The role of an umpire and a judge is critical. They make sure everybody plays by the rules. But it is a limited role." The parallel was only superficially appealing. An actual umpire, Gary Cederstrom, mocked it, explaining that "the strike zone is a living, breathing document." In constitutional law, the justices were not so much umpires as nine sluggers in the game.

Roberts himself knew the analogy had been glib. Four years later, on the same day Sotomayor was sworn in, one of Sotomayor's lower-court colleagues, Jon O. Newman, razzed the chief justice for oversimplifying what judges do. Balls and strikes are defined by a single rule, but a judge often has to choose among many, Newman wrote in an op-ed in the *Hartford Courant*. Sometimes the rules conflict. Sometimes the rules are unclear. Of course Roberts, a sports fan, knew that, but he wasn't going to say so. At a reception at the Court after Sotomayor's investiture, he pulled Newman aside. "I just want you to know I'm *still* calling balls and strikes," the chief said, letting on as well that newspaper clips about him speedily reached his eyes.

The umpire analogy wasn't original—Justice Robert H. Jackson had made the comparison more than a half century earlier, in 1951. But Roberts got deserved praise for talking a good game, which was the goal in confirmation hearings. The Senate, by a 78-to-22 vote, approved his nomination.

With the exception of his vote in both Obamacare cases, though, he has proven himself to be something other than a balls-and-strikes judicial minimalist. As chief, his ongoing twin agendas—to eradicate racial preferences and to deregulate political campaigns—boldly rejected contrary policies adopted by the democratically accountable branches of government. Congress and various localities had decided that race could be used, for example, to help desegregate schools or to achieve diversity in the workforce. Roberts insisted that itself was a violation of equal protection. Congress had also decided that money could corrupt campaigns. But Roberts thought restrictions on contributions violated "the whole point of the First Amendment." In both race and campaigns, as with gun control, the chief justice bore substantial responsibility for the Court's triumphalism.

ROBERTS HAD HIS CONSERVATIVE SKEPTICS—beginning with Samuel Alito and Clarence Thomas, who seethed to their law clerks, and to others in the conservative community, about Roberts's Obamacare vote. But on the liberal side of the Court, Ruth Bader Ginsburg was the undisputed leader—and after Justice John Paul Stevens's retirement in 2010, the most senior. That leadership position helped her become a folk hero, late in her more than 20 years on the Court. The wonder was that it hadn't happened sooner. Before joining the D.C. Circuit in 1980, she had been the preeminent appellate litigator for women's rights, winning five gender-discrimination cases before the Supreme Court—"the Thurgood Marshall of that cause," as Scalia put it when she was named to the *Time* 100 in 2015.

Like Marshall, the first African-American justice, Ginsburg masterminded a canny litigation strategy. Her favorite tactic was to argue on behalf of men who suffered discrimination. For example, in 1976 she challenged an Oklahoma law that allowed women, but not men, to buy 3.2-percent beer at age 18. The Supreme Court ruled 7–2 in Ginsburg's favor. By arguing against silly laws that hurt men, she was able to establish the broader "equal protection" principle that laws based on any gender stereotypes were probably unconstitutional. While histrionics were fine for politicians and protesters, she believed incrementalism worked better in the courts. Others made speeches—Ginsburg, as an advocate, made law.

But the similarities to Marshall ended there. Nobody had called the tall, burly Marshall reserved. His energy and storytelling combined with legal prowess and disregard of physical danger to make him a larger-than-life character. When he showed up at courthouses in Southern towns in the early 1950s—all 6-feet-2 of him—blacks "came in their jalopy cars and their overalls," according to his secretary. "All they wanted to do—if they could—was just touch him, just touch him, *Lawyer Marshall*, as if he were a god."

One Marshall biographer described his power this way: "No wonder that across the South, in their darkest, most demoralizing hours . . . the spirits of black citizens would be lifted with two words whispered in defiance and hope: 'Thurgood's coming.' "

Nobody ever said "Ruth's coming." At 5-feet-1 and barely 100 pounds, Ginsburg was a diminutive presence, almost hidden by her giant eye-glasses. She spoke carefully and precisely, like the law professor she had been for many years. "On and off the bench," one legal commentator wrote, "she always looked and sounded like the most dangerous weapon she could possibly be carrying would be a potato kugel." Opponents who dwelled on her physicality got what they deserved when they found themselves on the legal mat after an argument. Though colleagues and clerks recognized her warmth, outsiders could interpret her shyness as aloofness. The clerks from chambers of other justices loved to hear her war stories, but during many terms when she had groups of them over for high tea—complete with cupcakes served on china, with knives and forks—the opera music was usually playing so loud they had little chance of hearing her.

And yet whereas Marshall's star had waned once he joined the Court in 1967—after he retired in 1991, he was affectionately known best around the building for never missing "The Price Is Right" on weekday mornings—Ginsburg's grew. Though it was O'Connor in 1981 who was the first female justice (retiring in 2005), Ginsburg came to outshine her, turning into as close to a celebrity as the Court has ever had. Four times she's been honored with impersonations on "Saturday Night Live" and she's done pushups with Stephen Colbert on the "Late Show" (even if the colorful Justice Douglas did set a benchmark of sorts in 1956 by appearing on the popular prime-time game show "What's My Line?").

Part of Ginsburg's renown was self-generated, if unintentionally. She started to write more aggressively, in defense of freedoms she thought were being jeopardized by the Court's conservative majority. In 2013, a law student created the Notorious R.B.G. Tumblr online, "in tribute to Justice Ginsburg's fierce dissent" in the *Shelby County* voting rights case. "Notorious R.B.G." was a play on the late gangsta rap artist The Notorious B.I.G., who, as she liked to say, was also from Brooklyn, though he weighed three and a half times what she did and didn't have her collection of mezuzahs.

The meme took off, but she first learned about it only through her clerks. She's the only justice in history widely known by her initials. Her bobblehead is the hardest to find on the resale market. There's a best-selling mash-up of her career, *Notorious RBG: The Life and Times of Ruth Bader Ginsburg*—there she is in a full-color photograph in India, riding atop an elephant with her dear friend and opera pal Scalia; and in her robes with her husband in chef garb. There's also the recent *Ruth Bader Ginsburg Coloring Book* and *I Dissent: Ruth Bader Ginsburg Makes Her Mark*, a picture book biography for third-graders. (Several of the other justices thought these books crassly commercialized the Court and wished Ginsburg cooperated in fewer of them.) She stockpiles some of these items in her chambers—they're much better handouts than the official Gavel-Headed Supreme Court Pencils available in the gift shop on the ground floor. Near the Rothko on loan from the National Gallery, and a framed copy of the program for the 1895 gala at the Metropolitan Opera House in New York City that honored suffragist Elizabeth Cady Stanton's 80th birthday, Ginsburg proudly displays the snapshot of a bespectacled little girl dressed up on Halloween as the Notorious R.B.G.

Ginsburg also made the lifestyle pages for her fashion sense—the collection of judicial jabots, the fishnet gloves, the Ferragamo shoes, and the white ball gown and platinum wig she wore as an extra in the Strauss opera "Ariadne auf Naxos" at the Kennedy Center. Felicity Jones is playing her in an upcoming biopic, "On the Basis of Sex." At state dinners during the Obama administration, she was the one guest other than the president whom people wanted to sit next to. Ben & Jerry's has been petitioned to come out with "Ruth Bader Ginger." (There have been no requests for Plain Vanilla Alito.) At a talk at Notre Dame not long before Election Day in 2016, she was asked if her role was like being Queen Ruth.

"I'm not queen," she said, adding mischievously, "I'd rather be notorious." Which she certainly was after her comments about Trump during the 2016 campaign.

She might never have made it to the Supreme Court. Newly inaugurated President Bill Clinton appointed her in 1993 only after going through eight other names in a clown car process not uncommon in his administration. Within a few days of Justice Byron White's retirement announcement, Clinton decided he wanted Mario Cuomo, the governor of New York. Cuomo was progressive, a public intellectual, and a politician of stature like Earl Warren. Cuomo vacillated for days before turning the offer down, citing his duty to the New Yorkers who had elected him. Clinton's next choice: George Mitchell, the Democratic majority leader in the Senate. He wasn't interested either. Neither was Richard Riley, the secretary of education. Bruce Babbitt, the secretary of the interior, was the next possibility—and really wanted the job—but he had confirmation liabilities.

That was it for politicians, so Clinton's team turned to judges. The last in a series of four under initial consideration was Stephen Breyer, chief judge of the federal appeals court in Boston and a former top Senate aide to Ted Kennedy. Breyer had been on the appeals court for 13 years, confirmed with bipartisan support during the dying days of the Carter administration. He seemed to have the Court seat locked up until a disastrous interview with Clinton. Recovering from broken ribs and a collapsed lung in a bike accident that had hospitalized him, Breyer was off his game, and Clinton was unimpressed. Still, on the advice of staffers, a wavering president stuck with him. But the next morning, after questions came up about Breyer's tax records on employing a part-time housekeeper, he was finished.

Eighty-six days after White's retirement announcement, Clinton couldn't believe he had failed to name a replacement. "We're really at square one," he told Ron Klain, a White House lawyer who was centrally involved in judicial appointments and who had clerked for White. "We haven't consulted with Janet Reno. Call her and see what she thinks." Though she was the new attorney general, Reno had never been part of Clinton's inner circle and hadn't been involved in the process.

"I don't understand why Ruth Bader Ginsburg hasn't been at the top of your list," Reno said. "She's the most logical person to pick."

Ginsburg already had boosters, both in the Senate and in the academy. Her most strategic was her husband Marty, a leading tax lawyer who had been contacting Klain and others in the counsel's office daily to lobby for his wife. Even Scalia wanted her. She liked to tell the story about how, during all this, Scalia was asked, "If you were stranded on a desert island with a Court colleague, whom would you prefer, Larry Tribe or Mario Cuomo?" Both were noted liberals—Tribe as a Harvard law professor, Cuomo as a three-term governor. Scalia answered, "Ruth Bader Ginsburg."

But though Ginsburg had been on a White House list of 50 potential nominees that had been assembled early on in the administration—no more than "dinner-party ruminations," one staffer called it—her name had stimulated little interest. Some in the White House actually doubted her liberal bona fides, primarily because of the Madison Lecture she had given three months earlier at New York University that questioned what she labeled the "extraordinary" constitutional underpinnings of *Roe v. Wade*. The gist of her remarks was that the 1973 abortion ruling went "too far, too fast."

Her comments about *Roe* worried White House officials, and they knew they couldn't very well bring her in at that point and ask her to elaborate. In due course, they concluded they were overlawyering what she had written: Of course she'd be fine on the right to choose. Wary of relying on the take of advisers, Clinton himself read the NYU lecture and interviewed her. She was named the next day—the first Supreme Court nominee of a Democratic president in 26 years and, at 60, the oldest nominee since 1971. Within two months, she was confirmed uneventfully, in a 96–3 Senate vote.

Two decades later, Ginsburg's rock-star status—newly found, in her 80s—may have been partly why she dismissed suggestions during Obama's presidency that she retire and allow him to pick a successor who could serve on the Court for much more time than she had left. In 2009, 16 days into his first term, Ginsburg had surgery for early-stage pancreatic cancer. Even before the operation was disclosed publicly, the White House had learned of the diagnosis through the D.C. medical grapevine—an outrageous breach of doctor-patient confidentiality, but hardly unexpected in a close-knit company town like Washington. She recovered completely, just as she had from another cancer, of the colon, 10 years before.

Marking her 15th anniversary on the Court, Roberts playfully acknowledged her resilience "on the occasion of your reaching the midpoint of your tenure." The chief said she had "earned acclaim" for her "work ethic," her "precision with words," and her "total disrespect for the normal day-night work schedule adhered to by everyone else since the beginning of recorded history." Ginsburg could work so late that the Court guards had to unlock the doors for her to leave; she found herself doing more of that after Marty died in 2010. Even after getting home, she sometimes worked till well after midnight.

But the two cancers, along with her age, had led to a ghoulish whispering campaign among some liberals that she should retire, perhaps before Obama's 2012 reelection campaign or at least as the 2014 midterm elections approached. If the GOP were to reclaim the Senate, an Obama nominee to the Court might not be confirmable—or might not even get a hearing, as Garland later learned. Breyer, nearly six years younger than Ginsburg, wasn't subjected to the time-to-quit chorus. But both he and Ginsburg were in the mind of a Harvard law professor whose widely read *New Republic* essay in 2011 called on them to step down. "Both are unlikely to be able to outlast a two-term Republican," Randall Kennedy wrote. "Service comes in many forms, including making way for others." His was a "plea for realism, which is often difficult to muster in the face of the idolatry that suffuses popular thinking about the justices."

Well before the *New Republic* piece, the Obama administration had heard the rumblings—from former Ginsburg clerks and then through other back channels. Some of her friends had raised the subject with her, pointing out the possibility of a Senate flip, as well as the reality that since World War II only one party had won the presidency three terms in a row. By 2014, as the midterms neared, Obama himself was hoping Ginsburg would retire, despite their mutual fondness. Ginsburg addressed what her fans thought was a sexist attitude—and what she herself likened to a deathwatch. "When I forget the names of cases that I once could recite," she told one interviewer, "I will know." Until then, she said many times, "I will stay." If Trump served two terms, Ginsburg would be two months short of turning 92—and the oldest justice ever.

It's only natural to enjoy being notorious for as long as possible. Her cautious instincts—conspicuous both in the Madison Lecture and in how she litigated gender equality—were real. But in crucial cases—like *Obergefell*, the same-sex marriage case, in which she joined in the grandiloquent majority opinion authored by Justice Kennedy—she was as much an interventionist as the colleagues she chided.

CHAPTER 6

THE LEFT FLANK

NINE MONTHS AFTER GINSBURG'S APPOINTMENT, JUSTICE HARRY Blackmun retired, giving President Clinton another seat on the Court to fill. Breyer again was in the mix. But again it looked like he might come in second.

Clinton had gotten over how poorly Breyer had performed during his interview the year before. Both had written that episode off to Breyer's biking mishap. And whatever issues had existed about tax records for Breyer's household help were straightened out. Breyer's credentials and connections were so strong—and his confirmation chances so likely— that naming him seemed inevitable. But Clinton had his heart set on someone else: Richard Arnold, a federal appellate judge in Little Rock. (Bruce Babbitt, another also-ran for Ginsburg's seat, was the other of three finalists.) Arnold was every bit as distinguished as Breyer, and had been close to Clinton going back to the president's Arkansas days. Arnold had been a contender the year earlier, but was eliminated from consideration because of lymphoma, which had plagued him since the 1970s.

Now, Hillary Clinton pushed hard for Arnold again. Perhaps his health—and longevity—deserved another look. The president himself took the step of personally consulting with Arnold's physicians. The White House even drafted a speech announcing Arnold's nomination, though a speechwriter's email made clear the nomination wasn't a done deal; the subject line read, "Updated Version. Don't Assume a Decision. It's Chinatown." In the end—based on a medical evaluation and with Arnold's blessing—Clinton determined the gamble was too great. Arnold was out (and died a decade later at 68, of complications from the lymphoma).

Breyer was back in, and was nominated on the same day Arnold was ruled out. He would be confirmed easily, by an 87–9 vote. The whole process had taken less than half the time that Ginsburg's had. That should have been cause for celebration—especially at a White House that had promised this time would be "different"—but Clinton didn't savor the moment.

For inexplicable reasons, and informing Breyer only 30 minutes earlier that he'd been selected, Clinton made the announcement alone in the Rose Garden, opting not even to wait until Breyer could fly down from Boston. And unlike the lavish personal praise Clinton had intended to offer for Arnold—not only as "one of the outstanding jurists of our age," but for "his ability to quote Scripture in Latin, Greek and Hebrew, his competitiveness on the golf course, and his deep concentration when he plays cards"—the president was mechanical about Breyer. He did cite Breyer's academic and political pedigree—particularly his time in the late 1970s as chief counsel to the Senate Judiciary Committee, where he earned the respect of both Ted Kennedy, a Democrat, and Orrin Hatch, a Republican. But half of the president's remarks were about the Court candidates he didn't pick, Arnold and Babbitt.

About the nicest thing said about Breyer came from Scalia. "First Ruth, and now Steve?" he told a guest at Breyer's swearing-in ceremony. "It's almost enough to make me vote Democrat."

It's been that way for Breyer ever since, not quite earning the prominence of some of his colleagues. Though he had written varied thoughtful works articulating the role of the Court, they didn't sell like Sonia Sotomayor's memoir *My Beloved World*. And even within the lonely legal universe, the scholarship of other judges frequently garnered more discussion. Though usually a reliable liberal in the Court's most-watched decisions—and impassioned on such matters as the failure of capital punishment—he didn't inspire a following like the Notorious R.B.G.'s.

And finally, though his earnest pragmatism—born of temperament as well as his time on Capitol Hill—predisposed Breyer to seek consensus, he failed to achieve it in the big rulings like *Bush v. Gore*, on the 2000 presidential election; and *Shelby County*, on voting rights. Part of that was due to seniority. Even with more than 20 years on the Court, in cases in which he was in the majority, he couldn't control who got to write the opinion. That was because Ginsburg usually voted with him and, as the more senior justice, it was her call, unless an even more senior justice or the chief was in the majority. That was just how the Court worked.

Breyer deserved better, based on both his writing and his effort. But in a factionalized era it was his fate to be considered by many liberals, including sotto voce in the Obama White House, as a justice who sometimes yearned to command the middle and found himself getting run over. Progressive critics wanted more William Brennan; sometimes, they argued, you had to draw bright lines and take a firm stand on one side or the other. Sometimes you had to declare majestic moral principles rather than craft pedestrian rules intended to resolve only "the case before the Court." Had Hillary Clinton won the presidency and put a progressive on the Court, or even had Garland been confirmed, Breyer might have displaced Kennedy as the swing vote in some cases.

Confronted with the undaunted interventionism of other justices, Breyer's restraint just wasn't a match. He understood the disenchantment that those on the left had for him at times. He would smile and point out he was no Pollyanna, understanding that the country didn't always live up to the lofty goals inherent in the Constitution. In his 2005 book *Active Liberty*—a response of sorts to Scalia's originalist-textualist tract *A Matter of Interpretation*—Breyer acknowledged a national survey showing "that more students know the names of the Three Stooges than the three branches of government." But he maintained that conscientious judges should view the Constitution in a way that empowered citizens to govern themselves, through dialogue and engagement in the political process.

Judges, he wrote, "can make clear, above all, that the Constitution is not a document designed to solve" all problems. Rather, it "trusts people to solve these problems themselves. And it creates a *framework* for a government that will help them." That framework, according to Breyer, meant "democratically determined solutions, protective of the individual's basic liberties." The task of judges, he believed, was to use the Constitution to foster that democracy-based structure, while at the same time ensuring that elemental freedoms remained inviolate in the process.

Breyer's faith in institutions that helped "participatory self-government" to flourish was ruptured only once in his time on the Court. For him, *Bush v. Gore* represented the worst kind of injudicious interference, but his displeasure over it mostly ebbed. "You play the hand you're dealt," he liked to tell clerks who questioned how he handled being on losing sides. He remained the happiest warrior on the Court, doing the most public speaking, sometimes in spirited debates with Scalia over constitutional interpretation, one time before an audience of thousands. But Breyer has indicated on occasion his belief that diminished public confidence in the Court might be fallout from *Bush v. Gore*.

Practically all clerks love their justices. It's an intimate connection forged in the crucible of high-stakes legal matters—but Breyer's were especially close to him, drawn to his uninhibited, genial personality. He was a chef, a birdwatcher, a philosopher, and a buff of movies like "The Man Who Shot Liberty Valance." Equally at home with Proust and the Red Sox, he was an inveterate talker about both topics and a hundred more. His face was as expressive as Ginsburg's was not. Whatever sense of outrage he had about injustices typically was expressed as irony rather than malice. And he didn't take himself as seriously as other justices did. After he lost out to Ginsburg for a seat, when he went back to his court in Boston, he told another judge that "there's only two people who aren't convinced I'm going to be on the Supreme Court. One is me and the other is Clinton."

More than some of the justices, Breyer took a sincere interest in the lives of clerks. When they came into his office lined with rare leather-bound books, they often found a roaring hearth, even in warm weather. It made for an easy setting just to schmooze. Some justices saw their former clerks only at annual reunions or decennial birthdays. Breyer maintained deeper ties with his long after they departed for Wall Street, K Street, academe or the DA's office.

His clerks also simply found him entertaining to be around—like when he ate a "Breyer Burrito." Every few years the same thing seemed to happen at some Mexican-food lunch Breyer was having with them. As he was happily holding forth on whatever the subject was—liberty, equality or last night's box score—he would bite into a burrito that still had the wrapping paper on it. Ever the slightly distracted former Harvard professor, the lanky, jowly Breyer would pause for a second, quizzical, then go right back to talking and chewing the paper-covered burrito. The clerks wouldn't say a thing, but occasionally couldn't contain their laughter. They were similarly amused in the spring of 2017, when his cell phone went off in the courtroom during an argument. It was the second time it happened to him. Electronic devices in the courtroom are forbidden, even for justices. The chief later kidded Breyer he just might have to install a metal detector for Breyer.

Breyer's absent-mindedness played out elsewhere, as if the justice forgot that he wasn't in chambers. When he and his clerks dined at public restaurants near the Court, his enthusiasm sometimes got the better of him. He'd be talking so loudly in his mellifluous baritone—about a current case—that the clerks felt they had to warn him. One former clerk joked that if you wanted intel on a pending decision, "follow us to lunch."

On the bench, where he was one of the most active participants, he was wont to wander off into labyrinthine what-if questions with perplexed counsel. In a 2004 case on whether federal law could prevent states from allowing the use of marijuana for medical reasons, Breyer asked: "You know, he grows heroin, cocaine, tomatoes that are going to have genomes in them that could at some point lead to tomato children that will eventually affect Boston. . . . So you're going to get around all those examples?" In some years, the clerks ran a secret bingo game for courtroom arguments. The bingo card consisted of phrases commonly used by justices or by the lawyers arguing before them. The phrase you most wanted on your card? "Justice Breyer, if I understand your hypothetical correctly . . ." When a lawyer uttered those words one spring day, a clerk whispered to another, "Bingo!"

The justices, too, were fond of Breyer. Scalia asked clerks if he could get in on bingo. And there was a good reason O'Connor once selected him as the model for the jack-o'-lantern she directed her clerks to make for Halloween. They carved a grinning, bespectacled bald pumpkin—a dead ringer for Steve Breyer. It's still the standard by which other Halloween pranks at the Court are measured.

THERE'S NO EVIDENCE ANY CLERK has ever made a Sotomayor jack-o'-lantern. Though she was an ebullient presence inside the Court and out—her chambers were known for exuberant music and the aromas from the kitchen—some clerks found her a challenge to work for. For one thing, the hours were among the longest in the building. Other clerks made it home for a late dinner and had weekends to themselves, which wasn't always the case in Sotomayor's chambers. The D.C. subway system closes at midnight, and her clerks were thrilled when Uber made its launch in the city in late 2011. One of the main responsibilities of clerks is to write bench memos, which summarize for a justice the facts, issues and arguments in a case. Bench memos for most justices are under 10 pages; early on, bench memos for Sotomayor could run 70 to 80.

Sotomayor clerks thought their boss treated them like family, but this parent could be professionally insecure, especially in her first few years on the Court. She confessed to friends that the other justices knew more constitutional law than she did—and they let her know it. She was shocked by the lack of collegiality she encountered, compared to what she'd experienced at the federal appeals court in Manhattan. Even before she'd been confirmed, she was disappointed that none of the justices other than Ginsburg called her. To her clerks, doing a pumpkin with big hoop earrings just didn't seem like a good idea.

All the same, in less than a decade, and even given Ginsburg's star power, Sotomayor had emerged as a highly visible justice. Although she let on little about her view of life on the Court, she was eager to hawk her *My Beloved World*, an affecting, observant novelistic account of her upbringing in New York City public housing—and how she made it from there to Princeton, Yale, the Manhattan DA's office, and beyond. She was a publisher's dream. In between those pesky obligations at the Court, as well as swearing in Vice President Joe Biden in 2013, she was able to go on an 11-city book tour, costar with a Muppet, banter with Jon Stewart, salsa-dance with Jorge Ramos on Univision, and lead the New Year's Eve countdown in Times Square.

With more than 300,000 copies sold, *My Beloved World* became the best-selling book by any justice, present or past—eclipsing Thomas's *My Grandfather's Son* and O'Connor's *Lazy B.: Growing Up on a Cattle Ranch in the American Southwest*. Sotomayor's memoir also finally gave her financial breathing room, netting her more than $3 million and allowing her to get rid of credit card debt.

After *My Beloved World* came out, the clerks teased her about its success in the annual skit they put on for their bosses. In one routine, a clerk announced the Court that year had "not one, but two, bestsellers from the justices!" Turning first to Sotomayor, the clerk mentioned *My Beloved World*. Then the clerk walked over to Scalia—who recently had coauthored the esoteric *Reading Law: The Interpretation of Legal Texts*—and revealed the other bestseller: *Mi mundo adorado*, which was Sotomayor's as well, the Spanish version of her memoir. Scalia roared. It was the best bit in the skit, apart from the sight gag of another clerk dressing up as an accursed Breyer, in a bike helmet and a sling. (The justice had recently been in yet another bicycling accident.)

For the first few years after *My Beloved World*, it was the main topic Sotomayor wanted to talk about when she had clerks from other chambers over to hers for a brown-bag lunch. "But don't expect me to be talking about my sex life!" she once told the clerks, one of whom recounted afterward, "It was the very last time I wanted to hear 'justice of the Supreme Court' and 'sex life' used in the same sentence."

Sotomayor liked being the life of the party, and her persona was captured perfectly earlier that term at the Court's annual holiday party. Secretaries, police and other staff were already in the formal West Conference Room, where portraits of past chief justices filled the walls. Sam Alito walked in and obediently took his place in the long line at the buffet. Few said hello to the shy and distant justice, and he said hello to few. (One clerk, not Alito's, guessed Alito's best friend at the Court was Zeus, his springer spaniel who often accompanied him to chambers.) Whereupon, Sotomayor waltzed into the conference room. Yakking, greeting, beaming—all the more so given the buzz for her book—she headed straight to the front of the line, gloriously unaware of a line at all. She took some veggies and proceeded to hold court. A bemused Alito, watching the scene unfold, offered no reaction. It was just Sonia being Sonia. The two of them—four years apart in age—both grew up in working-class families, and both had gone to Princeton and Yale Law. But the similarities pretty much ended there.

The touching thing about Sotomayor—so sociable, so extroverted—was her dating woes. Divorced since 1983, she yearned for companionship and had done so long before joining the Court. It wasn't that she was lonely. She had a life filled with friends, extended family, godchildren and acquaintances in two neighborhoods—the hip U Street corridor of Washington and the West Village of Manhattan, where she kept her old condo and visited often. She even had gotten used to the scandalous reality that D.C. didn't have late-night takeout. She was the only justice to have dined with George Clooney and his wife Amal. Life was good. It was simply that she desired not to be single and that was an open secret at the Court.

Many who knew her remarked that her travails were a reflection not on her but on the state of gender inequality in society. For all the progress that had been made since Sotomayor came of age—she was one of three women on the Court during the 2017–18 term—the fact remained that many men were intimidated by accomplished women, especially if they were brighter than the men were. In a city full of politicians, lawyers, lobbyists, diplomats and eggheads, one might think it would be different now. Sotomayor didn't complain—she just kept looking.

Clerks didn't draw any conclusions about Sotomayor and the social scene. But it wasn't lost on them that the two most recent women appointed to the Court—Sotomayor and Kagan—were single, whereas the first two women, Ginsburg and O'Connor, were married and had children. The clerks weren't gossiping—in the way of clerks in prior terms who, along with some of their bosses, liked to tittle-tattle about the ascetic social ways of the famously single Justice David Souter. When it came to Sotomayor and Kagan, the clerks just didn't quite know what to make of it, and the single status of both was something they commented on. It also didn't escape the notice of clerks, female and male, that all the male justices were married. Or that it had been Scalia, the cultural traditionalist, who was the most vocal in telling his clerks that if they had family responsibilities, those took precedence over work.

ON THE BENCH, SOTOMAYOR ROUTINELY was the most fervid among the liberals, taking on a voice that the political left had hoped to hear from Ginsburg years earlier. Sotomayor had been outspoken, for example, in the 2016 Utah search-and-seizure case, as well as in matters of race, prison abuse, and prosecutorial and police misconduct. And she was reliable—the other justices who leaned left didn't have to worry that she would stray. Long term, at least as long as there was a Republican in the White House, Sotomayor represented the Court's left flank.

But President Obama had chosen her in the summer of 2009 not so much because of ideology as because, in his words, she would be a "legacy," allowing him to nominate the first Hispanic to the Court. "I'm the president—I want to make history," he told White House staffers. "This is one of the things I was elected to do." When his sights narrowed to Sotomayor, he explained that he was "trying to build a more inclusive society—where a Puerto Rican girl raised poor in the Bronx can grow up to become a Supreme Court justice." Her biography won her the seat. Four years earlier, George W. Bush had hoped to pick a Hispanic, but couldn't find the right candidate.

For Obama, naming Sotomayor, then 55, had the benefit of satisfying his base, which included Hispanics. And he genuinely believed that diversity—both demographic and in life experience—"fed excellence." But although academics and other federal judges thought well of Sotomayor, she wasn't considered in the first rank of available talent. While members of her own federal appeals court in Manhattan respected her zest and skill, they didn't confuse her with such past legends of that court as Learned Hand or Henry Friendly. Three weeks before she was nominated as a justice, Sotomayor was bad-mouthed in a two-page, single-spaced letter to the president from a famed liberal scholar at Harvard, Larry Tribe, who had been an Obama mentor at the law school. (The letter was leaked to the press more than a year later—to embarrass Tribe as much as Sotomayor.) While acknowledging her "demographic appeal" that "you don't need me to underscore," Tribe wrote, "bluntly put, she's not nearly as smart as she seems to think she is." Instead, Tribe touted Kagan for the job.

Scalia had done the same thing to a tablemate at the White House Correspondents' Association Dinner earlier that spring. For Breyer, he had offered his approval after the fact. This time, he wanted in on the action beforehand. "I have no illusions that your man will nominate someone who shares my orientation," he told David Axelrod, a top Obama adviser. "But I hope he sends us someone smart." Axelrod didn't ask for names, but the justice was happy to suggest one. "Let me put a finer point on it," Scalia said. "I hope he sends us Elena Kagan."

That wasn't a poke at Sotomayor specifically. But the two of them didn't become pals. In her second year on the Court, she attended the Christmas caroling session that Scalia always led. This was "Silent Night" fare, not "Jingle Bells." After a few songs, he asked if she had any requests. " 'Feliz Navidad!' " Sotomayor said. To which Scalia replied, slowly emphasizing each word, "We don't sing that song at *this* party." A few years later, she let slip how she felt about her colleague—or at least his views. Speaking to an audience at the University of Minnesota eight months after he died, she admitted, "There are some things he said on the bench where, if I had a baseball bat, I might have used it."

Obama already knew of Sotomayor—who earlier in her career, as a federal trial judge (appointed by the first President Bush), had ended the Major League Baseball strike in 1995—and he had her in mind even before he became the Democratic presidential nominee. Obama had read a lot of the judicial opinions of possible nominees. (In his presidency, Bill Clinton had read some as well. Donald Trump hadn't read a judicial decision in his life.) Only a few weeks after Obama's inauguration in January 2009, well before Justice Souter on May 1 faxed over his intention to retire, Obama specifically asked about Sotomayor at a staff meeting on judicial nominations. The new president assumed that with a Republican-to-Democrat changeover in the White House, a Court seat might open up. He figured it would be John Paul Stevens's—rather than Souter's—because Stevens at the time was 88, and his wife was ill as well. (In fact, Stevens never considered leaving in 2009.)

Of the four names Obama came up with himself, Sotomayor was the only one he didn't know personally. The other three—Kagan, soon to become solicitor general; Cass Sunstein, a prolific, eclectic legal scholar; and Diane Wood, a federal appellate judge in Chicago—all had been colleagues when Obama taught law at the University of Chicago. But "any conversation about a potential vacancy began with Sotomayor's name," recalled one of his advisers. "It was hers to lose." (Had Sotomayor botched her presidential interview, chances are Wood would've gotten the nod. Wood—along with Kagan and Janet Napolitano, the secretary of homeland security—were the only other candidates interviewed one-on-one by Obama.) If Obama had any reservations about Sotomayor, they weren't about whether she was the reincarnation of John Marshall—only that her votes on the Court would get it right (meaning left). Obama didn't want to wake up one day and think, "I'm Eisenhower—I picked the wrong person."

Sotomayor had heard the mutters that she wasn't smart enough and had advanced only because of affirmative action. But it wasn't until seven years after her appointment that she conceded the naysaying got to her. Appearing before a big Princeton audience in the spring of 2017, recalling as well the unattributed "reports that I was abrasive and not nice," she said, "I actually, seriously thought about pulling out of the process." It was only because of "tough love" and friends who told her "to stop wallowing in my self-pity" that she persevered.

Unlike the selections of Ginsburg and Breyer, Sotomayor's was efficient and clean. So was the rest of her path to confirmation. She met with a record 92 senators, aided as it happened by breaking an ankle at LaGuardia Airport two weeks into the process, as she rushed to fly to Washington for meetings. Because she could no longer get around the Hill easily, senators came to see her. Even those Republicans who had no intention of approving any Obama nominees were taken with her. She made eye contact, extended her arms, asked about family. She knew to say that she had this or that friend in a senator's state. Making a personal connection was something a politician could appreciate. Sotomayor even knew how to deal with Ted Cruz. All she had to do was mention the name of a past justice—preferably a conservative one—and Cruz would go on pedantically about everything he knew about that justice, in the process leaving little time for him to press Sotomayor on any substantive topics.

She hit only two bumps, dealing with ethnicity, gender and race. The bigger concerned what became known as the "wise Latina" line. "I would hope that a wise Latina woman with the richness of her experiences would more often than not reach a better conclusion than a white male who hasn't lived that life," Sotomayor had said in a 2001 lecture at the University of California at Berkeley. It was the same bit she had used in speeches going back seven years, all questioning an aphorism used by O'Connor and Ginsburg—that "a wise old man and a wise old woman will reach the same conclusion in deciding cases." Though judges aren't supposed to say such things, Sotomayor wasn't being the extremist that some claimed. She was only acknowledging that background matters—biological, personal and otherwise—and it's impossible for a judge to transcend it completely.

The other complication Sotomayor faced arose from a one-paragraph appellate ruling in 2008 that she had joined. The case dealt with white firefighters in New Haven, Connecticut. Black firefighters had passed a promotions exam at half the rate of whites. Worried about possible discrimination lawsuits, the city nullified the exam. White firefighters sued. Sotomayor, along with two other judges, ruled against them. During the pendency of Sotomayor's nomination, the Supreme Court, 5–4, reversed the ruling, concluding the white firefighters had been illegally discriminated against.

When it came time for a confirmation vote, neither the "wise Latina" line nor the firefighter case much mattered, though both gave cover to the 31 senators—all Republican—who opposed her. Her life story was that irresistible. "Wise Latina," she explained, had been an unfortunate "rhetorical flourish," and the short New Haven ruling was an instance of merely following precedent. Four years earlier, when Roberts had been confirmed, one senator who voted against him said the new chief had "retired the trophy" for performance by a judicial nominee. Roberts now thought he had an equal, at least in confirmation theater. At a social gathering not long after Sotomayor's swearing-in, he told Greg Craig, Obama's White House counsel, "I've been watching Supreme Court confirmations for a long time and have been involved in many myself. No one did it as well as you guys did it for Justice Sotomayor." That was high praise from Mr. Umpire himself.

As SOTOMAYOR HAD BEEN WHEN the first Court opening happened in Obama's presidency, Elena Kagan was in front from the outset for the second. Like Obama himself, as well as John Roberts and Merrick Garland, she was a product of the meritocracy. By itself, however, that wasn't decisive. In Kagan, then 50, Obama found someone he not only had known at the University of Chicago—she was the one who took on the task of maintaining the acquaintance—but who also shared his instinct to fuse liberalism with pragmatism. Even so, Kagan might have lost out if there had been an obvious alternative candidate with whom Obama could "make history."

When 90-year-old Justice Stevens retired in 2010, there were no such clear options. Many names were bandied about at the White House—including wild cards like African Americans Teresa Wynn Roseborough, general counsel of Home Depot (who earlier in her career had been a key lawyer for Al Gore in the litigation after the disputed presidential election of 2000); and Bryan Stevenson, an admired public interest lawyer in Alabama. But neither they nor other possibilities like academics Sunstein and Chicago's David Strauss—both close to Obama—gained any traction.

Although Kagan and Sotomayor, both New Yorkers, often voted the same way on cases, Kagan was more doctrinal, less attuned to real-world implications of a decision otherwise indicated by the law. Like Obama, Kagan was more head than heart. She wrote as well as anyone on the Court—her prose was as accessible and conversational as Roberts's—but she typically stayed away from the kind of incantations favored by Scalia and Sotomayor. That cool-headedness had helped her thrive as dean of Harvard Law School from 2003 to 2009, where she was able to soothe long-warring factions of the faculty, fashioning coalitions that helped the school mend its reputation. Before joining Harvard, she had served four years in the Clinton White House, where she also earned a reputation for being able to work both sides of an ideological aisle. "All-purpose brain in a place full of people who are more smart than wise," declared the *New Republic*.

Those political and policy skills, combined with her intense ambition, made even those in the White House peg her back then as a possible justice one day. "Elena and John Roberts wanted to get to where they are now and made decisions along the way," said a former colleague who's known her for years. "Both never said much controversial in public, both cultivated political patrons." Her yearbook picture at Hunter College High—a public school in Manhattan for the intellectually gifted—showed her in a judge's robe with a gavel and a quote from Justice Felix Frankfurter. (Her University of Chicago friends marveled at how someone so driven could be so scatterbrained that now and then she parked her car and forgot to turn the engine off.)

The only blemish on her record was a B– she got in first-year torts as a law student at Harvard. Five years later, when she applied for a clerkship with Justice Thurgood Marshall, one of her professors had to spend the better part of a paragraph in his recommendation letter explaining that the B– wasn't "the true reflection of her capacity." Marshall hired her and called her not just the customary grumpy nickname he bestowed on all clerks, Knucklehead—but also Shorty.

Kagan's main professional setback, apart from losing out for the presidency of Harvard in 2007, was when she left the deanship two years later to become the solicitor general in the Obama administration. That paved the way for her nomination to the Supreme Court the following year, but the job as SG was her second choice. She had hoped to be deputy attorney general, but it went to someone else. Being solicitor general—the federal government's top appellate lawyer, often referred to as "the 10th justice"—ended up working in her favor. She had had almost no experience practicing law, having been to court only a few times as a junior associate at a Washington law firm after she clerked for Marshall. As SG, she got to argue at the Court and further burnish her résumé.

At her confirmation hearings, she had shown she could be just as noncommittal as Ginsburg and just as disarming as Roberts. One of her answers turned out to be as memorable as the umpire line from the future chief justice. Senator Lindsey Graham wanted to know where she happened to be on Christmas Day 2009, when the "underwear bomber" Umar Farouk Abdulmutallab tried to blow up an Airbus 330 headed from Amsterdam to Detroit. "You know," Kagan said, pausing, aware she'd been handed a fine setup, "like all Jews, I was probably at a Chinese restaurant."

She had to navigate only one brief storm—over her sexual orientation. Even before she was nominated, rumors had circulated that the unmarried Kagan was a lesbian, which precipitated accusations that she was a liar in denying it. Columnists and bloggers had already weighed in—including a freelancer's piece on CBS News, quickly taken down, that Kagan would be "the first openly gay justice." The proliferating rumors gave editors an excuse to convert them into a seemingly respectable story. The day after Kagan was nominated, the *Wall Street Journal* published a large photo, in the middle of its front page, of Kagan playing softball while on the University of Chicago faculty. Though the caption didn't mention sexual orientation, there she was in pants and her short hair. (Why its law school chose to distribute that photo, only it knows.)

Two days later, the *New York Post* ran the same photo on a full page, minus any subtlety. DOES THIS PHOTO SUGGEST HIGH COURT NOMINEE ELENA KAGAN IS A LESBIAN? the headline had the gall to ask. The *New York Times* got around to posting the photo, too, but only in a piece about justices and their devotion to baseball—to which softball evidently was close enough. Maureen Dowd lampooned the whole thing in a *Times* column titled "Supremely Girly Girl"—which of course extended the story further.

The Obama administration grappled with how to handle the sideshow. On one hand, if sexuality was a private matter, should it even acknowledge the topic? The sideshow said more about the barkers than about whoever Kagan was or wasn't. But on the other hand, as a political matter, didn't the distraction have to be addressed? Administration officials felt whipsawed: Kagan was supposedly named because she was a lesbian; she was named despite being a lesbian; it's nobody's business if she's a lesbian, but why's she denying the claim? With a resentful Kagan's acquiescence, the White House chose to respond.

Ron Klain, an Obama adviser and Kagan's close friend from Harvard, decided to let another law school classmate attest to her heterosexuality—"outing" her as straight. "I've known her for most of her adult life and I know she's straight," Sarah Walzer told *Politico*, accompanied by the headline KAGAN'S FRIENDS: SHE'S NOT GAY. "She dated men . . . we talked about men—who in our class was cute, who she would like to date, all of those things. She definitely dated when she was in D.C. after law school, when she was in Chicago—and she just didn't find the right person." One of the things they talked about, according to Walzer, was how "it's an ongoing challenge for very smart women—there are not very many men who would choose women who are smarter than they are."

And then she made the point that should've been self-apparent. "There is this assumption that people make . . . about women who get to their 40s or 50s and never marry, that it must be because they're gay.

It's just usually that they don't get nominated for the Supreme Court and have everybody talking about them, so nobody really cares."

The White House got jeered for planting the *Politico* story. But the entire media-sown episode, though assuredly cringeworthy, passed and seemed to indicate that sexual orientation was no longer considered a basis for evaluating fitness for office. It was very different from the time in the 1990s when Justice Souter called a lower-court judge whose clerk was up for a position with Souter the next term. Souter had a question for the judge about the job candidate. "Well, I understand he's gay," Souter said. "Does this present a problem in your chambers?"

Although, as expected, most Republicans voted against her, Kagan breezed to a 63-to-37 Senate confirmation—becoming the first new justice in nearly 40 years who hadn't been a judge.

ONCE ON THE COURT, Kagan—even as the most junior member of the dissenting liberal bloc in key rulings on campaign finance (*Citizens United*) and voting rights (*Shelby County*)—took to the job easily. She also was part of the five-member majority that in 2015 declared same-sex marriage a constitutional right (*Obergefell*); by then, mercifully, not even the fringe press tried to insinuate she voted that way for any reason other than judicial conviction. Kagan liked to ask a lot of questions at oral arguments, which was a wily way to get in an early word to her colleagues about a case. That got around the fact that when they met in private conference after arguments to discuss cases and to hold a straw vote on a result, as the most junior justice, she went last.

She had a sense of humor as well, which helped when you were the newbie. The most junior justices often got stuck writing the "dogs," which was Court-speak for boring cases. In one especially insipid 9-to-0 case, the chief justice stuck Kagan with the opinion. To try wriggling out of writing it, in jest she threatened to dissent.

Kagan did her best to leaven her image as an all-work-and-no-play denizen of the ivory tower. In Q-and-As at law schools and bar gatherings, she made sure to flag her common touch. She had the same trainer as Justice Ginsburg and the best cross-jab on the Court; the best gift she ever received was a pair of Muhammad Ali boxing gloves; she was a devotee of Spider-Man and other comic book heroes; and in case anybody had forgotten, she'd shot a deer with Justice Scalia.

She also got mileage being known as the FroYo Justice. In recent times, the newest member of the Court was sentenced to the building's cafeteria committee, which oversaw fare at the public eatery on the ground floor. She called it a form of "hazing" but made the most of it, after learning from rank-and-file staffers of a clamor for a frozen yogurt machine. She had one installed (70 cents an ounce), to which nobody in the building proffered a dissent (though the cafeteria's chocolate chip cookies were another story). She got there just in time, considering Sotomayor's inauspicious tenure on the committee right before her. When the *Washington Post* in 2010 rated government cafeterias in D.C., the Court's received an F; "the food should be unconstitutional," the review said. Kagan first learned the politics of food at Harvard, instituting free coffee for students, who loved her for it. (Replacing her on the cafeteria committee, Neil Gorsuch confronted the crisis of the meatball subs. Somebody had switched out the marinara for shrimp cocktail sauce. He decreed the lunch food return to its originalist sauce.)

The odd part was that for all her deftness Kagan wasn't always so good at containing a less pleasant side to her personality. She wasn't mean—just bright and impatient with those who were less so. There were stories at Harvard about her being a "master pool shark" and "a yeller"—and those came from her allies. At the Court, her clerks found her similarly tough. Certain stories about justices get passed down and become part of Court folklore. The story told most about Kagan was how a law clerk gave birth—and returned to work within the week. As the narrative went, of course the justice hadn't demanded she come in, but she had created an environment in which a clerk might feel it was the best course. (The Court set up a nursery in a vacant second-floor office.) Notwithstanding any quibbles the clerks had, Kagan was known as a fine mentor and an unparalleled supporter when it came time for a clerk to look for the next job—in short, "not great to work for, but great to *have* worked for," as a clerk said.

Nobody expected Kagan to win over conservative justices by wielding nosh. To start with, she would have had to explain to some of them what a blintz was. But it was Obama's view that she had a knack for finding consensus and, as he put it, could "play varsity with the other eight." Clinton had hoped for the same kind of touch in Breyer. If Kagan could bring to the Court's conference table some of the skills she had demonstrated at Harvard, then perhaps she could be a latter-day Justice Brennan. That had been the counsel from Professor Tribe in his 2009 letter to Obama arguing in favor of Kagan over Sotomayor. As dean of the law school, Kagan had been able to persuade "a bunch of prima donnas to see things her way in case after case," Tribe wrote. Kagan's techniques, he said, "are precisely the same techniques I can readily envision her employing not just with justices like Kennedy but even with a justice like Alito."

That hope was a pipe dream. Brennan's interpersonal skills were unique. That was why at the annual luncheons President Reagan hosted for the justices, it was Brennan and Reagan who were the chummiest. After Brennan retired in 1990, he kept up a correspondence with his successor, David Souter, who sent Brennan postcards every summer from his home in New Hampshire. In one, Souter told of his climbing to the top of the mast of a 165-foot barkentine. To which Brennan typed back, "I can't say that I've climbed a 165-foot barkentine, or indeed that I've actually climbed aloft higher than a foot! I can't wait until your return."

There were Court cases in which Brennan's willingness to yield swaths of doctrinal ground—while preserving the core constitutional holding he was after—made a deal-making difference. But his influence can be overstated, especially when much of the time he began with a presumptive majority. The ends-justify-the-means Rule of Five works especially well when you begin with seven. Whatever divisions existed in the Warren Court—and they could be deep—they didn't come close to the polarization of the Roberts Court.

Besides, the institution didn't lend itself to politicking. Tradition dictated that a junior justice like Kagan lie relatively low. If two justices spoke at the same time during oral argument, the junior justice stopped talking. If two justices wanted to consult privately, it was ordinarily done in the senior's chambers. Perhaps just as important, the layout of the place didn't foster camaraderie. All the justices other than Sotomayor had their chambers on the main floor, and they did see each other at the conference and at lunch. But it was a big, isolating building. Each chambers had its own bathrooms, so the hallways allowed only random encounters. Most exchanges of ideas took place in typed memos. Many days could go by without one justice seeing any other; if there was any communication, it was indirect, through law clerks serving as agents. The idea that a single justice, Kagan or any other, might be able to bridge differences through personal chemistry was quixotic at best.

CHAPTER 7

THE RIGHT FLANK

Kagan at least aspired to influence. Thomas was fully content to be a lone wolf. On issues ranging from executions to affirmative action to race in jury selection, he outflanked even Alito on the right. Thomas said his opinions were a product of undeviating principle rather than rank partisanship, but his decisions almost always hewed to the conservative party line. He was with the conservatives in *Bush v. Gore, District of Columbia v. Heller, Citizens United, Shelby County,* and *Obergefell,* and in both Obamacare cases. Only in *Obergefell,* the same-sex marriage case, did his vote happen to respect the decisions of other branches of government—and in that case his deference happened to dovetail with what conservatives believed.

Scalia, for one, understood that originalism and textualism had interpretive limits. Comparing himself and Thomas—with whom he sometimes commiserated behind closed doors after the Court reached a decision they both abhorred—Scalia liked to explain: "I am a textualist. I am an originalist. I am not a nut." At least when it suited him, he acknowledged that stare decisis and historical judgment had roles in constitutional law. For example, Scalia conceded that maybe some punishments that were not "cruel and unusual" in 1791 would nowadays violate the Eighth Amendment.

By contrast, Thomas was a self-indulgent purist—or implicitly, by Scalia's terms, "a nut." If he thought a case should come out a certain way, that was how he wrote his opinion. Sometimes it was a dissent, sometimes it was a concurrence. Almost never, though, in any case of consequence did Thomas actually write the majority opinion. That was because he wouldn't brook nuance from a colleague or entertain compromise to win over a vote. If he was right, he was right. If a prior ruling of the Court was wrong, no matter how settled the law had become, it deserved to be scuttled.

Thomas's self-righteousness, though unflinchingly honest, didn't translate into influence, a truth exposed in his solitary dissents. In recent terms, his most important moment might have been in early 2017, when he got to swear in Mike Pence as vice president in the Trump administration. Thomas's supporters in academia and the legal profession, along with a few mainstream journalists, tried to sketch a different portrait. One of the administration lawyers who helped in Thomas's traumatic Senate confirmation battle in 1991, Mark Paoletta, later created one website after another to promote the justice's standing, as well as to counter affronts to his honor. At justicethomas.com, you can read pieces about Thomas, the "inspirational justice"; Thomas, "an American masterpiece"; and "Mr. Constitution." The website also took up the cause of rectifying the omission of any significant mention of Thomas at the Smithsonian's new National Museum of African American History and Culture. A different Paoletta website, confirmationbiased .com, set out to describe the "truth about" an unflattering 2016 HBO docudrama on Thomas's confirmation. Paoletta became chief counsel to Vice President Pence. Rather than through his judicial opinions, it is through his former clerks that Thomas had the most impact. By one count, one-fifth of them have gone to work for the Trump administration or have been nominated by Trump to the federal bench. No other justice comes close.

Despite attempts to lionize Thomas, though, he didn't help his own cause, not that it mattered to him. His conspicuous silence on the bench served only to make him appear more marginal. Other justices, current and past, found oral arguments invaluable in honing ideas. But Thomas, unlike his colleagues—who jockeyed to question lawyers throughout the hour assigned to each case—typically said nothing, except perhaps in a whisper to the justices on either side of him. Instead, he settled back in his chair, rubbed an eye, gazed at the ornate ceiling, and for all the grandeur of his surroundings, looked out of it. Until late February 2016, when Thomas spoke up in a desultory appeal involving misdemeanor convictions, a decade had passed since he last asked a question in court. According to the *New York Times*, it had been at least 45 years since another justice had gone even a single term without asking a question.

On this day, in his gravelly monotone, Thomas asked 11 in a row. Perhaps Thomas wanted to fill the void left by the loquacious Scalia's death two weeks earlier, especially since the case being argued tangentially involved the Second Amendment. But Thomas didn't explain his awakening. On many occasions, however, he had offered a range of reasons for his reticence: The other justices already talked too much; he was being courteous; he wanted to "allow the advocates to advocate"; he was self-conscious about the Gullah dialect he retained from growing up in rural Georgia; he'd been rattled in college and law school by more silver-tongued students. Pick one explanation or pick them all, but Thomas didn't waver from his reserve in the courtroom. And if not for his confirmation hearings, it oddly might have been the most familiar characteristic about him. (It would be another three years before he asked another question.)

At the time of Scalia's death in 2016, Thomas had been on the Court for nearly 25 years. After Anthony Kennedy retired in 2018, Thomas was senior to all his colleagues, even though he was only 70. After Thurgood Marshall in 1991 announced his retirement—failing to make good on his facetious threat to have clerks "prop me up on the bench" and "keep voting" in the event he died while a Republican occupied the White House—President George H.W. Bush selected Thomas to succeed him. (Waggish Marshall clerks liked to point out that a lifeless Marshall propped up on the bench would have asked no fewer questions than a silent Thomas.)

Before his appointment, Thomas had been an unexceptional federal appellate judge for 16 months and, before that, chairman of the Equal Employment Opportunity Commission (EEOC). His résumé was solid but hardly stellar. Like Marshall, he was African American. Yet Bush claimed he was naming Thomas not because of race but because he was "best qualified at this time." Their interview—at the Bush estate in Kennebunkport, Maine—lasted six minutes, after which they enjoyed crabmeat and English muffins. A year earlier, Thomas had been among a handful of candidates Bush considered to replace Brennan. Souter got that seat—perhaps because Thomas wasn't "best qualified" right then.

At 43, Thomas became the youngest justice since William O. Douglas was appointed in 1939 at 40. But even with more than a quarter-century at the Court, Thomas was still best known for his nationally televised confirmation hearings—the nastiest, most unthinkable, in U.S. history. He had been grilled about his views on substantive issues that contrasted him greatly with Marshall, a pillar of the civil rights movement. But it was his personal side that turned the second round of the hearings into a cauldron of race, gender, sex and politics.

A month after Thomas's initial testimony and two days before the scheduled Senate vote on his nomination, *Newsday* and NPR reported that a law professor named Anita Hill was accusing him of sexually harassing her when both of them were at the EEOC and the Department of Education. The accusations had been made in a confidential sworn statement to the Senate. Republicans attempted to discredit Hill and called news articles the product of a smear campaign. In his diary, President Bush called the accusations a "chicken-shit operation." Now, on Friday, October 11, 1991, Hill testified publicly before the Judiciary Committee. The substance of her charges was repulsive and riveting. Over the course of a weekend, 20 million TV households watched—and heard two wholly irreconcilable accounts of a workplace relationship, as well as far too much information about a porn star named Long Dong Silver.

At the Department of Education, according to Hill, Thomas talked to her "about acts that he had seen in pornographic films involving such matters as women having sex with animals, and films showing group sex or rape scenes." Sometimes, she said, he "told me graphically of his own sexual prowess." Later, after both had moved to the EEOC, came "one of the oddest episodes," which the committee chairman, Senator Joe Biden, knew would shock. Before Hill began, he had instructed Capitol Hill police "not to let anyone in or out of that door." The details were so salacious that those in the Senate gallery gasped when she described them.

Thomas had been drinking his usual Coke in his office, Hill testified. He "looked at the can and asked 'Who has put pubic hair on my Coke?'"

Why had she followed Thomas to the EEOC? Hill defended her decision this way: "The work itself was interesting"; "it appeared that the sexual overtures, which had so troubled me, had ended"; and "I was dedicated to civil rights work."

When Thomas returned to the witness table Friday evening—with its larger TV audience—he was apoplectic. He attacked his attackers, calling it a "travesty" that "dirt" and "sleaze" and "lies" had been "selectively leaked" to the media by the Judiciary Committee, "displayed in primetime over our entire nation." The hearings were "a circus" and "a national disgrace." (Never mind that Thomas himself helped Republicans look for "dirt" on Hill.) He then changed the subject. "From my standpoint, as a black American," he said, the hearings had turned into "a high-tech lynching for uppity blacks who in any way deign to think for themselves, to do for themselves, to have different ideas—and it is a message that unless you kowtow to an old order, this is what will happen to you. You will be lynched, destroyed, caricatured by a committee of the U.S. Senate, rather than hung from a tree." Most of that of course had nothing to do with Hill's allegations.

Biden, and the rest of the all-male (and all-white) committee, fumbled how to deal with the he-said/she-said narrative. Public opinion sided with Thomas, whose backers were better organized than Hill's, though there was a good argument to be made that Thomas might not have been confirmed if Biden had stage-managed the testimony of Thomas and Hill differently. Two days after the spectacle ended, Thomas was confirmed 52–48, the narrowest margin of approval for a justice since 1888. The nominee found out while soaking in a bathtub. "He shrugged at the news," according to *Resurrection*, an account of the confirmation ordeal by John Danforth, Thomas's main Senate sponsor. "Whoop-de-damn-do," Thomas himself recounted.

Whatever his lack of intellectual clout on the Court, Thomas now had a lifelong vote among nine. He became grayer and heavier—he had the best suspenders on the Court—and you never found him working out with Kagan or Ginsburg. But if he stayed reasonably healthy, in 2028 he would surpass Douglas's record of 36 years on the Court. With that kind of power, Thomas might have moved past the confirmation hearings, but he never let go of his umbrage. It was consistent with the scars he bore all his life. "In my 43 years on Earth," he told senators that Friday, "I have been able, with the help of others and with the help of God, to defy poverty, avoid prison, overcome segregation, bigotry, racism, and obtain one of the finest educations available in this country. But I have not been able to overcome this process. This is worse than any obstacle or anything that I have ever faced."

Thomas told the committee—and the country—that he would add "this" to his catalog of grudges. "My name has been harmed, my integrity has been harmed, my character has been harmed, my family has been harmed, my friends have been harmed. There is nothing this commit-tee, this body or this country can do to give me my good name back—nothing." It was a grievance he endlessly brought up at gatherings of conservative groups and in unguarded late-night exchanges with friends.

Long after the hearings, in appearances before simpatico audiences, Thomas's rancor was still manifest. Five years later, in a commencement speech at Rev. Jerry Falwell's Liberty University, Thomas deplored a culture of "victimization" and "a society saturated with complaint." He then recounted "the unpleasantness of my confirmation," and how he and his wife Ginni had gotten through only "by God's grace and on his mighty shoulders." Two years later, in July 1998, he was back at it. "I, for one, have been singled out particularly for bilious and venomous assaults," he told a gathering of the country's largest African-American bar association. Sixteen years after that, he explained to students at another Christian university that "the worst things that have been done to me, the worst things that have been said about me," were not by Southern racists but "Northern liberal elites." And in 2016, at a celebration of his

25 years on the Court sponsored by the conservative Heritage Foundation, Thomas argued that rather than debating issues in the "broken" culture of Washington, "we simply annihilate the person."

In Thomas's haunted world, the tormentors weren't only Anita Hill and the senators. The press was complicit as well. Thomas boasted to clerks that he no longer watched the news. He loathed journalists, whom he described as "universally untrustworthy." NPR's Nina Totenberg, who helped to break Hill's story, earned his singular disgust. In December 1999, he spoke at the annual dinner for the snarky DisHonor Awards given out by the conservative Media Research Center. The evening consisted of "roasting the most outrageously biased liberal reporting of the year." Thomas was there to send up a TV pundit, Julianne Malveaux, who had urged him to eat "lots of eggs and butter," so "he dies early, like a lot of black men do of heart disease." Thomas assured the rah-rah crowd that he was healthy and wished for Malveaux a life filled with her own artery-clogging food. But he couldn't resist a reference to Totenberg as an example of someone else who did him wrong—a decade before—and whom he would've liked to dis-honor in person. "I've finally had the opportunity to have my surgeon remove her many stilettos from my back," he announced gleefully. "I'd like to return them."

Thomas's fixation on the past reached its low point in late 2015. Every fall the Court hosts a private dinner to honor the federal judge receiving the Devitt Award, given by the Dwight Opperman Foundation, for "service to justice." The Devitt has been likened to a Nobel Prize for the American judiciary. Most of the justices, along with about 100 invited guests, attend. That year, Gloria Allred—the omnipresent women's rights lawyer—came as a friend of Julie Chrystyn Opperman, Dwight's widow. Allred has been called "a feminist avenging crusader or a deluxe ambulance chaser catching a ride on the latest tabloid scandal." It depended on whether she was representing you or suing you. Her L.A. law firm's website keeps a running tab of the multimillions it's earned in discrimination and sexual harassment lawsuits.

When Thomas saw Allred at the cocktail reception, he panicked. He knew who she was, and his first words to her were, "Are you here to serve me with papers?" The question flummoxed her. She wasn't involved in any matter involving Thomas or Hill. If she had been, a lawsuit wouldn't be commenced this way. But Thomas wasn't being funny. The whole episode was bizarre, unless one appreciated the depth of Thomas's anger and distrust. Whether that pain fed into his doctrinal obduracy was something only dime-store psychologists could address.

And yet within the Court itself, at the most casual level, he was everybody's favorite. While the personal was his nemesis in his path to becoming a justice, it worked to his benefit once he became a justice. Anybody you asked at the Court about Thomas mentioned his warmth, kindness and solicitude. He knew the names of the custodians and the elevator operators. You might not see him coming, but his booming belly laugh heralded his approach. If you were particularly lucky, he'd do his Darth Vader impression. When he heard that a close relative of a clerk or an employee was ill, he asked about it—and sometimes showed up, unannounced, at a local hospital to visit. At the end of each term, he took his clerks on a road trip to Gettysburg "to experience what Lincoln said and did"; the pilgrimage, he explained, was meant to juxtapose the template of Lincoln with the "lying" and "jadedness" of present-day D.C. When it came to hiring clerks, he was the least elitist among the justices. While others picked students from Top Ten law schools—or perhaps only Harvard and Yale—Thomas every so often reached down into the plebeian class of LSU, Creighton and the University of Utah.

Many clerks in other chambers cited the time Thomas took them to lunch as their best face time with another justice. The meal could last three hours, as he regaled them with tales not of constitutional law, but of his travels with Ginni in their 40-foot silver-hued RV colossus, complete with kitchen, satellite TV, and big leather seats up in front. Each summer, the couple drove around the country in what they called their "condo on wheels," in search of "the best of America." They attended NASCAR events and early-season football games of the Nebraska Cornhuskers. The great open road, Thomas told "60 Minutes," allowed him to flee "the meanness you see in Washington" and to take the opportunity to be "with regular folks." When he invited clerks back to his office after lunch to see his album of RV photos, they invariably followed.

Clerks from liberal and conservative chambers alike loved the stories and that Thomas shared them. Court outsiders might think of him as Mr. Hyde, but insiders viewed him as Dr. Jekyll.

It wasn't that clerks hadn't heard of the "unpleasantness" of Thomas's confirmation hearings (as one of his colleagues described it). Nor could the other justices have forgotten it. When, in the fall of 2016, a woman came forward on Facebook to accuse Thomas of groping her in 1999, it was impossible for those at the Court to miss the news—or the statement Thomas issued calling the claim "preposterous." Likewise, in February 2018, when *New York* magazine ran a cover story, "The Case for Impeaching Clarence Thomas"—based on fresh questions about his testimony at his confirmation hearings—other justices noticed. It simply was that in the small fellowship of the Court, you didn't bring those matters up, even as the national #MeToo movement took hold.

For the non-Thomas clerks—even those who believed Hill's version of events—it was less of a problem. You didn't work for him and wouldn't, so you could compartmentalize Good Thomas and Bad Thomas. One clerk caustically referred to him as He Who Must Not Be Named—after Lord Voldemort in the Harry Potter novels. The clerks who did work for Thomas didn't have to deal with any conflicting feelings. Virtually all of Thomas's clerks shared his ideology and presumably his views about his confirmation. Unlike most justices, who encouraged debate—Roberts, for example, valued curiosity more than rock-ribbed conservativism—Thomas frowned on dissent. "I won't hire clerks who have profound disagreements with me," he told a luncheon group early in his tenure. "It's like trying to train a pig. It wastes your time—and it aggravates the pig."

For the justices who had to work with Thomas, little good could come of dwelling on the past. Thomas was going to be their colleague regardless and an affable one at that. They were stuck with each other. One justice privately rationalized that Thomas and Hill "were both telling the truth." In another time, the justices were called "nine scorpions in a bottle"—a reference to the feuds among various FDR-appointed members of the Court. The current justices were keenly aware of the metaphor and wanted no comparisons.

SAMUEL ALITO WAS THE JUSTICE who most flew under the radar. He carried none of Thomas's burdens; he didn't have a meme or write a best-seller; he wasn't a swing vote; and he lacked Scalia's puckish prose. They didn't even recognize him in the town where he attended law school. In October 2014, Alito was in New Haven, Connecticut, to speak at Yale. He was then one of three alumni on the Court. He and his wife Martha-Ann stopped in for Sunday brunch at au courant Heirloom, right near campus. (Try the Hot Caramel Apple Doughnuts.) Too bad, no tables. The hostess had no idea who he was; he graciously didn't fill her in; and the couple left. Subsequently apprised that she had turned away a member of the Supreme Court, the hostess explained, "Well, he should have made a reservation. We get very busy for brunch."

Alito should have been less invisible, given that the Court pivoted definitively to the right with his confirmation in January 2006. His commitment to the conservative cause went back to his service in the Reagan administration, and then to his time as the top federal prosecutor in New Jersey and his nearly 15 years as a federal appellate judge there. Alito replaced O'Connor—a cautious conservative who sided with the liberals on 5-to-4 rulings about abortion, affirmative action, campaign finance, church-state relations, and the execution of minors. His appointment was the most important substitution on the Court since the Thomas-for-Marshall swap in 1991. None of the other swaps producing the Court's 2017–18 roster—Roberts for William Rehnquist as chief justice, Ginsburg for Byron White, Breyer for Harry Blackmun, Sotomayor for David Souter, Kagan for John Paul Stevens, Kennedy for Lewis Powell—represented as distinct a shift in the Court's alignment. Decisions that almost certainly would have gone in one direction under O'Connor—like *Heller, Citizens United* and *Shelby County*—now went the other way.

An uncharacteristically doleful Breyer took note, in a 2007 dissent he announced from the bench about whether communities could factor in race to preserve integrated schools. Alluding to Alito's arrival, Breyer declared, "It is not often in the law that *so few* have *so quickly* changed *so much*."

With Scalia gone, the argument could be made that Alito was the dream justice for conservative ideologues. Roberts had voted twice to uphold the constitutionality of Obamacare; Kennedy had written the decision that made same-sex marriage a constitutional right; and, fairly or otherwise, Thomas's behavior, on the bench and in the past, marginalized him. Alito had no taste for Scalia's all-embracing originalist philosophy; at best, Alito's worldview was as a textualist. But for the right wing, Alito always voted the correct way and without a lot of drama. Except in the case of same-sex marriage, he was altogether fine with the Court's contempt for the other branches of government. Seven years into Alito's tenure, an admiring law professor, Michael Stokes Paulsen, concluded that while "there are louder talkers, flashier stylists, wittier wits, more-poisonous pens, nobody on the Court had a more level . . . swing than Justice Samuel Alito." Writing in a scholarly religious publication, Paulsen called Alito "the most consistent, solid, successful conservative justice."

It might not have happened at all, given the tangled process that went into his selection. In the spring of 2005, the Bush administration knew a Court vacancy might be imminent. Chief Justice Rehnquist was fighting thyroid cancer, and one of his daughters had quietly notified White House officials that his prognosis was dire. He had considered leaving in 2003 even before he got sick. That was because he didn't want to roll the dice on his legacy if Bush lost reelection the following year and ceded to a Democrat the chance to name the next chief. Bush won, but by January 2005 Rehnquist was so ill that there was concern he wouldn't be able to administer the oath to Bush on Inauguration Day. (If it came to that, Bush indicated his preference for O'Connor as the substitute.)

But it was O'Connor, not Rehnquist, who on July 1, 2005, announced plans to retire. Eighteen days later, Bush initially nominated Roberts to replace her. The president had narrowed his choices to five conservatives: Roberts, Alito, Mike Luttig, J. Harvie Wilkinson III and Joy Clement. All were federal appellate judges: Roberts in D.C.; Alito in New Jersey; Luttig and Wilkinson in Virginia; and Clement in New Orleans. All five had been named to the bench by Republican presidents—Roberts and Clement by Bush himself, Alito and Luttig by Bush's father, and Wilkinson by Reagan. They were the best evidence of the long incubation cycle for becoming a Court candidate—and of why senators were ill-advised to gloss over lower-court appointments.

While able and amiable, Clement was the lone woman on the list and was there chiefly for that reason. Luttig and Wilkinson, at times rivals on the bench, were regarded as intellectual wunderkinds—both appointed before they turned 40—with vastly different temperaments. Luttig, a protégé of, and clerk for, Scalia, was a firebrand; Wilkinson, who had clerked for the centrist Powell, personified "courtly Southerner." Alito was the awkward nerd sometimes referred to as "Scalito," for sharing much of Scalia's ideology if not his style.

Roberts was then beginning his third year on the D.C. Circuit. Though his luster as an appellate litigator, as well as his service in Republican administrations, might have made him the universal favorite, some in the White House worried he hadn't written enough in his brief time as a judge to demonstrate his real stripes. As much as Bush sought to avoid a diehard dogmatist—what he derided as "a true believer" intent on blowing up Court precedents—he told his advisers he didn't want to repeat his father's error in picking Souter despite a scant record. Alito didn't have that liability. He'd been on the bench for 15 years and written hundreds of opinions; Luttig and Wilkinson also had comparably abundant judicial experience.

Accompanied by his terriers Barney and Miss Beazley, Bush conducted hourlong interviews with the five finalists and settled on Roberts, whose "quick smile" and "gentle soul" impressed the president, who saw himself as the ultimate "people person." Media reports of Roberts being a good guy didn't hurt. He had cultivated reporters. For years, he was known in press circles to be available for an off-the-record conversation, so much so that one admiring Washington regular commented, "John Roberts goes to lunch three times a day."

Bush and Wilkinson chatted about cross-training, the Founding Fathers, and Wilkinson's unsuccessful run for Congress at 25. But Wilkinson was older than the others and seemed too attached to lawyerly moderation in the style of Justice Powell. Luttig hoped to partake in an exchange about constitutional creed, which wasn't what interested Bush. It was a classic instance of a contender misreading the setting—and how that alone could torpedo his prospects. Luttig and Roberts interviewed with the president back to back. The two had been friends since their days in the Reagan administration, when both had helped O'Connor prepare for her confirmation hearings. Roberts and Luttig compared notes later that night, with Luttig still bewildered about Bush's questions. Alito, notwithstanding his consistent record, didn't leave much of an impression on the president either way. Clement, though on the bench somewhat longer than Roberts, displayed none of his command.

Vice President Dick Cheney—the administration's truest true believer—endorsed Luttig, though he acknowledged that nominating him would produce precisely the kind of bare-knuckle battle that Bush wanted no part of. The White House counsel, Harriet Miers, preferred Alito over Roberts, who seemed to her too Souter-ish. The attorney general, Alberto Gonzales—himself in the early running to succeed O'Connor until Bush took him out of consideration—was equivocal; he advised the president that there were good arguments for Roberts, Luttig and Alito. Most of the former Court clerks working at the White House pushed for Roberts, in part because they had seen his sparkle as a litigator. White House chief of staff Andy Card and political adviser Karl Rove also supported Roberts.

Days before Roberts's confirmation hearings were scheduled to begin in early September, however, Rehnquist died. Bush switched tracks and picked Roberts to be the new chief justice rather than to replace O'Connor. Scalia had told friends he dreamed of becoming chief, and Cheney pushed the president to consider him. But Scalia was too old to be a serious candidate and likely would have produced a confirmation conflagration. With O'Connor's seat open again, the administration needed another nominee.

The other finalists were still available. But Bush chose someone else. In making personnel appointments, he liked to ask, "Where's the diversity?" Wilkinson, Alito and Luttig—all white men—didn't represent it. O'Connor herself let that be known. The Roberts pick "was fabulous," she told a newspaper in Washington State after an afternoon of fly-fishing. "He's good in every way—except he's not a woman." More important, the president's wife Laura said publicly and privately that she hoped the next nominee would be a woman. Clement might have been a conventional choice, but Bush had already rejected her after her interview. Another woman, Priscilla Owen—a federal appellate judge in Austin, Texas—was a possibility, but Senate Democrats viewed her as a reactionary. So Bush looked into his own administration and picked the 60-year-old Miers.

She lasted only 24 days. It wasn't only her mediocre credentials, although they were meager by comparison to other nominees of the prior 35 years. Miers had served capably enough in the White House and before then as a private attorney in Texas—the first woman to run a big law firm in the state and to head the state bar, as well as Bush's personal lawyer. But that was about it. The bigger problem, though, was that Bush's base didn't trust her, despite his assurances that "I know her heart." The base was interested not in her heart but in how she'd vote. Was she the conservative they demanded or—ironically, given her concerns about Roberts—another Souter type? There was no way to know, because Miers hadn't been a judge or practiced constitutional law or shown any indication she had much thought about it. In the running list of potential justices dating to the Bush transition in 2000–2001, Miers's name had never appeared.

Her odds were therefore low at the outset and were further compounded by having a full-time job that left little time to cram for what would be grueling confirmation hearings. With few in the White House encouraging her to continue, and after being savaged by the legal community, Miers withdrew her name. Bush admitted his miscalculation, but he blamed others. "If I had it to do over," he wrote in his memoirs, "I would not have thrown Harriet to the wolves of Washington."

The road to Roberts had been smooth. But resolving the second vacancy was now becoming an embarrassment. Against the backdrop of the administration's highly criticized response to Hurricane Katrina at the end of that summer, the Miers episode made Bush look even more inept. He needed the Court seat filled without further drama.

THIS TIME AROUND, WILKINSON WAS ruled out, mainly due to age and approach, though it didn't help that he had given an interview, albeit benign, to the *New York Times* in the interim. Luttig's stock had continued to fall, despite hints that several conservative justices were hoping he'd be the nominee. Through back channels, White House officials were hearing from other judges on his appeals court that Luttig wasn't a team player. (This wasn't Wilkinson operating behind the scenes, but other judges who wanted it known that Luttig, though whip-smart, could be difficult.) And Bush still remembered his interview with Luttig. All this served to boost Alito's chances.

Alito, then 55, had backers all along. He was skilled, consistent and conservative. The issue was his manner, which never was mistaken for Roberts's effortless poise. Kindly put, Alito was a little weird, if also at times endearing. When Gonzales had an initial, get-to-know meeting with Alito—even before there were Court vacancies—Alito fidgeted, wriggled, and gave every appearance he wasn't ready for the spotlight. His suit didn't quite fit, and his hair looked like it had last been combed the night before. For Gonzales, who had already met with Roberts, the contrast was striking.

The endearing part showed itself a few months later. When the vetting got more formal, an administration official had to locate records from Alito's time as U.S. attorney for New Jersey. The official reached out to the current officeholder, Chris Christie (who later become governor). Christie wanted to relate office lore. When Alito served as an assistant prosecutor in the late 1970s, he was oblivious to the entreaties of the law librarian—a gregarious woman named Martha-Ann Bomgardner, who was Alito's behavioral opposite. She passed him a note in the library. They talked novels, Russian history, politics. She gave him her phone number. He didn't get the hint. "It took him, like, a million years," in Christie's telling, to call her. Well, not quite that long. Sam and Martha-Ann were married only seven years later.

Alito's interviewing style had improved since being vetted for the initial Court vacancy. This time, after meeting with the full administration screening committee (Cheney, Gonzales, Miers, Card and Rove), Alito actually emerged as the best performer, in the view of Cheney and Gonzales—even better than Roberts in terms of actual answers. And in Alito's interview with the president, he opened up a bit. All it took was Bush mentioning Alito's beloved Philadelphia Phillies. This conversation, along with the president's political needs and the consensus on his staff that Alito was, as an adviser put it, "the best pick on the draft board," led Bush to nominate Alito four days after Miers pulled out.

With Republicans controlling the Senate, the outcome was hardly in doubt. Even so, and despite having been coached to avoid squirms and eye rolls, Alito was a nervous witness at his hearings. He wasn't good at "speaking D.C.," as an administration handler said. In addition, Roberts was a tough act to follow. But Democrats overreached, unwittingly turning Alito into a sympathetic character. Deep into his third day of testimony in January 2006, having made no progress in challenging his positions on such matters as abortion and presidential power, the Democrats changed tack. They now pressed Alito on "character issues," such as his membership long ago in Concerned Alumni of Princeton (CAP), an organization that opposed coeducation, as well as affirmative action in university admissions. He had mentioned the membership when in 1985 he applied, successfully, for a promotion in the Reagan Justice Department, but in the hearings he recalled little about it, making sure to renounce CAP's racist and sexist statements.

A Republican senator, Lindsey Graham, offered Alito a lifeline. "Are you really a closet bigot?" he rhetorically asked.

"I'm not any kind of bigot—I'm not," Alito answered.

Martha-Ann was sitting a few feet behind him. She had been the stoic spouse throughout, as any confirmation set piece called for. The bigot question was apparently too much. She sniffled, then sobbed, then exited the committee room. The evening news caught it all. Democrats stopped asking mean questions.

The CAP kerfuffle, fanned by the press, helped make Alito despise journalists almost as much as Thomas did. He was sickened by articles about Thomas and what he thought was bias on the part of many reporters covering the Court. Alito liked to recount how the press in Canada was briefed on new rulings by the country's highest court. All the reporters were locked in a room, handed the written opinion, and then allowed to ask questions. "I thought it was a great system—until I found out that at the end they unlock the door and let them out," he deadpanned to an audience at the New-York Historical Society in November 2016.

Alito was confirmed 58–42, after an attempted Democratic filibuster (supported by then-senator Barack Obama) fizzled. The day after, Bush invited the new justice and his family to the White House. Taking Alito aside, the man who won the presidency in 2000 largely by fortuity again acknowledged the element of luck in career advancement. "Sam, you ought to thank Harriet Miers for making this possible," Bush told him, to which Alito replied, "Mr. President, you're exactly right."

Alito's time at Princeton, from 1968 to 1972—discussed briefly at the hearings in the context of CAP—had been formative. While others—like Sotomayor, four years after him—came away from that tumultuous period with an optimistic view of social progress, Alito had seen division and discord. "It was a time of turmoil at colleges and universities," Alito recalled in his opening statement to the Judiciary Committee, making clear which side of the culture wars he was on, even in his late teens. "And I saw some very smart people and some very privileged people behaving irresponsibly, and I couldn't help making a contrast between some of the worst of what I saw on the campus, and the good sense and the decency of the people back in my own community."

It was also at Princeton that Alito developed his passion for law. He'd come across the work of Alexander Bickel, the dapper Yale law professor who was the foremost constitutional scholar of his time. (Bickel died of cancer at only 49, in 1974, prompting an unusual tribute from the Supreme Court itself.) Though Bickel's personal politics were progressive, in the 1960s he became the academy's avatar of judicial self-restraint. He astutely spoke of "the countermajoritarian difficulty" presented by the Court's power to countermand popular governance in a democratic society. Influenced by his mentor Felix Frankfurter—who described him as nearly a "son-in-law"—Bickel worried about overly assertive justices and believed the Warren Court continually overstepped. In such mostly forgotten books as *The Least Dangerous Branch* and *The Supreme Court and the Idea of Progress*, he called on the Court to stay out of many disputes altogether and instead defer to the political branches, no matter what their failings might be.

That was exactly the view Alito had offered in 1985, when he sought to advance in the Reagan administration. "I disagree strenuously with the usurpation by the judiciary of decision-making authority that should be exercised by the branches of government responsible to the electorate," he wrote in his job application. More than 20 years later, at his confirmation hearings for the Court, he said Bickel's writing had provided him with a historical and theoretical basis for "my strong belief in judicial self-restraint." Bickel was the reason Alito chose to go to law school at Yale after graduating from Princeton. (The two of them never connected there—Bickel died during Alito's third year.)

Yet for all his professed admiration for Bickel, Alito, once on the Court, paid Bickel little heed. In a September 2015 speech at the George W. Bush presidential library in Texas, Alito mocked Bickelian notions of restraint and pragmatism. His view of stare decisis bordered on the cynical. The Latin phrase actually "means to leave things decided—when it suits our purposes," Alito told a Federalist Society luncheon. "Stare decisis is like wine. If it's really new, you don't want to drink it—it has to age for a while. If it's really old, it is very valuable, or it has possibly turned to vinegar. . . . It's not difficult for a judge to make the stare decisis inquiry come out however the judge wants it to come out." He conveniently left out those sentiments at his hearings a decade earlier. Not once did Alito mention Bickel or his writings in an opinion as a justice.

Only three weeks before the speech in Texas, Alito had traveled to NYU's Shanghai campus to talk about American democracy and the role of the Court in it. In a private session for guests and students, he implicitly referred to Bickel. "The judiciary is indisputably the least dangerous branch," he said, but "that does not mean we are not dangerous." After all, he added, the judiciary wasn't subject to the "checks" placed on the other branches.

After Trump won the presidency, Alito's truest colors materialized. In the spring of 2017, only 10 days after Gorsuch joined the Court, Alito appeared at the annual conference of the Third Circuit. That's the mid-Atlantic federal appeals court, based in Philadelphia, on which he sat before becoming a justice. The event in central Pennsylvania is for judges and lawyers. Most years they talk shop and it's an anodyne affair, without the presence of C-SPAN. But with hundreds in the audience, including journalists, what's discussed inside gets out. It was a measure of Alito's arrogance and tone-deafness that he spoke as he did.

"Having eight [justices] was unusual and awkward," he explained in his "fireside chat" with the chief judge of the circuit. "That probably required having a lot more discussion of some things, and more compromise and maybe narrower opinions in some cases than we would have issued otherwise." But now, he said revealingly, "we were back to an odd number." Who could possibly want "more compromise" and "narrower opinions" of the kind Professor Bickel would have counseled? Now that the conservative camp of the Court had a new member, certainly not Sam Alito. He knew how to count votes. And in Gorsuch, he had what quickly proved to be an ally who had even less interest in "more compromise" and "narrower opinions."

CHAPTER 8

DEUS EX MACHINA

UNLIKE SAMUEL ALITO—OR ANY OF THE OTHER JUSTICES DURING THE 2017–18 term, on the left or on the right—Anthony Kennedy made no pretense of being a minimalist. Appointed by President Reagan and the Court's longest-serving member at the time he announced his retirement in 2018—more than 30 years, just before he turned 82—Kennedy was the prototype for triumphalism. More than any other justice, he embodied what has made the Supreme Court the most dangerous branch. Though often described as its resident moderate, he was more radical than any of his colleagues when it came to exercising power. The others talked of restraint, if disingenuously. He did not. What Kennedy lacked in self-doubt he made up for in consistency. In key rulings—from *Bush v. Gore* to *Heller* to *Citizens United* to *Shelby County* to *Obergefell*—he came out on the side that disregarded what other governmental branches, federal or state, had done. He wasn't driven by partisan results as much as ensuring that the Court had the final word.

Kennedy had the great fortune of being that word himself. Because he happened to be the center of gravity of the Court—in the key rulings, most of the time—his vote often determined the outcome. That wasn't

because Kennedy was accomplished at cobbling together a majority. Nobody mixed him up with such giants of consensus as Earl Warren or
William Brennan. Nor was Kennedy a John Roberts, who on occasion
might try to marshal an argument based on the Court's institutional
needs rather than on interpretive consistency. Kennedy owed his influence simply to serendipity. Roberts was the chief justice, but as a matter
of power, it was the Kennedy Court over which he presided. Kennedy
represented a majority of one.

When Alito replaced Sandra Day O'Connor in 2006, the center
shifted. O'Connor used to be the swing vote—between a reliable liberal
alliance of four and a reliable conservative alliance of four that frequently
included Kennedy. Now it was Kennedy in control. In the O'Connor
days, if Kennedy didn't vote with the conservatives in a particular case,
chances were that O'Connor wasn't with the conservatives either. That
meant a 6-to-3 ruling that skewed liberal.

But with the Alito-for-O'Connor switch—and Alito dependably
with the conservatives—Kennedy typically dictated the result. Still on
the bench more than a decade after Reagan died, Kennedy was a telling reminder of a president's ability to shape history through Court appointments. Yet he claimed he had no unique station in the middle.
"Cases swing—I don't!" he protested to Harvard law students in 2015.
He rolled his blue eyes and waved a hand, as his face turned ruddier than
usual—an uncharacteristic expression of testiness. "I *hate* that term. It
has this visual image of these spatial gyrations."

Even if many of his votes were predictable, it was hard to pigeon-
hole Kennedy's politics. Like O'Connor, he was a staid, traditional Republican of the West. Returning home to Sacramento after getting his
Harvard law degree in 1961, he took over the private law practice of his
well-connected father, Bud. It was the early days of Reagan in the state
capital, and as a young lawyer, Kennedy got to advise the new California governor about a ballot initiative to curtail government spending.
The connection endured. It was Reagan who recommended to President
Ford putting Kennedy on the federal bench in 1975; at 38, he was the
youngest federal appellate judge in the nation.

On the Supreme Court, Kennedy's decisive votes—for example, on gun control in *Heller*, campaign finance in *Citizens United*, and voting rights in *Shelby County*—were consistent with a conservative Republican stance. But Kennedy also wrote *Obergefell*'s paean to liberty and love and personal identity. "The nature of injustice is that we may not always see it in our own times," he said. Those who wrote the Constitution "did not presume to know the extent of freedom in all of its dimensions, and so they entrusted to future generations a charter protecting the right of all persons to enjoy liberty as we learn its meaning." For Kennedy, that meant entrusting justices. In declaring a constitutional right to same-sex marriage, Kennedy's soaring majority opinion couldn't have been more progressive if Justice Brennan had reappeared to write it himself. The difference is that Brennan might've tried to dress up the ruling a bit more in legal-sounding language that wouldn't make his critics yowl.

Kennedy's core philosophy was less about being liberal or conservative than about being pro-judicial. He stood ready and eager to insert himself and the Court into matters of public policy that might better have remained with other government players. If he seemed to tack rudderlessly left and right, it was because his critics failed to recognize his destination. He wasn't in search of ideological purity—only justifying his place at the helm. Kennedy's view of his role also produced rulings that went far beyond resolving the individual issue at hand—in contrast to O'Connor, who tried, sometimes too much so, to draft opinions that gave judges wiggle room to deal with unforeseen situations. Her approach sometimes led to confusion, but it had the merit of modesty, limiting judicial mischief-making and encouraging legislative experimentation. By contrast, Kennedy wanted to speak with scope and sweep.

If he didn't like being called the swing justice, Kennedy positively reveled in the pivotal position in which it left him. He was thoroughly pleased in June 2012 when *Time* put a black-and-white close-up of his solemn face on its cover, with the banner "The Decider." He posed for the striking photo. His colleagues on the Court appreciated his polite manner. Law clerks, younger and raised in a different age, saw it as a patrician air, which created distance, perhaps intentionally so. Some years, he was the lone justice who didn't invite clerks from other chambers to lunch. Many of the clerks thought that was just his affected way, especially if they'd gotten to see his personal office. He had decorated his high-ceilinged chambers in just the style that made Harlan Fiske Stone back in 1935 snipe about the new building being "almost bombastically pretentious"—though Kennedy might have thought that a compliment. Whereas, for example, Elena Kagan's office contained no personal adornments—it had all the charm of a Marriott—Kennedy's had the finery of a throne room: deep-red walls with a matching carpet emblazoned with big gold stars.

FEW CLERKS HADN'T HEARD ABOUT the time back in June 1992 when Kennedy, for some reason, agreed to let a writer for *California Lawyer,* a trade publication, into those chambers just before he went on the bench. The Court was about to issue its ruling in a major abortion case in which Kennedy was the swing vote. On that morning, Kennedy could see down from his window to the protesters on the plaza in front of the Court. One sign read ABORTION STOPS A BEATING HEART 4,400 TIMES A DAY. Another, displaying a coat hanger, admonished: THIS IS NOT A SURGICAL INSTRUMENT. KEEP ABORTION SAFE. A dozen TV cameras waited for a Court announcement. Kennedy drank it all in. "Sometimes you don't know if you're Caesar about to cross the Rubicon or Captain Queeg cutting your own tow-line," he confided to the writer. Then the justice self-consciously requested solitude. "I need to brood . . . as all of us do on the bench, just before we go on." It was likely, though, that most of them didn't do it on cue.

Minutes after comparing himself to Caesar, Kennedy entered the courtroom to issue the abortion opinion he wrote with O'Connor and Souter. Officially, the opinion had no single author, but its first sentence was Kennedy's: "Liberty finds no refuge in a jurisprudence of doubt." For a brooder—someone whose tendencies might have produced an approach rooted in gradualism—the absence of doubt was remarkable. It also ran contrary to a credo among judges. Rather than proclaim certitude for the ages, they accepted that a "jurisprudence of doubt" better reflected their role as imperfect arbiter. Their muse was Learned Hand, an avowed skeptic, a legal theorist and an iconic minimalist for 50 years on the federal bench. "The spirit of liberty," Hand declared in 1944 in his most memorable speech, "is the spirit which is not too sure that it is right." An instinct toward caution made all the more sense given that justices over the years had expressed second thoughts over rulings they had joined.

Kennedy clerks still read the Caesar-Queeg magazine piece before beginning their year with him. It was a good introduction to a justice who seemed incapable of beginning conversations with his clerks with "I believe" when explaining his views on a case. Instead, it was, "the law says," with an occasional "history will judge us" thrown in. It was the Kennedy version of Breyer Bingo.

The awesome weight on his judicial shoulders was a self-dramatizing theme to which Kennedy the lawgiver continually returned, and basked in. In 1996 he wrote the majority opinion in *Romer v. Evans*, the first victory for gay rights at the Court. Despite a splenetic dissent by Scalia, the Court struck down part of the Colorado constitutional amendment that singled out homosexuals as a group that couldn't be protected by anti-discrimination laws. Three days after *Romer*, Justice Blackmun, now retired, sent Kennedy a congratulatory note. "Monday's decision took courage," he wrote. "You undoubtedly now will receive a lot of critical and even hateful mail. I have had that experience." As the author of *Roe v. Wade*, Blackmun surely had.

Kennedy could relate to such fearlessness—and he loved doing so. Replying to Blackmun, he wrote, "No one told us it was an easy job when we signed on."

In opinions, in speeches, in private comments, it was the same operatic story: Kennedy agonized, ruminated, pondered and deliberated about what to do. Assorted commentators took to calling him the Hamlet of the Supreme Court and Kennedy seemed to agree, telling one group, "You know Hamlet better than you know most real people." In the mid-1990s, he came up with the idea of staging "The Trial of Hamlet," an unscripted performance to settle whether the Danish prince was insane when he killed Polonius. Ever since, the show's been done regularly in Washington, Boston, Los Angeles and elsewhere, with Kennedy of course playing the hand-wringing judge every time.

In his cogitations about actual Court cases, he left out one question: Was it the job as a justice to be deciding? For Kennedy—who had been a judge for most of his professional life—perhaps it wasn't a question at all. It naturally fell upon him, and the rest of the justices, to step in and to speak. A few months after the Court took sides in the disputed 2000 presidential election—deciding in *Bush v. Gore* that the State of Florida had to stop its vote recount—Kennedy appeared before a House subcommittee that was considering the Court's budget request. His testimony might have been routine, but the subject turned to the Court's involvement in the election. "This was not the most difficult decision that the Court has made, for many of us," Kennedy told legislators. Then he dismissed the very notion of judicial abstinence. "Sometimes it is easy to enhance your prestige by not exercising your responsibility," he testified. "But that has not been the tradition of our Court." In that observation he was correct, obviously so. But it might have occurred to him that he was describing a failing rather than a virtue. Over the next 15 years, he reprised his central role in rulings on gun control, campaign finance and voting rights.

Kennedy's power was such that he didn't even have to seek out four other justices to command a majority. Because he sat between two opposed factions of four, Kennedy could wait for others to court him. John Paul Stevens, as the senior associate justice for years, strategically sought to lock in Kennedy when he seemed to lean toward Stevens's side. "I thought if he wrote it out himself he was more sure to stick to his first vote," Stevens explained. Many who wrote about the Court overstated the extent to which horse-trading was even attempted, beyond the circulation of successive revised drafts of opinions to some or all justices. But members of the Court on occasion sensed Kennedy was available for pursuit. Breyer, whose chambers have neighbored Kennedy's for more than two decades, was a recurrent pop-in, especially when a 5-to-4 ruling was on the horizon. Their relationship—rooted not only in proximity and improvisational instinct, but in age and in Californian upbringing—was closer than most at the Court.

FOR ALL HIS SELF-IMPORTANCE, Kennedy was the most accidental of recent justices. He joined the Court in 1988 as President Reagan's third choice for the seat given up by Justice Lewis Powell. After the Senate rejected Robert Bork, Reagan picked Judge Douglas Ginsburg of the D.C. Circuit—who, more quietly, seemed just as conservative and had the benefit of being 19 years younger than Bork. But Ginsburg lasted only nine days, forced to withdraw following disclosures that he had smoked pot in college and as a law professor at Harvard. A few days later, Reagan named the 51-year-old Kennedy.

Although there were other contenders—including Souter, then a 48-year-old justice on the New Hampshire Supreme Court—Kennedy was the favorite, in large part on the recommendation of Attorney General Ed Meese, who knew him from their California days. Kennedy had learned from Bork's mistakes. The nominee offered conventional, modulated views about stare decisis, the right to privacy, and respect for the other branches. With the Senate exhausted and with the backing of some liberal scholars who had opposed Bork, Kennedy sailed to a 97-to-0 confirmation.

He might have taken away some humility from the process. After all, his journey to the Court wasn't preordained. The day after Kennedy's nomination, Blackmun wrote him a note of congratulations, welcoming Kennedy to "a very exclusive organization called 'the good old #3 club.'" Blackmun had been President Nixon's third choice in 1970, after the Senate rejected Clement Haynsworth and G. Harrold Carswell. "You now qualify for the unusual but worthy distinction," Blackmun informed Kennedy. "It has served me to keep a little humble whenever Dottie [his wife] suggests that I might be getting too 'judgie.'" Blackmun could not pass up the chance to needle his colleagues. "The other characters around here do not qualify."

Kennedy had no interest in humility. In responding to Blackmun, he pointed out there was another member of the "#3 club": Joseph Story, who served from 1812 to 1845 and who historians considered one of the great justices. Kennedy had cast himself in elite company—before he even got started.

With Trump's victory in 2016 came renewed focus on Kennedy's special position. If he retired, Trump would get the opportunity to reshape the Court. Kennedy didn't receive the kind of pressure that Justice Ginsburg faced in 2014, but he couldn't escape all the talk. He helped fuel the speculation about his plans by privately musing about spending more time with his family, as well as finding time to write a memoir of his Sacramento days, which he hoped might bring in a generous advance. Of course, in Washington, private musings rarely remain private, which entertained Kennedy and led him only to muse more. (Even in 2012, he told several friends he might retire if Mitt Romney, the Republican, won the White House.)

Wherever Kennedy went to speak, the audience was divided into two camps—the few who uncouthly inquired about his "future plans" and those who merely wondered in silence. In late 2016, the Court hosted the annual dinner for the Devitt Award. With Kennedy there, a humongous birthday cake—with a chocolate gavel on top—was wheeled out and presented to him for his 80th birthday. Kennedy took note of the portraits of past chief justices on the walls of the West Conference Room. "I'm not the oldest one in here!" he said, with a grin that might just as well have meant, *Not yet.*

The Trump administration did its part to entice him to go. By naming Gorsuch—a former Kennedy clerk—to Scalia's seat, Trump hoped to telegraph to Kennedy that the Court was in good hands. If Kennedy left, the president would nominate someone like Gorsuch—perhaps even another Kennedy clerk, like Judge Brett Kavanaugh or Judge Raymond Kethledge. Nobody doubted that Kennedy liked to be wooed, but nobody knew whether such subtle signals from the administration meant a thing to him. Furthermore, to Kennedy, Gorsuch was hardly the ideal justice. He was acceptable, but his rigidity, no matter how well couched in civility, wasn't the Kennedy way.

Though Kennedy did let on to several individuals that he wanted Trump to win, if only to keep Hillary Clinton out of the White House, he also made it clear the new president wasn't his sort of Republican—or sort of person, for that matter. On a Saturday night in February 2017, Kennedy was feted again for his birthday, this time in the hills above L.A., at the Bel Air mansion of Julie Chrystyn Opperman, the patron of the Devitt Award. On both sides of the front door hung a 12-foot vertical vinyl banner portrait of the honoree; HAPPY BIRTHDAY, TONY! read a giant sign across the top of the door. For Kennedy, it was a fine crowd of not only family and former law clerks, but also a gospel choir; Emmitt Smith, the all-time NFL rusher; and Sarah Brightman, the top-selling soprano ever, who fortunately didn't perform her best-known hit, "Time to Say Goodbye."

The party took place around the time a lower federal court had blocked Trump's first executive order temporarily banning citizens of seven Muslim countries from entering the United States. In six minutes of remarks, after lauding the host and his own family, the tuxedoed Kennedy turned to Plato and Aristotle and the topics of "tolerance" and the "heritage of freedom." And then to much applause—and a few gasps—he paid tribute to the immigrants who had come to America over the generations. His 6-feet-3 frame slightly hunched, he quoted, slowly and wistfully, from the Emma Lazarus poem engraved on the plaque at the base of the Statue of Liberty: "Give me your tired, your poor, your huddled masses yearning to breathe free, the wretched refuse of your teeming shore. Send these, the homeless, tempest-tost to me, I lift my lamp beside the golden door." Anybody listening understood Kennedy was taking a veiled swipe at the brand-new president he had still hoped would win the election. (His views on immigrants notwithstanding, Kennedy's vote was decisive in 2018 when the Court, 5–4, upheld Trump's travel ban.)

As much as he might have wanted to retire then, Kennedy was characteristically torn. It wasn't as if he were hoping for a Democrat to win in 2020. But perhaps Trump would flame out before then and a more conventional Republican, like Mike Pence, might succeed him. One way or another, perhaps Kennedy's successor might be named by somebody other than Trump. Kennedy was also pulled in different directions by his children on the question of retiring soon. One son, Justin, was more conservative than he was, as well as friendly with Donald Trump Jr. Justin had no problem with the president naming his father's successor. But Kennedy's daughter Kristin, a New Yorker, was politically to the left of her father and urged him to wait out the Trump presidency. Complicating matters was the concern of Kennedy family members that in their view he was having memory issues, and that politics aside, years more on the Court would become increasingly difficult. By the end of the 2017–18 term, that view prevailed and Kennedy finally stepped down.

Who would replace Kennedy, and who would do the replacing, mattered to him. But there was another, maybe stronger, reason he had been ambivalent. As one Kennedy clerk put it, expressing what other clerks had intimated as well, "Why would you leave when you're running the country?" Such was the power wielded by the Supreme Court. It wasn't always so.

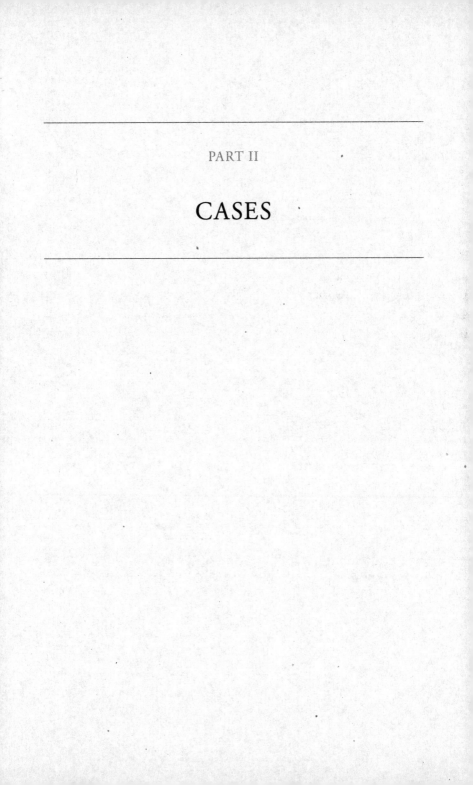

PART II

CASES

CHAPTER 9

SLEEPING GIANT

FOR MUCH OF AMERICAN HISTORY, THE SUPREME COURT WAS RELAtively quiescent. After the Revolution, after the failure of the Articles of Confederation, the U.S. Constitution was ratified. The country had a new operating system, dividing power between nation and states, and separating power at the national level among the three coequal branches of government. At the beginning, it was inconceivable that the justices would be the ones to declare new constitutional rights in that system. Until *Marbury v. Madison* in 1803, the Court even lacked authority to strike down acts of Congress, or acts of the president, as unconstitutional. Such authority, though suggested in the Federalist Papers, is nowhere stated in the Constitution. It was a seizure of power that Chief Justice John Marshall took upon himself, based on what he said the Constitution implied, as well as on the example that some state courts had already provided when it came to state statutes. Though not viewed at the time, or since, as especially controversial, Marshall's assertion of "judicial review" remained the most consequential instance of "judicial activism" in the Court's history. It is there that the rhetoric of "judicial supremacy" was born.

The other branches acquiesced in Marshall's power grab. But such assent was based on the expectation that the justices ruled on principle rather than whim. It had to be that way because the Court possessed neither sword nor purse, as Alexander Hamilton had famously written. Nor did the justices have the imprimatur of the ballot box. Securing their authority from principle ideally gave them special constitutional legitimacy—if they used the authority carefully and as long as they seemed to be acting neutrally.

Over the course of most of the 19th century, as the Court went about ascertaining its role, the justices confined their decisions mostly to striking the proper balance between federal power and state sovereignty. In 1810, in *Fletcher v. Peck*, the Court for the first time invoked the Constitution to invalidate a state law. Six years later, the justices ruled they had the power to review state court decisions if they involved federal law. Most important in this run of decisions, in 1819 the Court in *McCulloch v. Maryland* unanimously upheld Congress's power to charter a national bank and declared that states were helpless to tax it. Citing the Necessary and Proper Clause, but reading between the lines of the Constitution in its entirety, Marshall wrote: "Let the end be legitimate, let it be within the scope of the Constitution, and all means which are appropriate, which are plainly adapted to that end, which are not prohibited, but consistent with the letter and spirit of the Constitution, are constitutional."

The thrust of the early rulings wasn't about uncovering new substantive rights that were unenumerated in the Constitution, though the Court did make an occasional excursion into that minefield. In *Fletcher*, for example, the issue was whether the State of Georgia could interfere with a private contract. The justices said it could not, in part because the Constitution forbade any state from "impairing the obligation of contracts." But the Court also said "natural law" and "general principles which are common to our free institutions" restrained the state. Although such fuzzy language seemed an invitation to judicial freelancing, the Marshall Court stuck to its two main goals: solidifying the Court's institutional role and establishing federal power in a time of rising sectional fury over slavery.

It was not until the calamitous *Dred Scott v. Sandford* decision in 1857 that the Court veered from refereeing only the boundaries of its own supremacy. Under Chief Justice Roger B. Taney, the Court interposed itself directly into the substance of a political dispute. Since colonial days, the country had struggled with the social, economic, moral and electoral challenges presented by slavery. One key congressional effort to defuse conflict was the Missouri Compromise of 1820, which excluded the spread of slavery to certain American territories. By a 7-to-2 vote, the Court held the compromise unconstitutional—the first time since *Marbury* that it struck down a federal statute. According to Taney, the Missouri Compromise denied slaveholders a personal property right. That, he ruled, was a violation of "due process," even as he also left unquestioned that blacks were "beings of an inferior order, and altogether unfit to associate with the white race."

Universally considered by scholars as the Court's worst decision, *Dred Scott* inflamed abolitionist sentiment; set Abraham Lincoln on a path to his House Divided speech and propelled him to the presidency; and culminated in Fort Sumter four years after the ruling. (The actual ruling was effectively overturned by the Civil War itself, as well as by the passage of the Thirteenth, Fourteenth and Fifteenth Amendments in the five years after Appomattox.) In terms of constitutional doctrine, *Dred Scott* also represented the Court's first embrace of what came to be known as "substantive due process." The Due Process Clause of the Fifth Amendment states that no person may be "deprived of life, liberty or property" by the federal government "without due process of law." After the Civil War, the same open-ended language was added to the Fourteenth Amendment to constrain states. Before *Dred Scott*, it had generally been accepted that due process was procedural in nature—a ban on capriciousness, typically in matters of criminal prosecution. Before individuals could be incarcerated or executed, they were due such protections as notice, opportunity to be heard, and a neutral tribunal.

But that was it. The controlling word in "due process" had been "process." *What* the government could punish, or how it could otherwise treat you—say, by enslavement, or decades later, preventing you from getting an abortion or marrying someone of the same sex—seemed to have nothing to do with due process. The constitutional inquiry was about permissible means—*how* and *when*—rather than ends. *Dred Scott* began to change that. Now, when the Court determined that fundamental freedoms were implicated, due process could be used to grant substantive rights—even if the Constitution didn't explicitly mention them. There were some "liberties" so basic that no process would suffice to take them away. In *Dred Scott*, due process perversely meant the liberty of Americans to own slaves—surely an oxymoron. "Substantive due process" itself seemed a contradiction in terms—"sort of like green pastel redness," as the 20th-century constitutional scholar John Hart Ely put it.

THUS DELIVERED, SUBSTANTIVE DUE PROCESS remained dormant until the Progressive Era, nearly 50 years later. With the rise of cities and industrialization came laws regulating working conditions. Just after the turn of the century, in *Lochner v. New York*, the justices threw out a state statute setting maximum hours for employees in the baking industry. The owner of the Lochner Home Bakery sued, citing the Fourteenth Amendment's Due Process Clause. A 5-to-4 Court ruled that the law interfered with both an employer's and an employee's "liberty of contract." Only statutes designed to bar contracts to use property "for immoral purposes" or other "unlawful acts" were permissible. "Liberty" was coming to mean far more than protection from arrest and imprisonment; according to the Court, liberty encompassed broader values, which were up to the justices alone to identify and bless.

In dissent, Oliver Wendell Holmes Jr. ridiculed the Court for enshrining "an economic theory which a large part of the country does not entertain." He chastised his colleagues for encroaching on "the right of a majority to embody their opinions in law." Much as judges might think laws prohibiting commerce on Sunday or usury were "tyrannical," the Constitution didn't require their invalidation. Holmes's complaint wasn't over the results the Court reached—it was that the Court was involved at all.

Years later, Justice Stevens called Holmes's two-paragraph dissent "the most influential" in the Court's history. While some commentators have tried to defend *Lochner* as nothing more than neutral skepticism about government meddling in the affairs of individuals, the prevailing view remains that *Lochner* reflected the Court's values-laden "capitulation to big business" at the dawn of the modern age. Robert Bork himself called *Lochner* "the symbol, indeed the quintessence, of judicial usurpation of power." In substantive due process, the Court had created a whole new line of reasoning under which the justices could overturn legislation in favor of their own values.

For the next three decades, the Court cited *Lochner* in striking down nearly 200 state and federal laws as violations of "liberty" afforded by due process. Many of the laws were aimed at promoting worker health and safety, including legislation on child labor and minimum wages. Once in a while, the justices also rejected statutes that infringed on personal, rather than economic, rights. The most prominent examples were laws restricting foreign-language education (*Meyer v. Nebraska*) and requiring students to attend public schools (*Pierce v. Society of Sisters*), struck down as violations of substantive process; both, though, could have been decided simply under First Amendment principles protecting religion and expression. But cases like *Meyer* and *Pierce* were the exceptions. It was the laissez-faire capitalism sanctioned by *Lochner* that helped to bring on the Great Depression, beginning in 1929.

FDR's landslide election in 1932 signaled a turning point in the federal government's attitude toward regulation. As part of FDR's New Deal, Congress enacted a wave of laws to boost the economy, to reform the financial system, and to provide relief to the unemployed and the poor. But in its own surge, the Court pushed back, ruling that some of the legislation was an unconstitutional expansion of federal power. In 1935, in *A.L.A. Schechter Poultry Corp. v. United States*, the justices threw out the National Industrial Recovery Act, a centerpiece of the New Deal. Five other times that year and the next, the Court declared unconstitutional other New Deal legislation, along with a New York law on wages.

Roosevelt retaliated by proposing the Judicial Procedures Reform Bill of 1937. Better known as the Court-packing plan, it would have allowed presidents to appoint a new member of the Court, up to a maximum of six, for each sitting justice over the age of $70^{1}/_{2}$. (The number of justices is set by Congress, not the Constitution.) Bipartisan objections—that the president was threatening the Court's independence, and that the Court hardly needed more manpower—meant the bill went nowhere in Congress.

Within two months, however, Roosevelt's intimidation tactics apparently had worked—not on Capitol Hill but at the Court itself. A group of conservative justices, dubbed by the press the Four Horsemen, had led the resistance to the New Deal. The fifth vote was often provided by Justice Owen Roberts. But in *West Coast Hotel Co. v. Parrish*, upholding a minimum-wage law in Washington State, Roberts reversed course. This was the so-called switch in time that saved nine (though there's no conclusive evidence he did so because of the Court-packing plan, and some evidence the timing was coincidental). The Court had surrendered to the New Deal.

FDR, in office until 1945, ended up getting to fill all but one of the nine seats on the Court—all after he proposed to pack the Court. The *Lochner* era was dead. So, too, was the idea of substantive due process, at least in the realm of business regulation. Liberals exulted. Their victories in the cause for economic justice were secure. No longer would the justices substitute what seemed to be their own policy preferences for those of the people as expressed in legislative majorities. Conservatives despaired they had lost a mechanism by which to accomplish at the Court what had been denied in the ordinary course of politics.

The doctrine of substantive due process wasn't entirely dead. For example, in *Skinner v. Oklahoma*, when the Court in 1942 struck down a state law allowing compulsory sterilization of certain repeat-offender felons, Justice Douglas spoke of "fundamental" freedoms. But ultimately the Court overruled the law because it violated the Equal Protection Clause, since not all three-time felons were subject to sterilization. It wasn't until the 1960s that substantive due process came back in a new form, when the Court used it to scrutinize not legislation on economics but reproductive freedom. In the interim, while the justices by and large stayed out of the political bog, they twice intervened decisively. One case was notable; the other produced the most epic ruling since *Marbury*. Both were reasonable rulings, but their significance lay not only in the result but in the interventions themselves.

ON APRIL 8, 1952, in the middle of the Korean War, President Harry Truman seized control of most of the steel mills in the United States. He did so to avert a nationwide strike of steelworkers, which he had concluded would endanger the war effort. Truman based his executive order not on any specific statute but on authority implied in "the aggregate of his powers" in the Constitution, especially those that made him commander in chief of the armed forces. Two months later—a remarkably short time frame in constitutional litigation—the Court ruled that the president had exceeded his authority and commandeered that of Congress. Seizing private property in wartime "is a job for the nation's lawmakers, not for its military authorities," Justice Hugo Black wrote for the 6-to-3 majority. "In the framework of our Constitution, the president's power to see that the laws are faithfully executed refutes the idea that he is to be a lawmaker."

In a prophetic concurrence, Justice Robert Jackson acknowledged—and warned of—potential congressional timidity in the face of executive "personality" and "prestige." "I have no illusion that any decision by this Court can keep power in the hands of Congress if it is not wise and timely in meeting its problems," he wrote. "With all its defects, delays and inconveniences, men have discovered no technique for long preserving free government except that the executive be under the law, and that the law be made by parliamentary deliberations. Such institutions may be destined to pass away. But it is the duty of the Court to be last, not first, to give them up." In justifying the Court as arbiter, Jackson made clear that the other branches couldn't be left to their own constitutional devices to settle a political clash. For Jackson and others in the majority, the Court had to be the branch to resolve it. (In an analogous case two decades later, more momentously, the justices unanimously ordered President Nixon to turn over subpoenaed tape recordings in the Watergate scandal, swiftly leading to his resignation.)

The Steel Seizure Case, even if confined to its own unusual facts, further showcased the justices' growing role. Court cases are intertwined, even if the subjects seem different. Justice Breyer has commented that the Steel Seizure Case was an unspoken response to FDR's internment of Japanese Americans during World War II and the Court's refusal to declare the policy unconstitutional. Two years after the Steel Seizure Case, in 1954 the Court in *Brown v. Board of Education* conferred upon itself the task of ending the shameful practice of "separate but equal." In the broadest historical sense, *Brown* had been in gestation since the founding of the Republic.

Slavery has long been called America's original sin. Race was inextricably part of slavery. The Civil War was fought largely over slavery. The import of the three constitutional amendments quickly passed thereafter was race: the Thirteenth Amendment abolished slavery; the Fourteenth Amendment, in addition to making the Due Process Clause apply to state governments, adopted the Equal Protection Clause; and the Fifteenth Amendment guaranteed the right to vote without regard to "race, color, or previous condition of servitude." But state-sponsored racism endured in the South for another century.

In 1896, the Court in *Plessy v. Ferguson*—involving separate railway cars in Louisiana for blacks and whites—declared that "equal but separate" was constitutional, despite the Thirteenth and Fourteenth Amendments. There was an "underlying fallacy" in Homer Plessy's argument that "the enforced separation of the two races stamps the colored race with a badge of inferiority," according to the Court. "If this be so, it is not by reason of anything found in the act, but solely because the colored race chooses to put that construction upon it. . . . The argument also assumes that social prejudices may be overcome by legislation, and that equal rights cannot be secured to the Negro except by an enforced commingling of the two races."

Only Justice John Marshall Harlan I (grandfather of the justice who served from 1955 to 1971) dissented, famously so. Though he noted "a dangerous tendency" in increased "judicial interference" with "the will of the people as expressed by the legislature," he said the Court's failure to act would make *Plessy* "as pernicious" as *Dred Scott*. "Our Constitution is colorblind," Harlan wrote, "and neither knows nor tolerates classes among citizens."

Plessy exacerbated the legacy of slavery. The ruling legitimized a range of Jim Crow laws enacted by states during Reconstruction that mandated racial segregation in public facilities, transportation and schools. But the idea that separate facilities were in reality equal proved to be untenable. Apart from the inherent indignity of a divide based on race— being forced to ride "in the back of the bus"—African Americans were relegated to separate restaurants, hotels, bathrooms, and even public water fountains that were clearly inferior. Public schools presented the perfect illustration of how separate facilities were not equal.

Starting in the 1930s, Thurgood Marshall became the architect of the legal attack on *Plessy*. On behalf of the NAACP Legal Defense and Education Fund, slowly and strategically through the 1940s and early 1950s, the future justice filed lawsuits that challenged "separate but equal" in public education. First it was the mere availability of a separate law school in some states; next, unequal teacher salaries; then segregation generally in law schools and graduate schools. Marshall won some but not all cases. "You're whittling it away—you're cutting it down," he told an interviewer in 1977 for a Columbia University oral history project. "I was just methodically going down the road, going past bridge by bridge by bridge."

Marshall's efforts eventually turned to the biggest litigation target: grade schools and high schools. In the early 1950s, more than a third of states had legislatively authorized segregated public schools. In a broad assault, Marshall and other lawyers filed class actions across the country. The Supreme Court had already issued other equal protection decisions in the area of education that bode well for the justices' revisiting *Plessy*. In *Brown*, the Court did, though with trepidation on the part of many justices. Their dual threshold concerns were about drawing down the Court's institutional capital: Would the public think the Court was just acting as a political branch, and would the South obey an adverse ruling?

The justices also were divided on what exactly they should compel—and at what pace any changes should come.

The Court bundled pending lawsuits from Kansas, Virginia, Delaware and South Carolina. (A fifth case, arising in Washington, D.C., remained separate.) The titular case, *Brown*, involved black elementary school children in Topeka, Kansas, though *Briggs v. Elliot*, involving black students in both elementary and high school in Clarendon County in South Carolina, had the more representative facts in some ways. (Case names are often arbitrary; *Brown v. Board of Education* might easily have been *Briggs v. Elliott*. *Briggs* had come before the Court in early 1952, but the justices summarily sent the appeal back to a lower court to allow "further proceedings.")

But the real reason for avoiding the case was the upcoming presidential election. Though an FDR appointee and a New Deal liberal, Justice Frankfurter was the central voice counseling caution. Having observed as a professor what the *Lochner*-driven Court did to the New Deal early on, now he was overreacting as a justice to it. At a lunch with clerks, when asked why the Court ducked, he said, "Why, this is a social revolution that we're considering here!" If the Court did rule, "the two candidates will choose up sides on it," though "neither one will read the decision, of course, and it'll be thrown into a political scramble. . . . Is that the way you want this important question to be decided?"

Justice Stanley Reed, another FDR appointee, also worried about Court intervention. Discussing the case with one of his clerks, who favored a ruling that outlawed segregation, Reed remarked, "Are you one of those people who believes in krytocracy?" The clerk had to look the word up. It meant "government by judges."

BROWN, LIKE *BRIGGS*, had first come to the Court in 1952. The choice then was stark: Follow precedent and stay with the unsustainable *Plessy*, or extend more limited Court rulings on equal protection in higher education—and plunge the justices into the kind of political storm that so disquieted Frankfurter. But after hearing arguments, the justices again opted not to rule. They were divided—probably 5–4, in favor of overturning *Plessy,* by most accounts of what was said in their conference. The Court ordered the case to be reargued the following year, with particular focus on the history of the Fourteenth Amendment and what its drafters intended.

The delay paid off. Chief Justice Fred M. Vinson died in September 1953. When *Brown* was finally reargued, over three days that December, a new chief, Earl Warren, had taken over. Nobody was better suited to the task before the Court. Not only had he arrived with a reputation for integrity, he had the politician's touch for finding common ground. Warren—the longtime Republican governor of California—proved to be a maestro of internal politicking, at least in the exceptional case of *Brown.*

The new chief wanted the Court to overturn separate-but-equal—and to do so unanimously. A slim majority of the justices was prepared to act, but how far they were prepared to go was unclear. Instead of trying to force unity on the other justices or simply accepting a divided result, Warren gently worked the Court and waited. By avoiding an actual vote at conference, he gave each justice room to maneuver. He visited the others in chambers and had lunch with them frequently. Frankfurter yielded on his objections. So did Jackson, who had similar concerns about the Court abusing its power. When Reed appeared to be the last holdout, the story goes, Warren told him, "Stan, you're all by yourself in this now"—perhaps less a call for unanimity than empathy for a colleague from the border state of Kentucky. When the time came to vote, Reed joined the rest.

Warren assigned himself the task of writing the opinion. In a memo to the other justices, he stated his intention to write something "short, readable by the lay public, non-rhetorical, unemotional, and, above all, non-accusatory." But he said he was open to changes. As it turned out, few were needed. Warren's initial draft was close to the version all the justices approved at a rare Saturday conference. Two days later—on May 17, 1954—the Court announced its decision.

In a mere 13 paragraphs, writing an epochal opinion only eight months after President Eisenhower named him, the chief justice transformed the country—and the Court. Warren had succeeded in his desire to have something accessible: Less was more, though at that level of generality, the opinion read like an edict. "To separate [black children] from others of similar age and qualifications solely because of their race generates a feeling of inferiority . . . that may affect their hearts and minds in a way unlikely ever to be undone," he declared. Therefore, "we conclude that in the field of public education the doctrine of 'separate but equal' has no place. Separate educational facilities are inherently unequal."

As Warren announced the decision, the eyes of Justice Reed met those of Thurgood Marshall. Reed "was looking me right straight in the face," Marshall recalled, "because he wanted to see my reaction when I realized he hadn't written [a] dissent." One of Reed's clerks said there were tears running down the justice's cheeks.

For all the power of their words condemning segregation, the justices did not mandate an immediate remedy. It wasn't until the following year that the Court nebulously ordered that desegregation take place "with all deliberate speed." But the Old Confederacy was defiant. Over the decades—despite such highly publicized moments as President Eisenhower sending the 101st Airborne Division into Little Rock, Arkansas, to escort nine black students into Central High—it was hardly apparent that *Brown v. Board* had precipitated substantial reform. The Court had left the untidy business of implementing "all deliberate speed" to lower-court judges, who usually owed their appointments to patronage in the states where *Brown* had to be implemented. Even sympathetic judges didn't make for great administrators. They also lacked the resources to oversee the enormous task of any desegregation plan. Between bureaucratic reality and an intransigent political culture, *Brown* faced formidable headwinds from the beginning. Fifty years after the decision, much public education remained segregated—if no longer by government action, then because of geography, class, poverty and housing patterns. "With all deliberate speed" indeed.

At its heart, Earl Warren's ruling represented an ideal rather than

a result. Its primary power was symbolic, like Jackie Robinson breaking the race barrier in Major League Baseball. What Congress and the
White House had not accomplished since the Civil War (other than
President Truman's desegregation of the armed forces in 1948), the Supreme Court now had decreed in an instant. For the nascent civil rights
movement, and a complacent nation, that counted for a lot, whatever
the frustrations of "all deliberate speed" turned out to be. The Southern
backlash to *Brown* may have induced a backlash of its own, mobilizing
public opinion nationally and spurring the country to the Civil Rights
Act of 1964 and the Voting Rights Act of 1965, both of which probably
were more directly responsible than *Brown* for achieving a measure of
racial justice.

Brown was about public schools, but over time and then with aggressive legislation, integration came to the workplace, hotels, restaurants,
country clubs and much of American life. "Like poetry," Alexander
Bickel wrote eight years later, *Brown* "made nothing happen. But only
like poetry. Only as it may sometimes seem that nothing but power,
purposefully applied, can affect reality. . . . In fact, announcement of
the principle was in itself an action of great moment, considering the
source from which it came." "For African-Americans," said a leading
civil rights lawyer, *Brown* "divides American history into a B.C. and
an A.D." And for the Court—far more than exerting authority over
President Truman in the Steel Seizure Case or acquiescing in the New
Deal—*Brown* marked the beginning of a broader role in American life
that never abated.

Yet despite what it acknowledged as the unassailable correctness of the
result in *Brown*, the commentariat in coming years spilled a lot of scholarly blood over whether its reasoning was constitutionally persuasive. In
1958, in a series of lectures at Harvard, Learned Hand—considered the
greatest judge of his time and without doubt a champion of personal
liberty—attacked *Brown* on the same basis he had disparaged *Lochner*:
The Court had overstepped, acting as a "third legislative chamber." A
medley of leading law professors observed that *Brown*'s interventionism
seemed to be at odds with the left's prior fondness for judicial restraint.

Bickel himself had to devote some of *The Least Dangerous Branch* to defending *Brown* from these critics.

For its part, the Court had admitted that Fourteenth Amendment history was inconclusive about what the drafters meant by "equal protection," which was the Constitution's first mention of the idea of individual equality. *Brown*'s Footnote 11 cited years of social science research to bolster the Court's judgment that segregated schools harmed black students psychologically. That "modern authority" from experts was pretty much the only changed circumstance since *Plessy*, yet scholars showed that the methodology of some of the research was questionable. Years later, Clarence Thomas—Thurgood Marshall's successor on the Court—challenged the entire notion that students in an all-black school necessarily suffered psychological damage, saying that it rested "on an assumption of black inferiority." *Brown* was less analysis than proclamation, akin to Lincoln's in 1863.

Even with all the good-faith criticism of *Brown*'s doctrinal shallowness, it's easy enough to conclude that the Court got it right. The language of the Fourteenth Amendment—"equal protection"—seemed to demand an end to the racial caste system that slavery created and that invidious segregation laws preserved. That may not have been the consensus when the amendment was ratified in 1868 or at the time of *Plessy*, but constitutional text—written following a civil war brought on in part because of race—did provide *Brown* with a solid provenance. And even if sensible people might differ on the possible psychological or educational effects of segregation policy, the policy itself flatly contradicted what the Fourteenth Amendment demanded.

In the end, the justices may have folded into *Brown* their own sense of the country's moral and political needs—and their view that Congress and the states lacked the will to meet them. The justices were exercising their "legitimating" role, as political scientists described it. The people would follow a mandate because it came from the Court. But it wasn't as if the Court was entirely making it up based on some vaguely defined sense of fairness. Text and history were on the Court's side.

MARBLE TEMPLE:
The facade of the Supreme Court, shortly after construction
was completed in 1935.

HOMETOWN HERO: Neil Gorsuch greets folks during a Fourth of July parade in 2017 in Boulder County, Colorado, as his wife Louise looks on.

JOINT SESSION: President Donald Trump lectures Anthony Kennedy after Trump addressed Congress in February 2017. (Stephen Breyer is on the right.)

FATHER AND SON: John Roberts, after his investiture in October 2005, awaits his son Jack on the steps of the Court.

JUDICIAL TRIO (from left):
Sonia Sotomayor, Ruth Bader Ginsburg and Elena Kagan, 2010.

NOTORIOUS R.B.G.:
Ruth Bader Ginsburg
in chambers, 2014.

ORIGINALIST:
Antonin Scalia on
Fox News, 2012.

FULCRUM OF POLITICS:
Abortion demonstrators at
the Court, January 2018.

DEUS EX MACHINA:
Anthony Kennedy in
chambers, 2002.

SANCTUM SANCTORUM:
The justices' private
conference room, where even
law clerks are not allowed.

Sandra Day O'Connor at her confirmation hearings, 1981.

Clarence Thomas, 2016.

Stephen Breyer, 2016.

Samuel Alito with the Phillie Phanatic, 2006.

William J. Brennan Jr., 1986.

Earl Warren, 1967.

Oliver Wendell Holmes Jr., 1902.

Harry Blackmun, 1970.

CENTER OF THE STORM: The four-story-high courtroom, flanked by massive windows and 24 columns, is a magnificent setting.

NINE LAWGIVERS: The justices of the Supreme Court for the 2018–19 term (front row, from left): Stephen Breyer, Clarence Thomas, John Roberts, Ruth Bader Ginsburg, and Samuel Alito; (back row, from left): Neil Gorsuch, Sonia Sotomayor, Elena Kagan, and Brett Kavanaugh.

NEARLY A DECADE AFTER *Brown*, in a series of cases, the Court similarly got it right when it launched the reapportionment revolution. In 1962, in *Baker v. Carr*, the justices, 6–2, held that federal courts had a role in forcing states to correct inequities in the makeup of electoral districts. (The Court was down a justice.) Until then, the matter of voting districts had been exclusively up to state legislatures and Congress to resolve, because the Court found malapportionment to be a purely "political question," better left to legislatures. *Baker* led to the rule of "one person, one vote," fully articulated in *Reynolds v. Sims* in 1964, when the Court, 8–1, said representation had to be based chiefly on population rather than on territory. That meant states could no longer rely on outdated censuses to draw district boundaries—which typically meant that the votes of individuals in rural areas had greater weight than the votes of individuals in urban areas. Under the Equal Protection Clause, such inequality in voting power was unconstitutional, all the more when it served to deny minorities equal participation in the democratic process.

Frankfurter in *Baker*, and John Marshall Harlan II in *Reynolds*, cast the main dissents. They, and Bickel as well, believed the Court was straying into policy matters and reapportionment formulas it was ill-equipped to judge. By entering what he previously had warned was a "political thicket," Frankfurter wrote that the Court hadn't learned from self-inflicted trauma. Without mentioning *Dred Scott* or *Lochner*, he said *Baker* was "a massive repudiation of the experience of our whole past in asserting destructively novel judicial power." In *Reynolds*, Harlan, with uncharacteristic drama but admirable skepticism, cautioned: "The Constitution is not a panacea for every blot upon the public welfare, nor should this Court, ordained as a judicial body, be thought of as a general haven for reform movements."

Their instincts were sound. And Frankfurter and Harlan were presaging some of the adventurism of the Warren Court that soon followed. In the area of reapportionment, however, their qualms were misguided. There could be sound disagreements over the proper shape of an electoral district and which voters were packed into it—and whether such gerrymandering was motivated by permissible partisanship or illegal racism. After Congress enacted the Voting Rights Act of 1965, much litigation on those questions followed, including in the crucial case of *Shelby County* in 2013.

But on the less complicated issue of equality in numbers of voters within districts, both the constitutional directive and who should articulate it seemed quite clear. While the right to vote is not explicitly set out in the Constitution, it is implicit in the very structure of representative government. It's hard to imagine a system in which one vote counts less or more than another (except of course in the countermajoritarian U.S. Senate, where each state, no matter its population, gets two senators). It's equally hard to conclude that legislators can be solely entrusted with reapportionment, because, as Professor John Hart Ely noted, they have "an obvious vested interest" in whatever the status quo happens to be.

Under that circumstance, it fell on the Court to intervene to enforce the Constitution—to "clear the channels of political change" because "representative government cannot be trusted" to do so itself. Ely likened his approach to that of an antitrust regulator who intercedes not to "dictate substantive results" but only when the market is "systematically malfunctioning." Or to really be like an umpire, who acts "when one team is gaining unfair advantage, not because the 'wrong' team has scored." In theory (at least until *Gill v. Whitford* and *Benisek v. Lamone* in 2018), the Court could continue to stay out of challenges to partisan reapportionment that aimed only to give an advantage to a political party, rather than to deny one-person, one-vote. As long as election maps weren't drawn to thwart minority or ethnic participation, and as long as there was "an open political dialogue," the Court said reapportionment was for legislatures alone to consider. Warren rightly called *Baker* and *Reynolds*, more than even *Brown*, the most important rulings during his leadership.

Frankfurter, the most committed minimalist among the justices, retired after *Baker*. President Kennedy replaced him with Arthur J. Goldberg. The Court now tilted fully toward Warren's vision of an aggressive Court. What had begun in *Brown* with race expanded into other areas. In *New York Times v. Sullivan*, the Court in 1964 said the First Amendment constrained libel law and immunized the press from most liability unless it published falsehoods recklessly. The same year, in *Miranda v. Arizona*, the Court remade criminal procedure by devising rules for interrogating suspects. ("You have the right to remain silent . . ." For the rest, watch any episode of "Law & Order.") Both decisions could readily be justified by their reliance on express commands in the Bill of Rights—shorthand for the first 10 amendments—which the Court decided, piecemeal, apply not only to the federal government but also to the states. (It was by no means obvious why this should be so. Those who wrote the Bill of Rights didn't think it did apply to the states, though some thought it should. Over the course of several decades, the Court accomplished that result less by convincing analysis than by sleight of hand—declaring that the Fourteenth Amendment's Due Process Clause "incorporated" certain fundamental liberties protected in the Bill of Rights.)

In addition, in *Times v. Sullivan*, the justices were giving breathing room to journalists to criticize government, which in turn facilitated a more democratic political process. And in *Miranda*, the Court was protecting a class—criminal defendants—that the democratically elected branches were unlikely to look out for.

But as bold and granular as *Times v. Sullivan* and *Miranda* were, the Warren Court wasn't recognizing brand-new rights untethered to specific constitutional hitching posts. In the next series of cases, the Court turned itself loose. Back in 1961, the justices had heard a challenge to an old Connecticut law that criminalized both using contraceptives and providing medical advice about them. The statute applied to everyone, including married individuals. "An uncommonly silly law," Justice Potter Stewart later called it. But because the law wasn't enforced and because nobody suffered harm, the Court had ruled the appeal wasn't, in legal parlance, "ripe for adjudication" and so dismissed the challenge. Frankfurter wrote the opinion. Four years later, with Frankfurter gone, the issue was back—with litigants who had actually been arrested. In *Griswold v. Connecticut*, the Court, 7–2, declared the law unconstitutional. In so doing, the justices heralded the full-throated return of substantive due process, even as they tried to avoid saying so. This time, it was to protect not economic rights, as the Court had done in *Lochner*, but personal rights. Thus was created the morass of "privacy" and "autonomy" in constitutional law.

If the Court had any ambivalence, it seemed most evident in Harlan, the rigorously minded justice who throughout the years of the Warren Court tried to balance his reverence for individual rights with an instinct for judicial caution. That effort sometimes seemed self-contradictory. He was fully on board in *Griswold* and had wanted the Court to throw out the Connecticut statute four years earlier. In that prior case, he had written a landmark defense of substantive due process: "The full scope of the liberty guaranteed by the Due Process Clause cannot be found in or limited by the precise terms of the guarantees elsewhere provided in the Constitution. This 'liberty' is not a series of isolated points pricked out in terms of the taking of property; the freedom of speech, press, and religion . . . the freedom from unreasonable searches and seizures; and so on. It is a rational continuum which, broadly speaking, includes a freedom from all substantial arbitrary impositions and purposeless restraints." And yet only three years later, Harlan advised that "the Constitution is not a panacea for every blot upon the public welfare." So, for Harlan, which was it?

The Court had considered issues of sex, marriage and reproduction before. Back in 1942, when the justices in *Skinner* unanimously threw out a compulsory sterilization law for some repeat felons, the Court described procreation as "one of the basic civil rights of man." But Justice Douglas recognized that the Constitution didn't have a clause on that, so he relied on more conventional equal protection analysis, given that white-collar felons weren't subject to the law. In *Griswold*, no such out was available. The law applied to anybody, and so squarely posed the converse of *Skinner*—whether there was in effect a right *not* to reproduce. Douglas again wrote for the Court. Acknowledging the absence of any historical or textual mandate, he found a right of marital privacy implicit in the Constitution as a whole. In a metaphorical flourish, he announced that "specific guarantees in the Bill of Rights have penumbras, formed by emanations . . . that give them life and substance."

In citing those guarantees, in the First, Third, Fourth, Fifth and Ninth Amendments—for their "zones of privacy"—Douglas sought to ground *Griswold* in specific constitutional language. But the very idea of metaphysical penumbras and emanations doomed the effort. (Decades later, Justice Thomas mocked the whole endeavor, keeping on a couch in his chambers a pillow that read, "Don't emanate in my penumbras!")

Whether Douglas admitted so or not, the decision in *Griswold* was the handiwork of substantive due process. Douglas disavowed the notion that *Lochner* was reappearing in a different guise. "We do not sit as a super-legislature to determine the wisdom, need, and propriety of laws that touch economic problems, business affairs, or social conditions," he protested. By comparison, he said, the Connecticut contraception law "operates directly on an intimate relation of husband and wife and their physician's role in one aspect of that relation." Whether that distinction ought to amount to a decisive difference, of course, was the question, but Douglas treated it as the explanation.

Seven years later, in 1972, the Court extended *Griswold* to unmarried individuals. This time, in *Eisenstadt v. Baird*, some of the analysis was more dubious. The justices, 6–1, simply said that if *Griswold* was correct, there could be no "rational basis" under the Equal Protection Clause to treat unmarried people differently. (The Court was down two justices, because of the retirements of Black and Harlan.) Obviously the law involved was just as "silly." But Brennan, writing for the majority, then ventured into murkier terrain. "If the right of privacy means anything," he wrote, "it is the right of the *individual*, married or single, to be free from unwarranted governmental intrusion into matters so fundamentally affecting a person as the decision whether to bear or beget a child."

Fine sentiment though it was, this was a remarkable declaration. The Massachusetts statute in question didn't extinguish a person's freedom to forgo having a child—abstinence, for example, could still achieve that. Rather, the law interfered with the more limited freedom to have sex without having children. Did Brennan really mean that "if the right of privacy means *anything*," it was the freedom to have sex without having children? At best that was hyperbole; at worst it was the sort of freewheeling judicial flight that gave fits to Holmes, Hand and Frankfurter. To most judges—and to most Americans—if the right of privacy meant anything, it meant that the constable couldn't barge into your home, let alone your bedroom, in the middle of the night without a warrant or just cause.

Internal Court memos made clear that Brennan had more in mind than contraception when he chose to equate "privacy" with freedom from governmental "intrusion" into an individual's decision "whether to *bear* or beget a child." According to the private "case histories" his clerks prepared each term—in which they reviewed the intrigues behind the big cases—Brennan seemed to think that language would have "repercussions" in abortion appeals before the Court. Even if Brennan didn't refer to "due process" as such—for fear of losing part of his coalition that focused on equal protection—he was leaving its unmistakable scent. Though he made no mention of abortion, *Roe v. Wade* was already on the Court calendar, with a ruling just 10 months away. This was Brennan at his craftiest.

THE ORIGINS OF THE COURT'S tectonic shift in thinking could be traced to a footnote. In 1938, in the *Carolene Products* case, the Court had tucked in a thought for what 27 years later triggered the rebirth of substantive due process in its different form. In an otherwise trivial opinion on the interstate shipment of "filled milk" (what today might be called fake milk), "Footnote Four" became the most celebrated annotation in the Court's history. In the footnote, Justice (and later Chief Justice) Harlan Fiske Stone tried to differentiate why certain kinds of laws would be presumed constitutional and why others would be subjected to exacting scrutiny. It was, as one scholar put it, "the Court's first—and maybe only—attempt to say, systematically," when the justices should interfere with legislation. *Carolene Products* came just 13 months after the Court's "switch in time" scrapped *Lochner*. One might have thought it would take a bit longer for the Court to start thinking again about activism.

Footnote Four proposed that the Court be more vigilant in three types of cases: when the rights at stake were specifically mentioned in the Constitution (like freedom of expression and freedom of association); when a law singled out racial or religious or other "discrete and insular minorities" for "prejudice"; and when legislation interfered with normal political processes (like voting) for the purpose of entrenching those in power. Distinctly absent was any special vigilance for economic and property rights. The idea of *Carolene Products* was so compelling that, as Ely argued, the Warren Court could well have been called the "*Carolene Products* Court." Not only did Footnote Four foreshadow the reasoning both in *Brown* and in the reapportionment cases, it gave the Court a theory on which it could later resurrect substantive due process in *Griswold, Eisenstadt* and beyond.

The problem was that neither Douglas in *Griswold* nor Brennan in *Eisenstadt*—nor Stone in Footnote Four—convincingly explained why *Lochner*ian economic rights were not also entitled to extra vigilance. "The dichotomy between personal liberties and property rights is a false one," Justice Stewart thoughtfully wrote in 1972. "Property does not have rights. People have rights. Not all of those people are overlords of capitalism. The right to enjoy property without unlawful deprivation, no less than the right to speak or the right to travel, is, in truth, a 'personal' right. . . . A fundamental interdependence exists between the personal right to liberty and the personal right in property. Neither could have meaning without the other."

It's easy enough to caricature aggrieved property holders as sweatshop owners intent on exploiting minors and immigrants, but as Stewart pointed out, property rights also belonged to the owner of "a welfare check, a home [and] a savings account." Frankfurter saw the problem coming, years in advance. "Our power," he wrote in a 1943 dissent, shouldn't "vary according to the particular provision of the Bill of Rights which is invoked."

Lochner on the one hand, and *Griswold* on the other, seemed to represent an opportunistic double standard on the part of the Court and of theorists on both sides of the ideological divide. In a bygone age, liberals raged about the Court's failure to respect legislative choices, while conservatives hailed the Court's conviction. Then came the switch in time. Lo and behold: Liberals extolled Court intervention, while conservatives railed. Based on no principle other than expediency, the two swapped sides, adopting precisely the view they previously regarded as heresy. The respective hypocrisy of liberals and conservatives was matched only by the lack of self-awareness on both sides. "That the transition from one flawed substantive due process era to another occurred without evident irony or embarrassment is remarkable," wrote one commentator, J. Harvie Wilkinson III, himself a federal judge, whom George W. Bush nearly nominated to the Court.

Even with their rhetorical excesses and interpretive flimsiness, the Court's rulings on contraceptives could readily be rationalized. For all the vague talk of penumbras, there was something about the "sacred precincts" of the bedroom that demanded protection from government intrusion—especially when there were no compelling countervailing policy claims. That sexual intimacy was involved—which connoted First Amendment values of expression and association—only reinforced the rationale for Court intervention. More than a quarter-century later, even the arch-conservatives of the Court—Rehnquist, Scalia and Thomas— seemed to accept that *Griswold* had been legitimately based on "historical traditions of the American people."

Those arguments held much less sway in the next appeal before the Court based on substantive due process. In the case of abortion, there were powerful competing claims to a woman's privacy and autonomy. A fetus or an unborn child (depending on whose nomenclature one used) was at issue—abortion was not simply about the "freedom to do with one's body as one likes." Whatever a fetus might or might not be, it was "not nothing," as John Hart Ely wrote. A fetus didn't need to be a person to override a woman's supposed right to terminate her pregnancy at will. As Ely mordantly added: "Dogs are not 'persons'" under the Fourteenth Amendment, "but that does not mean the state cannot prohibit killing them." In short, when life, or its potentiality, merited protection was an issue on which people could reasonably differ.

Such quandaries of policy—call them legal, political or moral—were why democracies invented legislatures. And those quandaries were traditionally avoided by courts, for two reasons. First, legislatures were better able to collect facts, weigh choices, gauge public sentiment, make trade-offs, and draw lines; on a contentious subject seemingly unsus-ceptible to definitive resolution, the losing side could rest assured that it might prevail next time. Second, the Court preferred to risk its stature sparingly. On both counts—constitutional principle and institutional pragmatism—should the Court be intervening at all in the national de-bate over abortion?

In 1973, the year after *Eisenstadt*, the justices said it should. The case was called *Roe v. Wade*, which would remake the country's politics and judiciary. *Roe* signified the clearest entry of the Court (even now with Earl Warren gone and Warren Burger as chief justice) into what became known as the culture wars. It helped solidify the realignment of the major political parties, especially in radicalizing the Republicans; and it recast sedate Court confirmation hearings for the next four decades and counting. *Roe v. Wade* also was an inflection point for the Court itself—when the justices needlessly placed themselves in the middle of a matter best left to the democratically accountable branches. It was the moment that inaugurated the modern triumphalism of the Court—making it the most dangerous branch and, in so doing, undermining its legitimacy.

CHAPTER 10

THE RUNAWAY COURT

MUCH LIKE *BROWN V. BOARD OF EDUCATION*, *ROE V. WADE* HAD A CIRCU-
itous journey to the Court. There were actually two cases, considered
together: *Roe*, which challenged a 19th-century Texas statute criminalizing abortions other than to save the life of the mother; and *Doe v.
Bolton*, which challenged a Georgia statute that had additional exceptions for pregnancies that resulted from rape, that involved a "serious
defect" in a fetus, or that risked "injury" to the mother's "health" (which
had been interpreted to include psychological well-being). Physicians,
not mothers, were targeted—and physicians themselves had little claim
to privacy, which made the appeals different from *Griswold* and *Eisenstadt*. Both cases were initially argued in December 1971. But with two
Court vacancies unfilled—and with substantial internal disagreement
among the seven justices over the constitutional defects in the laws, and
how far a woman's right to privacy ought to go in the context of "bearing
a child"—rulings were deferred.

Justice William Brennan suspected they might also have been post-
poned because of presidential politics. According to his case histories,
Harry Blackmun and Warren Burger were "concerned about the im-

pact" *Roe* and *Doe* could have on the 1972 race between Richard Nixon and George McGovern. The cases were reargued the following year, with newly appointed Justices Lewis Powell and William Rehnquist in their seats.

The Court knew the abortion issue was brewing. Since the late 1960s, about a third of the states had either expanded their range of exceptions or repealed their abortion laws at least up to a certain stage in a pregnancy. Meanwhile, pro-choice advocates began looking to federal courts to achieve what legislatures had denied. Not only did the courts offer the prospect of victory, but if that victory had a constitutional dimension, it would be invulnerable to legislative interference. In early 1971, the first of those cases, *United States v. Vuitch*, made it to the Supreme Court. "Here we go in the abortion field," Blackmun declared in a memo to himself. He offered a tentative view of where he would come down. "I may have to push myself a bit," he wrote, "but I would not be offended by the extension of privacy concepts" to abortion. But the justices ended up avoiding the key question of whether there was a constitutional right to abortion (disposing of the appeal on other grounds). On the Friday after the Court ruled in *Vuitch*, however, it agreed to hear *Roe* and *Doe*.

In the 14 months that passed between December 1971, when the cases were first argued, and January 1973, when the decisions were handed down, Blackmun, their author, evidently paid no attention to whether the Court ought to be the branch to resolve the abortion debate. Nor did he seem to have especially strong views about a constitutional right to privacy or to personal liberty. That was more Brennan's passion. Instead, Blackmun conceived of his role as a benevolent, paternalistic expert committed both to ending the indiscriminate criminalization of abortion and to giving physicians greater discretion to treat their patients. After all, he had been in-house counsel to the Mayo Clinic before becoming a judge. He had even spent a week during the Court's summer recess of 1972 at the clinic's library researching the history of abortion. Who better to sort out the issue? Why have the unending back-and-forth disputation of the political arena when he, and the Court, could solve it once and for all?

On January 22, 1973, American constitutional law changed. That was the day *Roe v. Wade* came down. Knowing it would be a historic. Monday morning, Blackmun had invited his wife to the Court. With the self-drama that Anthony Kennedy would display two decades later, Blackmun had already reckoned in private musings that the Court would be promptly "excoriated" for its ruling, though his opinion contrasted strikingly with Warren's effort in *Brown* to win public acceptance of the decision. For this day, Blackmun had prepared a summary of his majority opinion. That wasn't unusual. His intention to distribute it to reporters, however, was. Brennan, backed by other justices, talked him out of it.

From his seat on the far right end of the bench, Blackmun read his summary: "We forthwith acknowledge our awareness of the sensitive and emotional nature of the abortion controversy . . . of the deep and seemingly absolute convictions that the subject inspires. One's philosophy, one's experiences, one's exposure to the raw edges of human existence, one's religious training . . . are all likely to color one's thinking."

There wasn't any mention of constitutional law, but it was a refreshingly candid admission of both the difficulty of the case and the fallibility of any justice. They were words one might have expected from storied jurists like Oliver Wendell Holmes Jr. or Learned Hand, who always worried about interceding. They were words that might have advised circumspection, as well as respect for legislatures that presumably had more experience dealing with "sensitive and emotional" controversies, and "absolute convictions," in diametric opposition. But not for Harry Blackmun or the other justices who joined his 7-to-2 opinion that declared abortion to be a fundamental right under the Constitution— thereby short-circuiting legislative debate, which was born of different "philosophies," "experiences," "exposure to the raw edges of human existence," and "religious training."

In his full 52-page ruling, Blackmun first reviewed the history of attitudes toward abortion since the Persian Empire, emphasizing that restrictions dated only to the 19th century. Next, he ran through the range of cases that touched on notions of privacy. There was Justice Louis Brandeis's celebrated dictum in a 1928 dissent about the "right to be let alone." There was *Skinner* in 1942, about the sterilization of felons, as well as cases on parents' rights to educate their children as they saw fit. There also was *Loving v. Virginia*, which in 1967 struck down state bans on interracial marriage chiefly on equal protection grounds. In that unanimous decision, the justices said antimiscegenation laws, even though applying equally to blacks and whites, were an "odious" and "invidious" racial classification. And there were the recent *Griswold* and *Eisenstadt* rulings on contraception.

From these cases, Blackmun announced without further explanation, emerged a "right of privacy" that was "broad enough to encompass a woman's decision whether or not to terminate her pregnancy." That right burst forth from the Due Process Clause of the Fourteenth Amendment—its "concept of personal liberty," according to Blackmun (though he seemed as much interested in the liberty of physicians, his fellow professionals, as in that of women). And that was it. With a wave of the judicial wand, without more of an accounting of why, abortion was placed in the pantheon of sacred American freedoms, with such rights as expression, religion, jury trials, and unsegregated public schools. Those rights, and others, had a basis in constitutional text or structure or history. Abortion did not, so it had to be read into a constitutional "concept of personal liberty." This was substantive due process, no doubt well intentioned, with a vengeance. The justices were discovering rights that seemed very distant from text or structure or history.

Nor could Blackmun attempt to root *Roe* in Footnote Four of *Carolene Products* and its explanation for why the Court should examine certain legislation more skeptically. Abortion didn't involve rights specifically mentioned in the Constitution. Abortion laws didn't single out "discrete or insular minorities," unless one suggested women were still firmly in that category. And the restrictions on abortion didn't interfere with regular political processes or the power of discontented citizens to find redress through them.

HAVING DECLARED ABORTION a constitutional right ipse dixit—and, by doing so, invalidating the laws of 46 states—all that was left for

Blackmun, at least in his own mind, was to map out a medical regime that the Court concluded would balance the irreconcilable interests of the woman and the fetus. Blackmun's only hint of humility was that he wouldn't be settling "the difficult question of when life begins." Conceding that "those trained in the respective disciplines of medicine, philosophy, and theology are unable to arrive at any consensus," he said, "the judiciary, at this point in the development of man's knowledge, is not in a position to speculate as to the answer." But apparently, it was in a position to devise detailed regulations, as if Blackmun had become a hospital administrator. In *Brown*, by contrast, the Court had proceeded gingerly, declining to order school desegregation right away; instead the justices asked parties for guidance, ordered another argument, and waited a year to come up with "all deliberate speed."

Guided by Brennan, as well as by four other justices who had indicated they would vote to void the Texas and Georgia statutes, Blackmun used his medical proficiency to codify a sliding-scale trimester approach. During the first trimester, the abortion decision would be left to the mother and her physician. Thereafter, government could regulate abortion to keep it safe for the mother. And only after viability, then generally thought to begin at the start of the third trimester, could government—in the name of the unborn—prohibit abortions, except when they were necessary to preserve the mother's life or health. Even if advances in technology would make viability a changing line of demarcation—a decade later, Sandra Day O'Connor, newly on the Court, would warn that the trimester framework was "clearly on a collision course with itself"—in political terms this sounded like an estimably balanced solution. One could imagine this type of proposal being worked out in a hospital committee or in a Senate cloakroom. The written negotiations between Blackmun and his colleagues had all the attributes of a legislative markup.

But as a matter of constitutional law, it was preposterous. There are various doctrinal containers on the ship of judicial interpretation: deference to other governmental branches; respect for legislatures as laboratories of experimentation; conscientious analogy to past rulings .

when recognizing new rights; an inclination toward the narrow over the broad; and fidelity to neutral principles, regardless of the result they dictate in a particular case. The canons are general and can even be in conflict: Deference, for example, can collide with neutral principles that necessitate judicial action. But Blackmun tossed all of them overboard.

Why was viability the "magic moment" at which a state's interest in the fetus prevailed? Blackmun's reply: "The fetus then presumably has the capability of meaningful life outside the mother's womb." But as John Hart Ely wrote, that seemed "to mistake a definition for a syllogism." In his own notes, Blackmun acknowledged that a constitutional rule built on trimesters was "arbitrary."

There were other analytical deficiencies in the opinion. Unlike in *Griswold*, the Court didn't try to ground its ruling in specific provisions of the Bill of Rights; the Due Process Clause, protecting "liberty," was plenty for Blackmun. And *Roe* certainly couldn't be justified as a decision barring the governmental snooping that was required to enforce the statutes in *Griswold* or *Eisenstadt*. A doctor's office, regulated by the grant of a state license, may be private, but it's not akin to the bedroom. Even if one accepts some generalized constitutional foundation for a "right of privacy"—penumbral or otherwise—just what is it exactly that puts abortion within its ambit? Saying the right "was broad enough to encompass a woman's decision whether or not to terminate her pregnancy" didn't begin to constitute an argument.

In Blackmun's *Roe*, "liberty" and "due process" created an interpretative smorgasbord from which the justices could choose the dishes they liked best. Carried to their extreme, those constitutional clauses appeared to give the justices free rein to obliterate laws simply because they happened to disagree with them. The Court clearly had not absorbed its own lessons about reading "liberty" and "due process" too expansively or uncritically. It was true that rulings invoking substantive due process dating to the early 20th century had said, for example, that states couldn't limit foreign language education or require students to attend public school. But these rulings were as much about settled First Amendment principles. *Roe* was fixed in far less.

The dissenters in *Roe*, along with a legion of scholarly critics in the decades since, feasted on its failings: the arbitrariness of the trimester approach; barely any discussion of a state's obvious interest in the continuing existence of a fetus; the gratuitousness of throwing out the entire Texas statute rather than only its most restrictive features; and the hypocrisy of resuscitating *Lochner*'s substantive due process without admitting it. (Early in his *Roe* opinion, Blackmun even cited Justice Holmes in *Lochner*, somehow claiming he was following Holmes in *not* second-guessing state legislative judgments.)

Yet look closely at the *Roe* dissent by William Rehnquist and Byron White. "If the Texas statute were to prohibit an abortion even where the mother's life is in jeopardy," Rehnquist wrote, there would be "little doubt" the statute would fall. But why's that? Could not a legislature conclude, for example, that the interests of a healthy fetus override those of a feeble mother? What if she was carrying twins? To the extent that even Blackmun admitted the Court wasn't going near "the difficult question of when life begins," why would the dissenters not honor a legislature's view that a fetus's "right to life" generally took precedence over a mother's interests? What if a legislature *required* abortions in the case of some fetuses—say, those that clearly wouldn't make it till birth? It was all well and good for Rehnquist and White to call *Roe* "an improvident and extravagant exercise of the power of judicial review," but the dissenters couldn't avoid inserting their own values. Their disagreement with Blackmun seemed mostly about result.

Among law professors, Ely wrote the most cutting critique of *Roe*, not long after it was issued. It wasn't just that Ely was a rising star in the legal academy—then at Yale, soon off to Harvard (and later dean at Stanford); he had been a prized law clerk to Chief Justice Warren, for whom he had earlier worked as a young staffer on the Warren Commission that investigated the assassination of President Kennedy. What rendered the Elysian evaluation so devastating was that it came from an acknowledged progressive who agreed with the outcome in *Roe*. Ely also had no problem with inferring a generalized constitutional right of privacy, "so long as some care is taken in defining the sort of right the inference will support." The "problem with *Roe*," he wrote, "is not so much that it bungles the question it sets itself, but rather that it sets itself a question the Constitution has not made the Court's business."

In the most quoted section of his *Yale Law Journal* essay, "The Wages of Crying Wolf," Ely admitted his progressive view—and stressed it didn't matter. *Roe*, he said, is "a very bad decision. Not because it will perceptibly weaken the Court—it won't; and not because it conflicts with either my idea of progress or what the evidence suggests is society's—it doesn't. It is bad because it is bad constitutional law, or rather because it is *not* constitutional law and gives almost no sense of an obligation to try to be." "Crying Wolf" proved to be greatly influential in academe—rightly so—and provoked other commentary from progressive scholars who might otherwise have let the faults of *Roe* go.

Twenty years after *Roe* and just three months before she was nominated to the Court, Ruth Bader Ginsburg—her generation's champion of women's rights—herself expressed laments about the ruling. The Texas statute criminalizing almost all abortions was among the most draconian. "Suppose the Court had stopped there, rightly declaring unconstitutional the most extreme brand of law in the nation, and had not gone on . . . to fashion a regime blanketing the subject, a set of rules that displaced virtually every state law then in force," she wrote, to the consternation of pro-choice advocates. "Would there have been the 20-year controversy we have witnessed?" Had the justices chosen a narrower path, settling for "no grand philosophy"—one that opened "a dialogue with, not a diatribe against, co-equal departments of government [and] state authorities"—the Court might have avoided the polarization caused by "a well-organized and vocal right-to-life movement."

According to Ginsburg, the justices also would have been wiser to ground *Roe* in a woman's right to equal protection, rather than in the amorphous concept of a right to privacy. Was not "disadvantageous treatment of a woman because of her pregnancy and reproductive choice" a "paradigm case of discrimination on the basis of sex"? Unlike contraception, which both men and women could use, only women faced pregnancy and only they were being forced by government to use their bodies as incubators. Without some control of their reproductive lives, the argument went, women were not as able as men to participate fully in society. It would've been a much better argument in favor of the result in *Roe* than what Blackmun had advanced. For starters, it was an argument.

Among the 12 justices who've been on the Court since *Roe v. Wade*, Ginsburg wasn't alone in criticizing the ruling. Two, Antonin Scalia and Clarence Thomas, in subsequent abortion decisions, urged the Court to overturn it completely. Other justices—and not just in the conservative bloc—have privately suggested they would never have voted for *Roe* in the broad way in which it was written. Of course, it's easy to say that anonymously, without consequence.

The actual *Roe* opinion was so unimpressive in constitutional grounding that a cottage industry developed around rehabilitating it much in the way Ginsburg proposed. A group of 11 widely known law professors published an entire book of doctrinal do-overs, *What Roe v. Wade Should Have Said*. Richard Posner, the iconoclastic federal judge (now retired), called *Roe* the "Wandering Jew of constitutional law," searching in vain for an explanatory "home."

Though Blackmun had anticipated criticism, he misread its lasting repercussions. Three months before *Roe* came down, as he continued to redo his opinion, Blackmun reflected on the probable fallout. "It will be an unsettled period for a while," he scribbled at the end of an outline. That prediction indicated either manifest naïveté or palpable vanity on the part of a justice far removed from the front lines of politics.

Roe turned the Court into a storm center ever after, though it took two presidential election cycles for the corrosive effects to set in. The ruling wasn't even the top story the next morning. The headlines were about the death of a former president, Lyndon Johnson. A day later, the news turned to the announcement of a cease-fire in Vietnam. That war eventually ended, but in time *Roe* would alter U.S. society, politics and the Court.

Brown v. Board of Education provides an instructive contrast. The other branches and the public outside the South largely accepted that watershed ruling, even as segregation persisted. While such acceptance by itself doesn't confer legitimacy on *Brown*, in theory the people weren't entirely disconnected from what their Court did. *Roe* yielded a different dynamic. After the ruling, the country's divisions over abortion—reflected in polls, political campaigns, and legislative reform or the lack of it—continued. More important, the acrimony pivoted toward the Court.

Blackmun himself was picketed and heckled in public appearances. He came to need bodyguards. Hate mail poured into his chambers for the two decades he remained on the Court. Other justices received unkind letters after controversial rulings on such topics as race, reapportionment, prayer in public schools, criminal defendants and Communist subversives. But the telegrams and postcards to Blackmun far surpassed them in number and wrath. He saved them all, including notes from other members of the Court who had gotten complaints. "I am getting anniversary letters on abortion," Justice Douglas wrote him a year after *Roe* in a note during an argument. "They are much nastier. . . . The best one is from a man who prays that my pacemaker will fail." The tens of thousands of letters seemed to become a point of pride for Blackmun, as he came to take ownership of a ruling about which he had been ambivalent at first.

Many hands went into the *Roe* written product, not the least of which were Brennan's. In offering advice, solicited and otherwise, and in writing *Eisenstadt* broadly, he played a major part, even if the respective papers of Blackmun and Brennan differ in suggesting how big a role it was. But when the *Washingtonian* magazine in 1993 published a piece titled "The Real Story Behind Roe v. Wade," implying Brennan was the master marionettist, Blackmun was irate. "Hogwash," he wrote on a Post-it that he stuck on a copy of the article he saved.

Antipathy to *Roe* extended beyond the personal to the institutional. Before the appeal came to the Court, activists on both sides of the abortion debate focused on state politics. Legislation and popular referendums had produced mixed results. Some states—like California in 1967, with the backing of the Republican governor, Ronald Reagan—liberalized their abortion laws. Other states declined to do so. In Michigan, in

1972, a ballot measure to permit early-term abortions was rejected by 22 percentage points. A few states that had adopted reforms faced pressure to repeal them. That same year, the New York State legislature voted to do so, foiled only by a veto by Governor Nelson Rockefeller, another Republican.

Some progressive critics of *Roe* became fond of arguing the ruling was all the more injudicious because it cut off abortion reform that by and large would have led to a national consensus if only politics had been allowed to run its course. "By relying on the courts to do their job for them," declared the *New Republic* five years after *Roe*, pro-choicers have "abandoned the process of democracy to the ardent right-to-lifers." *Roe*, the magazine said, "killed off the movement for abortion reform, by making it seem superfluous." The liberal essayist Barbara Ehrenreich called *Roe* "tragically premature." For "in the early 1970s," she wrote, there had been "no widespread feminist effort to reach out to, and *convince*, the undecided public of the justice of what we called abortion rights." The problem with that analysis was that it was hardly apparent that any pro-choice consensus was forming. More to the point, the analysis seemed irrelevant. The possibility of consensus wasn't much of an argument for the Court abstaining—just as the absence of that consensus didn't justify the Court intervening. The Court wasn't there to do the policy bidding of other branches.

For their part, *Roe*'s academic cheerleaders—or at least those who sought to minimize the institutional wreckage it caused—liked to argue that political ferment over abortion in the years before the ruling demonstrated that the turbulence following it had little to do with the actual decision. "*Roe* backlash" was a myth, according to its defenders. "Juricentric" explanations for the "deformed" politics that followed tended to forget about pre-*Roe* political and religious division, they insisted. The "pro-life" movement—newly branded as such after the ruling, the better to project a positive image—already had been mobilizing in some states, backed in particular by the Catholic Church. Maybe so, though there's no way to know if those efforts would have continued to gain traction in the absence of *Roe*. There's ample evidence of mobilization on the "pro-choice" side as well. But the mere fact of opposition to abortion before

Roe doesn't at all prove that rancor after it was simply a continuation of the earlier activity. After *Roe*, it was undeniable that pro-life efforts ramped up, and over time a vigorous anti-abortion crusade emerged. If nothing more, *Roe v. Wade* turned a gale into a hurricane—and demobilized pro-choice supporters who thought the battle had been won.

The apologia for *Roe* also ignored that pro-life ferocity was now going to be directed at a new target: the Supreme Court. *Roe*'s defenders missed the distinction. It was one thing to disagree with your opponents in the legislature, even on matters of life and death. But the struggle was ongoing. Abortion supporters won some, abortion opponents won others. What a legislature did or didn't do this session could always be revisited next round. All you needed was to win a few more votes. Such was politics, admittedly imperfect, at work—and what happened in many other countries as consensus of sorts was reached.

By banishing the moral debate from the political forum where it was best ventilated and where the loser recognized that tomorrow was another day, the justices in *Roe* shut off that safety valve in a democracy. Abortion was no longer fair game for compromise that worked itself out, state by state—offering the promise of adjustment that a one-fell-swoop Court pronouncement did not. Thus, even though the Court wasn't the sole cause of galvanizing pro-life forces, *Roe* gave the movement a jumpstart that would energize it since. Moreover, *Roe* offered a freer pass to activists to pander. They could talk about policies that, under *Roe*, could never be enacted.

After *Roe*, of course, most pro-life legislative lobbying would be pointless. There might be room for legislators to mandate a 24-hour waiting period before getting an abortion, or parental notification for minors, or spousal awareness or consent. These would be significant limitations to abortion. And pro-lifers could futilely demand that Congress and state legislatures pass a constitutional amendment overturning *Roe*. But the core issue of its legality had been taken off the table. In the face of an imperious Court, legislators were now irrelevant—and they knew it.

The neutering of legislatures was something that had concerned an important forefather of judicial restraint, James Bradley Thayer of Harvard Law School, back in the late 19th century. Thayer's disciples included Holmes, with whom he once practiced law; Louis Brandeis, who was a student; and Felix Frankfurter, who called Thayer "the great master of constitutional law"; as well as Learned Hand and Alexander Bickel. In 1893, even before *Lochner* had taken hold, Thayer had warned that overly aggressive courts would trivialize legislators, which in turn would "dwarf the political capacity of the people" and "deaden its sense of moral responsibility." If the public came to see judges as the principal guardians of its rights, then it wouldn't bother to direct its anger—"the thunderbolt of popular condemnation"—at legislatures for passing foolish laws. In addition, by focusing on constitutional litigation and the "fly paper" of courts, activists siphoned off resources from possible legislative reform.

And that was precisely what played out in the *Lochner* era; then during the New Deal, when laissez-faire conservatives sought out the justices; and later during the Warren Court, when liberals pursued judicial relief for laws they didn't like. Today, under Chief Justice Roberts, it's the conservatives again most often snubbing the legislature—that's what resulted in *Heller* and *Citizens United* and *Shelby County*. It wasn't that Thayer had blind faith in legislatures—or the people. He believed only that they were the most legitimate branch. "Under no system can the power of the courts go far to save a people from ruin," he wrote. "Our chief protection lies elsewhere." If the people wanted government by judiciary, they no longer had a democracy.

In recent years, there has been much rightful skepticism about the ability of Congress and state legislatures to do their jobs. But whatever their shortcomings, were they not probably in a better position to allocate resources to detailed research, extended debate and, on occasion, compromise? As a former Brennan clerk and later dean of Stanford Law School, Larry Kramer, tartly observed, all the Court does is read partisan briefs, hold oral argument, take a vote in the conference, and typically assign one inexperienced law clerk to deal with it.

The cloistered justices themselves didn't get the uproar over *Roe*. That was evident soon after the decision. According to Linda Greenhouse, the longtime Supreme Court reporter for the *New York Times*, Justice

Potter Stewart and an aide were driving from the Court to the White House for a swearing-in ceremony. The day was the anniversary of *Roe* a few years before. Spotting a noisy demonstration, Stewart asked what was up. The aide explained those were pro-life activists on the way to the Court. Stewart was clueless. "I don't understand," he said. "We decided that."

AFTER *ROE*, ABORTION ADVOCATES had little left to demand of anybody. Other than seeking funding for indigent women who wanted the procedure, they only had to play defense—their *Roe* triumph had the unintended consequence of lulling them into complacency while the pro-life movement gathered steam. "Pro-choice people went on a long siesta," the head of the L.A. chapter of Planned Parenthood told the *New York Times* in 1977. "The political organization and momentum that had changed laws nationwide dissipated in celebration of Court victory," one historian concluded.

Abortion opponents, however, fought a new kind of war, using different tactics and language. That meant going after the Court, making it their main political prize. The pro-life movement centered on chipping away at *Roe* in subsequent cases and on installing anti-*Roe* justices, which meant turning Senate confirmation hearings on Court nominations into proxies on *Roe*. It also meant some presidential candidates now started to make the Court a key political issue, for the only way to get rid of *Roe* (or retain it) was to appoint the right justices. Before *Roe*, prolifers had to wage a battle on multiple fronts. In *Roe*, as Ginsburg put it in 2013, the Court gave them "a single target to aim at."

The enduring politicization of the Court far exceeded what happened to it after *Brown v. Board of Education* or, for that matter, after *Dred Scott*. That politicization alone undercut the claim by *Roe* apologists that ideological and party realignment already underway meant the ruling didn't have far-reaching ramifications. Far from ending the abortion controversy, *Roe v. Wade* was both unifying and polarizing. For many activists on the right, abortion provided the all-consuming issue that the Vietnam War had provided for the left. And with legislatures eliminated as a vehicle for finding a middle ground, positions hardened.

There were abortion opponents in both Democratic and Republican ranks. But the GOP was the more logical launching point for the new pro-life movement. Republicans generally were more conservative than Democrats on social issues, more accommodating on religious interests, and more welcoming to evangelicals. The incipient Religious Right thus had but one party to affiliate with. Just as some scholars have suggested that ideological backlash due to *Roe* was exaggerated, they say blaming *Roe* for radicalizing the GOP was historical overkill. The Republican Party was already veering rightward. Rev. Jerry Falwell and the Moral Majority were coming anyway. "Rockefeller Republicans"—those in the party, like Nelson Rockefeller, who had long held moderate to liberal views on cultural issues and other domestic policies—were on their way out. Reagan's ascension to the presidency seven years after *Roe* would have happened, regardless.

These scholars had a point, showing that *Roe* alone didn't further drive in the wedge between the parties. Yet *Roe* not being the exclusive cause hardly means it wasn't a cause. The parties may indeed have been realigning, a progression that could be traced to *Brown v. Board of Education*, as Southern conservatives fled Democratic ranks. But *Roe* hastened the GOP turn to the right and its metamorphosis into the stridently pro-life party it has been since the 1980s. Republicans worried about a range of issues, from school prayer and crime, to affirmative action and the Equal Rights Amendment, but nothing came to transfix movement conservatives more than abortion. For the GOP, *Roe* became the Great White Whale.

It didn't happen overnight. But one wouldn't have expected otherwise, given numerous other conservative flashpoints. The Catholic hierarchy issued the expected condemnations of *Roe*. Eight months after the ruling, the National Conference of Catholic Bishops called for a "grassroots pro-life organization" to coalesce on a "right to life" constitutional amendment to overturn *Roe*. In 1974, a Senate subcommittee held hearings on various versions of an amendment; according to one count, 68 versions had been introduced the prior year. But many non-Catholic religious activists reacted more moderately. Even some evangelicals, like the Southern Baptist Convention, initially committed to "a middle ground between the extreme of abortion on demand and the opposite extreme of all abortion as murder." During the 1975 Senate confirmation hearings for John Paul Stevens—nominated to the Court by President Ford to replace Justice Douglas—not a single question was asked about *Roe*. Obsessing over it during confirmation hearings didn't really begin until Sandra Day O'Connor in 1981.

Within the Republican Party, reactions to *Roe* had yet to reach critical mass. President Nixon issued no public comment when *Roe* was announced. (Oval Office tapes released many years later indicated he was uncertain. On the one hand, he believed abortions might promote "permissiveness"; on the other hand, he thought they might be necessary, like "when you have a black and a white, or a rape.") Ford, his successor, offered little more, ambivalent perhaps because his wife Betty vocally supported abortion rights. In a letter to the archbishop of Cincinnati, for example, he triangulated, stating he had "consistently opposed" *Roe* because it constituted "abortion on demand," but any right-to-life amendment had to "recognize and provide for exceptional cases." His support for an amendment was predicated less on the morality of abortion than simply on returning its regulation to state control.

In 1976, during the GOP's presidential primaries—its first since *Roe*—Ford similarly tried to stay away from it. But his opponent, Ronald Reagan, pushed hard to the right, demanding a constitutional amendment. Never mind that Reagan, as California governor nine years earlier, had signed a reform bill that led to hundreds of thousands of abortions in the state. Before the first primary, *Newsweek* predicted abortion could be "1976's sleeper issue." Reagan had come to understand the power of abortion—and what the Court had wrought—as a wedge issue. Although Ford prevailed in the primaries, Reagan had established himself as "the darling" of pro-life groups. And the Republican platform that year, despite urging "a continuance of the public dialogue on abortion," called for a constitutional amendment "to restore protection of the right to life for unborn children."

In the general election campaign, abortion came up only sporadically, since neither candidate placed as much primacy on it as Reagan had in the primaries. For his part, Jimmy Carter, the Democrat, successfully navigated the issue most of the time. He was an overtly religious, born-again Christian and personally opposed abortion, though, like Ford, he waffled on a constitutional amendment. While that was enough to capture traditional liberal states, he wound up winning the election chiefly because of the support of Southern evangelicals.

BUT THE 1976 CAMPAIGN WAS A HARBINGER. Despite *Roe* lacking a major role in the outcome of the race, the ruling demonstrated that a core of voters, especially in the GOP primaries, cared deeply about "the rights of the unborn." It was beside the point that those voters didn't constitute a sizable percentage. These were the new single-issue voters, who terrified pro-choice Republican politicians who supported federal funding for Medicaid abortions. Pro-lifers "are a very significant force," Senator Bob Packwood of Oregon explained. "They are people who are with you 99 percent of the time—but if you vote against them on this issue it doesn't matter what else you stand for." Not that long after, the evangelical magazine *Christianity Today* warned of merging single-issue morality with politics. "Too narrow a front in battling for a moral crusade, or for a truly biblical involvement in politics, could be disastrous," an editorial stated. "It could lead to the election of a moron who holds the right view on abortion."

Overall public opinion, however, wasn't shifting. According to Gallup in 1975, a significant majority of the country continued to favor legalized abortion in at least some cases (and has continued to do so ever since). But the frustration and fervor of opponents was contagious; soon enough, they were able to get a majority of states to enact new abortion restrictions. Had *Roe* never happened—had abortion remained a decentralized, legislative battle, even in the context of the larger culture wars—future presidential races might have been very different. And

members of Congress would not have been as polarized on the narrow
fiscal issues about abortion that the Court had left to them.

By the next presidential election, in 1980, evangelicals had turned on
Carter. Whereas in 1976 polls indicated that nearly 50 percent of evangelical voters chose him—far more than had backed prior Democratic
presidential candidates—that percentage now plummeted. One pollster
suggested that Carter would have won the popular vote had it not been
for the Religious Right. Carter was in electoral trouble for reasons having nothing to do with abortion: the Iran hostage crisis, high interest
rates, energy shortages, Soviet aggression, and a primary challenge from
Senator Ted Kennedy. But abortion, too, was an issue. Throughout his
term, even though Carter hadn't endorsed *Roe* and even though he opposed federal funding for abortion, he refused to support a constitutional amendment overturning *Roe*. It also helped the pro-life cause that
the number of abortions had gone up since *Roe*—no surprise, but the
data nonetheless made real what in 1973 remained abstract. Many evangelicals viewed as unforgivable the refusal of Carter—the Sunday school
preacher from Plains, Georgia—to be more with the pro-life cause.

Much as Reagan had shown in 1976, conservative activists learned
that abortion could be exploited to unite voters already predisposed
against Carter. It was that shrewd opportunism that forged the Religious Right. Strategists in the conservative movement, from Richard
Viguerie and Phyllis Schlafly to the avowedly religious Falwell and Paul
Weyrich, had direct electoral evidence that anger over *Roe* could motivate evangelicals. In the 1978 midterm elections, pro-life Republicans in
Minnesota took the governor's mansion and both Senate seats; officials
in both parties agreed abortion played a large role in the outcome. In
Iowa, the pro-choice Democratic incumbent in the Senate lost, despite
leading in the polls for months by at least 10 percentage points; on the
Sunday before the election, pro-life groups distributed 300,000 pamphlets at church services across the state. In New Hampshire, the pro-
choice Democratic senator lost as well.

The religious historian Randall Balmer makes the case that abortion
was merely a convenient pretext for conservatives who were incensed

over federal policy and court rulings that denied tax exemptions to segregated private schools. To de-elect Democrats, it was a lot easier to or-
ganize conservative Republicans around abortion—with its overlay of
traditional values, religious freedom and states' rights—than around
racial policy. But Balmer's argument fails to appreciate that without
Roe v. Wade, political activists, evangelical and otherwise, wouldn't have
had nearly as good a hook. It's a chicken-and-egg problem.

Reagan himself didn't always embrace abortion with the zeal of a
convert. He didn't have to. As late as August 1980, three months before
the election, when he addressed 15,000 evangelicals at a rally in Dallas,
he left out any mention of abortion. Instead, he spoke in soothing tones
about the "awakening" of "Religious America"—"perhaps just in time
for our country's sake"—and "the incontrovertible fact" that "all the
complex and horrendous questions confronting us" have "their answer"
in the Bible. "I know you can't endorse me," he told them, "but I want
you to know that I endorse you." His was a different approach than
Falwell's, which proclaimed abortion as the first of the five major "sins
of America" (followed by homosexuality, pornography, humanism and
"the fractured family"). But Reagan knew that the audience in Dallas
and elsewhere understood what he was talking about.

Even without consistent *Roe* rage, and with his acknowledgment that
he wasn't exactly a regular churchgoer, Reagan could be the beneficiary
of evangelical ire at President Carter—and at the Court. Nearing the
end of his presidency, Reagan appreciated what the pro-life movement
had done politically. "Many of you have been attacked for being single-
issue activists," he told a gathering of right-to-lifers at the White House
in 1987. "But I ask . . . What single issue could say more about a society's values than the degree of respect shown for human life at its most
vulnerable: human life still unborn?"

Had *Roe* not happened, many evangelicals would still have been frustrated over a cultural landscape that had nothing to do with abortion.
"Women's lib" (as it was then labeled), cohabitation, recreational drug
use, church-state relations—all provided ideological veins for conservative activists to mine. Abortion, though, was singularly different not
only because it tapped into a life-and-death absolute, but because it had

been taken away from the forum in which political discord was customarily hashed out.

By 1980, ANY STRANDS OF GOP moderation on abortion had disappeared. The party platform continued to clamor for a constitutional amendment. And rather than concede that the question of abortion was "one of the most difficult and controversial of our time," as it had done in 1976, the platform now demanded that judicial nominees respect "the sanctity of innocent human life." This was the first mention of a so-called litmus test for service on the bench. It all but required candidates to pledge explicit opposition to *Roe* as a condition for getting the job— and it was the genesis of the corruption of the Supreme Court appointments process.

Every four years, Republicans have looked to dial up the bombast. The 2016 platform, which invoked abortion 36 times, claimed that "unborn babies can feel excruciating pain during abortions" and demanded bans on its "cruelest forms"—"especially dismemberment abortion procedures, in which unborn babies are literally torn apart limb from limb." It also called for impeachment of federal judges who "unconstitutionally usurp" legislative prerogatives on abortion (among other issues). The party's nominee, Donald Trump—who over the years had repeatedly expressed pro-choice sentiments—vowed to appoint only anti-*Roe* justices. The Court in *Roe* alone didn't create those positions, any more than it was responsible for the GOP's hard turn to the right and the rise of Reagan. But *Roe* surely was an accelerant.

Meanwhile, the Court since *Roe* has necessarily remained in the fray, generating fresh tumult over the regulation of abortion, as well as the Court's role specifically. The justices have heard cases dealing with state and federal legislative efforts to limit abortions further, as well as the occasional case challenging *Roe* itself. In 1980, the Court ruled that Congress had the power to deny Medicaid funds for abortions—the so-called Hyde Amendment. Eleven years later, the Court said Congress could bar clinics that received federal funds from discussing abortion with patients—the so-called gag rule. In the most important post-*Roe* case, on the final day of its term in 1992, *Planned Parenthood v. Casey*, the Court refused to overturn *Roe* but significantly modified it. In a bitterly fragmented 5-to-4 vote, the Court struck down part of a Pennsylvania statute that ordered a married woman to notify her husband of her intent to have an imminent abortion. That provision imposed an "undue burden" on the woman, according to the Court.

But in creating that standard, the justices were discarding their declaration in *Roe* that abortion was a "fundamental" right that could be restricted only to serve a "compelling state interest." Under that more exacting test, most restrictions early on in a pregnancy were unconstitutional. Now, with only an "undue burden" test, some restrictions would henceforth be valid. In *Casey*, the Court also upheld statutory provisions requiring a woman to wait 24 hours before an abortion and to give a heightened level of consent—provisions that the Court only a few years earlier had struck down in two cases. The justices also repudiated the trimester framework altogether, instead focusing on viability alone.

The main *Casey* opinion, unusually, had three coauthors: Anthony Kennedy, Sandra Day O'Connor and David Souter—the "troika," as a Blackmun clerk designated them. It was the opinion that memorably began with Kennedy's language that "liberty finds no refuge in a jurisprudence of doubt." This was the passage that had caused him to brood to a journalist about "crossing the Rubicon." But there was a more remarkable passage, in which the Court declared that "only twice in our lifetime" had it called on "the contending sides of a national controversy to end their national division by accepting a common mandate rooted in the Constitution." *Roe* was the second time. *Brown v. Board of Education* was the first.

The analogy was ludicrous, and yet the Court took the equivalence further. Just as the justices, under attack, had stuck by the initial *Brown* decision—when a year later, in 1955, they set out how the desegregation ruling should be implemented—the Court in *Casey* found itself having to defend "the central holding of *Roe*" largely because doing otherwise would signal "a surrender to political pressure." So, having thrust itself into the political muck 19 years earlier, the Court now had no option but to remain mired, lest it appear to yield to the stresses it inevitably faced as a result of its initial choice. That wasn't exactly a resounding constitutional rationale, especially when part of *Casey* did overrule two of the Court's own recent rulings. Nor did the Court try to distinguish how *Brown*, in overturning the "separate but equal" doctrine of *Plessy* that had lasted 58 years, wasn't a "surrender to political pressure."

Blackmun, the author of *Roe*, was on the periphery of *Casey*—representing a view about the wisdom of *Roe* that had passed. He joined the *Casey* troika, at least where they invalidated parts of the Pennsylvania abortion law. "When so many expected the darkness to fall," he wrote, "the flame has grown bright." Kennedy, O'Connor and Souter, he said, deserved praise for "an act of personal courage." But in warning that *Roe* was in peril, his theatrical concurring opinion was much more about being the self-anointed guardian of *Roe*, the last of its seven-justice majority still on the Court. As he neared the end of his tenure, *Casey* was his final *cri de coeur*.

The troika's approach in *Casey*, according to Blackmun, was "worlds apart" from the approach of Chief Justice Rehnquist and Justice Scalia, who in dissent with Justices White and Thomas urged that *Roe* be overturned. But, Blackmun said, "the distance between the two approaches is . . . but a single vote. I am 83 years old. I cannot remain on this Court forever, and when I do step down, the confirmation process for my successor well may focus on the issue before us today. That, I regret, may be exactly where the choice between the two worlds will be made." There of course had been a third option. The Court might have decided originally not to leap in, instead entrusting resolution to the political process and democratic compromise.

Back and forth the Court has gone on abortion—from *Roe* in 1973, to *Casey* in 1992, to striking down a statute on so-called partial-birth abortion in 2000, but disowning that ruling only seven years later after Alito took O'Connor's seat. The juxtaposition of the latter two cases illustrated just how malleable—and flawed—the "undue burden" standard of *Casey* was in practice. The two cases also demonstrated that, for the all the talk of principles, Court rulings sometimes came down to head counts. O'Connor out, Alito in—presto chango, the vote was different.

In late June 2016, in *Whole Woman's Health v. Hellerstedt*, the Court unexpectedly struck down a Texas statute, H.B. 2, which placed two strict limitations on abortion providers. One restriction required physicians who performed abortions to have admitting privileges at a nearby hospital. The other required abortion clinics to have the same equipment and staffing as ambulatory surgical centers. Together, these TRAP rules—targeted regulation of abortion providers—would likely force the majority of clinics in the state to close, particularly in rural areas. That was the whole point, according to pro-choice advocates. Not so, said defenders of H.B. 2—it was merely intended to protect women's health. Scalia had died 18 days before the case was argued. So it was assumed the Court would split 4–4. That made sense: The four liberals—Ginsburg, Breyer, Sotomayor and Kagan—would reject the law; the three conservatives—Roberts, Thomas and Alito—would uphold it; and Kennedy, in the middle, would side with the conservatives. Kennedy had deemed an abortion restriction to be unconstitutional only once—in *Casey*; in both partial-birth cases, for example, he had voted to restrict late-term abortions.

But Kennedy joined the liberals in striking down H.B. 2. By a 5-to-3 vote, the Court found the Texas requirements imposed an "undue burden." Breyer, writing for the majority, said that neither provision of the Texas law "confers medical benefits sufficient to justify" the "substantial obstacle in the path of women" seeking an abortion. Ginsburg wrote separately to emphasize that Texas was using women's health as pretense—to undo *Roe* and *Casey* without having to admit it. Given that other medical procedures, including childbirth, were "far more dangerous to patients," yet not subject to H.B. 2, "it is beyond rational belief" that H.B. 2 was anything more than an effort to make getting an abortion more difficult. Even though he made the difference in the case, Kennedy wrote nothing, choosing instead to assign the opinion to Breyer. Were the facts in *Hellerstedt* so egregious concerning Texas's intent that Kennedy believed he had no choice? Had he altered his view about what constituted an "undue burden"—and come full circle since the time when, as a young lawyer, he had decried *Roe* as "the *Dred Scott* of our time"? The inscrutable Kennedy wasn't saying.

In the nearly 50 years since *Roe*, *Hellerstedt* represented a high-water mark of Court support. But tides ebb and flow. Roberts and Alito have never squarely had the opportunity to consider the status of *Roe*. (Alito, as a lower-court judge, had in a dissent voted to uphold the spousal-notification requirement that the Supreme Court struck down in *Casey*.) Nor has Gorsuch. Thomas was the only current justice who had voted to overturn the ruling. As long as Kennedy remained on the Court, along with the liberal quartet, *Roe* looked secure—even if Roberts, Alito and Gorsuch all voted to overturn it. But with Kennedy's retirement in 2018, and with Republicans still in control of the White House and a filibuster-less Senate for judicial nominations, *Roe* now faces its greatest danger since *Casey* in 1992.

WHEN *ROE V. WADE* ARRIVED at the Court in 1973, it's not as if the justices were forced to issue the ruling they did. Judges aren't algorithms, merely executing programmed commands. The Court had three easy alternatives to what it chose to do in *Roe*—all in the service of Louis Brandeis's admonition half a century earlier that "the most important thing we do is not doing."

First, the justices could have adopted Alexander Bickel's strategy of "prudence," for the sake of both democracy and the Court's own standing. That might have meant striking down the extreme Texas abortion law on narrow grounds, while at the same time upholding the more reasonable Georgia statute at issue in the companion case, *Doe v. Bolton*. This, Richard Posner has argued, could well have "accelerated the movement to reform state abortion laws and brought us close to where we are today (abortion freely available in liberal states, but very difficult to obtain in conservative ones) without the political turmoil engendered by *Roe*." Even if the justices sometimes do recognize constitutional rights that are then safe from political intrusion, a continual interplay between the Court and legislatures (both state and federal) is part of what produces sound constitutional law.

Second, the Court might have put off making any decision about abortion—for example, by concluding the *Roe* appeal was insufficiently "ripe" for adjudication. The justices could have done so and said no more. Or they might have written briefly that for now it was best to give legislatures wide berth to find a political solution. There is a time and a place for saying nothing at all. Bickel preached what he called the "passive virtues," which were discretionary tools to avoid deciding a case. Inaction was especially appropriate when the political branches could in theory work things out—and even better when they were actually doing so in some states. In "staying its hand," Bickel said, the Court best conserved its power for when it was truly needed.

It wasn't that Bickel desired a weak Court. Precisely the opposite. He understood that restraint was a means to an end—it served to enhance the justices' ultimate authority, to be harnessed at moments like *Brown*. In *Roe*, restraint would have meant leaving intact varying lower-court decisions and allowing more courts to continue to wrestle with the issue. There likely would have been conflicting decisions in different regions of the county, but the legal system contemplated, and more than tolerated, the inconsistency—all the more when it served a more important goal. Sometimes the inconsistencies even worked themselves out, and an outlier court moved back to the center of gravity.

Finally, the Court might have declared that the regulation of abortion wasn't a matter for the judiciary, which would have effectively undone lower-court rulings that had struck down abortion laws. State legislatures, and perhaps Congress, would then have been mostly free to legislate as they liked. All three alternatives—a narrow ruling that invalidated the Texas statute, no ruling at all, and a ruling that would take federal judges out of the process—would have allowed the justices to avoid the havoc they wreaked in *Roe*. All three were compatible with a robust, eminently sound belief that abortion should be legal and widely available—just not by judicial fiat.

Roe isn't *Brown*. Attempts to equate the two in constitutional legitimacy—how can you applaud *Brown* but vilify *Roe*?—fail even the laugh test. The cases involved wholly different contexts, histories and constitutional questions. Defending the one doesn't demand defending the other.

Liberals rejoiced in *Roe* for a generation. They romanticized a Court that did social justice, notwithstanding the demands of self-government. If there were risks that the other side would win control of the Court and use its power to return to the days of *Lochner* or otherwise act illiberally, that was a worry for a different day. In the rest of the 1970s, and then the 1980s and 1990s, liberals won cases and lost cases—more in the latter category as Republican presidents filled most of the Court vacancies. In 1995, for example, the Court, for the first time in six decades, struck down a federal statute on the ground that Congress had exceeded its powers under the Commerce Clause. Ever since the New Deal, the Commerce Clause—giving Congress power to "regulate commerce" among states—had been the constitutional basis for exercises of vast national regulatory power. In *United States v. Lopez*, which involved the Gun-Free School Zones Act of 1990, the Court, 5–4, ruled that a federal ban on firearms near schools showed an insufficient connection between school violence and interstate commerce.

Lopez represented an early hint from an increasingly conservative Court that it would have little regard for legislative judgment, in Congress or elsewhere. Five years later, the Court made plain that *Lopez* was no aberration. In *United States v. Morrison*, the justices, 5–4, struck down part of the Violence Against Women Act. Passed by Congress in 1994, that statute provided a federal civil remedy for victims of gender-motivated violence. But despite substantial congressional fact-finding that such crimes had an impact on commerce, the Court said they were not "in any sense of the phrase, economic activity." Though reasonable policy makers might differ on that, the justices trusted only themselves to make the call.

Liberals got their truest comeuppance, justly enough, in the aftermath of a presidential election. Long ago, they had dispensed with respect for the political branches of government. Now in 2000, control of one of those branches—the White House—was in dispute. Who would decide between Texas governor George W. Bush, the Republican, and Vice President Al Gore, the Democrat? Not Congress, not the state (Florida) that held the pivotal electoral votes. The Court, now conservative, would. And the left would learn that what was good for the left was good for the right. If *Roe v. Wade* amounted to judicial overreach, *Bush v. Gore* was a judicial disgrace. The two are ignoble bookends in contemporary American jurisprudence.

CHAPTER 11

REVENGE OF THE RIGHT

THE DISPUTED ELECTION OF 2000 SEEMS A LIFETIME AGO—BEFORE 9/11
and the age of terror, before Barack Obama and gridlock, before Donald
Trump and chaos. Unless you wanted to engage in the game of imag-
ining what the country might look like had Al Gore become the 43rd
president, did it really matter anymore how the election was resolved?

For the Supreme Court, in *Bush v. Gore*, it surely did. No other ruling of the current era, including *Roe v. Wade*, so undercut the Court's
legitimacy. It's true enough that George W. Bush took office peacefully.
There were no riots in the streets. Many citizens, along with their representatives, sneered, but they obeyed, just as they ultimately had after
Brown and *Roe*. In 1832, President Andrew Jackson did ignore a Court
decision concerning the Cherokee Nation—"Well, John Marshall has
made his decision, now let him enforce it," Jackson may have said—but
such outright insubordination was the exception. The Court's dominion
over American life had become so reflexively ingrained in the public
mind that the justices' intervention in *Bush v. Gore*—even if wrong in
the first instance—was assumed: Who else was going to take care of
the mess?

The question was a sign not so much of strength in constitutional architecture as of collective disengagement with how government was supposed to work. Few hollered at the Court in the sustained way that followed *Roe*. That was because the dispute, unlike the one about abortion, was over something incapable of replication. After all, an election involving 6 million votes that essentially ended in a tie was a statistical accident. But *Bush v. Gore* nonetheless produced an insidious result. It confirmed the cynical assumption of many—elsewhere in government, as well as among the public generally—that the justices sometimes were no more than undeclared partisans.

And no other decision seemed to shatter the fiction within the Court itself that its members performed their duties independently of politics, operating above the petty machinations of the other branches. Even if one charitably concluded the justices exercised no conscious partisan choice between Republican and Democrat, the fact was that in *Bush v. Gore* the justices demonstrated total contempt for Congress. Both the Constitution itself—the Twelfth Amendment—and a federal statute called the Electoral Count Act identified Congress as the final arbiter of a disputed presidential election. Each provision had been adopted following a deadlock: the Twelfth Amendment after Thomas Jefferson and Aaron Burr in 1800 were tied in the Electoral College for nearly three months, and the Electoral Count Act after three states had chosen competing slates of electors in the 1876 election between Samuel Tilden and Rutherford B. Hayes. In drafting the Electoral Count Act, Congress had specifically decided that the Court should play no part in a dispute. Yet in *Bush v. Gore* the Court leaped in, and a submissive Congress allowed itself to be rolled.

The justices didn't talk about the ignominy of *Bush v. Gore* among themselves. It was not a topic they lingered over in commencement addresses or in their memoirs. But ask them, and a few—on both sides—will tell you that no other ruling haunts them more. Not because it resulted in Bush becoming president—that probably would have happened anyway had the Court stayed out of the battle—but because of the institutional scar it left. Among law clerks each year, *Bush v. Gore* was the one recent high-profile ruling that virtually all agreed had stained the institution.

The official tally in the decisive state of Florida was 2,912,790 votes for Bush to 2,912,253 votes for Gore—a difference of 537, or less than a one-hundredth of 1 percent. But Bush really won by a single vote, cast by Anthony Kennedy, in a 5-to-4 ruling by the Court. Sandra Day O'Connor and the three hard-line conservatives—William Rehnquist, Antonin Scalia and Clarence Thomas—sided with Bush as well. But in essence it was one justice who got to pick the president.

Election Night 2000—Tuesday, November 7—was a dramatist's dream and everyone else's nightmare. Polls had indicated a close contest nationally and that Florida could be the tipping state. Just before 7 p.m. Eastern, all the major TV networks within a 12-minute span announced Gore as the winner of Florida's 25 electoral votes. He was on his way to the total of 270 he needed in the Electoral College. "If we say somebody's carried a state," explained anchor Dan Rather about CBS's state-of-the-art predictions apparatus, "you can pretty much take that to the bank!" Three hours later, all the networks issued retractions. Apparently, the organization conducting exit polls for the networks had imperfectly modeled the number of expected absentee ballots. Software gremlins were also at play; in one county, Gore's electronic vote total at one point stood at *negative* 16,000.

Shortly after 2 a.m., the networks declared Bush was the winner in Florida and thereby the president-elect. Here was Rather again: "Sip it, savor it, cup it, photostat it, underline it in red, press it in a book, put it in an album, hang it on the wall!" Only Peter Jennings at ABC hedged, saying Bush would be president "unless there is a terrible calamity." Jennings didn't have to wait long. The networks had relied on a 50,000-vote margin for Bush that existed at the moment they made the call. But numbers continued to come in, and the 50,000 shrank to 18,000 to 6,000 to 1,000 to 200—it was like watching a Tom Clancy thriller in which the timer on a bomb ticks ever closer to zero. Gore, who had initially called Bush to concede right after the network announcements, called him back to retract. That led to a testy exchange between the two candidates that culminated in Gore's "You don't have to be snippy about it!"

With actual returns, rather than projections, showing a virtual dead heat, the networks had little choice but to withdraw their declaration. Completing a surreal night, they moved Florida from the REPUBLICAN column to UNDECIDED. The big jigsaw piece in the lower-right corner of their electronic TV maps turned back to white, surrounded by the blues and reds of states long resolved. The Electoral College was now at 266 votes for Gore and 246 votes for Bush. "We don't have egg on our face," cringed Tom Brokaw on NBC. "We have an omelet." The networks had blown the electoral call twice. Print media made their own mistakes. The *New York Times* ran off more than 100,000 copies of an edition announcing, BUSH APPEARS TO DEFEAT GORE, before literally stopping the presses and redoing the front page.

Thus began the great Bush-Gore recount that went on for 37 days. The Democrats wanted only to keep recounts going. The Republicans did all they could to run the clock out. Each side claimed the higher moral ground, but if Gore had led or if Bush had trailed, each would have adopted the opposite position. Realpolitik didn't constitute hypocrisy. Invoking principle, even though you would abandon it tomorrow, did.

The action in the state shifted among 67 counties, from local canvassing boards and various courthouses to the state legislature and the governor's mansion. But lurking over all of it like a vulture was the U.S. Supreme Court, which got involved to some extent more than half of the 37 days of the recount. Twice the Court agreed to hear appeals by Bush after he lost in the Florida Supreme Court. Chief Justice William Rehnquist seemed to know it would turn out that way. He loved to run betting pools, for the NCAA basketball tournament, for the Super Bowl, for which case would be decided last each term—it didn't matter. But after Election Day 2000, he sent out a memo to Court employees cautioning them not to bet on a presidential victor.

Once lawsuits began flying, it was Kennedy who followed them with the most anticipation. He even provided his colleagues with written updates, as if they weren't already following developments. As he typically was the first member of the Court to arrive each morning—sometimes by 6—the others would find his updates waiting. Kennedy's interest stemmed in part from his duty to oversee emergency petitions from federal courts in the Southeast. But he also was just hoping. No justice was more eager to second-guess other governmental actors—and here Kennedy might score a hat trick: the Florida Supreme Court, the Florida legislature and Congress. This, he believed, was an impending constitutional crisis—a Chicken Little fear further propagated by hyperventilated TV coverage.

There was no such crisis. A crisis, for example, would be if the commander in chief refused to transfer the reins of power after being defeated. The Constitution and federal law set up procedures for resolving a contested presidential election. And none of the procedures involved the Supreme Court. This was the system properly, if lumberingly, at work.

As the Florida dispute slogged on, in New York City Jane Ginsburg was at a luncheon at Columbia University's law school, where she taught. A couple of reporters at her table were discussing the election. One asked the other, "Can you imagine being a justice these days and wondering if this storm is headed your way?" Professor Ginsburg overheard them. She smiled, then interjected, "Yes, actually," she said. "I can." Her mother was Justice Ruth Bader Ginsburg.

Each side had its gripes. Democrats objected to the actions, and inaction, of Katherine Harris, Florida's secretary of state and a political ally of the governor, Jeb Bush, who was the brother of George W. Harris's chief interest was in swiftly certifying an election result that had George W. in the lead. Republicans didn't like how Gore was cherry-picking the counties in which to seek recounts.

Litigation began on parallel paths—one in state court, one in federal. The first suit was actually filed by the Republicans, despite their claims later that it was Gore the crybaby who rushed to court. Republicans had vented for decades about how disgruntled Democrats always headed there when they couldn't get what they wanted through the political process. That was the complaint of Robert Bork, Antonin Scalia, Ronald Reagan and a cavalcade of intellectuals who made a living reprimanding the judicial excesses of the 1960s and '70s. *Roe* was their smoking gun for Democrats' disrespect for democracy.

But now that Democrats were pursuing the political process—through recount procedures established by Florida law—Republicans wanted the game moved to a different playing field. While talking about "states' rights" (or "federalism," which had no overtones of the Old South) and demonizing federal courts were great fodder for conservatives on the Federalist Society lecture circuit, the Bush campaign contended those topics had no place in this particular battle in this particular state.

Six days after the election, Bush's lawyers appeared in the federal courtroom of Judge Donald Middlebrooks in Miami to preempt possible action by state judges who Bush thought would be predisposed to Democrats. Middlebrooks had been appointed by President Clinton, but was widely respected in Florida political circles. Bush's position was simple: He wanted to stop all manual recounts on the grounds they were "unreliable," "subjective" and "inevitably biased," and therefore unconstitutional. Papers in the case had been filed 48 hours earlier, but Middlebrooks had already thought it through. Right after the hearing, he issued a 24-page ruling against Bush.

Though the arguments before him were "serious," Middlebrooks wrote, this was a "garden-variety election dispute." The threshold question, he said, was who should consider them. And he decided it wasn't him. Under the Constitution, "responsibility for selection of [presidential] electors . . . rests primarily with the people of Florida, its elections officials and, if necessary, its courts." But what of Gore's decision to pursue recounts only in counties likely to harvest net votes in his favor? Wasn't selective recounting itself a violation of "equal protection of the laws"—especially if different counties applied different standards in evaluating improperly punched paper ballots (like those with "dimples" or "hanging chads")?

No, said the judge. "The state election scheme," he wrote, was "reasonable" and "appeared to be neutral." That made it ordinarily immune from federal intervention (in contrast to, say, practices aimed at depriving racial minorities of the right to vote). The procedures strived "to strengthen rather than dilute the right to vote by securing, as near as humanly possible, an accurate and true reflection of the will of the electorate." And Article II of the Constitution itself delineated the authoritative role of states, rather than the federal judiciary, in determining how presidential electors were chosen. An electoral system run by localities was wise, according to Middlebrooks. "Rather than a sign of weakness or constitutional injury, some solace can be taken in the fact that no one centralized body or person can control the tabulation" of an entire election. "The more county boards and individuals involved in the electoral regulation process," the judge wrote, "the less likely it becomes that corruption, bias or error can influence the ultimate result."

Middlebrooks had crafted the most scrupulous legal opinion of those 37 days. Little noticed at the time or since, it was a ringing exposition of judicial modesty, of staying in the wings when the crowd demanded a command appearance. His ruling was subsequently upheld by a federal appeals court, and the Supreme Court never addressed it. Middlebrooks understood the virtue of *not* deciding cases. "Federal judges," he wrote, "are not the bosses in state election disputes."

A WEEK LATER, the Gore legal team filed suit in state court to stop Harris from certifying the election returns until manual recounts had been completed in the four counties that Gore had selected. Democrat-backed litigation on recounts followed elsewhere in the state. The Florida Supreme Court quickly stepped in to block Harris and unanimously ordered her to include the results of recounts in her tally. Bush appealed to the U.S. Supreme Court. One of his lawyers, George Terwilliger, well described why. "The first thing they teach in law school is, 'Give me the court, and I'll give you the ruling.'" Terwilliger called the Florida Supreme Court "result-oriented, philosophically liberal and politically Democratic." He could have added that Gore's legal team considered the

U.S. Supreme Court result-oriented, philosophically conservative and politically Republican.

Few scholars expected the justices to go anywhere near a state election dispute, even if it involved the presidency. Norms of judicial humility had changed, but the experts agreed it would be institutional hubris to grant cert. Ginsburg told clerks the Court wouldn't touch the election "with a 10-foot pole"—right before the Court took the case. One of Bush's lawyers, a top appellate practitioner in Washington who had previously served in two Republican administrations, thought otherwise. He flew down to Florida's capital, Tallahassee, to offer advice. His name was John Roberts, and he turned out to be right. To the horror of Justices Ginsburg, Stevens, Souter and Breyer—who became the dissenters in *Bush v. Gore*—the Court on November 24 accepted this initial appeal out of Florida, called *Bush v. Palm Beach County Canvassing Board*. It was the first in a cascade of blunders by the justices.

Court arguments normally are scheduled months in advance, giving parties a chance to brief the issues fully and offering justices the opportunity to size up the issues. However, for this case, argument was set for only a week hence—an expedited calendar used only in extraordinary situations like the Pentagon Papers Case in 1971 or the Nixon Tapes Case in 1974. An unresolved presidential election necessitated haste, but with haste came the amplified possibility of sloppy analysis.

Bush wanted the Court to hear his claim about equal protection—that varying recounting standards violated the Fourteenth Amendment because voters were denied an equal voice. But the justices declined. Not only was it premature because Middlebrooks's ruling was still pending before an appeals court, but such a question would also open a Pandora's box. There were 3,141 counties in the United States. Most contained multiple municipalities, each of which might have separate voting precincts. All used different machines, ballot designs, instructions and personnel. Lines could be short in some neighborhoods, around the block in others. Polls were open for 12 hours in some places, 15 in the next. Many of the disparities disproportionately affected African Americans. Such impact had always been a benchmark of equal protection jurisprudence. African Americans tended to live in poorer areas, which had less reliable voting equipment. In a close election, variations related to race might far exceed whatever nonracial differences might be revealed in a recount. Did the Court really want to get into whether any such variances could amount to constitutional transgressions—and to do so on a ridiculously short clock?

Not for the moment, the justices decided. Instead, they agreed to consider only the more obscure issues raised in Bush's appeal. First, was federal law violated when the Florida Supreme Court extended the state's deadline for certifying a winner? Similarly, was a state court barred from clarifying what marks on a ballot represented an actual vote? The federal law in question was the Electoral Count Act of 1887, which served to block states from changing the rules of a presidential election after Election Day. Congress enacted the law to avoid a rerun of the stalemate of 1876 between Tilden, the Democrat, and Hayes, the Republican. If a state satisfied the Electoral Count Act—its "safe harbor" provisions— then Congress had to accept its slate of electors when it officially counted electoral votes in January. The safe harbor provisions also included a deadline for having all electors in place; for the 2000 election, the deadline was December 12. The other issue the justices agreed to consider was jurisdictional: Had the Florida Supreme Court violated Article II of the Constitution, which gives state legislatures exclusive power to specify how electors were chosen? Did that mean state *courts* could have no part in the process?

That was the legal minutiae. What the justices really wanted to know was whether the Florida Supreme Court was trying to steal the election—by reaching a pro-Gore result and then contorting the law to accomplish it. In fact, the Florida court was acting reasonably. It was simply trying to ensure that every legally cast vote got counted, just as state law envisioned—and not so different from what other states required. In Bush's Texas, for example, state law "preferred" manual recounts to electronic counts. As long as a ballot showed evidence of "any clearly ascertainable intent of the voter," the ballot would be accepted. Bush, as governor, had signed the law. While Texas didn't control Florida elections, and it might be that both states had unconstitutional statutes, the existence of Texas's law, and others like it, undermined Bush's argument.

The safe harbor provisions were also easy to dispense with. The Florida Election Code, created of course by the legislature, was a mishmash. Provisions conflicted with each other. What actually was "the law" on Election Day, and to what extent was a subsequent interpretation by a state court a forbidden "change"? A court's decision to harmonize contradictory election provisions might be only the everyday exercise of statutory construction that courts did for a living.

Moreover, the safe harbor itself wasn't a *requirement* at all—not of the U.S. Constitution or of the Florida constitution or of Congress itself. The Florida Election Code made no mention of it. All the safe harbor did was grant a *benefit* to a state that sailed in under certain conditions. But a state might still decide that it preferred to count all its votes rather than enjoy immunity from congressional scrutiny of its electors. And the Florida Supreme Court was reasonable to conclude it had a role to play in resolving ambiguous state election law. Even if Article II of the Constitution dictates that "state legislatures" control the "manner" of selecting electors, the "manner" includes the passage of prior legislation—whose final interpretation is the province of the judiciary.

While the Florida Supreme Court's opinion ordering further recounts wasn't a model of clarity, it should have been good enough for the justices in Washington to let it pass. That was especially so if one concludes the U.S. Supreme Court had no business in the case to begin with. Article II said "each state" was in charge of its own presidential electors. Even if a state court got it wrong, wasn't that preferable to federal intervention over this most sacrosanct of state prerogatives, as Article II itself recognized?

On December 4, a mere three days after they heard oral argument, the justices stepped away from the precipice. Kennedy wanted most to keep his hand in the game. "We must be very careful to preserve the role of the Court," he had warned during argument. Stevens, especially, thought the Court should have no role other than to return the matter to Florida and allow state processes to run their course. Scalia and Thomas wanted all litigation terminated and Bush in effect declared the winner. Instead, the Court unanimously settled for something in the middle. That meant punting the case back to Tallahassee and asking

REVENGE OF THE RIGHT 225

the Florida Supreme Court for a rewrite that better accounted for federal law and the Constitution. It was the appellate equivalent of a shot across the bow—or as a clerk put it, "across the distinctly port side of a lower court."

The justices said nothing about why they were opining at all, considering that the Constitution made Congress the ultimate master of the Electoral College. If there was a dispute about electors, should not Congress sort it out if the Florida authorities didn't? There also wasn't a single mention of equal protection in the Court's unsigned opinion, though that issue lay in wait. Some of the conservative justices did anticipate that, if need be, equal protection would be the constitutional sword they used to dispatch Gore. But at that point, none of the justices much wanted to see the mess wind up back before them. The Court had avoided equal protection mostly because the justices recognized it would be divisive. The last thing they needed was a 5-to-4 fracture over the presidency.

The other telling thing about the case was how little effort Gore's lawyers themselves put in urging the Court to exercise institutional self-control. Where were references to such beacons of restraint as Felix Frankfurter and John Marshall Harlan II, Learned Hand and Alexander Bickel? It was as if it never occurred to Gore's side—which, after all, staunchly supported interventions like *Roe v. Wade*—that restraint was a credible argument anymore. Just ask Gore's chief lawyer in the case, Harvard Law School's Larry Tribe. "Judicial restraint," he wrote years earlier in the preface to his consummate treatise on constitutional law, "is but another form of judicial activism." In that view, for Bush or for Gore, the Court would reign supreme. Such was the disrepute into which judicial minimalism had fallen.

THERE'S AN OLD JOKE AMONG STATE JUDGES: Saint Peter is running things at the Pearly Gates when three doctors arrive and ask to be let in. "Who are you?" Saint Peter asks the first.

"I was a neurosurgeon," he replies.

"Too many here already," Saint Peter says, and dismisses him.

The second man identifies himself as a cardiologist, and he, too, is rejected.

When the third starts walking off before even being questioned, Saint Peter asks, "What about you?"

"Psychiatrist—you don't need me here."

"Actually, we do," Saint Peter answers. "We need someone to talk to God—he thinks he's a Supreme Court justice."

One member of the Florida Supreme Court told the joke privately when the case was bounced back from Washington. But the judges didn't take the hint. In Tallahassee, a different phase of the litigation was underway: Gore's challenge of Harris's certification of the election. A local judge decided against Gore. So, three days after the ruling in Washington, the dispute was right back at the Florida Supreme Court. Under immense time pressure, they had to think on the fly. Should they widen the scope of recounts, and if so, should they announce counting standards? Both might ward off equal protection problems, but the latter might generate safe harbor issues. Unlike in the first appeal, the Florida Supreme Court was deeply divided.

The next afternoon, by a 4-to-3 vote, the court ordered an expanded recount. Now, all "undervotes" had to be evaluated statewide—and it had to be done within a few days if the state was going to heed the safe harbor provision. Undervotes were ballots that a voting machine read as having cast no vote. That might have happened because voters really cast no vote ("none of the above," in effect), or because they didn't fully punch out the hole on a ballot or fill in the little circle with enough pencil. Determining voter intent fell to mere humans and required each ballot to be examined by hand. There were 40,000 to 60,000 undervotes, depending on definitions.

Democrats were elated. "This decision is not just a victory for Al Gore," proclaimed Bill Daley, chairman of the campaign. "It is a victory for fairness and accountability in our democracy itself." Yet despite "democracy itself," Daley added, "all of these matters should be resolved by the Florida judiciary—not by the politicians." From the son of the boss of political bosses, former mayor Richard Daley of Chicago, it was crowning proof of how judicialized our politics had become. Would James Madison ever have imagined that a presidential election would come down to a duel between two supreme courts?

The Florida ruling contained a grab bag of defects. Rather than only direct each county's canvassing board to divine the "clear indication of the intent of the voter," wouldn't it have been better to spell out uniform criteria for doing so? It was true that the Florida Election Code already stated that "intent of the voter" was the standard. But the language begged the question. And why not also recount the roughly 100,000 "overvotes"—ballots that a machine indicated had cast multiple votes? What if someone wrote on a ballot, "Oops, I voted for Smith and Jones, but I prefer Jones"? There couldn't be any doubt there. And frankly, to be consistent, why not manually inspect all 6 million ballots in the state, impractical as that might be?

None of those weaknesses made the ruling indefensible. It simply was flawed, which wasn't surprising. There couldn't be a perfect ruling when the subject matter involved imperfect technology, imperfect voters and imperfect human evaluations of voter intent—decentralized in 67 counties. But degree of difficulty hardly dictated that judges and legislators shouldn't seek the fairest count. Insisting, as the Bush team did throughout, that machine counts were better than manual recounts didn't even add up to an argument.

The question was who got to render the final decision. If the Florida Supreme Court had hoped to keep the justices in Washington at bay, the omissions in its ruling did the opposite. Even though this case technically was separate from the earlier appeal, the Florida judges had unwisely failed to address the justices' instruction to explain themselves better. Some of the Florida judges privately explained later they weren't flouting Washington. They were just swamped. But to some of the justices, the Florida Supreme Court was looking more and more like a renegade.

Back in Washington, several justices watched the Florida judicial proceeding on TV, which was ironic, given what they thought of cameras in their own courtroom. The justices had just begun a holiday recess, but they were back in business that Friday night. Within a few hours of the Florida ruling ordering a statewide recount that would begin Saturday morning, Bush's lawyers churned out a petition to the justices. It asked not only that the Court again step in, but also that it halt the recount immediately. The emergency request got filed with the Court's "death clerk," who normally handled last-minute pleas from death row inmates for stays of execution. That same evening, Stevens saw Breyer at a Christmas party. "I guess we'll have to meet tomorrow—it'll take us about 10 minutes," Stevens said. He assumed there wasn't a chance the Court would block the recount. Some of Gore's top aides told the candidate the same thing.

In Tallahassee that Friday, both houses of the Republican-controlled state legislature prepared to hold a special session the following week that would award Florida's electors to Bush. The ruling by the Florida Supreme Court made such a move more likely. For if Gore pulled ahead in the recount, the same court might direct Harris to certify him the winner, then order the governor to sign the formal documents for the Electoral College. If both state officials refused, the court itself might execute the documents. The governor had previously said that "no judicial power exists" to compel him to send along a Gore electoral slate. It was the only time in the dispute that any official threatened to defy a court, which was another reflection of the judiciary's primacy. Officials routinely did end runs of legislative and executive commands, but the courts were off limits. That was why judges were wise to conserve their power by leaving political disputes to the two political branches.

If the legislature did ignore the Florida Supreme Court and went ahead with a Bush slate, that could mean two slates of electors going to the Electoral College and a resulting deadlock—just as in 1876—which would require Congress to sort out a winner in January, presumably in time for Inauguration Day.

The pathology among Florida's three branches of government—and the chance it would metastasize to Congress—unnerved all the participants. But their fears were misplaced. A resolution might have taken time, and the process surely would have looked chaotic. But no blood would have been shed, no states would have seceded. The process would have been no more and no less than what we signed up for in a democracy. Whatever decision Congress reached on our behalf, it was answerable. If we disagreed with the resolution, we could vote its members out of office soon enough. We can't do that to Supreme Court justices.

ANY EMERGENCY STAY WOULD BE drastic and extraordinary. Litigants had to convince the U.S. Supreme Court that they would likely win once an appeal was fully presented. But that alone was insufficient, because the justices often knew how a case was probably going to come out when they decided to take it in the first place (even though under Court rules it takes only four votes, not five, to grant cert). So litigants also had to show they would suffer "irreparable harm" if a stay were not granted.

The first requirement turned out to be easy for Bush. The Court had heard *Bush v. Palm Beach County Canvassing Board* a week earlier. Back then, the discussion among the justices in the conference left little doubt there was a 5-to-4 majority in reserve in Bush's favor. It was the second requirement that rightly worried Bush's lawyers. How could they argue that including legal votes would irreparably injure Bush? It might be politically mortifying, but that wasn't the Court's problem, all the more when a stay would stop the recount and make the clock even shorter. A stay was meant only to maintain the status quo. But if you let the condemned inmate go to the chair, there was no way to undo it. Was the possibility of a small lead for Bush becoming a small lead for Gore the equivalent?

Bush's petition to the Court warned that "the entire electoral process under our federal/state dual scheme was now threatened" because "whatever tabulations" ensued would be "incurable in the public consciousness, and once announced, cannot be retracted." That was utter nonsense. The Constitution and federal law allowed for the very possibility that a state's electoral votes wouldn't be counted. But the Court bought it, in the most intemperate decision of the election saga. On

Saturday afternoon, December 9—only seven hours after the recount began—the justices issued the stay, blocking further counting. If the looming safe harbor deadline was an actual requirement, the stay effectively made Bush the president-elect. Oral argument, for what it might be worth, was set for Monday morning.

The vote was 5–4. The deceptive unanimity of the Court's prior ruling was gone. The four liberals laid bare the breach. Stevens—joined by Breyer, Ginsburg and Souter—took the rare step of writing a dissent to the stay. It was exceptional enough for the Court to declare ahead of time where it stood on an appeal, but publishing a dissent this early on evidenced a depth of indignation seldom heard at the institution.

This was the moment during the dispute when the Court's credibility—challenged during such lows as *Dred Scott* in 1857, *Plessy* in 1896, and the *Korematsu* ruling in 1944 that upheld the internment of Japanese Americans during World War II—dissolved again, in our own times. That loss of credibility was more consequential than a single presidential election. The four dissenting justices were disconsolate. "To stop the legal counting of votes," Stevens wrote, the majority departed from "venerable rules of judicial restraint." On questions of state law, he said, "we have consistently respected the opinions of the highest courts of the states. On questions whose resolution is committed at least in large measure to another branch of the federal government, we have construed our own jurisdiction narrowly." Blocking the recount, Stevens concluded, "will inevitably cast a cloud on the legitimacy of the election."

It was a bit rich to hear liberals bellyaching about restraint—just as it was to see the conservatives trampling the independence of states—but Stevens was correct. If there was irreparable harm to be done, it was that the stay would amount to a verdict for Bush before the appeal was heard.

This was more than Scalia could bear. If dissents to a stay were unusual, concurrences to a stay were unheard of. A stay order was typically an unsigned sentence or two. Writing to explain a stay smacked of gloating. But what Scalia possessed in wit he lacked in discretion. Stevens knew it and got Scalia to reveal his emotions. None of the other justices in the majority joined Scalia, and on a less frantic schedule, they might've tried talking him down. Taking the bait, he wrote: "The counting of votes that are of questionable legality does in my view threaten irreparable harm to [Bush], and to the country, by casting a cloud upon what he claims to be the legitimacy of his election."

Both sides, then, at least agreed that any ruling by the Court would "cast a cloud" on electoral legitimacy. It just depended on whose parade the rain would fall on. In Scalia's view, "the public" couldn't handle more. It was the Court's job to put the political process out of its misery. Bush's "election" wasn't even a question. Indeed, Scalia had wanted the recount stopped the night before the Court granted the stay. He tried to convince his colleagues to reverse the Florida ruling immediately— without giving Gore the chance to respond. It was an unprecedented, brazen display of partisanship on the part of a justice.

The majority of five granted the stay more out of fear for the five than concern for the country. Had the justices not done so, the recount would have continued and Gore might've pulled ahead. If the Court then had to invalidate the counts, the lead would revert to Bush. That could make the justices look even worse than they did by blocking the recount before it got rolling. The Court routinely reversed the status quo, most dramatically when it reinstated death sentences that had been thrown out by lower courts; typically, in those situations, the inmates were then executed. The only difference was that heinous killers, unlike a presidential candidate, had no constituency to offend.

The stay stunned Gore, but he remained a prisoner of the Court's mystique. Minutes after the stay, using his BlackBerry pseudonym "Robert Stone," he sent an email to senior campaign staff, entreating them to "Please make sure that no one trashes the Supreme Court." He also wasn't stupid. He believed that Kennedy or perhaps O'Connor might still be flipped during oral argument, turning a 5-to-4 loss into a 5-to-4 win. There was no purpose in taunting the bear.

But Alice in Wonderland had arrived: Decision first, legal reasoning afterward. O'Connor was already disgusted—with both what she viewed as a mutinous Florida Supreme Court and the incompetence of Florida voters. Manual recounts were folly, she thought. And if voters couldn't follow instructions—"for goodness' sake!" as she later put it during the argument—she saw no reason to save them. There was another explanation for her attitude: She wanted Bush to win. It wasn't just that she was a loyal Republican—earlier in her career, she had been the GOP majority leader of the Arizona Senate. Several publications, for example, reported that on Election Night she had told friends that Gore's apparent victory "was terrible." There was also the greater problem of succession. If Gore were in the White House, and if she wanted the next justice to be named by a Republican, she'd have to wait at least four years before retiring. And she did want off the Court, to care for her ailing husband John.

Siding with Bush for reasons of succession was bad enough. But it was worse if one believed what her husband revealed a few months after *Bush v. Gore* was decided. At a large charity dinner, he told another guest that Sandra had voted as she did—even though "she knew it was wrong"—in the hope that she would be able to retire sooner. That was inconsistent with what she had said at the Court—that she had real objections to what was happening in Florida. But it would have been inconceivable for her to acknowledge to colleagues or clerks—or to herself—that she consciously chose Bush over Gore despite knowing it was wrong to do so. (The dinner guest, who has bipartisan connections, was willing to disclose the conversation only years later because time had passed, John had died in 2009, and O'Connor had retired.)

To the extent her husband's health had affected her judgment, the cruel result was that O'Connor was forced to stay for four more years anyway. Due to the opprobrium *Bush v. Gore* received—which long baffled her—she didn't retire until 2005, a year after Bush won reelection. In the interim, John's health had deteriorated further.

Under other circumstances, O'Connor might have been the ideal member of the Court to weigh the case. At the time, she was the only justice who had held elective office. Prior eras included former senators, governors, attorneys general and others outside the cocoon of judicial life. Of the 31 justices appointed between 1922 and 1971, fewer than half had prior judicial experience; of the nine justices appointed by FDR, only three had been judges. But the Court that decided *Bush v. Gore* was dominated by judicial veterans. That meant most of the justices had little firsthand appreciation of how politics worked, of why politics had value in a democracy. (The post-O'Connor Court is the first ever to lack even a single member who had served in elective office. Rather than seeing that insularity as a deficiency, Chief Justice Roberts has lauded it, believing it somehow makes for justices who stick to "legal arguments" rather than making "policy" choices.)

Considering O'Connor's position—and given that Rehnquist, Thomas and Scalia weren't open to persuasion—the only justice in question after the stay was Kennedy. In characteristic fashion, from that Saturday to the final ruling three days later, he sent different signals to colleagues and clerks. Breyer especially worked him. After the fact, Souter privately acknowledged he had thought Kennedy was winnable. Meeting with students at Choate a month later, Souter said that if there had been more time, he hoped to bring Kennedy into a coalition in the same way Kennedy joined him, along with O'Connor, back in 1992 in the *Casey* joint opinion that had upheld *Roe v. Wade*.

If he'd had "one more day—*one more day*," Souter told one of the Choate participants, he believed he might have prevailed.

Kennedy, though, stuck with the majority and never seriously considered abandoning it. Responding to Souter's musings, Kennedy later said if *he* had had one more day, "I might have persuaded *him*."

The internal Court enmity over *Bush v. Gore* called to mind the line from half a century earlier about "nine scorpions." Apart from the pay, the job of being a justice was certainly the best in the legal profession. It offered power, job security, a short docket, a regal office, rank at a nice restaurant but anonymity at Whole Foods, summers away from Potomac swelter, and never having to deal with clients. Yet the Court could be a cage. Although the justices get along personally, they have to deal with each other, in close proximity, for years. A case with the stakes of *Bush v. Gore* tested their kinship.

AFTER ORDERING THE STAY, the Court agreed to consider three questions during oral argument. Both issues from the earlier appeal were still open: the safe harbor statutory provision (with its deadline of

December 12) and the constitutional clause about the role of state legislatures. But this time, equal protection—which the justices sidestepped
in Round 1—was on the table. The Court may fairly put off issues when
the facts justify it. But in this instance the Court had left itself open to
accusations it had rigged the game. If the justices avoided equal protection a week before, only to take it up in the bottom of the ninth
inning—when Electoral College deadlines might leave no more time for
recounts to be conducted in a way that satisfied equal protection—the
justices were guilty of either awful planning or diabolical cunning.

Once again, the issue that the justices didn't bother to ask was whether
they ought to be involved at all. And even more glaring, Congress, across
the street, remained silent. The Florida legislature, for example, had filed
an amicus curiae brief that urged the justices to do nothing to circum-
scribe its prerogatives. Such "friend of the court" briefs were common.
So, where was Congress, which had the role both under the Constitution and under federal statute to resolve presidential elections? After the
Hayes-Tilden fiasco of 1876, Congress had set up an entire process to
handle exactly the situation posed by Bush and Gore in 2000. But in a
test of its own supremacy, in which it had the most to lose in terms of
institutional power, a cowed Congress was a no-show. Given so many
years of unchallenged pronouncements about judicial supremacy, that
was hardly a revelation.

Some members of Congress actually announced they were relieved
the Court took on the dispute. This abdication of responsibility, of
course, was less about faith in the justices than about the legislators'
dread they might have to act—and be held accountable by voters. Republicans knew that if the Court ruled against Bush, they still controlled the House of Representatives, which under the Constitution had
the final word over the presidency. So, to them—apart from defending the very idea of separation of powers—there was nothing to lose
from the Court diving into the pool. Democrats recognized that even if
Gore won at the Court, he would lose in the House, so what was the
point of trying to wrest the dispute from the Court, where he might win
and get some leverage? Several justices observed this bipartisan reluctance and concluded it gave them more justification to intervene. But

Congress wanting out of its obligations was itself the best evidence it was the correct institution to confront the storm. Congress was accountable.

At 11 a.m. sharp on Monday, December 11, the justices left their robing room in the chief justice's chambers and slowly proceeded across the hallway to their entrance in the back of the courtroom. It was only about 10 steps. But on this historic day, a few law clerks made sure to gather to witness the walk—or what some clerks have referred to as the "duckling crossing." Ted Olson, the well-known Washington litigator, opened the argument for Bush. He wanted the justices to focus on the presumed impudence of the Florida Supreme Court, but to the justices, the constitutional and statutory questions about changing the Florida election rules seemed minor. The justices wanted to hear about equal protection.

Tactically minded, Breyer was the justice to drill it home. Knowing the conservatives were likely to invoke equal protection to justify ending the recount for good, he now offered a compromise that might pull Kennedy away. Breyer told Olson he was willing to concede an equal protection violation because of "different standards in different places," and then asked, "What in your opinion would be a fair standard?" If that could be resolved, Breyer wanted to resume the recount, ignore the December 12 deadline, and give Florida until December 18, the date the Electoral College met.

Given the questions to Olson, Gore's lawyer—David Boies, the New York trial specialist—assumed, correctly, that equal protection was the ballgame. Kennedy got him to acknowledge there had to be a "uniform standard." But, Boies insisted, that standard was simply "whether or not the intent of the voter is reflected by the ballot." Though such intent was a subjective determination, he was correct. Kennedy saw it as a dodge. "That's very general," he told Boies. "Even a dog knows the difference in being stumbled over and being kicked. . . . From the standpoint of the Equal Protection Clause, could each county give their own interpretation to what intent means?" Yes, Boies replied.

Kennedy couldn't believe it. "This is susceptible of a uniform standard," he said, "and yet you say it can vary from [recount] table to table within the same county?"

Boies had dug himself a hole. If he proposed uniform rules about, say, hanging chads, he'd be tacking close to the shoals of the Electoral Count Act and out of the December 12 safe harbor he had admitted was significant. Boies wanted it both ways and ended up satisfying nobody. There really was no way out of the conundrum, other than to say Florida already had an established rule: to determine the intent of a voter. Existing law had no equal protection issue with different voting technologies. So, even though Florida counties might wind up evaluating the same kind of paper ballot differently, that hardly seemed a constitutional problem.

There was one other, more technical issue that Boies failed to raise. Rehnquist wanted to know how a recount could be completed by the December 12 deadline, which the stay had made impossible. Boies should have mentioned "tolling," which was a commonplace judicial remedy. It "stops the clock" when unusual circumstances, beyond the control of the parties, dictate that a time constraint can't be met. Here, if December 12—tomorrow—was considered the deadline (however erroneously), the justices could easily just push it back by exactly the interval that had passed between the stay on Saturday, December 9, and when the Court chose to rule. The fixation on December 12 was wrong from the beginning. Twenty states, including California, wound up not making the deadline anyway. December 18, when the Electoral College met, was an alternative. So was January 6, when Congress assembled to tally the electoral votes. But Boies never offered fallback dates.

Even Inauguration Day wasn't a drop-dead cutoff. The Twentieth Amendment, passed in 1933, provided that Congress could select an acting president if nobody was yet "qualified" for the job. The speaker of the House, a Republican, was next in the statutory line of succession, but not the required choice. As one scholar suggested, "Surely Bill Clinton would be willing to stay on for a few more weeks." Were the odds high that Congress would call on the Twentieth Amendment? Obviously not. Could Gore easily have mentioned it to any court worried about December 12? Of course. The game for Gore was always to buy more time.

At half past noon, *Bush v. Gore* was adjourned, and the nine justices went into their private conference. Meanwhile, in Tallahassee, committees in each house of the Florida legislature passed resolutions that, if approved by the full bodies, would appoint a Bush slate of electors—regardless of the outcome at the Court. In the whirl of activity on this last Monday of the 37 days, the most unlikely participant was the Florida Supreme Court. Acting as if they wished to be in Washington defending their honor themselves, the judges issued a revised opinion in the first election appeal—the ruling that the U.S. Supreme Court had tossed back a week earlier. By a 6-to-1 vote, the judges explained that when they extended the deadline for certifying the election, they simply were reconciling conflicting election statutes that had been enacted long before the present election took place. With *Bush v. Gore* pending at the U.S. Supreme Court, the effect of the Florida ruling might have given the justices, yet again, another chance to get out of the way. Instead, they ignored the ruling.

FOR A DAY AND A HALF, the justices bumbled their way through to six different opinions. The outcome—no more recounts and no more tries for the Florida Supreme Court—wasn't in doubt, though some justices and clerks at the time thought it might be. Kennedy's clerks in particular worried about his wandering doctrinal eye—if he had any consistent philosophy other than being the lawgiver—and sought to keep him away from Breyer. Though O'Connor wanted somehow to be part of a middle ground, Breyer recognized she wasn't open to more recounts. Thomas said he pulled his first all-nighter since law school.

The bilateral dramas were aggravated by the squeeze of time. Because the pressure to get a decision out was so intense, the justices didn't have the chance to review each other's final drafts—which was why the ultimate product read as tortuously as it did. It was less than the sum of its parts. It was also why the four dissenters weren't able to unite to produce a single opinion. If all the justices agreed on little else later on, they recognized their work in this defining case wasn't their best.

On Tuesday night, just before 10, the Court ruled. The justices did so not from the great courtroom—the way other decisions came down—or in any other fashion that signified what they were doing. Instead, they went home beforehand, through the basement garage, in the stealth of the night. The ruling failed to include the usual summary at the beginning—there just wasn't time. That's why the Florida Supreme Court had released its opinions differently, with a spokesman announcing if a lower-court decision had been either upheld or overturned. The U.S. Supreme Court simply put out stacks of the 65-page ruling in the press office and left it to the media to figure things out, which they attempted to do in real time, on live television, shivering in the December air outside the Court. It was like the Clue board game for constitutional law—Anthony Kennedy in chambers with a quill pen. It was a fitting last act both for the Court and for the media.

Just as they had on Saturday when they halted the recount, the justices split 5–4 for Bush. Sure enough, they based their manufactured rationale on equal protection. Because there weren't uniform standards, the recount was unconstitutional. And because the Court said the deadline of December 12 had to be honored—it happened to have only two hours left at this point—there was, darn it, just no time to return the case to Florida.

The main opinion was unsigned, but Kennedy had drafted most of it. Because the proposed statewide recount seemed to "value one person's vote over that of another," it denied their votes "equal dignity." He even had the temerity to invoke *Reynolds v. Sims*, the 1964 Warren Court decision establishing one person, one vote. That principle—to facilitate an electoral say for all—seemed to cut directly against what Kennedy was now saying. In his mind, it was better to *exclude* ballots that weren't susceptible to a mechanistic determination of voter intent.

But he never explained why subjectivity in this one area of the law was a constitutional problem. Courts tolerated subjectivity all the time. How, for example, was assessing a witness's testimony in a trial different from interpreting "marks or holes or scratches on an inanimate object"? Well, according to Kennedy, "the fact-finder confronts a thing, not a person" when assessing ballots rather than witnesses. But that hardly was a difference. Nor did Kennedy apparently think through what he really meant by equal protection. What, exactly, was the harm of County A counting a dimpled chad and County B not doing so? The worst that could happen was that ballots in County B would be wasted. There was the same probability of an undercounted ballot going for Bush or Gore. Neither would suffer greater injury—unless the bigger risk was to Bush because he was ahead. Kennedy's assertion sounded a lot like Scalia's lame makeweight to justify the stay.

The basis for Kennedy's objection to manual recounts was all the more unconvincing because the alternative was to do nothing. Leaving all undervotes uncounted did treat them equally, but that outcome seemed particularly unreasonable if the undervotes weren't caused purely by human error. What could account for punch-card ballots registering undervotes up to eight times more often than optical-scan ballots (the ones that look like an SAT answer sheet)? That seemed like the result of physical design, in which case the disparity in error rate itself raised equal protection problems, throwing into question the validity of the vote in the entire state. There simply was no good reason for different voting systems, other than to indulge budget and inertia—which surely were inadequate justification to undercut what Kennedy called the "fundamental" right to vote. As Breyer pointed out in dissent, "Voters already arrive at the polls with an unequal chance that their votes will be counted." Based on Kennedy's logic, one could argue that manual recounts were constitutionally *mandated* because of the inherent unfairness in voting systems.

Each of the four liberals wrote a dissent. Breyer and Souter acknowledged an equal protection issue—which is why many Republicans wrongly claimed it was a 7-to-2 ruling—but said Florida could fix it. Ginsburg and Stevens at last argued that the Court shouldn't be opining anything other than that it was ill-advised to opine.

REHNQUIST HAD WANTED TO WRITE the main opinion. It wasn't about exercising his privilege to do so if he was part of the majority. It was

about his title—chief justice of the United States—lending weight to a
ruling, as Earl Warren had done in *Brown*. However, Rehnquist couldn't
find four other votes. The day before, he had circulated a draft opinion
that berated the Florida Supreme Court for a ruling that was "perhaps
delusive." But he recognized he had to address his own hypocrisy, the
pot attacking the sins of the kettle. He had made his reputation defending states from federal intrusions. "In most cases, comity and respect for
federalism compel us to defer to the decisions of state courts on issues
of state law," he wrote. This case, though, was no "ordinary election,"
but one for "the only elected officials who represent all the voters in the
nation." Scalia and Thomas joined the opinion, but neither Kennedy
nor O'Connor wanted any part of the chief's language, which was why
Rehnquist's opinion was only a concurrence.

The net effect of the splintered majority was to underscore that although the five agreed on a result, they couldn't agree on a reason. A
constitutional diktat without principle might resolve the immediate dispute, but it eroded faith in the Court, especially when the five justices
awarding the presidency to the Republican all happened to be appointees of Republicans. The weakest element of both the majority opinion
and Rehnquist's concurrence was that neither ever explained why the
Court was the correct branch to intervene. Congress wasn't even mentioned. Any branch that settled the election was going to be pilloried by
half the country. That implacable division should have given the Court
all the more inducement to stay away. Stevens's sorrowful dissent drove
home the point. "Although we may never know with complete certainty
the identity of the winner of this year's presidential election," he wrote,
"the identity of the loser is perfectly clear. It is the nation's confidence in
the judge as an impartial guardian of the rule of law."

The Court hadn't learned. In earlier episodes, it was always the failure of the justices to justify their involvement that did them in. Such was
the lesson of 1876, when the vote of a single justice, sitting on a special
electoral commission, bestowed the presidency on Hayes. *Roe v. Wade*
illustrated what happened when the patina of principle, developed over
many years—in a case like *Brown v. Board*—disappeared from a ruling.

Now, *Bush v. Gore* showed what the institution stripped of apparent neutrality looked like. The astonishing thing about the case was that in this once-in-a-century political standoff, in which the Court should have gone out of its way to say why it should be the one to step in, it offered nothing. Such unexplained arrogation of power, more than vulgar partisanship, was the hallmark of the case.

So, too, was scorn for a state court. The majority's "federal assault on the Florida election procedures," Stevens wrote, was rooted in a "lack of confidence in the impartiality and capacity" of state judges. It was one thing to distrust courts in the South during the 1950s and '60s, when judges sometimes defied federal civil rights laws; in such cases, the justices intervened. But the Florida Supreme Court was hardly of "the Jim Crow South," as Ginsburg pointed out. Moreover, the Florida court had applied election law "liberally," recognizing absentee ballots that a more technical reading would've rejected. That benefited Bush. Had the Florida court ruled the other way, Gore would have taken the lead by thousands of votes. As the scholar Jack Balkin wrote, none of the justices in the *Bush v. Gore* majority complained about "*this* change in Florida law."

The most disingenuous part of the majority opinion was its jaw-dropping disclaimer. Here the Court was issuing what read like a bold pronouncement, Warren Court style, about the importance of equal protection in electoral matters. In theory, the ruling might reshape the conduct of most American elections. But no, Kennedy said, the ruling was "limited to the present circumstances," a snowflake that melted before it reached the ground. "Limited to the present circumstances" was about as convincing as the "penumbras" and "emanations" of an earlier Court ruling about the constitutional basis of marital privacy. The justices had enough confidence in their logic to decide the presidency today, but it wasn't sound enough to be used in a gubernatorial race tomorrow. And indeed *Bush v. Gore* has been cited in only one Court case since (a tangential reference in a Thomas dissent).

Lightning bolts just weren't the Court's way. Because it decides so few appeals, and because its rulings are the law of the land, the Court selects cases that will have sweeping application. One-off rulings like *Bush v. Gore*—in "the same class as a restricted railroad ticket, good for this day and train only," as a justice put it in a 1944 dissent—not only squandered the Court's time, but opened it up to suspicion that decisions were driven by results. Scalia himself had said as much just a few years before, in a lone dissent in the ruling that made the Virginia Military Institute coed. The Court "does not sit to announce 'unique' circumstances," he wrote. "Its principal function is to establish precedent—that is, to set forth principles of law that every court in America must follow." Yet *Bush v. Gore*, the Court commanded, had no precedential value. Its presidential value, however, was immeasurable.

It made sense that the majority wouldn't stand by its improvised ruling for the long haul. Conservatives had long been loath to use the Fourteenth Amendment to expand voting rights. Kennedy and the other four justices knew what their ruling might unleash in the hands of future liberals. "The problem of equal protection in election processes generally presents many complexities," Kennedy wrote. Well, yes, a sudden, extemporaneous revolution of equal protection doctrine was "complex." Following its logic, *Bush v. Gore* might discredit every statewide election in America. Standards were standards, whether for recounts or for the initial counts we call elections. And so the ruling was "limited to the present circumstances."

Announcing a profound change in the law that conveniently benefited Bush—and then disavowing the change—came across as unadorned favoritism. At whatever level of consciousness, the goal seemed to be to install a Republican in the White House, where for the next four years he could anoint the justices' new colleagues. *Bush v. Gore* was the ultimate conflict of interest for the justices, in which the conservatives seemed to act to consolidate their 5-to-4 majority. This was the Court trying to pack itself. Whatever else one thought of *Roe v. Wade*, nobody imagined that the seven justices in its majority acted out of selfishness.

"Equal protection" was a sham in *Bush v. Gore*. Did the majority seriously believe the ruling would be the same in a hypothetical *Gore v. Bush*, in which Gore led by 537 votes and Bush sought a recount? Assume in this alternate scenario that the Florida Supreme Court blocked any recounts. Bush would have appealed to the justices to "count all the votes." It was fair to guess that the five conservatives would not have paid tribute to equal protection. Rather, they would have done precisely the converse of what happened in *Bush v. Gore*—either set counting standards themselves or ordered the Florida court to do so. They would have ignored the December 12 deadline without hesitation. And the four dissenters likely would have figured out a way to call for the end to the whole thing and to hand the presidency to Gore. Nobody would be applying for judicial sainthood.

Kennedy ended his opinion, straight-faced, with a peroration about how "none" stood "more in admiration" than the justices of "the Constitution's design to leave the selection of the president" to "the people." The claim was laughable, for it was the political process that Kennedy, most especially, didn't respect. Congress, elected by "the people," could not be entrusted to settle the election. Why was it up to the Court? Kennedy blamed the litigants. "When contending parties invoke the process of the courts," he wrote, "it becomes our unsought responsibility to resolve the federal and constitutional issues." That was overwrought hooey. The justices were forced to hear nothing. Accepting jurisdiction in the 2000 election showed not respect for the rule of law, but the hubris of kings. Nobody "forced" Kennedy or the other four to hear *Bush v. Gore*. Nobody "forced" them pick a president. In the first instance, they had to choose who chose—Congress or the Court. And the justices chose themselves. Bickel would have been appalled. One law professor called *Bush v. Gore* "almost a parody of the Bickelian notion of judicial restraint." Bickel's "passive virtues" had been turned into the "passive-aggressive virtues."

What Bickel had appreciated that the *Bush v. Gore* majority did not was the Court's limited reserve of institutional capital. If the justices had mythical status in American government, it arose in part from their distance. By choosing not to act—even in this peculiar situation—they could have demonstrated the resilience of the other, political branches. On the most politically charged question—who would be president—the justices could have shown respect for, rather than doubt in, those branches. Indeed, *Bush v. Gore* seemed in the same league as *Dred Scott*.

A commentator had written of the latter: "A question which involved a Civil War can hardly be proper material for the wrangling of lawyers." The same might be said about a question that involved a presidential election.

Bush v. Gore could have been a shining moment for the Court. Instead, the Court couldn't wait to rush in, twice. Foolishly, the justices believed their involvement would ennoble the outcome. It did not. The justices succeeded only in sullying the Court's reputation.

Seventeen years later, Chief Justice Roberts recognized the problem, though in a very different context. In an important case about the constitutionality of extreme gerrymandering based not on geography but on maximizing partisan advantage, he worried about making the Court the arbiter. "We will have to decide in every case whether the Democrats win or the Republicans win," he pointed out during the argument in *Gill v. Whitford* in the fall of 2017. "If you're the intelligent man on the street and the Court issues a decision—and let's say the Democrats win—that person will say, 'Well, why did the Democrats win?'" Even if the Court explained that the Constitution compelled the answer, that person "is going to say that's a bunch of baloney. It must be because the Supreme Court preferred the Democrats over the Republicans." According to Roberts, that would cause "very serious harm to the status and integrity" of "this Court in the eyes of the country." That sure sounded like an indictment of what the Court had done in *Bush v. Gore*. But it's a pretty good bet that had Roberts been on the Court at the time of *Bush v. Gore*, he would have been part of the majority.

HAD THE COURT NOT INTERCEDED, and had a statewide recount in Florida not produced an outcome that both candidates blessed, the dispute would have landed in Congress on January 6—and Bush would have won anyway. That made the intervention of the five justices even less rational.

The denouement might have looked like this: If Congress had had two slates of Florida electors before it—one sent by the state legislature, the other by the state supreme court—the Senate and the House would each have had to choose a slate. That was how the Electoral Count Act drew it up. The GOP-controlled House would go for the Bush slate. But with the incoming Senate divided 50–50 between Democrats and Republicans, the body's presiding officer got to break the tie. The Constitution made that individual the vice president, who was still in office until January 20. Gore would be in the position of deciding in favor of himself.

But according to the Electoral Count Act, the Senate was supposed to pick the slate that that had been "ascertained" by the governor. That would've meant a Bush victory—unless the Florida Supreme Court declared the governor's signature a nullity and ordered another executive— perhaps the state attorney general, who was a Democrat—to sign in his place. Or perhaps the Florida court itself would have simply "ascertained" a slate. It would've been uncharted political terrain and spellbinding theater, but squarely within the contemplation of those who wrote the Electoral Count Act. The likely result: continued deadlock.

If the House and Senate failed to agree on a slate, the Twelfth Amendment would have kicked in, requiring the House to name the president. Again, Bush would've won. But the Senate got to choose the vice president. Gore's tiebreaker would've gone to Lieberman (who also, as a senator, would have voted for himself). For many Americans, a Bush-Lieberman coalition would have constituted rough justice.

Could a completed Florida statewide recount have produced numbers that all sides accepted, obviating the need for congressional resolution? That was unlikely, given the range of reasonable counting standards available. In the months that followed *Bush v. Gore*, media and academic organizations conducted studies of the ballots and reached a consensus. If *all* disputed ballots—undervotes as well as overvotes— had been counted, Gore would have won. But if only undervotes were counted—which is all the Florida Supreme Court directed—Bush would still have been ahead, thereby rendering extraordinary congressional action unnecessary.

DIFFERENT JUSTICES DEALT WITH the ruling's aftermath in their own ways. The very next day, Thomas told high school students in Washington that a justice's partisan preferences had played "zero" part, and to suggest otherwise was "like slurring the process." Rather, he said, "the last political act we engage in is confirmation"—which of course was contradicted by the reality that most healthy justices who retired chose to do so when the White House was controlled by the party with which they were associated. Rehnquist, stopping by the Court's press office that afternoon, endorsed Thomas's view. Others just snickered. Writing in the law review of Thomas's alma mater, one scholar asked whether he also "believed in Santa Claus, the Easter Bunny, and the Tooth Fairy." There was nothing surprising about Thomas's protestation. Accusing your colleagues of partisanship, let alone acknowledging your own, demolished the idea that the justices serve on a principled Court. Such was the way around any cognitive dissonance.

Over the years, Scalia was defiant, predictably so but no less hypocritically. It wasn't that he believed the Court had made an intellectually plausible equal protection argument—he reportedly told a colleague it was "a piece of shit." He simply presumed the justices had to act—"an easy case, it really was," he claimed. It was as if Scalia believed the Court's choice was little different from its decision to intervene in school segregation. "We were the laughingstock of the world—the world's greatest democracy couldn't conduct an election," he told Charlie Rose, omitting where it was in the Constitution he unearthed a "laughingstock of the world" clause that allowed the Court to disregard explicit text that left to Congress the resolution of electoral disputes for the presidency. "Some court was going to decide it," he said matter-of-factly. Sometimes Scalia had a more smug response when asked about *Bush v. Gore*. "Get over it!" he declared. Souter confided to friends that he never did, so embarrassed was he about the ruling.

Only O'Connor publicly came to regret her vote. At first, she couldn't fathom why anybody might be so upset the justices intervened. An article in *USA Today* six weeks after the ruling especially caught her attention. The piece detailed the "lingering bitterness" among law clerks. Her obliviousness to how the ruling played was understandable, even if she once had been a ranking politician in Arizona. The Constitution's structure planned it that way, isolating justices from the body politic. Even the dumbest senators had a sense of their constituencies. A decade later, in retirement, O'Connor still seemed to have little patience for the criticism, telling a conference in Aspen that "it wasn't the end of the world . . . so forget it."

But by the spring of 2013, she found she hadn't been able to. Her tone was different, perhaps because of the Court's unrelenting interventionism in other areas since, and perhaps at 83 she had developed more humility. "Maybe the court should have said, 'We're not going to take it—goodbye,'" she told the *Chicago Tribune* editorial board. *Bush v. Gore* "gave the Court a less than perfect reputation" and "stirred up the public." And though Florida judges "kind of messed up" some of their rulings, she admitted, "probably the Supreme Court added to the problem at the end of the day."

If only she had spoken up 13 years earlier.

By the time of the 2000 election, *Roe v. Wade* had been the bête noire of the American right for nearly three decades. For justices like Scalia and Thomas, the ruling epitomized the sins of an activist Court, adrift from its constitutional moorings. In *Bush v. Gore*, the Court came full circle. Constitutional law had become the continuation of politics by other means. The lesson for conservatives was Justice William Brennan's Rule of Five. *Roe* was of course about abortion, whereas *Bush v. Gore* was about an election. But they were flip sides of the same coin at the Court: "If you have five votes here, you can do anything." Though *Roe* hadn't been overturned, the conservatives in *Bush v. Gore* got even sweeter revenge. The raw power exercised in the former had come home to roost in the latter—poetic justice of a sort. One who lives by the judicial sword dies by the judicial sword.

Roe was based on substantive due process, *Bush v. Gore* on a dishonest view of equal protection. But the interpretive mechanisms weren't the point. Both liberals and conservatives now had fully embraced judicial triumphalism.

CHAPTER 12

JAMES MADISON MADE US DO IT

FOR ALL ITS SINS, *BUSH V. GORE* HAPPENED ONLY DUE TO AN ELECTORAL freak. Neither the justices nor the politicians planned to have the Supreme Court deciding presidential elections. But *Bush v. Gore* nonetheless reflected an attitude and an arrogance that continued to embolden the Court. Several months before the ruling, Gallup reported that 62 percent of Americans approved of the way the Court did its job. The percentage has been lower ever since.

In late 2005, a young and ambitious conservative, John Roberts, succeeded William Rehnquist as chief justice. Just as important, a few months later, a young and ambitious conservative, Samuel Alito, replaced Sandra Day O'Connor, the first time in 34 years that two justices had joined the Court in a single term. O'Connor's retirement provided a pivotal opening for the judicial right. When Kennedy was with Roberts and Alito—and with the votes of Antonin Scalia and Clarence Thomas secure—conservatives would now have a majority to drive a true counterrevolution to what they viewed as the judicial excesses of the prior 70 years.

Choice targets abounded: abortion rights, the sprawling regulatory state, racial preferences, criminal defendants, enemies of religion. But the cause that most lathered a lot of conservatives was the Second Amendment. *Roe v. Wade* provided the playbook—to achieve in court what could not be accomplished in legislatures. For most of American history, the Second Amendment hadn't been a source of controversy, so apparent was it to judges and scholars that an individual "right to bear arms" conferred by the Constitution was little more than a fund-raising slogan for the National Rifle Association (NRA). Despite that consensus, as well as many gun control laws enacted over the decades, the Court would soon declare otherwise, in *District of Columbia v. Heller*. It was an important Scalia majority opinion, but more significantly *Heller* revealed that the new Roberts Court had substantive objectives to realize.

Many constitutional clauses are general, but they're designed to be. The Fourth Amendment's ban on "unreasonable searches and seizures" expressed unambiguous values, even if courts were left to fill in the details. Likewise, the Fourteenth Amendment's guarantee of equal protection has been the measure of social fairness ever since the Civil War. But the Second Amendment was another matter—a single sentence mashing together four phrases and commas, the connection among which was anybody's guess. It would have flunked a fifth-grade exercise in sentence diagramming.

The Second Amendment was more Rorschach test than self-revealing pronouncement. Despite what sworn originalists and textualists claim, the Constitution doesn't interpret itself any more than Holy Scripture does. The 27 enigmatic words of the Second Amendment read in full: "A well regulated militia, being necessary to the security of a free state, the right of the people to keep and bear arms, shall not be infringed." That's the entire thing. But how does a "well regulated militia" relate to the rest of the sentence? If the Framers weren't being paid by the word, it must be in there for some reason. Does it envelop the right to bear arms? If the right to bear arms has a life of its own, isn't the militia clause useless? Who are "the people," and in what capacity do they have this arms-bearing right? Doesn't "well regulated" contemplate *regulation*? In short, was the amendment about an individual right to own weapons, or a collective right of defense tied to the existence of a militia?

For the first 217 years of American history, the answer was that the amendment protected the collective, militia-based right, in the service of security. Individuals were relevant only in the context of the collective. Militias were part of the colonial tradition. Americans particularly distrusted a standing army—and rightly so. They had just fought against the British version in the Revolution, during which King George III's troops often seized the guns and ammunition of private citizens. After the Revolution, most white men were required to keep arms and "muster" them publicly as part of a local militia responsible for both public safety and defense (against Indians and foreign powers). It was this right to possess arms that the newly independent Americans wished to be enshrined in the Bill of Rights. Back then, militias had none of the modern connotation of survivalist brigades living in the woods (even if the idea of protecting insurrectionist impulses did seem rather antithetical to a constitution establishing a government).

The Constitution mentions the word *militia* not only in the Second Amendment, but in three other places. Congress, for example, was granted the power to "call forth" militia to "suppress insurrections and repel invasions," and the president was declared "commander in chief of the army and navy of the United States, and of the militia of the several States." The Second Amendment was meant to emphasize that, despite those federal contexts, state militia could not be disbanded.

Through the 19th century, and even with the temporary creation of a conscripted Union Army during the Civil War, militia continued to be a staple of defense and culture. Over time, however, as the need for a permanent national army became obvious, especially during the Spanish-American War in 1898, the importance of state militia waned. By the end of World War I, the national army had nearly 300,000 troops, 17 times more than in early 1861. Even so, the militia tradition continues to the present day, in the form of a modest army called the National Guard in each state. (The National Guard is controlled by respective state governors, but can also be mobilized by Congress or the president for federal duty.)

Gun restrictions were nothing new. In the 1700s and 1800s, even after the Civil War, black men generally weren't allowed to own guns.

In the Wild West, in such gunslinger towns as Dodge City (Kansas) and Tombstone (Arizona), newcomers had to surrender their firearms to the sheriff. Restrictions became more prevalent in the decades after the Civil War, often in response to the perception that crime was a burgeoning threat. There were various sociological explanations for the rise in crime: urbanization, the end of the frontier, a demoralized population, and Prohibition. Sometimes a notorious episode produced new laws. The St. Valentine's Day Massacre in 1929—in which Al Capone took out seven members of the North Side Gang in Chicago—has been called "the most famous machine-gun incident of all time." It led to FDR's National Firearms Act of 1934, one of the first major pieces of federal gun control. The law regulated the most deadly weapons—machine guns, sawed-off shotguns and silencers used by gangsters like Capone, and Bonnie and Clyde. The statute taxed the weapons, required their registration, and most important, banned their transport across state lines.

FIVE YEARS LATER, the National Firearms Act became the subject of the Supreme Court's first significant gun appeal. To secure its ongoing efforts to curb gun violence, the federal government wanted the Court's blessing against any Second Amendment problem. There wasn't widespread belief in a constitutional impediment to the law, but when Congress expanded the law in 1938, the House Ways and Means Committee received thousands of letters from gun enthusiasts, some of which cited the Second Amendment. The tale of Jack Miller—arrested in the Ozarks, in 1938, for possession of an unregistered sawed-off, double-barrel shotgun—made for a good test case.

Born in 1900, Miller was the kind of two-bit, 240-pound thug who filled the pages of pulp crime novels. By the time of his 1938 arrest, he had been a gambler, a bouncer, a moonshiner, an informant, a getaway driver on a string of bank heists, and a killer, though on that last one he'd been defending a woman in a bar. At his trial, the judge understood the government's desire to get the right case to the Court. He dismissed the firearms charge against Miller on Second Amendment grounds, and the Feds promptly appealed. (It was a different age of litigation. When he found out the Court had taken the appeal, Miller's lawyer wired the clerk: "UNABLE TO OBTAIN ANY MONEY FROM CLIENTS TO BE PRESENT AND ARGUE CASE." So the government argued alone, which didn't help Miller's chances.)

In the spring of 1939, in *United States v. Miller*, the justices unanimously ruled for the government. From its perspective, that was the good news. The bad was that the Court's opinion was "an impenetrable mess," as a commentator described it. Justice James McReynolds said the case turned on the language of the Second Amendment—whether there was sufficient connection between "the preservation or efficiency of a well regulated militia" and Miller's possession of a sawed-off shotgun. McReynolds found there was not. Such a weapon simply could not be thought of as "ordinary military equipment"; nor could "its use contribute to the common defense." With the "obvious purpose" to "assure the continuation" of militia power, McReynolds wrote, "the declaration and guarantee of the Second Amendment were made. It must be interpreted and applied with that end in view." (Miller never served time. In keeping with his luck, before the Court ruled, he was found dead by a creek in Oklahoma, shot multiple times with a .38.)

Nobody confused McReynolds's writing with that of Oliver Wendell Holmes Jr. But the essence of *Miller* seemed clear: Militias were the point. When the Second Amendment was ratified, standing armies were "strongly disfavored." Instead, "adequate defense of country and laws could be secured through the militia—civilians primarily, soldiers on occasion." So, no individual right to bear arms existed apart from what was necessary to constitute a citizen army. The ruling confirmed conventional wisdom—legal and academic—until that point. And thereafter, that view remained unremarkable for a generation.

It wasn't until the urban violence of the 1960s, and the assassinations of the Kennedy brothers and Martin Luther King Jr., that Congress passed more gun laws. The Gun Control Act of 1968 banned interstate trafficking of most firearms, ended the importation of military-surplus weapons, and expanded the categories of individuals deemed too risky to own guns. The attempted assassination of President Reagan in 1981 led to congressional passage of the Brady Bill a dozen years later. Named for Reagan's press secretary, James Brady, who was shot in the head during the assassination attempt and spent the rest of his life confined to a wheelchair, the bill imposed a five-day waiting period on gun buyers and required states to do background checks. Then, in 1994, as part of the largest crime bill in U.S. history, Congress outlawed the manufacture and possession of a range of assault weapons. The Clinton administration's focus on lethality recalled the Depression-era machine-gun culture and the adoption of the National Firearms Act in response.

Noticeably absent in the debates over the Brady Bill and the assault weapons ban was any preoccupation with the Second Amendment. Nor had the Supreme Court, or any other court, provided any suggestion that it believed *Miller* had been wrongly decided in 1939. Gun control remained the preserve of the democratic process. Some measures were enacted, some were rejected, a few were repealed. Presidents of both parties came and went, their respective positions on crime and weapons turning on both ideology and events. Resorting to the courts never entered the discussion. Political participants on both sides assumed that gun policy would be worked out legislatively, as it had been since the Revolution—no matter the crises after the Civil War; during Prohibition and then the Depression; and amid the turbulence of the 1960s.

On occasion, the language of the Constitution was summoned, but more as a mantra than an argument. As far back as 1975, Reagan had talked up Second Amendment rights. Running to the right in his bid for the 1976 GOP presidential nomination, he wrote a piece for *Guns & Ammo*, a magazine for firearms enthusiasts. The incumbent president, Gerald Ford, who had survived two attempts on his life, backed gun control. Reagan, who had signed strict gun measures while governor of California, now switched sides (as he had done on abortion). He first recited the line about how "the automobile is the greatest peacetime killer in history," yet "there is no talk of banning the auto." Next, he asked if rising crime was due to "the criminal's instinctive knowledge that the average victim no longer has means of self-protection." But then he assumed the role of historian and scholar. "Our nation was built and civilized by men and women who used guns in self-defense," he wrote.

"We may not have a well-regulated militia, but it does not necessarily follow that we should not be prepared to have one." And there ended the analysis. "The Second Amendment," Reagan concluded, "is clear, or ought to be. It appears to leave little, if any, leeway for the gun control advocate." One could almost hear a director yell, "Cut and print!"

Reagan won the presidency four years later, and in that landslide, Republicans took control of the Senate for the first time in 27 years. There was some ferment about the Second Amendment, but it went nowhere. For example, the Senate Subcommittee on the Constitution commissioned a study on "The Right to Keep and Bear Arms." One year and 150 pages later, under the direction of Senator Orrin Hatch, it proclaimed newfound truths: "What the Subcommittee on the Constitution uncovered was clear—and long lost—proof that the Second Amendment . . . was intended as an individual right of the American citizen to keep and carry arms in a peaceful manner, for protection of himself, his family, and his freedoms."

Never mind that what the Republicans had "uncovered"—down the block at the Library of Congress—were such items as the papers of James Madison, even though the draftsman of the Bill of Rights, the report recognized, was "now dead for two centuries." There simply was yet to be a political groundswell for fundamentally changing what most folks thought about a right to bear arms. In late 1988, nearing the end of Reagan's presidency, the Justice Department issued a white paper on 15 areas of constitutional doctrine it deemed ripe for Supreme Court consideration. Entitled "The Constitution in the Year 2000," it included discussions of abortion, presidential authority, freedom of religion, equal protection, and discrimination based on sexual orientation. The report didn't say a thing about the Second Amendment.

The mainstream view about the amendment's limited reach was conveyed most emphatically by Warren Burger, of all people. The conservative chief justice, appointed by President Nixon, had retired in 1986. He was peeved by the attention the amendment had been getting. In 1990, writing in the Sunday newspaper supplement *Parade*, he called the amendment an anachronism, created at a time that a state militia, "like a rifle and powder horn, was as much a part of life as the automobile is today." But "with two world wars and some lesser ones," militia had given way to vast national armed forces. A year later, Burger, typically a dull interviewee, let loose. Appearing on national TV, when asked about gun rights, he took out a pocket copy of the Constitution and fumed that the Second Amendment had been "the subject of one of the greatest pieces of fraud—I repeat the word 'fraud'—on the American public by special interest groups that I have ever seen in my lifetime." He invoked the automobile analogy that Reagan and others had used. "If the militia, which was going to be the state army, was going to be 'well regulated,' why shouldn't 16- and 17- and 18-, or any other, age persons be regulated in the use of arms the way an automobile is regulated?"

ALTHOUGH SELF-STYLED ORIGINALISTS AND TEXTUALISTS claimed that constitutional meaning was fixed, the old view of the Second Amendment slowly but relentlessly came into question. The "special interest groups" that Burger derided—chiefly the deep-pocketed, well-organized NRA—influenced both political incumbents and their challengers. Throughout his presidency, Reagan kept up the Second Amendment drumbeat, and few Republicans protested. Others joined in the rehabilitation effort. Writing in the *Washington Post* in 1990, the columnist Michael Kinsley quoted a contrarian colleague: "If liberals interpreted the Second Amendment the way they interpret the rest of the Bill of Rights, there would be law professors arguing that gun ownership is mandatory."

Academics, especially the libertarians among them, published stacks of self-referential pieces on law and history that echoed what Hatch's subcommittee had "uncovered." Some of the scholarship just happened to be funded by millions of NRA dollars, which also eventually endowed the Patrick Henry Professor of Constitutional Law and the Second Amendment at George Mason University's law school. (After Scalia's death, the school was rechristened the Antonin Scalia School of Law until someone there realized the acronym would be ASSoL. The school quickly became just the Antonin Scalia Law School.) In addition, the NRA bankrolled an essay contest for law students and paid book reviewers to write favorably about the Second Amendment. All of it was a brilliant fusion of partisanship and scholarship, which helped to give the Court's ruling in *Heller* a veneer of academic respectability.

Crucially, the independent scholarship of three established left-leaning law professors—Larry Tribe of Harvard, Akhil Amar of Yale and Sanford Levinson of the University of Texas—offered validity to gun rights activists. Levinson's 1989 article, "The Embarrassing Second Amendment," stood out and was cited by activists as proof their position wasn't off the wall. In fact, Levinson hadn't endorsed the view that the amendment conferred a categorical private entitlement to own firearms. All he suggested was that the "right to bear arms" language had to be taken seriously, writing, "For too long, most members of the legal academy have treated the Second Amendment as the equivalent of an embarrassing relative, whose mention brings a quick change of subject." Though enforcing the Second Amendment might have "social costs," he said, so did enforcing the First, with all the hate speech it shielded. Levinson imputed bad faith to his fellow liberals, supposing that their stance derived from "the perhaps subconscious fear that altogether plausible, perhaps even 'winning,' interpretations of the Second Amendment would present real hurdles to those of us supporting prohibitory regulation." There was a credible alternative: Maybe his colleagues just didn't think all the revisionism about the amendment had negated its actual text, history, purpose or subsequent judicial appraisal.

Behind much of the drive to rewrite the meaning of the amendment was the NRA. The organization was founded after the Civil War to promote training and safety and, by 1900, hunting and the great outdoors. ("Great" was in the eyes of the beholder—nobody asked the elk.) Only later did the NRA turn to politics. And even then, it supported the 1934 and 1968 gun laws. It was not until 1977 that Second Amendment absolutists took over the NRA, at its annual meeting—voting out what passed for moderate leadership, in the midnight "Revolt at Cincinnati."

The group's radicalization was a long time in the making, but made sense within the context of the broader culture wars and the Republican Party's turn to the right. NRA membership had tripled to 1.9 million in the 16 years between the Watts riots of 1965 and Reagan's first inauguration. The new NRA initially focused on states, where many gun laws had been passed and which most gun control advocates ignored. Roused, the NRA in 1980 endorsed a presidential candidate for the first time: Reagan. At NRA headquarters outside Washington, as the author Michael Waldman observed, FIREARMS SAFETY EDUCATION, MARKSMANSHIP TRAINING, SHOOTING FOR RECREATION no longer appeared in big letters on the facade. Now, it was just about THE RIGHT OF THE PEOPLE TO KEEP AND BEAR ARMS, without a word about a well-regulated militia.

In every presidential election after 1980, the NRA endorsed the Republican or energetically opposed the Democrat. After George W. Bush's election in 2000, his new attorney general John Ashcroft, at the urging of the NRA, upended decades of Justice Department policy. Ashcroft, himself an NRA member, stated in a letter read at its annual convention in May 2001: "The text and the original intent of the Second Amendment clearly protect the right of individuals to keep and bear firearms."

At the Supreme Court, Clarence Thomas also began to sow a change. In a 1997 case, the justices had to decide the constitutionality of the Brady Bill's requirement that local authorities conduct background checks on prospective gun buyers. By a 5-to-4 vote, the Court struck down that provision on grounds of federalism, saying Congress had violated the sovereignty of states. While Thomas joined the majority, he filed a lone, gratuitous concurrence about the Second Amendment. The Constitution, he advised one and all, placed "whole areas outside the reach of Congress' regulatory authority," like the First Amendment's blanket prohibition on legislators from abridging freedom of speech or freedom of religion. The Court's "most recent treatment of the Second Amendment" had been 58 years earlier. Citing "a growing body of scholarly commentary"—some of it paid for by the NRA—Thomas said "perhaps" the time was coming when the Court would acknowledge, "as the amendment's text suggests," that the "right to bear arms" was "a personal right."

How far the law had come, how fast it had changed. Thomas had shown that constitutional interpretation and politics were dynamic and symbiotic. The one affected the other. The Constitution was indeed alive, not that Thomas or Scalia or other originalist-textualists would dare admit it. *Brown v. Board of Education*, for example, surely had helped to alter the country's attitudes about race, particularly as they were reflected in such legislation as the Civil Rights Act of 1964 and the Voting Rights Act of 1965. But public views about race also helped to spur the Court to announce *Brown* in the first place.

In the matter of the Second Amendment, in a matter of decades, NRA agitation had produced a sea change. By exploiting academia, public relations and electoral engagement, activists had transformed Burger's "fraud on the public" into an idea that at least one justice now bought. Political wishes were now constitutional claims. Public opinion, too, had come around. According to Gallup, nearly three-quarters of Americans in 2008 believed the Second Amendment guaranteed the right to own a gun, period—independent of a state militia. Politicians in both parties, including a young Democratic senator from Illinois named Barack Obama, espoused support for at least a limited individual right—which of course was an argument militating against judicial involvement, since the political process was on the case.

THOMAS'S CONCURRENCE HAD AN AGENDA. He was sending a signal to movement lawyers to bring another test case to the Court. But it wasn't as easy as it sounded. They had tried. A few years after Thomas's opinion, a federal court cited it and said the Second Amendment demanded re-evaluation. The Supreme Court, however, in 2002 declined to hear the case, in part because Thomas and others recognized they lacked the votes to declare a new constitutional right. Such was the head count with O'Connor still there. A ruling that refused to extend *Miller*, the 1939 case, could devastate the Second Amendment cause. The Court didn't like to continually revisit issues, lest it appear that constitutional law was dependent on mere personnel. Better to hold off.

The optimal test case would involve a sympathetic plaintiff—not, for example, a drug dealer or bank robber. And the best law to challenge would be the most restrictive—say, a ban on all handguns, no matter the circumstance. The case would also ideally be handled by lawyers well acquainted with appellate practice, which would provide the best tactical opportunity to build a favorable record in lower courts. And one would need some luck—with court proceedings not taking place right after a school massacre. Activist constitutional litigation could fail not just on the merits, but if any of these ingredients were absent.

Getting the right appeal before the Court consumed NRA lawyers. They were cautious. When they started to game the timing of a test case, O'Connor was still on the bench. Would she, or one of the older liberals, be gone by the time the Court granted cert, perhaps a couple of years away? And who would the replacements be?

But as experienced and turf-conscious as the NRA was, it couldn't control all gun litigation. Beginning in the summer of 2002, three libertarian lawyers embarked on their own journey to the Court. At the Institute for Justice, a public interest law firm in suburban D.C., Clark Neily III and Steve Simpson were convinced the time was right, even with NRA misgivings at the beginning. *Heller* was their brainchild. Because their firm couldn't fully finance the litigation, they asked a friend with equally strong convictions—and money to spend—to help. His name was Bob Levy, and he became a key part of the campaign. A self-made multimillionaire, Levy had sold his financial-database firm in 1987 and decided to go to law school at 49. With fierce opinions about the Bill of Rights, he became an author and TV pundit on constitutional issues and was a board member of both the Federalist Society and the Cato Institute, a prominent D.C. libertarian think tank. Levy agreed to join, as did several other lawyers. (Because *Heller* was considered a civil rights case and because Levy won, he was later awarded legal fees and reimbursed for some expenses, paid for by the D.C. government.)

Their litigation strategy was savvy and painstaking. They decided to find an array of demographically diverse plaintiffs in the District of Columbia, which had a long-standing ban on owning handguns, even if kept at home for self-defense. As the strictest gun law in the country, it was the most vulnerable to a Second Amendment challenge. The plaintiffs would not be gun-toting miscreants but law-abiding citizens who wanted to protect themselves and their families. As Levy explained at the time, they would be far from the "usual suspects" plucked from the gun lobby. The libertarian lawyers spoke of their lawsuit being modeled on the work of Thurgood Marshall in his march toward *Brown v. Board of Education*. Because of jurisdictional technicalities, Dick Anthony Heller, 61, became the main plaintiff. As a security guard for a federal office building, he already lawfully carried a pistol at work, but he was denied a license to keep it at home in his high-crime D.C. neighborhood.

In early 2003, the lawyers filed suit in federal court in Washington. A judge threw the case out in 2004, citing "years of unchanged Supreme Court precedent" and "the deluge" of lower-court opinions "rejecting an individual right to bear arms." On appeal, after a two-year procedural delay, the D.C. Circuit ruled for Heller, in early 2007. The D.C. Circuit had once been the most liberal appellate court in the country, but Republican appointments had turned it around. According to the court, "the people" to which the Second Amendment referred had to mean citizens individually. Otherwise, the disappearance of Founding-era militia would render the amendment a "dead letter." The individual right to bear arms "existed prior to the formation of the new government" and was broad enough to include not only "resistance" to "the depredations of a tyrannical government," but also self-defense against "private lawlessness." The right was subject to "reasonable restrictions," but not the "virtual prohibition" D.C. had imposed.

With its law annulled, the D.C. city government faced a dilemma: Adopt a more lenient statute, or appeal to the Supreme Court and risk a harsh ruling that would become the law of the land. Many advocates of gun control urged the former. The Court was too much of a gamble. Thomas's views were clear; Scalia had made similar comments in a book; Roberts, when he was on the D.C. Circuit, had unsuccessfully tried to get the Court to reassess the Second Amendment. But the city, calling the case "quite literally a matter of life and death," decided to appeal—a decision it came to regret. More than five years after Neily, Simpson and Levy hatched their idea, the justices granted cert.

The justices' decision to hear the appeal was itself aggressive, reflecting a partisan agenda. The lower federal courts were yet to be widely divided, and might never be. There was hardly a raging national debate about total bans on firearms. Alexander Bickel, for one, might have advised the justices to ignore the case, leave the D.C. City Council to rewrite its law, and see what happened. Bickel surely would have questioned whether the Court's institutional reservoir had been wisely tapped.

THE ORAL ARGUMENT, IN MARCH 2008, was a trip back in time. Much of the discussion centered not on modern matters like urban violence, or even such traditional tools of constitutional interpretation as precedent. Instead, the justices cast their sight way, way back—not just to the moment of the Second Amendment's ratification in 1791, but to English legislation against Scottish highlanders; to the 18th-century English jurist William Blackstone; and all the way back to the English Bill of Rights, passed by Parliament in 1689. Justice Kennedy wondered if the history of hunting might be relevant to the phrase "keep and bear arms." Didn't the amendment have to do with "the concern of the remote settler to defend himself and his family against hostile Indian tribes and outlaws, wolves and bears and grizzlies, and things like that?" Not so much, the lawyer for the District of Columbia replied.

But the terms of debate—originalism in full blossom—were Scalia's. And he was having the doctrinal time of his life. When Justice Souter asked about "current crime statistics" and "the murder rate in Washington, D.C., using handguns," Scalia interjected: "All the more reason to allow a homeowner to have a handgun!" When Justice Breyer mentioned "80,000 to 100,000" Americans "killed or wounded in gun-related" incidents every year—and asked if it was "unreasonable" for a city to react by outlawing handguns—Scalia chimed in before Heller's lawyer could respond: "You want to say yes—that's your answer!"

The court was flooded with amicus curiae briefs—66 in all, ranging from elected district attorneys and the American Academy of Pediatrics that supported the handgun ban, to 33 states and Vice President Dick Cheney (as well as the NRA) that opposed it. But the most compelling brief came from a group of historians, led by the Pulitzer Prize winner Jack Rakove of Stanford. "Historians are often asked what the Founders would think about various aspects of contemporary life," their brief concluded. "Such questions can be tricky to answer. But as historians of the Revolutionary era we are confident at least of this: that the authors of the Second Amendment would be flabbergasted to learn that in endorsing the republican principle of a well-regulated militia, they were also precluding restrictions on such potentially dangerous property as firearms, which governments had always regulated when there was 'real danger of public injury from individuals.'"

But Scalia—the originalist, who said he prized what words meant at the time they were written—apparently had little use for scholars versed in the details. Historians "were just as 'causey' as anybody else," he told the journalist Marcia Coyle three years after *Heller*. "They won't gather to submit a brief . . . unless they care which way it comes out." Did "anybody else" include justices of the Supreme Court?

It seemed so, when the ruling was announced in late June 2008, on the last day of the Court's term: The Second Amendment guaranteed an individual's right to keep a gun, at least "in defense of hearth and home." The vote was 5–4. The ideological scorecard was the usual: Scalia, Roberts, Thomas, Alito and Kennedy in the majority; Souter, Breyer, Stevens and Ginsburg in dissent. Displaying atypical diplomacy, Scalia acknowledged that the justices' historic declaration was controversial. The Court was "aware of the problem of handgun violence," he said, "but the enshrinement of constitutional rights takes certain policy choices off the table." It might be "perhaps debatable" that "well-trained police forces provide personal security," but "what is not debatable is that it is not the role of this Court to pronounce the Second Amendment extinct."

Scalia devoted 43 of his 64 pages to poring over the pre-20th-century history, as if the sheer welter of references unequivocally established the right that he seemed to presuppose. It was a far cry from Earl Warren's 13 paragraphs in *Brown*, but mass alone doesn't make an argument. As one *Heller* critic, himself a judge, later put it: "The range of historical references in the majority is breathtaking, but it is not evidence of disinterested historical inquiry. It is evidence of the ability of well-staffed courts to produce snow jobs." And what about the 1939 Court precedent? Scalia swatted *Miller* away by saying it hardly denied a private right to own guns. Rather, he said, the Court had then addressed only certain kinds of extreme weapons.

Scalia claimed to be able to discern so clear an intent in the amendment that any contrary legislative interpretation was impossible. The views of "the people" as represented by the D.C. City Council of 2008 had to yield to "the people" of the Second Amendment, speaking 200 years later through Scalia and four other justices. The mention of "militia" in the clumsily worded amendment was merely a "prefatory statement of purpose," which did not at all govern the "operative clause" about "the right of the people to keep and bear arms." But merely "prefatory" didn't mean irrelevant—and what did owning a handgun in 2008 have to do with a militia? In the National Guard, a handgun probably wasn't even your main weapon. For Scalia, it simply wasn't possible that the Second Amendment was obsolete. And so he decoupled its two main clauses. The right to own a musket for military service had been transmuted into a right to keep a Smith & Wesson .44 at your bedside.

In dissent, Stevens pounced, more than willing to engage Scalia on originalist terms. Relying on historical evidence as well, Stevens reached a different conclusion—and more persuasively. Calling Scalia's majority opinion "strained," he demonstrated that old documentary materials hardly proved the outcome the Court now chose to enforce. Considering the degree of specificity that "well regulated militia" reflected, if the amendment intended to cover "hunting or personal self-defense," why, Stevens asked, didn't its drafters just say so? Actually, as he pointed out, those drafters, in the context of writing state constitutions, had considered—and rejected—including a provision protecting a personal right to bear arms. That omission, he said, was the better gauge of original intent. (In the spring of 2018, Stevens, long retired, called for outright repeal of the Second Amendment.)

Breyer, in a separate dissent, mostly stayed out of the historical debate, opting instead to do the more conventional, pragmatic, case-by-case balancing of interests he knew best—and which Scalia (as well as Roberts, Thomas and Alito) regarded as unprincipled. Breyer agreed with Stevens that any 18th-century private right to own arms was coextensive with keeping them for militia purposes. "Self-defense alone, detached from any militia-related objective, is not the amendment's concern," Breyer wrote. For him, the equally important point was that D.C.'s law, "which focuses upon the presence of handguns in high-crime areas, represents a permissible response to a serious, indeed life-threatening, problem." After "extensive public hearings" and "lengthy research," the "more knowledgeable," accountable officials of D.C. had concluded that "the easy availability of firearms in the United States has been a major factor contributing to the drastic increase in gun-related violence and crime over the past 40 years." Under those circumstances, and all the more so given the ambiguity in the Second Amendment, the Court was wrong to "second-guess" the D.C. legislature and "take from the elected branches of government the right" to determine solutions to urban homicide. In *Heller*, it was Breyer, more than any other justice, who showed institutional deference.

Breyer might have done well to quote the master, Alexander Bickel. "As time passes, fewer and fewer relevantly decisive choices are to be divined out of the tradition of our founding," Bickel wrote in *The Least Dangerous Branch*, 46 years before *Heller*. "Our problems have grown radically different from those known to the Framers."

CRITICS OF THE RULING had a field day with Scalia, who so often had gone to town on those he disagreed with. The catcalls came from both left and right, fairly so. Liberals said he was a fraud. Several conservatives were less kind, saying he was a colossal hypocrite. Scalia himself dismissed any notion that he had manipulated history to realize a political end. No, no, he said. He was just a vessel of the Founders— James Madison made him do it. *Heller*, he later told an interviewer, was the ultimate "vindication of originalism." But it was not. Scalia's selective "originalism" sounded like the spacious, adaptable "living" Constitution he preached did not exist. Most centrally, how could Scalia legitimately use so many external sources from so many time periods to determine what the amendment really meant? Was that not precisely the kind of subjective interpretive frolic that he blasted his colleagues for? "Good for me but not for thee" seemed to be Scalia's motif of judging.

He apparently had forgotten his own words, twice. Five years earlier, the justices in *Lawrence v. Texas* struck down a state law that criminalized gay sodomy. Scalia dissented, scathingly. The Court, he wrote, "has taken sides in the culture war, departing from its role of assuring, as neutral observer, that the democratic rules of engagement are observed." What the state legislature had chosen to do was "well within the range of traditional democratic action, and its hand should not be stayed through the invention of a brand-new 'constitutional right' by a Court that is impatient of democratic change." It is, Scalia said, "the premise of our system that those judgments are to be made by the people, and not imposed by a governing caste that knows best." How, then, was D.C.-style gun control not "well within the range of traditional democratic action"? And what was the difference between the culture war over guns and the culture war over homosexuality?

Reva Siegel, a liberal scholar at Yale who frequently wrote in defense of *Roe*, answered these questions incisively in a widely cited article in the *Harvard Law Review*. Scalia, she said, simply applied different labels, which wasn't the same thing as articulating a distinction. When Scalia was championing a partisan cause, it was "fidelity to law," whereas when his liberal colleagues did so, it was "injecting their values into judging." When he declared "a brand-new 'constitutional right,'" Siegel observed, he insisted he wasn't taking a side in the culture war—he was "rescuing" the Constitution "*from* the politics of the culture war."

Sixteen years before *Heller*, in *Casey*—the abortion ruling that upheld *Roe*—Scalia in dissent had similarly gone off about the perils of an "Imperial Judiciary" that "foreclose[s] all democratic outlet for the deep passions this issue arouses," thereby eliminating "the political forum that gives all participants, even the losers, the satisfaction of a fair hearing and an honest fight." Quoting Lincoln's First Inaugural, he wrote: "If the policy of the government upon vital questions affecting the whole people is to be irrevocably fixed by decisions of the Supreme Court . . . the people will have ceased to be their own rulers, having to that extent practically resigned their government into the hands of that eminent tribunal." Gun control would have seemed like a "vital question," best kept away from meddlesome judges "injecting their values into judging" and denying the people a "political forum." Justice Brennan had it right when he wrote about originalist theory in its infancy, back in the 1980s—"arrogance cloaked as humility," he called it.

The liberals' attack on *Heller* didn't surprise Scalia. And he didn't appear to care. What came from the right was another story. Two prominent conservative federal judges—J. Harvie Wilkinson III and Richard Posner—eviscerated Scalia's opinion. They used the sharpest analytical instrument available to conservative jurists: a comparison of *Heller* to *Roe*. Wilkinson in 2005 had been one of George W. Bush's finalists for the Court. Had he made it there over John Roberts or Samuel Alito, *Heller* wouldn't have happened. Nominations matter.

"The *Roe* and *Heller* Courts are guilty of the same sins," Wilkinson wrote in the *Virginia Law Review*. "Each represents a rejection of neutral principles that counseled restraint and deference to others regardless of the issues involved. . . . Each represents an act of judicial aggrandizement: a transfer of power to judges from the political branches of government—and thus, ultimately, from the people themselves." Even on policy issues on which reasonable folks could differ, the message of both *Roe* and *Heller* was for Americans to "bypass the ballot and seek to press their political agenda in the courts."

Wilkinson was especially critical of Scalia's misuse of originalism. Rather than representing its "triumph," *Heller* could "just as easily be seen as the opposite—an exposé of original intent as a theory no less subject to judicial subjectivity and endless argumentation as any other." Not that he had any sympathy for the liberal *Heller* dissenters. Their "claims of dedication to democratic processes," Wilkinson wrote, could "hardly be squared with decades of overturning legislative restrictions on abortion." But he said their "new restraint" wasn't as bad as the *Heller* majority's "new activism," because "vociferous opposition to *Roe* placed upon conservatives a special obligation" not to repeat the sins.

According to Wilkinson, Scalia's hypocrisy was most evident in *Heller* when he spelled out acceptable gun restrictions, despite what the rest of the opinion concluded about an individual's right to bear arms. Scalia declared that laws barring possession of firearms by felons and the mentally ill were still okay. So were restrictions on firearms in "sensitive places such as schools and government buildings." It sounded reasonable enough—if you were drafting a statute. But Scalia wasn't a legislator and in any event was supposed to be interpreting the Second Amendment, which offered no such qualifications. Alluding to *Roe*, Wilkinson wrote, "the Constitution's text, at least, has as little to say about restrictions on firearm ownership by felons as it does about the trimesters of pregnancy. The *Heller* majority seems to want to have its cake and eat it, too." (Scalia's logic tied him in knots in the years following the ruling. Asked on Fox News in 2012 about what weapons could be regulated, he said the Second Amendment "obviously" doesn't apply to cannons because they're not "arms" to "bear." But, he added, "I suppose there are handheld rocket-launchers that can bring down airplanes that will have to be decided.")

Ever the provocateur, Posner also charged Scalia with making *Roe*'s mistake by "nationalizing" a permanent outcome when ordinary political processes would allow different approaches to an issue based on "local differences in relevant conditions or in public opinion." While political activists naturally preferred one decisive judicial victory to fights in Congress, 50 states and hundreds of localities, that didn't mean the Court had to indulge the preference. And Posner showed far more contempt than Wilkinson for what Scalia had wrought. In another article, Posner savaged Scalia's lifework of making originalism an accepted conceptual tool. The title of Posner's piece: "The Incoherence of Antonin Scalia." Scalia accused Posner of "lying" in the "hatchet job" of a review, to which Posner shot back, "I did not." Did not! Did, too! These were two of the finest legal minds in the nation.

Heller APPLIED ONLY TO the federal government (which legally included D.C.). Two years later, in *McDonald v. Chicago*, along the standard ideological fault lines, the Court extended the ruling to states and localities.

But neither decision proved to have significant impact on legislation. Because other laws were not as extreme as D.C.'s, they were able to withstand constitutional challenge. Scalia's qualifiers—about who could own a gun, where it could be carried, and what firearms were "dangerous and unusual"—were sufficiently broad to allow most gun restrictions. Literally gun-shy, the justices have stayed out since. The most important skirmishes in lower courts have been over carrying loaded guns, either openly or concealed. Most regulations, especially on concealed weapons, have been upheld by most courts.

At least two justices have disagreed with the limited effect of the gun rulings. In late June 2017, the Court declined to hear a case out of California in which a federal court had upheld a state ban on most members of the public carrying any firearms. Thomas, joined by the newly arrived Neil Gorsuch, filed an eight-page dissent. Despite *Heller* and *McDonald*, they said, the Court's repeated denials of cert had turned the Second Amendment into "a disfavored right." By contrast, they noted, since *McDonald* in 2010, the justices had heard 35 First Amendment cases; such a "discrepancy" was "inexcusable." Thomas and Gorsuch had special disdain for what they viewed as the elitism of the other justices. "For those of us who work in marbled halls, guarded constantly by a vigilant and dedicated police force, the guarantees of the Second Amendment might seem antiquated and superfluous. But the Framers made a clear choice: They reserved to all Americans the right to bear arms for self-defense. I do not think we should stand by idly while a state denies its citizens that right, particularly when their very lives may depend on it."

Despite the Thomas-Gorsuch cry for all-out judicial aggression, the Court seemed several votes away from overturning more major gun restrictions; even Gorsuch declined to join a Thomas dissent in early 2018 that thundered on about the Court's "continued inaction" on the "cavalier," "dismissive" and "defiant" treatment of the Second Amendment by lower-court judges—and how abortion rights, by comparison, were taken more seriously.

But those who argue that *Heller* has turned out to be inconsequential miss a larger point. For one thing, the ruling picked up where other Court rulings left off in denuding the other branches of government.

Gun laws, wise or not, were the product of democracy—elected representatives addressing hard choices (or not). Some laws, including a new one in D.C., were enacted after *Heller*, but most were leftovers. A feckless post-*Heller* Congress did little, in part because it might have figured the Court would defeat new laws anyway. The main action continued to be in the courts—more business for the federal judges who used to be conservatives' favorite villains. Neither grassroots activists, nor legislators themselves, had much incentive to take on the nasty business of compromise and conciliation. After mass shootings such as those at the Mandalay Bay resort in Las Vegas in October 2017, or the Marjory Stoneman Douglas High School in Florida in February 2018, countless legislators lined up to insist the Second Amendment left them powerless to take action.

But more important, *Heller* had symbolic resonance, transcending any specific effect on this or that law governing the 300 million guns in the country. *Like Roe v. Wade* 35 years earlier, *Heller* triumphantly discovered a right where none was obvious in the Constitution—when it would have been better to defer to other branches. Like *Bush v. Gore* eight years earlier, *Heller* marked a fresh appetite for confrontation on the part of the Roberts Court's ascendant conservative flank. Here anew the Court was rejecting the promise of self-rule. Scalia himself described the institutional hubris—in a same-sex marriage case five years after *Heller*. Spirited public debate, he wrote in *Obergefell*, demonstrated "the beauty of what our Framers gave us"—"a system of government that permits us to rule ourselves." By halting public debate, the Court "pawned" that "gift" in order "to buy its stolen moment in the spotlight."

Anybody who thought that reinventing the Second Amendment might be a one-off from the new Court soon learned otherwise.

CHAPTER 13

FOR THE LOVE OF MONEY

TWO YEARS AFTER *HELLER*, THE ROBERTS COURT TOOK ON CAMPAIGN finance regulation in *Citizens United*. What, if any, were the limits on corporate spending on elections? *Citizens United* was a tougher case than *Heller*. It implicated not an ambiguous constitutional provision about guns, but the First Amendment's resolute protection of expression. If money enabled speech, then the more that corporate spending was regulated, the less speech entered the marketplace. Some liberals who supported the goal of reducing money's influence on campaigns nonetheless found themselves opposing restrictions on corporations. The spending at issue in *Citizens United* was by a conservative nonprofit organization to make a "documentary" about Hillary Clinton for use during the 2008 presidential campaign. The country's leading First Amendment lawyer, Floyd Abrams, said "criminalizing a movie about Hillary Clinton" was "a constitutional desecration." He argued in the Supreme Court against the government restrictions.

In *Citizens United*, two great values recognized by the Court—public confidence in the political process and the inviolability of free expression—clashed. But despite their different subject matter, *Citizens*

United and *Heller* were of a piece: They both involved challenges to well-established statutes enacted by legislators trying to deal with hard questions. As in *Heller*, the justices in *Citizens United* chose to override the judgment of the people.

THE HISTORY OF REGULATING SPENDING in political campaigns dates to colonial times. After 26-year-old George Washington, in his successful 1758 race for the Virginia House of Burgesses, tried to win over voters by serving them "a hogshead and a barrel of punch," the legislature passed a law to forbid such inducements. Over the course of more than 200 years—but especially during Theodore Roosevelt's presidency at the turn of the 20th century—Congress tried to curtail possible corruption in campaigns: barring politicians from soliciting civil service workers; requiring disclosure of contributions; and limiting corporations and labor unions in their contributions to (and expenditures on) candidates. But most of the laws were toothless, providing little means of enforcement. And so it remained until the 1970s.

By then, most candidates campaigned through TV, and the need for advertising cash skyrocketed. Money talked louder and longer. After the abuses in the 1972 presidential election and ensuing Watergate scandal, Congress passed stronger reforms and established the modern regulatory structure for campaigns. There were more rules for "political action committees" (PACs), which pooled money that could in turn be used on campaigns. And an independent agency, the Federal Election Commission (FEC), was created to administer the rules. Most important, the new laws set strict limits on contributions.

In 1976, the Supreme Court considered the conflict between these laws and the First Amendment for the first time. The crux of *Buckley v. Valeo* was that it acknowledged the link between money and speech—that in campaigns the amount of the former determined the extent of the latter. "Virtually every means of communicating ideas in today's mass society requires the expenditure of money," the Court said. "Unlimited political expression" that was still "subject to a ceiling on expenditure" was "like being free to drive an automobile as far and as often as one desires on a single tank of gasoline." The question was which way that observation cut. In the name of free expression, should anybody get to spend any amount on a campaign—or would the absence of regulation lead to moneyed voices drowning out others?

The Court split the difference. For expenditures, it said, the First Amendment allowed candidates themselves to spend overall whatever they wanted. But contributions *to* individual candidates were a different matter. Because they were only "a general expression of support for the candidate"—rather than the contributor's actual "communication" of "the underlying basis" for support—limits on contribution were acceptable. So Congress could set a cap on how much someone could contribute to any one federal candidate. In distinguishing between contributions and expenditures, the Court gave Congress latitude to legislate against "the reality or appearance of corruption inherent in a system permitting unlimited financial contributions"—while at the same time accommodating First Amendment interests.

It was hardly an ideal result. Treating contributions and expenditures differently ended up destroying half of the system that Congress had established. But at least it reflected some judicial deference to the other branches. The gaping loophole left by *Buckley* concerned "issue advocacy." *Buckley* said expenditure limits applied only to communications that "in express terms" advocated "the election or defeat" of an "identified" candidate. If an ad didn't use any of the so-called eight magic words listed in a *Buckley* footnote—*support, defeat, elect* and so on—then the ad (or film or whatever) was exempt from campaign finance law. That formalistic distinction is what allowed those unremitting TV spots during campaign season that never quite told the voter whom to vote for. So, a partisan group's 30-second ad exalting candidate Smith's love of blueberry pie wasn't subject to expenditure limits. Nor was a commercial stating candidate Jones behaved like a war criminal. But any sentient viewer understood the respective ads' take on Smith's and Jones's fitness for office.

The funds that poured into issue advocacy came to be called "soft money." The proliferation of big contributions led Congress to pass the

Bipartisan Campaign Reform Act of 2002, popularly known as McCain-Feingold (after its chief Senate sponsors, Republican John McCain and Democrat Russ Feingold). The law had two key parts: It restricted the ability of political parties themselves to receive soft money, and it aimed to close the *Buckley* issue-advocacy loophole. Now, corporations (and unions) were barred from funding most "electioneering communications"—which were candidate-specific ads broadcast in the 30 days before a primary and in the 60 days before a general election (exactly what would be at issue in *Citizens United*).

While the law was labeled "bipartisan," the politics behind it reflected the standard partisan divide over money in politics. Most Republicans, in defense of free markets and constitutional rights for corporations, opposed regulation. Most Democrats, citing the integrity of elections, favored it. The First Amendment aspect presented the quandary. Both liberals and conservatives treasured freedom of expression, though not always consistently. Republicans were happy to take a tough stand on, say, smut, but not the appearance of political corruption. When it came to campaign finance, Democrats were fine with dissociating money from the idea of speech.

The year after McCain-Feingold passed, the Supreme Court in *McConnell v. FEC* upheld most of its provisions against a First Amendment challenge brought by GOP senator Mitch McConnell. The vote was 5–4, along familiar lines, with Sandra Day O'Connor—the former state legislator—as the swing vote, siding with the liberal bloc. The majority said limits on contributions and spending had only incidental impact on free speech. Moreover, "reams of disquieting" congressional findings had shown the subtle harms of soft money and big money, which not only correlated with electoral victory, but meant preferential access to officeholders. The dissents argued simply that unless corruption was demonstrable—pretty much a quid pro quo bribe—most of the McCain-Feingold reforms were unconstitutional. The majority's looser definition of corruption "sweeps away all protections for speech that lie in its path," Anthony Kennedy wrote.

For proponents of vigorous campaign finance restrictions, the halcyon days were few. A mere four years later, in 2007, the Court did a U-turn, and the conservatives prevailed. In *FEC v. Wisconsin Right to Life*, the justices ruled that the ban on corporate issue ads during election season violated the First Amendment, as long as the ads didn't explicitly endorse or oppose a candidate. "Where the First Amendment is implicated," Chief Justice John Roberts wrote, "the tie goes to the speaker, not the censor." Perhaps, he said, the earlier ruling in *McConnell* could still be constitutionally rationalized. Maybe "express advocacy" ads and their "functional equivalent" both posed dangers to the political process that Congress was allowed to address. But in *Wisconsin RTL*, Roberts claimed, any advocacy in the ads was too disconnected from specific candidates. "Enough is enough," he wrote.

His position was absurd. Created by a pro-life nonprofit, the ads inveighed against senators who were using the filibuster "to block federal judicial nominees" of the pro-life president, George W. Bush. The ads were to run during the blackout period before the 2004 election in which one of those senators, a Democrat, was up for another term. It was entirely clear whom the pro-life ads were opposing—not even close to Roberts's debatable "tie." But because the ads didn't actually mention the Democrat, they weren't the "functional equivalent" of "express advocacy." Such was the chief's justice position.

So, under the First Amendment, the specific ads in the case could not be barred. But there remained the theoretical possibility that barring other ads might still be constitutional. McCain-Feingold lived on, moribund but not buried. Roberts professed to be drawing a line. But as the dissent pointed out, and despite Roberts's protest to the contrary, there really wasn't any way to square *Wisconsin RTL* with *McConnell*. Scalia, who voted with the chief, called him out for trying to have it both ways. "This faux judicial restraint," Scalia seethed, "is judicial obfuscation."

As in *McConnell*, the vote in *Wisconsin RTL* was 5–4, except it went the other way. Nothing of substance had happened in the interim. The facts on the ground were the same. Congress hadn't backed down on its findings about the effects of soft money. All that had changed was the Court's roster. Though Roberts had succeeded William Rehnquist as chief, it didn't matter in this case. But Samuel Alito had replaced O'Connor, and that made all the difference. ("Gosh," O'Connor said the week after *Citizens United*, "I step away for a couple of years and there's no telling what's going to happen." A year later, she acknowledged, "sadly," that she would have voted the other way in *Citizens United*, believing that the Framers in the First Amendment "were talking about the rights of individuals, not corporate entities.")

Three years after *Wisconsin RTL*, in 2010, Roberts no longer tried to play the judicial minimalist. In *Citizens United*, he joined the hard-line conservatives, along with Kennedy, to defang much of campaign finance law and, at least in tenor, transformed American politics.

CITIZENS UNITED, THE CONSERVATIVE NONPROFIT behind the lawsuit, was part of a rich tradition. Political organizations—left and right—were formed to proselytize, strategize and often demonize. Even the last came with the blessing of the First Amendment, which protected all opinions and most accusations short of libel. It didn't make for pretty politics or an informed electorate, but it surely beat a system of censorship. Far better that individual citizens, rather than the government, decided what views were worthy. The verdicts of the people were called elections.

Founded in 1988 by followers of Ronald Reagan, Citizens United described its mission as restoring "the founding fathers' vision of a free nation, guided by the honesty, common sense, and good will of its citizens." The group liked to do so by going after Bill and Hillary Clinton. In 1992, when he was running for president, Citizens United produced an ad that urged voters to "get to know Bill Clinton." All they had to do was dial a number, and for $4.95, they could hear a snippet of his taped calls with a lover, Gennifer Flowers. By 2007, when it appeared certain Hillary was going to run for president, Citizens United decided to make a documentary about her. It aspired to be a right-wing "Fahrenheit 9/11," the 2004 polemic about George W. Bush by liberal filmmaker Michael Moore. Its architect was David Bossie, the head of Citizens United, who had dedicated his career to Clinton-bashing. (Bossie later served as deputy campaign manager for Donald Trump's presidential run.) "Hillary: The Movie" was the result.

Its cast of politicians, journalists and all-purpose "opinion makers" variously described Hillary as "venal," "ruthless" and "sneaky," in addition to "being driven by power" and "steeped in sleaze." The 90-minute combination of horror show and unintentional parody made it look like a co-production of Alfred Hitchcock and Mel Brooks. Citizens United wanted to distribute "Hillary" in part through video-on-demand on cable. The FEC ruled the movie was an electioneering communication covered by McCain-Feingold. That essentially prevented its broadcast during the 2008 Democratic presidential primaries, chiefly between Hillary Clinton and Barack Obama. Citizens United challenged the FEC's ruling, and the Supreme Court agreed to hear the case.

Like *Brown v. Board of Education* and *Roe* and *Bush v. Gore*, it was another important appeal that made two trips to the Court. The first, in a March 2009 argument that resulted in no published opinions, didn't suggest *Citizens United* would be a big deal. Ted Olson, who had won *Bush v. Gore*, began by telling the justices that First Amendment freedoms were being "smothered" by McCain-Feingold—"one of the most complicated, expensive, and incomprehensible regulatory regimes ever invented by the administrative state." But he mostly wanted to argue only that the FEC erred in its specific decision on "Hillary: The Movie." He said McCain-Feingold addressed "short, punchy" ads and simply wasn't meant to apply to this kind of documentary. As a result, he said, the First Amendment issue wasn't paramount.

But the conservative bloc of the Court, given *Wisconsin RTL*, wanted to go all the way. *Citizens United* presented the opportunity to discard the *McConnell* ruling and to finally declare whole sections of McCain-Feingold unconstitutional. This was the quintessence of the emerging Roberts Court. Whatever the chief had counseled about minimalism during his confirmation hearings, *Citizens United* showed beyond doubt that his Court had ideological agendas. If precedent or an instinct toward judicial modesty got in the way, so be it.

One long exchange during the argument crystallized what the case represented for conservatives. The interrogators were Alito, Kennedy and Roberts. Their victim was Malcolm Stewart, the Justice Department lawyer defending McCain-Feingold. Alito began by asking why the law necessarily applied only to video-on-demand electioneering communications, like "Hillary: The Movie." What about DVDs or Internet distribution—or a "campaign biography" in "a public library"? If those contained "the functional equivalent of express advocacy," could their corporate funding be banned? Instead of trying to confine McCain-Feingold to TV ads—the Court had long ruled that broadcasting, because its spectrum was limited, was subject to more regulation than other media—Stewart hedged.

That wasn't enough for Alito, who couldn't believe that Stewart didn't attempt to limit the law's reach. "That's pretty incredible," Alito noted.

Kennedy took up the attack. Again, Stewart accepted the premise—and with it the possibility that political speech in America was about to become less free. So Roberts, still the best litigator in the courtroom, drove home how dangerous—and dubious—the government's position now seemed. "If it's a 500-page book" that "at the end" states, "Vote for X," Roberts asked, "the government could ban *that*?"

Sure thing, Malcolm replied, corporate funding for that book could be a felony because it was "express advocacy."

Nobody actually believed McCain-Feingold purported to criminalize book writing. The FEC had never intimated it. And, anyway, this appeal was limited to a documentary. Stephen Breyer and John Paul Stevens made these points to try to rehabilitate the government's defense of McCain-Feingold. But the cause was lost. Three of the five conservative justices had succeeded in placing the specter of book banning over campaign finance regulation. These three made plain they were pursuing the broadest possible First Amendment inquiry. With Antonin Scalia and Clarence Thomas having already indicated they would void key provisions of McCain-Feingold, there were five votes to allow unlimited corporate spending on issue ads, just as long as the ads were "independent" of the campaigns themselves.

Yet no ruling came that spring of 2009. According to multiple published accounts, the justices, 5–4, were prepared to rule very broadly in favor of Citizens United. Kennedy and Roberts each had drafted opinions that might speak for the Court. Roberts's draft was narrow, building on *Wisconsin RTF*. Historically, the Court's decisions flow from what came before. There's an almost Newtonian momentum to them. But as Scalia had done in *Heller*, Kennedy's draft tossed aside any notion of incrementalism. He was ready to strike down much of McCain-Feingold, as well as to reverse the 2003 *McConnell* ruling and a 1990 precedent. Alito, Thomas and Scalia preferred Kennedy's aggressive approach.

However, David Souter, who by then had announced he was retiring, indicated to the chief he was not only dissenting, but that he thought the Court was acting illegitimately. He was furious, in a way that those who knew him hadn't seen since *Bush v. Gore*. A decision to invalidate McCain-Feingold was one thing—dismissive of Congress, disrespectful of precedent and intensely partisan. But, Souter protested, the Court was doing it in a way that undercut itself as an institution. Citizens United itself hadn't even asked for what the Court was now offering, and so the government hadn't been given a full opportunity to brief the issues. Whether the conservatives had planned all along to use the case to strip down McCain-Feingold—or whether a broader ruling materialized after Malcolm Stewart's book-banning debacle—didn't matter. In effect, Souter was accusing the umpires of changing the strike zone.

The charge made Roberts uneasy. Ever the strategist, playing a long game, he got his colleagues to agree to issue no ruling at all. Instead, *Citizens United* would be reargued. The clash between the First Amendment and corporate campaign spending would then squarely be before the justices.

REARGUMENT CAME IN EARLY SEPTEMBER, which was unusual because the Court begins each term on the first Monday in October. (The justices wanted to be sure the issue was resolved before the November 2010 midterm elections.) There were two different cast members. Justice Souter was gone, replaced by Sonia Sotomayor. And this time, the government was represented by the new solicitor general, Elena Kagan, who herself would join the Court a year later. Sotomayor, hearing her first case, was as skeptical of Citizens United's position as Souter had been. Kagan, arguing the first appellate case of her life, at least disavowed Stewart's answer about book banning. "The government's answer has changed," she informed the justices, which drew a few smiles on the bench and tee-hees from the courtroom audience.

Four months later, in January 2010, it was clear that neither Sotomayor's arrival nor Kagan's debut had changed a thing. The Court simply did what it would have done back in June. Kennedy wrote for the 5–4 conservative majority. Stevens wrote the dissent for the liberals, of which Sotomayor was now part. The core of *Citizens United* was that Congress could no longer ban independent political expenditures by corporations (as well as by nonprofits, unions and other entities that pooled resources). It didn't matter if such entities engaged in direct electoral advocacy. Instead of saying only that Jones behaved like a war criminal, an ad could add, "Don't vote for Jones." Nor did it matter when the ad appeared. As long as expenditures weren't "coordinated" with a candidate (whatever that meant), corporations and other entities could raise and spend unlimited amounts. The expenditures weren't donations to a candidate—they were considered pure political speech, just like distributing leaflets in the town square.

"If the First Amendment has any force," Kennedy declared, "it prohibits Congress from fining or jailing citizens, or associations of citizens, for simply engaging in political speech." By "associations," he meant corporations, large and small. The result of the ruling was to unleash major sums of new money into politics. "Super PACs"—efficient ways to pool the money—were the spawn of *Citizens United* (and a related lower-court ruling two months after it).

In that year, 83 Super PACs spent only $63 million, most of it on ads, most of them negative. By the end of the 2016 presidential year, 2,394 Super PACs spent more than $1 billion on federal elections alone (and raised $700 million on top of that)—again, most of it on negative ads. (Seven percent more was spent on Republican candidates than Democrats.) Do the math: that's a lot of "speech" uttered by a small number of organizations, Yes, the organizations consisted mainly of individual donors, but, no, those individuals weren't Mom and Pop U.S.A. Most Super PAC money came from a few hundred wealthy individuals.

And of course the idea that the Super PACs were wholly detached from the candidates they served was something out of Never-Never Land. Indeed, staffers for some candidates quit to go create Super PACs that did the bidding of those same candidates. In terms of possible corruption, it made no sense to think candidates would be less in the pocket of a Super PAC donor than of a direct donor. If it walks and talks and spends like a supporter, it's someone to whom the candidate might feel beholden. Although individuals after *Citizens United* still were limited in the amount they could directly contribute to a candidate, the existence of Super PACs effectively gutted that constraint. Far from simplifying a tangled body of campaign finance law, *Citizens United* muddled it even more.

But politicians and pundits have wildly overstated the granular impact of Super PACs, as well as *Citizens United* generally. Dire predictions about "opening the floodgates to corporate cash"—whether it materialized or not—missed the point. If details mattered, so did unfairly blaming the ruling, year after year, for every sin of campaign financing. In fact, money spent by Super PACs, though significant, was still dwarfed seven times over by the overall amount spent on elections. And most Super PAC funds came *not* from corporations or big labor, but from individuals. While those individuals were fatcats like Charles Koch and George Soros, they presumably didn't lack for access and influence anyway. And before *Citizens United*, they were already allowed to spend unlimited amounts on elections, as long as they didn't coordinate with a campaign. McCain-Feingold wasn't aimed at them—only at corporations and other entities. (Traditional business corporations themselves were never an issue. Because they didn't want to alienate their customers or clients, those corporations weren't the ones pouring money into campaigns.) In short, *Citizens United* did not by itself poison the political tap. By then, the water already tasted pretty bad. Money was the issue, not just corporate money.

Citizens United did allow corporations to pool money in Super PACs that then used the war chests to buy TV ads—which would otherwise be too costly for anyone other than the richest individuals. Aggregating wealth made it that much more powerful. And by eliminating the 30- and 60-day windows, the ruling enabled more ads to appear, right up to Election Day. But most important, *Citizens United* signaled to the plutocracy that the Court was fully taking a laissez-faire approach. After telling the political culture that all bets were off, independent campaign expenditures shot up. It just wasn't due to those big bad corporations.

IN *CITIZENS UNITED*, KENNEDY AND STEVENS went back and forth about how free speech and campaign finance regulation might properly be balanced. For Kennedy, there wasn't any gray area. Regulation equaled censorship. And "the censorship we now confront is vast in its reach," he warned. "The government has muffled the voices that best represent the most significant segments of the economy." Perhaps such voices, "of manifold corporations," represented the kind of "factionalism" abhorred by the Framers, "but the remedy of destroying the liberty of some factions is worse than the disease." Instead, "the people" should be "entrusted" to judge "what is true and what is false." Talk of censorship, however, was misplaced. Censorship implied that specific viewpoints were banned, rather than certain *means* of expression being restricted. Congress didn't seek to limit Republicans or Democrats, conservatives or liberals. Rather, it aimed to cleanse a political process that, to many rank-and-file citizens, looked rigged.

Stevens, in 90 anguished pages, said Kennedy didn't appreciate the threat of actual corruption, as well as the public perception of it, that went back to the time of Teddy Roosevelt. "While American democracy is imperfect," he added, "few outside the majority of this Court would have thought its flaws included a dearth of corporate money in politics." In what was the last major dissent of his nearly 35 years on the Court, Stevens mocked Kennedy's cavalier conviction that no amount of money from special interests could taint "faith in our democracy."

More significant than the Kennedy-Stevens disagreement on the merits of McCain-Feingold was what they thought about the Court's role in determining the law's fate. Kennedy had long shown he had no problem with Court interventionism. It didn't matter if he was overriding a legislature or a state court or an earlier decision of the justices.

Stevens, on the other hand, insisted the Court had engineered an unnecessary outcome, reaching out to tread on legislative privileges. He took up the baton from Souter, accusing Kennedy and the majority of the worst kind of judicial activism: "assertion over tradition"; "absolutism over empiricism"; "rhetoric over reality"; and favoring "broad constitutional theories over narrow statutory grounds." "Rules of judicial restraint," Stevens wrote, "used to cabin the Court's lawmaking power." Some of his words came from the dissent Souter had drafted in the spring of 2009 but never got to publish. "Essentially," Stevens concluded, "five justices were unhappy with the limited nature of the case before us, so they changed the case to give themselves an opportunity to change the law." Stevens's denunciation of conservative hypocrisy was a continuation of what he had said in *Heller* two years earlier—and in *Bush v. Gore* eight years before that. Then again, the absence of judicial restraint was a keystone of *Roe* a generation earlier.

While Roberts was perfectly content to be in the *Citizens United* majority on the specifics of campaign finance, he didn't have to do the dirty work himself. He assigned the opinion to Kennedy, who gladly agreed to write it. Kennedy never met a First Amendment plea he didn't like, and he certainly didn't mind being the decisive fifth vote again in a landmark case. Roberts, instead, used his concurrence to focus on judicial restraint. He was defensive, all the more so given the grief he continually received over his I'm-just-calling-balls-and-strikes bit at his confirmation hearings. He felt a need to explain why the Court was justified both in overturning recent precedent and in rejecting congressional judgments.

Stare decisis, the chief justice acknowledged, was "the preferred course." And quoting the mighty Justice Oliver Wendell Holmes Jr., he said that questioning the constitutionality of an act of Congress was "the gravest and most delicate duty that this Court is called upon to perform." But on both counts this case—isn't it always *this case?*—was exceptional. Stare decisis was "neither an inexorable command, nor a mechanical formula of adherence to the latest decision." Otherwise, "segregation would be legal, minimum wage laws would be unconstitutional, and the government could wiretap ordinary criminal suspects without first obtaining warrants." And with due respect to Congress's decision to pass McCain-Feingold, there just was "no way" for the Court to avoid the First Amendment issue in *Citizens United*. "Our obligation faithfully to interpret the law," Roberts wrote, required the Court to act boldly. That at least was the assertion—and could be used to undo decades of a lot of settled doctrine in many areas of constitutional law. All it took was five votes.

Six days after the ruling, President Obama condemned the Court, apparently buying in to the "floodgates" narrative. "With all due deference to the separation of powers," he said in his first State of the Union address, *Citizens United* "reversed a century of law that I believe will open the floodgates for special interests, including foreign corporations, to spend without limit in our elections." Below him in the House chamber, six black-robed justices in the front rows watched and listened. One of them, Sam Alito, grimaced and shook his head. He was part of the *Citizens United* majority under fire. And poor Sam was distinctly unaware of the ways of PR.

"Not true," Alito seemed to mutter. TV cameras caught it.

Citizens United became part of the next news cycle, which was how the White House planned it. "With all due deference to the separation of powers" was impromptu on Obama's part, perhaps because he caught sight of the justices just below. But the rest was calculated—the president's language about *Citizens United* appeared in drafts of his speech. While Obama, in a radio address, had already chided the Court ruling, the State of the Union would be heard by far more people. Yet neither he nor staff could have anticipated Alito's response—and Obama was surprised by it, as well as by the contretemps that followed.

The State of the Union is the president's show, and Alito's display was a breach of decorum. But there was plenty of commentary that Obama shouldn't have rebuked the justices to their faces. Even Roberts objected. The chief justice told law students at the University of Alabama that "the image of having the members of one branch of government standing up—literally surrounding the Supreme Court—cheering

and hollering while the Court, according to the requirements of protocol, has to sit there expressionless, I think, is very troubling." Roberts,
and other justices, wondered why any of them kept attending States of
the Union. Orrin Hatch, a Republican senator, called Obama "rude."
(Other justices perfected the art of the stone face. At President Trump's
first State of the Union, in January 2018, when he congratulated himself
for appointing "a great new Supreme Court justice," cameras showed
Neil Gorsuch staring blankly ahead. "Never play poker with this man,"
suggested several Twitter observers.)

Alito, privately, didn't let the matter go. Perhaps he took it personally,
since Obama, as a senator, had voted against his confirmation. Nearly
three years after the State of the Union fuss, late in Obama's 2012 reelection campaign against Mitt Romney, Alito was riding in a van with
clerks on his way back from an event. Alito's no conversationalist. There
were stretches of awkward silence. But as they drove by the Capitol,
unprompted, he looked out the window and said, "You know, I hope
Romney does win the election." He paused, then added dryly, "Because
then, if I don't go to the inauguration, no one will care."

The solicitor general's office at Justice was also less than delighted
about what Obama had done. Although most justices learn to have thick
skins most of the time, some of the government lawyers who argued at
the Court thereafter wondered if any of the conservatives were a little
frostier. Maybe Obama had been impertinent, or maybe the leader of
one branch of government had only been dramatically confronting another. But nobody's authority was challenged. The most revealing aspect
of the criticism of Obama was that the branch he was taking on was
the Court. It was another example of believing the temple at One First
Street was above and apart from politics. Who did the president of the
United States think he was making the Court look like just another political institution? Of course, *Citizens United* did that all by itself.

EVEN SO, THE RULING HAD ITS MERITS. To some degree, money does
enable political speech. In the age of mass media, passing out pamphlets

on the street was quaint at best. Lincoln and Douglas live wouldn't get the numbers of a high school football game on local cable. If you wanted to reach a large audience now, election ads were the way, and ads cost money. Incumbents, being the safe choice, might draw the most financial backing, making it that much easier for them to stay in office. But insurgents at least had the opportunity to go after the money—and perhaps overcome the power of incumbency. If the First Amendment was Darwinian—allowing the marketplace of ideas to determine who spent what, and which ideas won out—then congressional regulation only warped the competition.

It wasn't even self-evident that Congress was correct that big money drowns out other voices. In *Wisconsin Right to Life*, Scalia had made that point about false assumptions. There was "wondrous irony" in "both the genesis and the consequences of [McCain-Feingold]," he wrote in a concurrence. Despite the presumed "corrosive and distorting effects" of "immense aggregations of wealth," corporations and other entities were "utterly impotent to prevent the passage of this legislation." He noted further that restricting corporations might concentrate more power in the rich, who were left untouched by McCain-Feingold. "While these wealthy individuals dominate political discourse," Scalia said, "it is this small, grass-roots organization of Wisconsin Right to Life that is muzzled."

It didn't take a cynic to believe that some in Congress supported McCain-Feingold because it *benefited* incumbents. Rather than "unclogging" channels of communication and change, the law became an "accessory" to "majority tyranny." That's how the scholar John Hart Ely famously described legislation that deserved Court intervention. That, he wrote, was part of the compelling reasoning behind Footnote Four of *Carolene Products*.

Moreover, a lot of spending restrictions seemed to assume voters were morons, so gullible that they would vote for the candidate who blared the most ads at them. The data might show a correlation between money and electoral success, but that sounded less like the fault of money than those who permitted it to dictate their selections. If you voted for the zillionaire-funded hack because she ran the most ads, you ultimately had only yourself to blame. All the 30-second spots in the world hadn't forced you into it. Maybe you should vote *against* a candidate on the ground he spent an obscene amount to try to win. So the argument for letting the First Amendment run free—in the form of cash that facilitates speech—can be a good one.

Ted Olson, the lawyer who argued *Citizens United*, had a favorite way to illustrate how, in his view, a regulation like McCain-Feingold got its First Amendment priorities wrong. Alluding to other Court decisions that championed the right of free expression, he asked, "Why is it easier to dance naked, burn a flag, or wear a T-shirt profanely opposing the draft, than it is to advocate the election or defeat of a president?" That, he said, "cannot be right."

The problem with that analysis was that duly elected legislators disagreed with it. Congress concluded that at the very least corporate cash produced an appearance of corruption, which in turn undermined faith in elected representatives. The restrictions in McCain-Feingold (and other laws going back a century) were a reasonable effort to counter the possibility of harm to the electoral process. That evil surely seemed greater than that posed by naked dancers, burned flags or profane T-shirts—or marches by the Nazis or the Ku Klux Klan—which was why those expressive activities were granted constitutional protection even when legislators thought otherwise. To think of those respective choices in terms of *Carolene Products*, are corporations (or, for that matter, rich people or even gun owners) really the type of "discrete and insular minorities" that demanded Court protection from a tyrannical legislature? General Motors doesn't seem in quite as much need of a judicial shield as African-American schoolchildren in the South.

If one believed legislators acted only in self-interest, and if McCain-Feingold was enacted to entrench incumbents, that would have provided another *Carolene Products* justification for the justices to jump in. But such cynicism excluded the possibility, and evidence, that Congress acted in good faith. Maybe legislators thought the political system had become infected by special interests, and that limiting at least corporate money might be an effective disinfectant. Such motivation might also be born of self-interest. In the long run, the public wasn't likely to see as legitimate a Congress overrun by special interests or perceived to be. The point is that high-minded or cynical explanations for McCain-Feingold weren't mutually exclusive.

At the end of the day, as with most provisions of the Constitution, enforcing the First Amendment requires a balance. "Congress shall make no law . . . abridging the freedom of speech" doesn't truly mean "no law." That's why, as Holmes declared, one couldn't falsely shout fire in a theater. Disclosing atomic secrets could land you in jail for life. A civil suit for slander could result in bankruptcy. Speech (and press) didn't always win. Some rights are subordinate to others. The marketplace of ideas that Kennedy trumpeted had never been entirely unfettered. Having a First Amendment didn't mean you could weaponize it.

Campaign finance restrictions were a close case. One might even call it a tie, to use the words of John Roberts. In such a case, the tie should have gone to Congress, where ongoing adjustment could happen and democratic consensus might build. Congress was the appropriate co-equal branch not because it necessarily was wisest or fairest, but because it most directly, however imperfectly, reflected the "consent of the governed" that Thomas Jefferson celebrated in the Declaration of Independence. Only from the "consent of the governed" did government derive its "just powers." A well-known federal judge, J. Harvie Wilkinson, had called *Heller* and *Roe* two peas in a pod. "The losers in *Heller*—those who supported the D.C. handgun law, or, more accurately, supported the D.C. voters' right to enact it—have cause to feel they have been denied the satisfaction of a fair hearing and an honest fight," he wrote, invoking the words of Scalia. Wilkinson might have added *Citizens United* to the list.

The ruling was not the cause of all that afflicts politics. But *Citizens United* was altogether emblematic of the Court's arrogance about judicial supremacy. Yet again it had swept into the political thicket, taking unto itself an issue that would have been better left to the democratic branches. Worst of all for the Court, *Citizens United* had the perverse effect of bestowing ownership of the problem on the justices. They weren't chiefly to blame for the ills of politics, but their ruling made a lot of people in the country think they were.

CHAPTER 14

A DISDAIN FOR DEMOCRACY

THE ROBERTS COURT FACED A RANGE OF SUBJECTS IN ITS FIRST 10 years—the war on terror, the rights of criminal defendants, the reach of the Internet, Fourth Amendment privacy, capital punishment and national health care. In particular, rulings that curbed presidential power in the 9/11 era might be viewed as prime examples of Court triumphalism. But unless one believed the president had unchecked constitutional authority over enemy combatants, the rulings were simply unremarkable reminders that the president—be it George W. Bush or Barack Obama—was not a king. (That was especially so when Congress, for example, had established rules governing military commissions, which were to be used instead of civilian courts for some prisoners. And to the extent that access to regular courts was considered a fundamental right for most prisoners, it made sense that courts couldn't be excised from the process of determining when.) The constitutional principle of "separation of powers" could similarly be seen at work in decisions about a president's power to dictate immigration policy.

All these cases on presidential authority, though, were very different from *Heller* and *Citizens United*, which represented intrusions on traditional legislative prerogatives. And no subject better illustrated the Court's presumptuousness than race. *Shelby County v. Holder* in 2013 represented the pinnacle of that jurisprudence. That ruling said as much about the Court's view of itself as the underlying decision that drove a stake through the Voting Rights Act of 1965.

Race had a long history at the Court. *Dred Scott* and *Plessy* in the 19th century represented unenlightened times, *Brown* very much the contrary. But *Brown*, in its pronouncement that "separate but equal" was "inherently unequal," articulated only an ideal. In the more than half a century since, the country struggled with how to achieve racial equality in fact. Could the federal government adopt policies that intruded on the rights of states to make their own choices? Could blacks and whites be treated differently in the service of equality? How much authority did Congress have under the three Civil War Amendments on affirmative action and anti-discrimination policies? And was it up to Congress or the Court to determine what laws were constitutionally tolerable?

Voting rights became a primary battleground. Without the actual power to cast a ballot, citizens had little chance to participate in the political process and bring about change. The sanctity of the political process, according to the Court, was central to its thinking in *Bush v. Gore* and *Citizens United*, for example. Yet African Americans for 100 years after the Civil War, particularly in the South, still didn't have the same voting rights as whites. That disenfranchisement happened despite both the Fifteenth Amendment's guarantee of the right to vote and *Brown's* promise of racial equality.

The Fifteenth Amendment's directive was short and clear: "The right of citizens of the United States to vote shall not be denied or abridged" by the federal government or any state "on account of race, color, or previous condition of servitude." But the legacy of slavery and Reconstruction would not be overcome so easily. After the amendment was ratified in 1870, many states contrived ways to circumvent it. In some jurisdictions, African Americans were either legally disenfranchised or subjected to intimidation by the Ku Klux Klan and other groups, so they wound up registering to vote at rates far below those of whites.

Some lawsuits reached the Supreme Court, which several times invalidated various exclusionary tactics. But case-by-case litigation had limited effect on defiant states and no effect on jurisdictions that weren't defendants. And states that concluded they wouldn't be able to forever suppress the black vote turned to gerrymandering to minimize its impact. The big reapportionment cases of the 1960s—*Baker v. Carr* and *Reynolds v. Sims*—established the principle of "one person, one vote," but did not aim to address partisan gerrymandering. (Both in the fall of 2017 and the spring of 2018, the Court took a fresh look at the question, but ultimately punted on the constitutional issue.)

Unlike many other constitutional amendments that lacked explicit means for compliance, the Fifteenth provided, "Congress shall have power to enforce this [amendment] by appropriate legislation." After a century of local efforts—almost always in the South—to thwart African Americans from voting, Congress passed appropriate legislation.

Spurred by civil rights leaders as well as events, President Johnson in March 1965 offered up a bill that would become the Voting Rights Act. LBJ, a son of the South, did so eight days after "Bloody Sunday," when nonviolent demonstrators in Alabama were attacked by state and local police on the now-iconic Edmund Pettus Bridge. Marching from Selma to Montgomery, the demonstrators fought for the right to vote. LBJ's speech, before a joint session of Congress, has been called his greatest. Its singular moment came when Johnson declared, "We shall overcome"—which was the anthem of the civil rights movement. In Selma, watching on TV, Martin Luther King Jr. wept.

Signed into law in August, the Voting Rights Act of 1965 (VRA) was a crucial accomplishment of the civil rights movement and of President Lyndon Johnson's Great Society. The law aimed to destroy the barriers that continued long after passage of the Fifteenth Amendment. The most important VRA provisions barred literacy tests and other devices that disenfranchised racial minorities. It also imposed federal oversight on those jurisdictions that had engaged in persistent discrimination. In essence, the law distinguished between states that had behaved well and those that had not—this was discrimination itself, but with legal justification. The affected states loathed it. Apart from chafing at federal monitoring generally, the Voting Rights Act seemed to be a continuation of Reconstruction, a century after the fact. In *Shelby County*, the Court considered whether continued federal oversight was permissible or whether Congress had exceeded its bounds.

BUT THERE WAS A LARGER context to *Shelby County*, which culminated nearly a decade of undisguised hostility by the Roberts Court toward racial preferences. Gun rights were a divisive issue, but only to relatively few. Campaign finance mattered in elections, but those were annual occurrences. Race, however, pervaded American life. How the justices dealt with it offered a telling portrait.

Six years before *Shelby County*, the Court had made clear its new attitude toward racial discrimination and government efforts to remedy it. The case was called *Parents Involved*. The issue was a voluntary integration plan in Seattle (and a related plan in Louisville, Kentucky). The context was not the Fifteenth Amendment, but the Fourteenth Amendment's guarantee of equal protection. Cases like *Brown* had involved school districts that engaged in "de jure segregation"—abject, old-fashioned discrimination against African Americans that was rooted in official government policy. By contrast, the districts in Seattle and Louisville had long been largely segregated because neighborhoods were segregated and students typically attended school near their homes. Neighborhoods turned out like that—"de facto segregation"—because of individual choices rather than government edict.

To achieve more integration, Seattle and Louisville decided to consider race in assigning students to schools. In Seattle, students were allowed to apply to any high school. Because some became oversubscribed, the district had to use tiebreakers, one of which was race. The goal was to keep each school roughly in line with the racial mix of the overall student population. That could mean whites or nonwhites would be favored in a particular school in a given year, depending on parental preferences.

(In Louisville, the district used race in both elementary school assignments and transfer requests.)

Various parents sued, claiming a violation of equal protection. In their own defense, the school districts cited two Court cases from four years earlier that allowed race-conscious classifications so long as they were "narrowly tailored" to advance a "compelling government interest." That was the Court's way of saying it would permit racial classifications if at least five justices agreed with a school's plan. The bar would be high, but not insurmountable. In the key case, *Grutter v. Bollinger*, the Court in 2003 approved an affirmative action plan at the University of Michigan law school that included race as one factor in "holistic" admissions. If a heterogeneous student body was a legitimate goal, then something beyond grades, test scores and recommendations could be considered.

Justice Sandra Day O'Connor led the 5-to-4 majority. Government "has a compelling interest in attaining a diverse student body," she wrote, in one of her last pivotal opinions. The Court was confirming what it had said a quarter-century earlier in the 1978 *Bakke* decision, its first major affirmative action case. "It has been 25 years" since the Court "first approved the use of race to further an interest in student body diversity," O'Connor wrote. "Since that time, the number of minority applicants with high grades and test scores has indeed increased. We expect that 25 years from now, the use of racial preferences will no longer be necessary to further the interest approved today."

In *Parents Involved*—with O'Connor gone—the Court concluded that 25 years was too long. The justices, 5–4, rejected the voluntary plans in Seattle and Louisville, reversing what lower federal courts had ruled. Respect for precedent had disappeared. The facts of racial disparity hadn't changed. But the dramatis personae of the Court had. Gone, too, was any deference to the judgment of local lawmakers, who in these cases were seeking not to perpetuate segregation but to foster integration. It wasn't that five justices thought the moment that O'Connor envisioned had arrived. Rather, the majority believed, the earlier *Grutter* ruling was deeply flawed, perhaps even wrong, though they didn't say so. Instead, they suggested, *Grutter* had nothing to do with *Parents Involved* because *Grutter* involved an "array of qualifications and characteristics" besides race, whereas in *Parents Involved* race alone was "determinative." It wasn't much of a distinction. Because Samuel Alito had replaced O'Connor, Anthony Kennedy now cast the deciding vote. Clarence Thomas and Antonin Scalia also joined the majority, with Thomas alone declaring that "racial imbalance is not segregation" and couldn't by itself justify the voluntary plans to mitigate the imbalance.

But it was Chief Justice John Roberts who chose to write for the Court. He invoked *Brown* five times, insisting that historic decision commanded the outcome. "When it comes to using race to assign children to schools, history will be heard," Roberts wrote. The chief then provided the capstone in *Parents Involved*. "The way to stop discrimination on the basis of race," he wrote in a line that became an instant classic, "is to stop discriminating on the basis of race." Never mind that he lifted the language, without attribution, from an opinion in a lower court's consideration of the lawsuit—an appropriation that Breyer called out without even having to mention Roberts's name.

Breyer was less subtle in the rest of his dissent. The ruling left him shaken. He was not a justice to show passion in his opinions. Going back to when he taught at Harvard and worked for Senator Ted Kennedy, his interests in the law were about deregulation, economics and government structure. But in *Parents Involved* he saw a Court turning away from the commitment, yet unfulfilled, of *Brown*. He expressed his dismay using the most effective weapon in a justice's arsenal: He spoke from the bench after Roberts announced the Court's decision.

Oral dissents were rare—only a handful each term. Though justices typically laid out in writing their analytical objections to a ruling, a dissent from the bench served as an exclamation point. It might include lines from the written version, but it allowed for a display of emotion—pauses, cadence, facial expression—that a page couldn't convey, as well as language perhaps less suited for posterity. Many of the justices believed that for all the care that went into written opinions, it was the delivery of occasional, unofficial summaries from the bench—for both dissents and concurrences—that provided the clearest window on their colleagues' thinking.

For an uncommonly long 21 minutes, Breyer spoke. "It wasn't that long ago that people of different races drank from separate fountains, rode on separate buses, studied in separate schools," he said. "In this court's finest hour, *Brown vs. Board of Education* challenged that history and helped to change it. For *Brown* held out . . . the promise of true racial equality, not as a matter of fine words on paper, but as a matter of everyday life." To invalidate the voluntary Seattle and Louisville plans, he concluded, "is to threaten the promise of *Brown*." *Parents Involved* was a decision "that the Court and the nation will come to regret."

Without ever mentioning the two new justices by name, he underscored how their arrival had created a new Court. Reading the sentence slowly, drawing out the key words, he said, "It is not often in the law that *so few* have *so quickly* changed *so much*." Breyer believed his *Parents Involved* dissent to be the most important opinion in his more than 20 years on the Court.

John Paul Stevens, also in dissent, excoriated Roberts for calling on *Brown* to make his case. Race-conscious efforts to voluntarily integrate schools, he said, were not the same as race-conscious efforts to mandate segregated schools. There was a "cruel irony" to citing *Brown*, given that in 1954 "it was only black schoolchildren" who were ordered "where they could and could not go to school based on the color of their skin." By contrast, "the history books do not tell stories of white children struggling to attend black schools." Stevens said Roberts's "rewriting" of *Brown* was akin to Anatole France's observation, "The majestic equality of the law forbids rich and poor alike to sleep under bridges, to beg in the streets, and to steal their bread." Stevens kept up the attack, concluding, "It is my firm conviction that no member of the Court that I joined in 1975 would have agreed with today's decision." With that parting shot, he reminded Roberts that one of those justices was William Rehnquist, Roberts's predecessor as chief and for whom he had clerked.

It was true that Kennedy's concurrence—the critical fifth vote— potentially tempered the impact of *Parents Involved*. He didn't agree that the Fourteenth Amendment had to be colorblind. Instead, he wrote that "de facto resegregation in schooling" and "racial isolation" were problems that school districts could constitutionally address, as long as the solutions were "narrowly tailored." He mentioned, for example, that "strategic site selection of new schools" and "targeted" recruiting might be acceptable, even if race-conscious—as long as placement decisions about individual students weren't based on race. (Six years later, in *Fisher v. University of Texas*, Kennedy similarly aimed for a middle ground, reaffirming that race could be a factor in university admissions as long as it wasn't the only factor.)

Breyer responded that alternatives mentioned by Kennedy had already failed in Seattle and Louisville. But his was a broader point. "I do not claim to know how best to stop harmful discrimination; how best to create a society that includes all Americans; how best to overcome our serious problems of increasing de facto segregation, troubled inner city schooling, and poverty correlated with race," he wrote. "But, as a judge, I do know that the Constitution does not authorize judges to dictate solutions." Rather, he said, "the Constitution creates a democratic political system through which the people themselves must together find answers." They did that through legislatures, city councils and school boards. "The Court should leave them to their work." It was "for them to decide whether the best way to stop discrimination on the basis of race is to stop discriminating on the basis of race." More than just pulling back from *Brown*, it was the Court's institutional arrogance that Breyer was indicting.

Sonia Sotomayor wasn't a justice when *Parents Involved* was decided. She didn't join the Court until two years later, becoming its second current minority member. But when she did come on, she bided her time to answer the chief justice's views on race. The opportunity arrived in 2014 in *Schuette v. Coalition to Defend Affirmative Action*. Sotomayor herself had benefited from race-conscious admissions at Yale Law School, just as Justice Thomas had. "To doubt the worth of minority students' achievement when they succeed is really only to present another face of the prejudice that would deny them a chance even to try," she recalled in her autobiography.

Now, in *Schuette*, Sotomayor called Roberts's maxim on stopping discrimination "a sentiment out of touch with reality." "Race matters," she wrote in a fiery dissent. "Race matters in part because of the long history of racial minorities' being denied access to the political process. . . . Race matters for reasons that really are only skin deep, that cannot be discussed any other way, and that cannot be wished away. Race matters to a young man's view of society when he spends his teenage years watching others tense up as he passes, no matter the neighborhood where he grew up. Race matters to a young woman's sense of self when she states her hometown, and then is pressed, 'No, where are you *really* from?' . . . Race matters because of the slights, the snickers, the silent judgments that reinforce that most crippling of thoughts: 'I do not belong here.' "

And then Sotomayor addressed Roberts directly. "In my colleagues' view, examining the racial impact of legislation only perpetuates racial discrimination. This refusal to accept the stark reality that race matters is regrettable. The way to stop discrimination on the basis of race is to speak openly and candidly on the subject of race. . . . We ought not sit back and wish away, rather than confront, the racial inequality that exists in our society. It is this view that works harm, by perpetuating the facile notion that what makes race matter is acknowledging the simple truth that race *does* matter."

Roberts took offense. Simmering, he wrote a brief reply. "To disagree with the dissent's views on the costs and benefits of racial preferences is not to 'wish away, rather than confront' racial inequality," the chief said. "People can disagree in good faith on this issue, but it similarly does more harm than good to question the openness and candor of those on either side of the debate."

The debate intensified as the Court tackled voting rights.

THE VOTING RIGHTS ACT OF 1965 was a perfect illustration of the role that the Framers intended for the legislative branch. Congress identified a problem, crafted a solution that worked, and periodically updated the law to account for changed factual circumstances. And though the VRA boldly established federal control over voting matters, which traditionally were the province of states, the statute received wide praise. On signing an extension of the VRA in 1982, President Reagan said it "proves our unbending commitment to voting rights . . . the crown jewel of American liberties, and we will not see its luster diminished."

Section 2 of the VRA provided the bottom line, barring racial discrimination in voting nationwide, applying to all states and localities. Section 5—in theory, a temporary provision—imposed additional hurdles on certain jurisdictions that had historically engaged in discrimination and had low voter turnout as an apparent result. These jurisdictions were required to earn federal approval—called "preclearance"—before they could make any changes to voting procedures. The rationale of Section 5 was that relying on lawsuits filed under Section 2 wouldn't be enough to ensure full compliance.

The preclearance requirement initially applied to six states in their entirety and part of one other. Later, three more states, as well as parts of six others, became subject to Section 5. Most of the "covered" jurisdictions were in the South, but also included were localities in such places as California and New York. To change their voting procedures, the jurisdictions had to show the U.S. attorney general (or a federal court in Washington) that a change had neither discriminatory intent nor discriminatory effect. A jurisdiction—whether an entire state, or only a county, city, town or other political subdivision—could "bail out" of Section 5's strictures if it had a spotless record for the prior decade. But the point was to place the burden on certain jurisdictions, in advance, to show they weren't discriminating—rather than on African Americans, in piecemeal litigation after an election had already happened, to show that jurisdictions were. Even when plaintiffs won those suits, victory didn't remedy their lost opportunity to vote.

The VRA required Section 5 to be reauthorized regularly. Congress did so four times, in 1970, 1975, 1982 and 2006. The most recent authorization passed the Senate by a 98-to-0 vote, and the House, 390–33. President George W. Bush signed the renewal, which was scheduled to last to 2032. In its fact-finding for the 2006 extension, Congress heard from more than 60 witnesses representing different views, and assembled a massive evidentiary record about racial discrimination in covered states. But much of the evidence Congress cited in 2006 dated to the 1975 extension, which itself was based on elections in 1972 or earlier.

That was a long time ago—and a fact that in *Shelby County* would come back to haunt legislators.

Between 1984 and 2013, nearly 200 covered jurisdictions were granted bailouts. It was the rule, rather than the exception, for a petitioning jurisdiction to win. Between 1965 and 2013, the Justice Department received 556,000 proposed individual changes in voting procedures, and it precleared virtually all of them. But the procedure was burdensome, taking time and money. And for jurisdictions not eligible for a bailout, complying with the VRA took effort as well. Moreover, the statute had teeth when it needed them. For example, before *Shelby County*, states had been denied the ability to implement voter ID requirements, reduce early-voting periods, toughen voting-reinstatement rules against felons, and redraw voting districts—all because the Justice Department or a federal court found the changes to be discriminatory in their application.

Nonetheless, states (and their subdivisions) continually litigated against the VRA for reasons beyond merely saving the millions in compliance costs—or to regain the opportunity to disenfranchise minorities. The states detested being under the thumb of the federal government, regarding Section 5 as a symbol of shame. That complaint—whether it was described as federalism or states' rights—was as old as the Republic. When Section 5 was last reauthorized, a Republican congressman from Georgia spoke for many. "Congress is declaring from on high that states with voting problems 40 years ago can simply never be forgiven, that Georgians must eternally wear the scarlet letter because of the actions of their grandparents and great-grandparents," said Lynn Westmoreland, who opposed reauthorization. "We have repented and we have reformed."

FOUR TIMES, THE COURT HAD upheld the VRA's constitutionality. The year after it was enacted, for example, the justices declared the law a rational response to the "unremitting and ingenious defiance" of the Fifteenth Amendment by Southern states intent on "perpetuating voting discrimination in the face of adverse federal court decrees." But in 2009 the Roberts Court agreed to revisit the question. In the *Northwest Austin* case, a small utility district in south-central Texas challenged Section 5. The municipal district had its own elected board and was required to obtain preclearance before it relocated poll locations.

As in other constitutional litigation like *Heller* (or *Brown v. Board of Education*, for that matter), a private advocacy group, rather than the actual litigant, was the impetus behind *Northwest Austin* (also called *NAMUDNO*). The organization was the conservative Project on Fair Representation, a one-man show that sought to contest "racial and ethnic classifications and preferences" in American society. An indefatigable former stockbroker named Edward Blum founded the organization, which recruited the Texas utility district just days after the latest VRA reauthorization (and later backed the plaintiffs in the *Fisher* affirmative action case and *Shelby County* itself). Blum liked to call himself "Yenta the matchmaker" in constitutional litigation. "I find the plaintiff, I find the lawyer, and I put them together, and then I worry about it for four years," he explained in one interview.

Given the Court's ruling two years earlier in *Parents Involved*, there seemed to be five voices sympathetic to changing course on Section 5, if Kennedy would join Roberts, Scalia, Thomas and Alito. In particular, Breyer and Ginsburg worried about a Court that was on the verge of a perilous retrenchment on race. The oral argument confirmed that apprehension—that a majority of justices believed the discriminatory world of 1965 was long gone. The argument also exquisitely reflected the Court's scorn for Congress. For most jurists, the lopsided Senate and House votes in favor of reauthorizing Section 5 might have called for deference. For Scalia, it was cause for suspicion. "You know," he informed one of the lawyers defending Section 5, "the Sanhedrin [the ancient Israeli judicial body] used to have a rule that if the death penalty was pronounced unanimously, it was invalid, because there must be something wrong."

Scalia then questioned the entire premise of legislation itself, which operates on majority rule. "Do you ever seriously expect Congress to vote against a re-extension of the Voting Rights Act?" he asked. "Twenty-five years from now? Fifty years from now? When?"

His implication appeared to be that because the other branch couldn't be trusted to make judgments *he* deemed rational and responsible, the Court would have to do so. In short, Scalia trusted himself more than he trusted the citizenry or the representatives it elected. Was this the same justice who just 24 hours later in a ruling on gay rights would castigate the Court's intervention? In that case, *United States v. Windsor,* which struck down the federal Defense of Marriage Act, Scalia dissented, saying, "We might have let the People decide." In overriding Congress, the majority in *Windsor* had "cheated both sides, robbing the winners of an honest victory, and the losers of the peace that comes from a fair defeat. We owed both of them better." Evidently, what the justices owed to "the People" depended on which side of the culture wars the issue fell.

Kennedy, ever secure in second-guessing other governmental actors, joined Scalia in questioning congressional competence. "Congress has made a finding that the sovereignty of Georgia is less than the sovereign dignity of Ohio?" he asked. "The sovereignty of Alabama is less than the sovereign dignity of Michigan? And the governments in one are to be trusted less than the governments in the other?" Boring in on the lawyer arguing for the Justice Department, he advised, "You have a very substantial burden if you're going to make that case." It might have been a fair point about federalism—except for the existence of the Fifteenth Amendment itself and the legislation that Congress passed under its command.

Justice Kennedy also wanted to know why Congress in 2006 hadn't seemed to take seriously the possibility that historical practices of discrimination had lessened. Did not the election of Barack Obama, the nation's first African-American president—six months before the argument—suggest progress? Had Congress dug deeper and updated the VRA's coverage formula, might not the list of covered jurisdictions be different? The problem with that argument was that Congress passed scores of bills based on debatable evidence and the Court left those statutes untouched.

After *Northwest Austin* was argued, there were likely five votes to strike down parts of the VRA based on a theory of "equal" state sovereignty. But Roberts—ever shrewd, and genuinely concerned about the

Court appearing unduly aggressive—maneuvered his colleagues to a narrower decision. Rather than resolve the constitutional question right now, he again opted for the long game, as he had done in the conference in *Citizens United* that same month. When the Court in June 2009 released *Northwest Austin*, its very next announcement in the courtroom was that *Citizens United* would be reargued later that summer. Such patience—or "faux judicial restraint," as Scalia called it in an earlier context—was easy enough to do when your tenure on the Court might be 30 years or more.

BY AN 8-TO-1 VOTE IN *Northwest Austin*, the Court ruled that the Texas utility district was indeed eligible for a bailout from Section 5, even though it was a tiny political subdivision within a larger county. The VRA makes no mention of such entities, and the Court's decision was, to be charitable, creative. But it allowed Roberts to play diplomat, with all the justices other than Thomas going along. (Articulating the most radical view, Thomas wanted to strike down Section 5 immediately.) Though the broader constitutional issue "has attracted ardent briefs from dozens of interested parties," Roberts wrote, "the importance of the question does not justify our rushing to decide it. Quite the contrary: Our usual practice is to avoid the unnecessary resolution of constitutional questions."

An instinct of "avoidance" was in the best traditions of minimalism, preached early on in American history by Chief Justice John Marshall and echoed by such later justices as Oliver Wendell Holmes Jr., Louis Brandeis and Felix Frankfurter. Many times, but not much of late, the Court had steered clear of big questions, preferring to let the elected branches handle them or to allow lower courts to explore them further. Roberts himself, on the job for eight months, told graduating law students at Georgetown in May 2006 that deciding cases "on the narrowest possible ground" helped ensure that "we not embarrass the future too much." In announcing *Northwest Austin* from the bench, Roberts even offered an olive branch to Congress, saying, "We appreciate that the members of Congress take the same oath we do to uphold the Constitution."

The beauty of Roberts's approach was that he got to dance at two weddings at the same time. By taking a pass on the constitutional question, he provided the guise of modesty, disinclined as he was to cause massive disruption in a system that had been in place for four decades. If Congress acted, he might look like a genius. Commentators praised the chief's prudence. "Roberts blinked," blogged a leading expert on election law.

That view failed to see a broader agenda. The chief barely hid it, using his opinion to get in his shots about the VRA. Even if the statute remained for the moment, Roberts had already made clear he believed, as he had declared the year before: "It is a sordid business, this divvying us up by race."

Those attitudes harked back to what Roberts had written in 1982 while working at the Justice Department. Roberts urged the Reagan administration to take an "aggressive stance" against efforts to strengthen statutory protections for minorities. He claimed proposed changes would amount to "a quota system," resulting in "reverse discrimination." When Reagan agreed to compromise, Roberts complained in a memo that "we were burned." (Roberts later said those views reflected only him being an advocate for a client.) His views—which realized full voice in *Parents Involved*, *Northwest Austin* and *Shelby County*—seemed to turn the venerated idea of *Carolene Products* on its head. Whereas *Carolene Products* aspired to protect "discrete and insular minorities," Roberts was suggesting that it was the resentments of majorities that deserved judicial solicitude. As various commentators noted, all five justices in the Roberts Court rulings in *Parents Involved*, *Northwest Austin* and *Shelby County* were appointed by President Reagan or worked in his administration.

Although "the historic accomplishments of the Voting Rights Act are undeniable," Roberts proclaimed in *Northwest Austin* that "things have changed in the South." Black voter turnout and black registration rates now approached "parity." "Blatantly discriminatory evasions of federal decrees" were rare. Minority candidates held office "at unprecedented

levels." During oral argument, Roberts had pointed out that 99.98 percent
of requests for preclearance were granted. That, he suggested, meant
the requirements were "sweeping far more broadly" than necessary. The
lawyer for the Justice Department said no, the high percentage meant
Section 5 was a deterrent, to which Roberts replied, "Well, that's like
the old elephant whistle. You know, I have this whistle to keep away the
elephants. . . . There are no elephants, so it must work." It was another
great line, but its logic seemed to apply to any coercive legislation: How
can one ever prove a causal link between a prohibition and the absence
of the proscribed conduct?

The chief acknowledged that improvements in black participation
were "no doubt due in significant part to the Voting Rights Act itself,"
but it was "a very different nation" than the one that passed the VRA.
Any "current burdens" had to be justified "by current needs," he said.
Whether they did, however, was "a difficult constitutional question we
do not answer today."

Tomorrow was a different story. Roberts was letting Congress off
the constitutional hook for now, but he was warning legislators to fix
the VRA to the Court's liking. They could rethink the coverage formula for Section 5 and then update it—or else, next round, the Court
wouldn't be so deferential. The blame, though, would be on Congress,
as the argument had it. One observer called this the "doctrine of one
last chance"—"avoidance on steroids, but with an expiration date." The
irony was that Roberts's play seemed to invite future legal challenges
against the VRA. If that were so, his ruling wasn't really about judicial
deference at all. It was about setting up Congress, giving future litigants
a roadmap, and paving an easier way for the Court to kill off the VRA
entirely. None of the liberal justices had even countered his extended
critique of the VRA. If Congress ended up doing nothing, he had laid
the groundwork for decisive judicial intervention. And if that happened,
nobody could fault the justices next time.

Lawmakers didn't even see the trap. Predictably, they did nothing. It
was a polarized age to begin with. And it would be a political challenge
for most legislators to appear soft on racial discrimination—which had

been Scalia's point during the argument in *Northwest Austin*. The door was open for the right jurisdiction with the right Section 5 grievance. *Shelby County* would be the case that made it to the Court in the next go-round that Roberts seemed to have so well foreseen.

EDWARD BLUM, WHO HAD SET *Northwest Austin* in motion and was frustrated when the Court wriggled out, quickly began searching for the best case to finish the job. He found Shelby County, Alabama, a predominantly white, fast-growing Republican suburb of Birmingham. For decades, Shelby had the reputation as the "moonshining-est" county in the state; "every joke having to do with bootlegging in Alabama has a Shelby County twist," according to a 1935 newspaper account. It was ideal for Blum's purposes because—unlike the Texas utility district (and many other jurisdictions)—it wasn't eligible for Section 5 bailout; Shelby had previously made electoral changes without seeking preclearance, in violation of the law. A court would have to face the VRA's constitutionality head-on.

The amazing thing about the case was how easily it might never have happened. It hadn't dawned on county officials themselves to fight the VRA. That was because of how ingrained the statute was, as well as the reality that litigation cost a fortune. After *Northwest Austin*, Blum approached the county with the idea of going to court. He said that his nonprofit, which was funded by foundations and wealthy individuals, would pay all the bills. (As it turned out, because there didn't need to be a trial or other time-consuming fact-finding, the actual costs totaled only about $250,000.) Blum himself had done the digging in online Justice Department filings to find the right jurisdiction. If Shelby didn't go along, Blum had a county in Mississippi that was game.

In April 2010, Shelby filed suit. Two lower courts ruled against the county, with one stating, "Congress drew reasonable conclusions from the extensive evidence it gathered and acted pursuant to the Fourteenth and Fifteenth Amendments, which entrust Congress with ensuring that

the right to vote . . . is not abridged on account of race. In this context, we owe much deference to the considered judgment of the people's
elected representatives."

The Supreme Court agreed to hear Shelby County's appeal. The argument, in February 2013, replayed some of the historical debate reflected in *Northwest Austin*: about the vestiges of slavery, the progress of
civil rights, congressional authority and the autonomy of states. Echoing
what he had said four years earlier, Scalia pooh-poohed the overwhelming votes in the Senate and House to reauthorize Section 5. To him,
they were less the evidence of belief in a "continuing need for this piece
of legislation" than of the "perpetuation of racial entitlement." Scalia
apprised the solicitor general, Donald Verrilli, that "whenever a society
adopts racial entitlements, it is very difficult to get out of them through
the normal political processes. . . . And I am fairly confident [Section 5]
will be reenacted in perpetuity unless—unless a court can say it does not
comport with the Constitution. . . . Even the name of it is wonderful:
the Voting Rights Act. Who is going to vote against that in the future?"

It was striking that none of Scalia's tirade had anything to do with
the originalism he had so eagerly embraced in *Heller* five years before.
Whereas his "normal political processes" seemed to be part of the bar-
gain of self-governance reflected in the Constitution, his "perpetuation
of racial entitlement" sounded more like a stock line from a campaign
speech. Even if Congress was lazy or cowardly, was that not its privilege
in the constitutional scheme of things? Scalia couldn't handle Congress
being Congress. For him, Congress's apparent submission to what was
politically prudent made its decisions unlawful.

Sotomayor stewed over Scalia's loaded assessment of Congress and
the statute. She waited for the right moment in the argument. When
the county's lawyer, Bert Rein, returned to the lectern for the rebuttal
phase of his argument, she didn't even allow him to begin. Staring down
at Rein from the bench, and without referring to Scalia by name, she
asked, "Do you think that the *right to vote* is a racial entitlement in Section 5?" Rein could only respond, "I think that the world is not perfect."

Kennedy, naturally, wanted to play the part of super-legislator. He
recognized that Congress had four times renewed the VRA. "But times

change," he said. "The Marshall Plan was very good, too," referring to massive U.S. support to help Europe recover after World War II. If Alabama was to amend its discriminatory ways in the 21st century, he asked, "Is it better off doing that if it's an independent sovereign or if it's under the trusteeship of the United States?"

Breyer tried to offer Kennedy a different historical narrative. When the VRA was enacted in 1965, according to Breyer, it was in the context of "an old disease"—200 years of slavery, followed by 80 years of Jim Crow. Now, there had been more than four decades with the VRA in effect, and the statute had "helped a lot." It did so by exercising federal coercive power selectively—which was why not all 50 states were subject to preclearance. "Of course it was aimed at treating some states differently than others," Breyer said. "What do you think the Civil War was about?"

Roberts, jettisoning the fig leaf of deference in *Northwest Austin*, also wanted to take on Congress. The coverage formula it readopted in 2006 appeared downright irrational to him. "Do you know which state has the worst ratio of white-voter turnout to African-American-voter turnout?" he asked Verrilli.

"I do not" was the answer.

The chief noted it was Massachusetts, which wasn't a suspect state under the VRA. By contrast, he said, Mississippi—which was a covered jurisdiction—had the best ratio, "where African-American turnout actually exceeds white turnout." Considering the statistics, Roberts bluntly asked Verrilli, how could the Justice Department suggest "that the citizens in the South are more racist than citizens in the North"? (The day after the argument, the Massachusetts secretary of state accused the chief of "using phony statistics.")

Roberts's questions, like those of Kennedy, were nothing more than judicial disagreements with congressional judgments. What such disagreements had to do with constitutional law was something the justices didn't explain—and that was the larger issue in *Shelby County*. What was the institutional role of the Court in this dispute? Interested parties could differ on how far the modern South, as well as the rest of the nation, had come since the Civil War—and whether the onus placed by the VRA was still appropriate. That really wasn't the question. Instead, the issue was who got to decide. During one exchange, Rein told the Court that "the problem to which the Voting Rights Act was addressed is solved . . ."

"That is the question, isn't it?" interrupted Justice Elena Kagan. "But who gets to make that judgment really? Is it . . . the Court or is it Congress?"

"Congress can examine it, Congress can make a record," Rein replied. But it was "up to the Court to determine whether the problem indeed has been solved."

"Well," Kagan said, "that's a big, new power that you're giving us—that we have the power now to decide whether racial discrimination has been solved? I did not think that that fell within our bailiwick."

Her restraint was a wise ideal. But it had little to do with real life. From *Roe* to *Bush v. Gore,* from *Heller* to *Citizens United,* the Court had concluded its bailiwick was vast and wide. Racial discrimination was just another area in which the justices trusted themselves most.

THE COURT DOESN'T ANNOUNCE WHEN decisions will be handed down. But as a term draws to a close, if any of the big cases are left, veterans of the Court scene know to be there to see history made. On June 25, 2013—the penultimate day of the term—the pews in the 400-seat courtroom were full. The solicitor general was there, along with two of his recent predecessors. So was retired Justice Sandra Day O'Connor, in a VIP section—perhaps to see firsthand what her absence on the Court meant. *Shelby County* was the last ruling of the morning, and it surprised nobody. The shock would have been if the Court stepped back from the brink.

The justices ruled, 5–4, in favor of the county. The battle lines were the same as in *Northwest Austin* and so many other important cases. The four liberals—Ginsburg, Breyer, Sotomayor and Kagan—dissented. The four conservatives—Roberts, Scalia, Thomas and Alito—were in the majority. Kennedy was the fulcrum. But while he had sided with the Court's liberal bloc in other cases on race—*Fisher* just the day before, and *Parents Involved* six years earlier—in *Shelby County* he was resolute. Despite efforts by the liberals, Kennedy didn't brood this time and the outcome in *Shelby County* was never in question. Kennedy liked to impress on his clerks year after year that for him "the will of the people" was paramount. Yet when their choices resulted in an outcome he didn't like—or in this instance, they failed to exercise their will at all—he was altogether willing to impose his own. For Kennedy, self-government was sacred, except when it wasn't. And when it was his vote that made the difference, so much the better. No justice was more taken with the rhetoric of judicial supremacy.

What the Court had threatened in *Northwest Austin* became reality in *Shelby County*. Roberts wrote for the majority, just as he had in other key race cases. No policy issue was more important to the chief than racial discrimination—and whether the Court's word on it should be last. "Our country has changed," Roberts wrote, offering up as proof the fact Selma itself now had an African-American mayor. If Congress didn't revise the VRA, the justices would—now declaring that the VRA's dated coverage formula was unconstitutional. Absent any formula to follow, Section 5 was dead. No longer would any jurisdiction have to get federal approval to change its voting practices. Section 2 remained: Litigants could still sue after the fact. And Congress was free to come up with a new formula, though in that unlikely event, it was hardly apparent that the Court in a future case would be more forgiving. Some of the conservative justices were open to deeming preclearance to be entirely unconstitutional; Thomas had already staked out that position.

Any semblance of constitutional "avoidance" had vanished. Roberts's self-professed restraint in *Northwest Austin* was gone, replaced by a disregard for prior rulings, along with his primers on the history of the South and the purpose of the Fifteenth Amendment. Most of all, his opinion overflowed with disdain for Congress and democracy itself. "The Fifteenth Amendment is not designed to punish for the past; its purpose is to ensure a better future," the chief wrote. "Congress—if it is to divide the states—must identify those jurisdictions to be singled out on a basis that makes sense in light of current conditions." And in case lawmakers had forgotten, Roberts reminded them of the ticking clock he had set: "We made that clear in *Northwest Austin*." Congress's "failure to act leaves us today no choice" but to strike down part of the VRA. Apparently, there was a time limit for democracy.

So why did Roberts, two years later in *Obergefell*, ridicule the idea that justices "could impose their will" based on a failure to act? Quoting his mentor and predecessor, Chief Justice Rehnquist, Roberts wrote, "Surely the Constitution does not put either the legislative branch or the executive branch in the position of a television quiz show contestant so that when a given period of time has elapsed and a problem remains unresolved by them, the federal judiciary may press a buzzer and take its turn at fashioning a solution."

Roberts's use of "no choice" was fanciful, considering that four of nine justices disagreed. The constitutional basis for *Shelby County* was no more persuasive. For all their failings, *Heller* aimed to root itself in the Second Amendment, and *Citizens United* claimed the mantle of the First. By comparison, *Shelby County* barely tried to find a constitutional anchor. It certainly wasn't in the Fifteenth Amendment, from which the VRA emerged. According to Roberts, *Shelby County* derived from the "fundamental principle of equal sovereignty among the states," a line that had first appeared in *Northwest Austin*. He had come up with the phrase as a baseline against which to measure the VRA's differentiation between states. Emphasizing the ostensible indignity that the VRA created, he now asked how it could be that a handful of states had to "*beseech* the federal government for permission to implement laws that they would otherwise have the right to enact and execute on their own."

In fact, as Ginsburg pointed out, an early VRA case, in 1966, had discussed "equality of states," but stressed it applied only "to the terms upon which states are admitted to the Union, and not to the remedies for local evils which have subsequently appeared." (In an article for *Slate* the day after *Shelby County*, a well-known federal judge called "equal sovereignty" a principle of constitutional law "of which I had never heard—for the excellent reason that . . . there is no such principle.")

"Equal sovereignty" denied the reality that Congress routinely treated states differently. California received a new freeway, but Alaska got a national park. Were these spending programs now constitutionally suspect? Even within the four corners of the VRA, Roberts's pronouncement made little sense, because he accepted that Section 2—which barred racial discrimination in voting—burdened states that had higher minority populations. If Alabama still faced more lawsuits than Vermont, why wasn't Section 2 also unconstitutional? "Equal sovereignty" didn't mean a whole lot. At best—and worst—it evoked the complaints the Confederacy once had.

STILL, THE PROBLEM FOR GINSBURG and the other dissenters was that the chief had been able, unchallenged, to slip the phrase into *Northwest Austin*. The *Shelby County* dissent behaved "as if our decision in *Northwest Austin* never happened," Roberts wrote. In the interest of harmony, and perhaps because they weren't thinking far enough ahead, none of the *Shelby County* dissenters had objected. Their protest now was a little late. Roberts had already laid the foundation, from which *Shelby County* seemed like a logical next step. Roberts cited *Northwest Austin* 27 times. This was the chief justice, ever maneuvering, at his tactical best.

Ginsburg wrote the sole dissent, from a ruling she thought among the worst the Court had reached during her tenure—worse even than *Bush v. Gore*, which applied only to a single election. She regarded her dissent as among her finest. It was so strong that the other dissenters granted her the floor by herself, the better for the four to speak in a unified voice.

Much of what Ginsburg said could have been published in *Northwest Austin*, had the constitutional question not been shelved. "The grand aim" of the VRA, she wrote, was "to secure to all . . . a voice in our democracy undiluted by race. As the record for the 2006 reauthorization makes abundantly clear, second-generation barriers to minority voting rights have emerged in the covered jurisdictions as attempted *substitutes* for the first-generation barriers [like literacy tests] that originally triggered preclearance." Roberts, she charged, made "no genuine attempt to engage" with that legislative record. "One would expect more from an opinion striking at the heart of the nation's signal piece of civil-rights legislation." The "sad irony" of the opinion was "in its utter failure to grasp why the VRA has proven effective."

"History did not end in 1965," Roberts had written for the majority. "What's past is prologue," Ginsburg replied.

Then, in a veiled comeback to the chief's bit about elephant whistles, she offered her own analogy. Roberts's view that the VRA was no longer needed was "like throwing away your umbrella in a rainstorm because you are not getting wet." Her line went viral, and "It's Still Raining" became a battle cry for fund-raising by liberal advocacy groups.

As much as challenging Roberts on the merits of the VRA, Ginsburg wanted to address the institutional problem. "We see the issue as a 'who decides' question," she said from the bench, just as liberals had pointed out in *Bush v. Gore, Heller* and *Citizens United*—and conservatives had complained in *Roe v. Wade*. Ginsburg compared the First and Fifteenth Amendments. Whereas the former instructed Congress to "make no law" abridging the freedom of expression, the latter was "of a distinctly different thrust." It vested in Congress the power to affirmatively enforce the right to vote (just as the Fourteenth Amendment left the specifics to Congress on equal protection). The language of the Constitution recognized that lawmakers were best positioned to handle the details of enforcing the broad goals. In her 1993 confirmation hearings, Ginsburg had told senators, "We must always remember that we live in a democracy that can be destroyed if judges take it upon themselves to rule as Platonic guardians." In *Shelby County*, even more than in *Heller* and *Citizens United*, that scenario was playing itself out.

"By overriding Congress's decision" to renew the VRA, she concluded, "the Court errs egregiously." There was not even the formal "I dissent." For Ruth Bader Ginsburg, this was about as surly as it got.

When Ginsburg announced her dissent from the bench, she gave in to the temptation of sounding like a politician herself. Referring to Martin Luther King, she noted that "the great man who led the march from Selma to Montgomery, and there called for the passage of the Voting

Rights Act, foresaw progress even in Alabama." Quoting King, she said, "the arc of the moral universe is long . . . but it bends toward justice if there is a steadfast commitment to see the task through to completion." It was a rousing courtroom moment, but Ginsburg would've sounded even better confining herself to a doctrinal indictment of the ruling.

REASONABLE PEOPLE MIGHT HAVE DISAGREED on the relative costs and benefits of the preclearance regime the Court struck down in *Shelby County*. And nobody knew for sure what voting rights would look like in the absence of oversight of certain states. Maybe the political risks of appearing to discriminate would now be too great. Maybe after-the-fact Section 2 enforcement would be enough. Maybe even the South had changed for good.

But the immediate aftermath of *Shelby County* proved otherwise. Within an hour of the ruling, Texas, heretofore a covered jurisdiction, revived a voter ID law that had been denied preclearance under Section 5. North Carolina soon imposed its own voter ID rules, reduced early voting, and altered registration procedures; a lower federal court eventually threw out the changes that, in its view, "target African Americans with almost surgical precision." Other states went to work as well, closing polling places in some black neighborhoods and cutting back on voting hours. So far, the Court has chosen not to weigh in on the post–*Shelby County* laws. But the new restrictions seemed to be the latest evidence of the South's "unremitting and ingenious defiance" of the Fifteenth Amendment that the Court dating to 1966 had recognized as a legitimate basis for the VRA. These were exactly the rippling "second-generation barriers to minority voting rights" about which Ginsburg had warned.

Defenders of the various laws claimed the restrictions had nothing to do with race—only the integrity of elections. Slightly less disingenuous supporters claimed the laws were really aimed only at suppressing Democratic votes, not African-American votes as such. But the idea of the VRA as an inequitable anachronism was manifestly false. Roberts was wrong. Ginsburg, who wanted to leave it to Congress, was right. It was a fair criticism of Congress that it, characteristically, failed to act after *Shelby County* (although its failure to act debunked Scalia's assertion that Congress would never pass up the chance to vote for voting rights). But among the problems with Supreme Court triumphalism was that it helped to debilitate lawmakers. Why bother expending political capital if the justices across First Street were just going to substitute their judgment for yours?

The week after *Shelby County* was argued—following the justices' vote in conference to gut a historic act of Congress—Kennedy was in Sacramento for the dedication of a library in his name at the federal courthouse. He was asked generally about the Court's role in resolving so many political issues. "It's a serious problem," he said. "A democracy shouldn't be dependent for its major decisions on what nine unelected people from a narrow legal background have to say." Kennedy never saw the irony—or the hypocrisy. Roberts surely drove the train in *Shelby County*, but he was able to do so only because Kennedy was aboard. Without him, Roberts wouldn't have had a fifth vote.

Kennedy would return to center stage in *Obergefell v. Hodges*, the Court's next milestone ruling—that cemented his legacy as both judicial interventionist and self-proclaimed sentinel of gay rights. Because of the Court's alignment, he owned national policy over it. As one scholar put it: "This is Anthony Kennedy's country. The rest of us only live here." No matter one's view on gay rights, *Obergefell* was another illustration of why the Supreme Court had become a dangerous branch.

CHAPTER 15

ROE BY ANY OTHER NAME?

NOT SO LONG AGO, FEW TOPICS MADE THE COURT MORE TWITCHY THAN matters of sex. In the heyday of obscenity prosecutions in the 1970s, the best part of each term for several justices was getting together in a darkened room to watch porn films that were exhibits in First Amendment appeals. Between reels of "Sexual Freedom in Denmark," which included scenes of actual sex, Thurgood Marshall, for example, turned to Harry Blackmun and asked, "Well, Harry, I didn't learn anything—how about you?" John Marshall Harlan II, nearly blind, needed to bring a clerk with him to narrate the steamy scenes. "You don't say," Harlan sometimes exclaimed. But according to *The Brethren*, the classic insider account of the Burger Court, most justices didn't attend the screenings, finding the mere idea of the films distasteful.

Cases involving homosexuality presented greater challenges. In the 1960s and '70s, gay rights had yet to become part of mainstream culture and weren't something much discussed at the all-male Court. If sexual orientation came up at all, it was considered more an aberrant behavior than a human characteristic, ripe for discrimination and governmental intrusion. When the Warren Court first took on the constitutionality of contraception bans, some justices likened homosexuality to adultery and incest. Ten years later, in *Doe v. Commonwealth's Attorney*, the justices affirmed, without even issuing an opinion, Virginia's criminal statute against sodomy, at least between gays—even if between consenting adults in private. The right to privacy that *Roe v. Wade* discussed a few years earlier was deemed irrelevant.

Another decade passed before the Court reconsidered the issue, in *Bowers v. Hardwick*, a prosecution out of Georgia. Cases like *Heller* and *Citizens United* had their origin in methodical strategy by true-believing ideologues who were willing to violate the law as a way to challenge it. Michael Hardwick, a 29-year-old gay bartender in Atlanta, was just unlucky.

One night in 1982, outside a bar, Hardwick was cited for carrying an open bottle of beer. Because his summons included the wrong court date, he didn't show, and a judge issued an arrest warrant. When a police officer arrived at Hardwick's apartment one morning weeks later, he was let in by a guest. The officer found Hardwick in a bedroom engaged in oral sex with another man. Both men were charged with sodomy, a felony under Georgia law, though seldom prosecuted unless it involved coercion or public acts.

Sodomy was the kind of word that a lot of people had to look up to learn what it actually meant. Georgia defined it as an act "involving the sex organs of one person and the mouth or anus of another," though law enforcement there, and in other states, commonly understood it to apply only to homosexuals. The term *sodomy* itself, deriving from the biblical city of iniquity, suggested an affliction rather than an ordinary practice engaged in by straights and gays alike. The local DA was content to drop the sodomy charge, but Hardwick agreed to make his arrest a test case. *Bowers v. Hardwick* reached the Supreme Court in 1986.

The justices who voted to hear the appeal had different motivations. Warren Burger and William Rehnquist wanted to spell out what *Doe v. Commonwealth's Attorney* had left implicit—that the Constitution didn't protect gay sex. Byron White was concerned that lower federal courts would issue conflicting rulings. Several of the liberals thought

ROE BY ANY OTHER NAME? 317

Roe provided sufficient principle to extend constitutional rights to gay men and women, and the liberals worried that in a second Reagan term the Court was likely to grow more conservative. "Things are just going to get worse," William Brennan told a clerk. But another liberal, Blackmun, thought taking the case risked damage to *Roe*, which had come to dominate his thinking on any case that could be used to impugn it. *Bowers* involved substantive due process—just as *Roe*, and *Griswold* and *Eisenstadt* before it, had. Blackmun persuaded Brennan to change his mind about granting cert. But by that point, Marshall had already agreed to do so and didn't want to be seen, again, as Brennan's lackey. In the end, an odd constellation of votes brought *Bowers v. Hardwick* to the Court: White, Burger, Rehnquist and Marshall. Jurisprudence can make for strange bedfellows.

The courtroom argument reflected the gulf among the justices, as well as how archaic the discussion sounds today. *Gay* or *gay rights*—now everyday, neutral parlance—were never spoken. Nor did they appear in the ruling. Blackmun emphasized that Georgia had never applied its law to married couples, and the last prosecution of any kind there happened before World War II. If there was a constitutional right to private consensual sodomy, Rehnquist wanted to know, then what about polygamy and adultery? Burger asked about incest "in the privacy of the home." Lewis Powell took the same tack. "You emphasize the home and so would I if I were arguing this case," he said, addressing Hardwick's lawyer. But what if Hardwick had been arrested in "a motel room or the back of an automobile or toilet or wherever"? Powell had long been the Court's moderate—personally tolerant and doctrinally pragmatic. But the case bedeviled him, illustrating how homosexuality was foreign to many of the justices. "Sexual activity between men was something he did not comprehend," according to Powell's authorized biography. During Powell's personal deliberations, he asked one of his clerks about the details.

"Are gay men not attracted to women?" asked the 78-year-old Powell.

"They are," the clerk offered, in disbelief he was having this conversation with the gentlemanly justice. "But," he continued, "there is no sexual excitement."

"None at all?"

"Justice Powell, a gay man could not get an erection to have sex with a woman."

"Don't you have to have an erection to perform sodomy?"

"Yes," the clerk explained, "but that's because of the sexual excitement."

When the clerk also told Powell that about 10 percent of the male population was gay, he was astounded. "I don't believe I've ever met a homosexual," Powell said.

The clerk himself was gay. Powell had as clerks 18 gay men and four lesbians during his 16 years on the Court—the most of any justice at that time, according to a 2001 survey. But none were open about it. (Today, gay and lesbian clerks typically are.)

In the conference, Powell initially voted to reverse Hardwick's conviction, but changed his mind six days later. Part of his reason was procedural. Hardwick hadn't been tried or sentenced—so his constitutional argument seemed premature. More centrally, though, Powell wasn't convinced, as he later wrote in the ruling, that behavior "condemned for hundreds of years has now become a fundamental right." Powell's flip-flop captured his torment; in effect, he noted to himself, the Court was split "$4^1/_2$ to $4^1/_2$." He became the decisive vote in the 5-to-4 decision to uphold the constitutionality of the sodomy statute.

In his majority opinion, White barely concealed his contempt for gays. He had asked a clerk to write a considered draft, but became impatient when it didn't arrive fast enough. So White dashed off the opinion himself, in 13 brutal paragraphs. It showed. "Proscriptions against [homosexual] conduct have ancient roots," he wrote. All 13 colonies had outlawed sodomy; half the states still did. "No connection between family, marriage, or procreation, on the one hand, and homosexual activity, on the other, has been demonstrated," he said. So it "is, at best, facetious" to claim that a constitutional right "to engage in such conduct is 'deeply rooted in this nation's history and tradition' or 'implicit in the concept of ordered liberty.'" White's opinion, as one historian put it, "dispatched the issue and those affected by it with the same sympathy that he would have shown an opposing tackler in his football days."

Burger, in a concurrence, jeered at Hardwick's argument as grounded on "personal preferences" that "cast aside millennia of moral teaching."

Brennan initially decided to write a dissent, as he often did in big cases (which was why Marshall sometimes thought of him as an "opinion hog"). But Blackmun prevailed on Brennan to let him handle the main dissent. Blackmun assailed the Court's "almost obsessive focus on homosexual activity" at the expense of seeing a larger dimension. "Only the most willful blindness could obscure the fact that sexual intimacy is 'a sensitive, key relationship of human existence, central to family life, community welfare, and the development of human personality.'" (He slyly took that quote—without attributing it—from a majority opinion that Burger had written in an obscenity case.) The case wasn't really about sexual activity, Blackmun wrote, but rather about "the right most valued by civilized men, namely, the right to be let alone. . . . It is revolting to have no better reason for a rule of law than that . . . it was laid down in the time of Henry IV."

Bowers v. Hardwick was widely vilified. Gay rights groups called it a latter-day *Dred Scott*. Law professors wrote about it, disparagingly, more often than about any case since *Roe*. The *Boston Globe* called it "preposterous and contradictory," based on "homophobia rather than law." The solicitor general in the Reagan administration, Charles Fried—a loud critic of *Roe*—said Justice White had been "stunningly harsh and dismissive." Those conservatives who did defend White did so largely because they believed that attacking *Bowers* meant ratifying *Roe*. As time went by, White's 31 years on the Court became reducible to one opinion. Powell, who retired a year after *Bowers*, came to rue his vote. Asked about the ruling by a law student four years later, in 1990, he admitted, "I think I probably made a mistake in that one." That might have reflected an underlying conviction on his part—or that *Bowers* had earned so much scorn.

IN 1987, ANTHONY KENNEDY took Powell's seat. That set the stage for the demise of *Bowers*, given Kennedy's relatively expansive views on gay

rights in his pre-Court years in Sacramento. But a transformation in
social attitudes helped, too. Even with anxiety over AIDS, and efforts
by some in the Religious Right to blame the disease on homosexuality,
Americans were becoming more tolerant of differences in sexual orientation. Popular culture both influenced and reflected growing acceptance.
YEP, I'M GAY, declared a *Time* cover story in April 1997, in which the
sitcom star Ellen DeGeneres explained why she was coming out. The
resulting "Ellen effect" helped to make gay men and women visible and
less threatening. They worked in your office; they lived in your neighborhood; they had families. Kennedy had known that for years. Being
gay was about human identity, not sexual practice. *Homosexual*, which
emphasized *sex*, was supplanted in the lexicon by *gay* and *LGBT* (for
lesbian, gay, bisexual and transgender).

In the world of constitutional law, views quickly changed as well.
Just as there had been conservative backlash to *Roe*, there was both a
liberal and a libertarian backlash to *Bowers*. Had Robert Bork, rather
than Kennedy, replaced Powell, the Court's views on gay rights might
well have remained retrograde. Sandra Day O'Connor, who was part of
the *Bowers* majority, might not have modified her views. But Kennedy's
arrival, together with shifts in cultural outlook, set the Court on a new
path. *Romer v. Evans* in 1996 was the first way station.

Four years earlier, Colorado referendum voters added Amendment 2,
as it was known, to the state constitution. The amendment nullified
all state and local laws that barred discrimination based on sexual orientation. Several municipalities—including liberal bastions Aspen and
Boulder—had passed anti-bias ordinances that regulated employment,
housing and education. The amendment also blocked all future anti-bias
enactments—legislative, executive and judicial. A group called Colorado
Family Values, partly funded by the billionaire Philip Anschutz, drove
the effort to put the amendment on the ballot. The gist of its campaign
was that bias-discrimination laws granted gays "special rights." Not only
were such rights themselves discriminatory, the argument went, but
gays were already a disproportionately powerful special interest group.
The state supreme court struck down Amendment 2. Citing the federal Constitution, the court ruled that the amendment denied gays the

"fundamental right to participate equally in the political process." (That seemed to ignore that the amendment was adopted by vote, 53 percent to 47 percent—the essence of "the political process.")

With Kennedy leading the way, the Supreme Court, 6–3, agreed with the Colorado court. The justices could simply have declined to hear the case, but Kennedy got them to review what the state court had done and then to endorse it. In effect, the justices were atoning for *Bowers v. Hardwick*. Although they oddly failed to mention *Bowers* at all, they had destroyed its principal rationale—that the law could treat gays differently just because they were gay. "A state cannot so deem a class of persons a stranger to its laws," Kennedy wrote. "A law declaring that in general it shall be more difficult for one group of citizens than for all others to seek aid from the government is itself a denial of equal protection of the laws." He was joined by the four liberal reliables—John Paul Stevens, Ruth Bader Ginsburg, Stephen Breyer and David Souter—plus O'Connor.

Antonin Scalia's dissent was petulant—even for him. Joined by Rehnquist and Clarence Thomas, he described "homosexuals" not as a historically persecuted minority but as a group with "high disposable income," "enormous influence in American media and politics," and "disproportionate political power"—the last of which, he noted, "though composing no more than 4 percent of the population," won nearly half the vote on Amendment 2. He compared "homosexual conduct" to such other "reprehensible" conduct as "murder" and "cruelty to animals."

Scalia was no less respectful of the majority in *Romer*. He called Kennedy's opinion "terminal silliness," "hand wringing," "false," "comical," "long on emotive utterance," and "nothing short of insulting." He trotted out Rehnquist's polygamy analogy from *Bowers*. By the majority's reasoning, Scalia asked, if Amendment 2 "impermissibly targeted" gays, didn't it mean that a law prohibiting polygamy should be in doubt? (*No* was the easy answer, given the implicit coercion in polygamous relationships historically.) He also derided his colleagues for ignoring the precedent of *Bowers*. "If it is rational to criminalize the conduct," Scalia wrote, "surely it is rational to deny special favor and protection to those with a self-avowed tendency or desire to engage in the conduct." And for

Scalia, *Bowers* surely was still good law—"unassailable, except by those who think that the Constitution changes to suit current fashions."

That was the crux of Scalia's rage. The opening sentence of his dissent charged Kennedy and the majority with taking sides in an unabating partisan battle. "The Court," he wrote, "has mistaken a Kulturkampf for a fit of spite," somehow analogizing to Prussian policies against the Catholic Church in the 19th century. Striking down Amendment 2 was "an act, not of judicial judgment, but of political will." Belittling his colleagues, Scalia—the graduate of Harvard Law School—wrote that "when the Court takes sides in the culture wars, it tends to be with the knights rather than the villains . . . reflecting the views and values of the lawyer class from which the Court's members are drawn."

Perhaps for a judge, the only sin worse than behaving like a politician was acting like a hypocrite. So how was it that Kennedy and the majority had exercised "political will," but Scalia was not, years later, in *Heller*, *Citizens United* and *Shelby County*? Why was the democratic process sacrosanct when it curtailed gay rights, but wholly unworthy when it came to gun control, campaign spending and the Voting Rights Act? In *Heller*, *Citizens United* and *Shelby County*, Scalia and his conservative colleagues seemed to be exercising precisely the kind of political will he ranted about in *Romer*. It didn't require much imagination to suppose that in *Romer* Scalia just happened to side with the voters of Colorado, whereas he didn't agree with Congress or the D.C. City Council in the others. In the alleged Kulturkampf, there could be little doubt which side he was on.

DESPITE SCALIA'S EFFORT TO DRESS Amendment 2 up in "traditional attitudes," its provisions were just as repellent as those in the Georgia statute had been in *Bowers*. The title of the amendment itself, "No Protected Status Based on Homosexual, Lesbian, or Bisexual Orientation," conveyed a meanness that went beyond "traditional attitudes." The problem with Kennedy's majority opinion wasn't so much its ultimate conclusion, but the explanation for it. Normally, before invoking equal protection to strike down a law, the Court first had to determine the status of the individuals being adversely affected. If the class deserved special protection—racial minorities were the obvious category, given the Fourteenth Amendment—then the Court would apply "strict scrutiny" to evaluate a law's constitutionality. This was Footnote Four of *Carolene Products* in action: "Discrete and insular minorities," all the more when normal political processes weren't likely to protect them, warranted special judicial sensitivity. In most other situations, laws deserved deference and needed only to have a "rational basis." In most Fourteenth Amendment litigation, once "strict scrutiny" was implicated, a law was doomed; if rationality was the test, a law typically was upheld.

Did Amendment 2's classification of gay citizens subject it to strict scrutiny? Kennedy didn't say. Instead, he explained that the amendment lacked any "rational relationship" to legitimate governmental purposes. "Its sheer breadth is so discontinuous with the reasons offered for it," Kennedy wrote, that the amendment "seems inexplicable by anything but animus." Hatred, he declared, couldn't be a rational basis for legal distinction. But the argument seemed circular. Couldn't there be an alternative explanation for the amendment? The ordinances enacted by localities outlawing discrimination based on sexual orientation were clearly reasonable exercises of democratic will. So, too, presumably, would have been their repeal by the localities. There's no Fourteenth Amendment requirement that legislative rights be a "one-way ratchet." The gears of change can work in reverse.

Maybe localities would decide, on second thought, that their ordinances intruded too much on the prerogatives of private landlords and employers, or that they unfairly provided gay citizens with protections not granted to other classes. Maybe reversing course was a product of animus, but it wasn't the only possible explanation. Moreover, not every kind of discrimination was actionable. Employers could prefer applicants who looked better. Bad hair wasn't a suspect classification, as Scalia derisively observed during oral argument. The Supreme Court had never identified sexual orientation as a suspect category—akin to race or religion or gender. And it didn't do so in *Romer* either.

So, wasn't it up to Colorado to decide if sexual orientation deserved to be listed as a forbidden basis of discrimination, as Aspen, Boulder and other municipalities had decided? If municipalities declined to pass anti-bias ordinances in the first place—because of, say, hatred—would *that* be a basis on which to claim a violation of equal protection and to demand the creation of an affirmative Fourteenth Amendment right? And assuming municipalities were allowed to change their minds, why should a state constitutional provision accomplishing the same democratic result be any different?

The way to salvage Kennedy's opinion was to point out that Amendment 2 did more than return the state to the status quo before local anti-bias laws were enacted. As Kennedy himself indicated, it created a new reality by singling out a group for "disfavored" treatment. Perhaps it's just semantics to argue that eliminating a right that had been temporarily granted to gays now turned them into outcasts. That had been the substance of Scalia's dissent—that the absence of "preferential treatment" hardly amounted to a denial of equal protection. But Scalia conveniently ignored the resulting reality.

Under the amendment, heterosexuals—as well as "everyone else in the world," from "hot-dog vendors to fat people," as the scholar Akhil Reed Amar put it—could still seek the passage of specific anti-discrimination laws to protect themselves. But gays no longer could, even though it was they—more than, say, hot-dog vendors—who, in Kennedy's words, might "need" such laws "most." Here again was the shadow of *Carolene Products*. Because Colorado unjustifiably targeted its gay citizens for disparate treatment, the Court reasonably concluded that Amendment 2 violated the Constitution. The amendment was "at once too narrow and too broad," Kennedy wrote, identifying persons "by a single trait" and then denying them "protection across the board." But whether the Court had to insert itself and say anything at all was another matter. The Colorado judiciary had already solved the issue—the state lost—and such sinister amendments were hardly marauding the national landscape.

———

SEVEN YEARS AFTER *Romer*, in June 2003, the Rehnquist Court erased the stain of *Bowers* completely. *Bowers* had not only become a badge of second-class citizenship for gays, but also was used to justify discrimination in immigration proceedings, military discharges, teacher dismissals, and adoption and custody hearings. Now, in *Lawrence v. Texas*, the justices explicitly declared *Bowers* bad law.

Like *Bowers*, *Lawrence* began in a bedroom. Late on the night of September 17, 1998, Houston police were called to investigate a "weapons disturbance" at a local apartment. Inside, officers reported finding John Geddes Lawrence Jr., 55, and Tyron Garner, 31, having consensual sex. The two men were arrested and charged with "deviate sexual intercourse," an act that Texas law had defined as oral or anal sex between individuals of the same gender—and for 25 years had criminalized. By now, Texas was one of only four states to do so; another nine punished non-homosexual sodomy as well. Virtually all Western countries, generations earlier, had stopped punishing any kind of sodomy. Lawrence and Garner were convicted by a justice of the peace and each fined $195. Relying on *Bowers*, an appellate court upheld the convictions. (No weapons were found, and later reports indicated the defendants weren't having sex. Both details suggested the charges were based as much on Lawrence and Garner being of different races as being gay. For his part, the prosecuting DA, Chuck Rosenthal, was forced to resign after admitting "pharmacological impairment" and an affair with his secretary.)

The Court heard the case in March 2003. Given *Romer*, there was every expectation the justices would be receptive to the claims of Lawrence and Garner. The visitors' pews in the courtroom were filled with an estimated 200 gay men and women, many of them prominent members of the D.C. legal community. It no longer seemed "at best, facetious" (as White had put it in *Bowers*) that the Court might grant some degree of protection to intimate private conduct between same-sex couples. The lawyer for the two men, Paul Smith—who had clerked for Powell four years after *Bowers* and subsequently came out as gay—argued that the Texas law violated both equal protection and due process. The first point was narrower—that the Constitution did not permit disparate treatment of gays and straights. That view seemed to grant the possibility that a sodomy law in theory could be equally, and therefore fairly, applied. But the latter point—fundamentally based on a libertarian ideal of "being left alone"—returned the Court to the wonderland of substantive due process.

Even though the Equal Protection Clause could have given the Court the easier way to dispose of the case, most of the argument focused on due process. In part that was because Smith wanted *Bowers* overturned. It was also because Scalia wanted to establish that a state should be allowed to express its moral disapproval by prohibiting certain behavior. If a state could do so, gays had no liberty argument. Smith acknowledged that American history reflected little support for gay rights specifically. But the better focus was on "a tradition of respect for the privacy of couples in their homes, going back to the founding." Citing contraception and abortion, Smith said, "The Court's decisions don't just look at history, they look at the function that a particular claimed freedom plays in the lives of real people."

Scalia scoffed. "I don't know what you mean by the function it plays 'in the lives of real people,'" he told Smith. "*Any* law stops people from doing what they really want to do."

As in so many other cases, the question came down to the justices picking and choosing which rights they wished to consecrate. Smith described that exercise as "reasoned judgment to identify a realm of personal liberty that involves matters central, and core to, how persons define their own lives." It was an honest acknowledgment that the history of interpreting constitutional provisions meant more than executing objective commands. It was the kind of acknowledgment, for example, that Scalia never considered later in *Heller*. But Smith's statement did open up the Court to the charge it was again substituting its own preferences for those of the people of a particular state. "Texas has the right to set moral standards," Rosenthal, the DA, said.

Breyer tried to corner Rosenthal. His "question" was classic Breyer, quoting a famous Mother Goose nursery rhyme, to considerable courtroom cackling: "So . . . the justification for this statute . . . is simply, 'I do not like thee, Doctor Fell, the reason why I cannot tell.'" Breyer was showing that, when it came to the bedroom, a state had to be more than arbitrary in its assertion of morality.

Rosenthal was perplexed. Breyer tried again: Could Texas say "it is against the law at the dinner table to tell really serious lies to your family"?

"Yes, they can make that a law," Rosenthal replied, but he conceded that "there would be no rational basis for the law."

Scalia tried to help the overmatched Rosenthal: "I don't know of a 200-year tradition of laws against lying at the dinner table."

Breyer got so frustrated with Rosenthal that toward the end of the argument he pleaded for a "straight answer." He didn't intend it as a pun—which brought the house down even more. Thomas, seated to his right, quickly filled him in, which made Breyer smile. It was more pure Breyer.

Scalia and Breyer performances aside, nothing in the argument indicated how a ruling would shake out. If, as most assumed, there was going to be a fifth vote to expand gay rights, it would be O'Connor's or Kennedy's. O'Connor spoke only three times and confined herself to the equal protection question. Kennedy, too, seemed unmoved by the broader issue.

But that was why reading a lot into oral arguments was misguided. Though the justices who do speak may provide an unguarded glimpse into their thinking—unfiltered by subsequent hedging—the arguments reveal only so much. When the ruling in *Lawrence v. Texas* was announced, on the last day of the term, it was Kennedy who wrote the majority opinion. He went big, glossing over the equal protection issue and diving right into substantive due process.

"Freedom extends beyond spatial bounds," he began. "Liberty presumes an autonomy of self that includes freedom of thought, belief, expression, and certain intimate conduct. [This] case involves liberty of the person both in its spatial and more transcendent dimensions." This was unalloyed Kennedy, the Court's metaphysicist-in-residence. The opening recalled his words a decade earlier in *Casey*, the 1992 case that upheld *Roe v. Wade*. "At the heart of liberty is the right to define one's own concept of existence, of meaning, of the universe, and of the mystery of human life," he wrote back then. "These matters, involving the most intimate and personal choices a person may make in a lifetime, choices central to personal dignity and autonomy, are central to the liberty protected by the Fourteenth Amendment."

Kennedy said the Court's "obligation" was "to define the liberty of all, not to mandate our own moral code." Cases like this one were no more about a gay person's "right to engage in certain sexual conduct" than a married person's "right to have sexual intercourse." Because the 1986 sodomy ruling in *Bowers* "demeans the lives of homosexual persons," the Court threw it out altogether. "*Bowers* was not correct when it was decided, and it is not correct today," Kennedy wrote. The latter was significant enough in undoing a precedent of only 17 years, but the former mea culpa was something the Court just didn't do.

His prose was beautiful, spiritual, poignant. It voiced why gay individuals had a societal claim to something more than avoiding persecution—that their relationships were no less loving than those that straights had. The problem was that Kennedy's words didn't quite explain what they had to do with constitutional law, unless embedded in the Fourteenth Amendment was some generalized principle of libertarianism. But how far would such a notion extend? Like Justice Brennan's words in *Eisenstadt* in 1972, and like Justice Blackmun's in *Roe* the following year, Kennedy's meditation on "personal dignity and autonomy" didn't seem tethered to much more than what five justices happened to favor. Kennedy might have been better off simply saying that the Constitution didn't allow the government to poke its nose into the bedroom without overriding justification, and that the typical prosecution for sodomy demanded government snooping. That was why the contraception rulings in *Griswold* and *Eisenstadt* were easily defensible—and among the reasons why *Roe* was not. *Lawrence* fit nicely into the *Griswold-Eisenstadt* continuum.

THE VOTE IN *Lawrence* was 6–3, with the justices lining up as they had in *Romer*. Although O'Connor refused to renounce her vote in *Bowers*, she joined the majority in striking down the Texas sodomy law, but only as far as it violated equal protection. Rehnquist, Scalia and Thomas dissented, but only Scalia in the conference pushed to uphold the Texas law. In his dissent, he resumed his *Romer* diatribe.

Once again, Scalia wrote, the majority had "taken sides in the culture war." Though he insisted he had "nothing against homosexuals," he wanted it known that "many Americans do not want persons who openly engage in homosexual conduct as partners in their business, as scoutmasters for their children, as teachers in their children's schools, or as boarders in their home." The *Lawrence* ruling wasn't constitutional law as much as "the product of a Court" that had "largely signed on to the so-called homosexual agenda." According to Scalia, there couldn't be any other explanation for the justices' overriding the democratic wishes of the citizens of Texas. Of course, in the decade that followed, he made no mention of any "so-called guns agenda" or "so-called fatcat-campaign-spending agenda" or "so-called voting-suppression agenda" when he decided in *Heller*, *Citizens United* and *Shelby County* that "traditional democratic action" wasn't good enough.

Undoubtedly, Scalia thought the distinction in *Lawrence* was illegitimately discovering rights implied in the gauze of the Due Process Clause, whereas those other rulings had a basis in constitutional language. But that kind of distinction was just another iteration of the originalist-textualist trope that Scalia proved a master of manipulating. Even so, it didn't stop him from laughing at the whole enterprise of substantive due process. Of course Texas's law "imposes constraints on liberty," he wrote. "So do laws prohibiting prostitution, recreational use of heroin, and, for that matter, working more than 60 hours per week in a bakery." And yet those laws, he pointed out, obviously were not constitutionally infirm.

Scalia's fury at Kennedy's reverie on liberty went back to the *Casey* abortion ruling in 1992. The logical endpoint of its "famed sweet-mystery-of-life passage," as Scalia mocked it, was "the totality of our jurisprudence." For "if the passage calls into question the government's power to regulate *actions based on* one's self-defined 'concept of existence, etc.,' it is the passage that ate the rule of law." As he usually did, Scalia had a point, but he oversold it and thereby undercut his warning about freelancing judges. It was also unconvincing under the circumstances. Because even if Kennedy's grandiose words were mostly overlooked, conventional doctrine still rendered Texas's law unsupportable.

Scalia's line about a "homosexual agenda" stalked him for the rest of his career. One of his clerks, Gil Seinfeld, who served during the *Lawrence* term, later said the dissent—and that line in particular—was evidence of "an angry man railing against a world that was changing around him in ways he found profoundly unsettling." In a revealing remembrance of the justice on his death—titled "The Good, the Bad, and the Ugly"—Seinfeld explained that he filled the role of resident "counter-clerk." Scalia had hired him "in spite of" his instincts being "profoundly different from the justice's." In fact, Seinfeld so disagreed with Scalia about *Lawrence* that he asked to have nothing to do with it. "I didn't want to help hone the justice's arguments or improve his prose," Seinfeld explained. While Scalia always involved all four of his clerks in drafting, he told Seinfeld no problem. But to the extent Seinfeld was the sole liberal in an otherwise true-believing chambers, his decision to sit *Lawrence* out may have removed a key brake on Scalia's anti-homosexual wrath. A year after, another Scalia counter-clerk wondered, "What would have happened if someone had said: 'Justice, not for nothing, but if you say 'homosexual agenda,' that's where half of people will stop reading"?

One section of Scalia's dissent did prove to be partly prescient. If promoting "majoritarian sexual morality" was no longer the government's business, then *Lawrence* "effectively decrees the end of all morals legislation." That, he said, could mean the end of laws against adultery, obscenity, prostitution, adult incest and bestiality. To that parade of horribles, Scalia added same-sex marriage. "The Court today pretends that . . . we need not fear judicial imposition of homosexual marriage," he wrote. "Do not believe it." Scalia accused the majority of dishonesty in claiming that "this case 'does not involve' the issue of homosexual marriage." That was true "only if one entertains the belief that principle and logic have nothing to do with the decisions of this Court."

If he intended his lecture to ridicule the inevitability of same-sex marriage, he accomplished just the opposite. In the years that followed, Scalia's dissent was the launching pad for many legal arguments in support of it. The fact he might have helped his prophecy come true drove him bananas.

THE IDEA OF SANCTIONED gay marriage in the United States dates to the early 1970s—chiefly in the context of condemning it. In 1971, the Minnesota Supreme Court ruled that same-sex marriages were not required by state law, and the justices chose not to hear the appeal. Phyllis Schlafly, the conservative activist, based part of her opposition to the Equal Rights Amendment on the claim it would legalize gay marriage.

Nearly two decades later, as the gay rights movement strengthened, cities and states began to recognize "domestic partnerships" and "civil unions." These arrangements provided gay couples with some of the preferences given to their heterosexual counterparts: tax breaks, access to insurance and pensions, and adoption and inheritance rights. But these new forms of recognition did not bestow the full spiritual and legal benefits of the marital bond. A widely read *New Republic* cover story in 1989, "Here Comes the Groom: A (Conservative) Case for Gay Marriage," helped to advance the argument. "Legalizing gay marriage would offer homosexuals the same deal society now offers heterosexuals: general social approval and specific legal advantages in exchange for a deeper and harder-to-extract-yourself-from commitment to another human being," wrote Andrew Sullivan, a conservative commentator. "It's one of the richest ironies of our society's blind spot toward gays that essentially conservative social goals should have the appearance of being so radical."

The argument didn't get far. In 1993, the Hawaii Supreme Court did rule that under the state's constitution, same-sex couples could be denied marriage licenses only if there was a "compelling state interest." The court sent the case back to a lower court to consider that issue. But the chance that same-sex marriage would be granted constitutional protection anywhere led to a boomerang: 39 states eventually adopted statutes or constitutional amendments that restricted marriage to opposite-sex couples. (Hawaii did the same.) And most important, in 1996 Congress overwhelmingly passed the Defense of Marriage Act (DOMA). The key section of that ironically named statute, signed into law by President Clinton, defined marriage for federal purposes as a heterosexual union only. The definition affected a partner's eligibility for Social Security payments and more than a thousand other federal benefits. Crucially, DOMA also excused states from having to recognize out-of-state same-sex marriages.

Along with various state measures, DOMA temporarily quieted any significant national move toward gay marriages. But in November 2003—only five months after *Lawrence v. Texas*—the Massachusetts Supreme Court declared that the state constitution guaranteed the right to same-sex marriage. "Whether and whom to marry, how to express sexual intimacy, and whether and how to establish a family—these are among the most basic of every individual's liberty and due process rights," the court said. Massachusetts thus became the fifth jurisdiction in the world to authorize gay marriage. The ruling was a watershed—akin to "the Berlin wall coming down" for gay men and women—and it turned marriage into a central issue for gay activists. Public opinion yo-yoed after the ruling, but during the next decade, many state courts and legislatures increasingly embraced same-sex marriage.

Ultimately, in 2013, the U.S. Supreme Court got involved, agreeing to hear appeals on two questions in separate cases: whether DOMA violated the Constitution, and whether same-sex marriage itself deserved constitutional status. The route to *Obergefell*, first plotted in *Romer*, was set.

The DOMA case, *United States v. Windsor*, had its origins in the 44-year relationship between Edith Windsor and Thea Spyer. They had met in 1963 in a restaurant in Greenwich Village and then danced all night. In time, they dated, moved in together, traveled and loved. Early on, they considered themselves "engaged"; Windsor wore a diamond brooch, rather than a ring, to avoid unwelcome questions about her "fiancée." In 2007, as Spyer's health deteriorated due to multiple sclerosis, they flew to Toronto and got married. (Canada had legalized same-sex marriage in 2005.) At the time, Windsor was 77 and Spyer was 75. Two years later, Spyer died. Her will named Windsor as sole heir. But the

IRS, citing DOMA, denied her the exemption from estate taxes that straight spouses received. Instead, she got a federal tax bill for $363,000, and another bill from New York State for $275,000. Windsor sued, arguing DOMA was unconstitutional. Two lower courts sided with her. The government appealed, and the Supreme Court agreed to hear the appeal.

Meanwhile, in California voters had approved a ballot initiative in 2008 that defined marriage in heterosexual terms only. But that same year, the California Supreme Court ruled that under the state constitution "marriage" had to include same-sex couples. Later that year, voters approved a measure, Proposition 8, which undid the ruling by amending the state constitution to bar same-sex marriages. Gay couples sued in federal court, arguing that Prop 8 violated the Fourteenth Amendment.

A two-week federal trial followed in 2010. Because state officials declined to defend Prop 8, the task was left to its private sponsors—a fact that later proved to be critical. The trial was highly publicized, in part because the lead lawyers together opposing Prop 8 were Ted Olson and David Boies, the celebrated adversaries in *Bush v. Gore* in 2000. They said their lawsuit was in the tradition of *Brown v. Board of Education*. After testimony from experts on marriage, history and various social sciences—as well as from gay couples themselves—Judge Vaughn Walker found that Prop 8 violated both equal protection and due process. A federal appeals court agreed, relying heavily on *Romer* and Prop 8's ostracizing of gay couples. The U.S. Supreme Court could have let it go at that and denied cert, but chose to hear the case, formally titled *Hollingsworth v. Perry*.

Rulings in the DOMA and Prop 8 cases, both 5–4, were announced on the same Wednesday in late June 2013. In *Windsor*, the DOMA case, the Court took another step toward full recognition of gay marriage. But in the Prop 8 case, the justices carefully ducked the question. Taken together, the rulings suggested the Court had the votes, but not yet the will, to declare same-sex marriage a constitutional right. Some critics regarded the latter as timidity. Instead, it was a rare, laudable instance of institutional humility.

In the Prop 8 case, the justices simply found that, on second thought, they lacked authority to hear the appeal. Since the plaintiffs in the initial lawsuit had won, they had nothing left to ask for. State officials in California once again refused to defend Prop 8. So the only complaining parties on the appeal were Prop 8's private sponsors, and according to the Court, they weren't an acceptable stand-in for the state. The justices dismissed the appeal, effectively leaving intact Judge Walker's ruling that Prop 8 was unconstitutional. California now joined a dozen other states (and D.C.) that permitted same-sex marriage, but the ruling didn't extend to other jurisdictions.

THE COURT'S NONDECISION DECISION WAS a fine example of Alexander Bickel's "passive virtues" in operation. That was particularly so because had the Court taken on Prop 8 directly, the justices would have been badly split, which the Court's odd lineup in the dismissal showed. Half the dissenters (Anthony Kennedy and Sonia Sotomayor) would have voted to strike down Prop 8 on constitutional grounds, and half (Sam Alito and Clarence Thomas) would have voted to uphold it. There could be no middle ground; all that these four agreed on was the opponents of Prop 8 were entitled to "their day in court." But worse than producing a riven Court, a definitive ruling would have foreclosed the ability of other actors in society to keep experimenting. While the Court seldom seemed to grasp the concept anymore, there was benefit in its not interjecting itself. By giving states, lower courts and the public itself the chance to continue wrangling, the justices could conserve their prestige. It was even possible that a consensus reached away from the marble temple might prove to be more durable, all the more since the Court in theory could go either way on the underlying question.

In *Windsor*, the other ruling on gay rights that day, the Court did act, striking down the key section of DOMA, which had defined marriage for purposes of federal benefits. As he had in *Romer* and *Lawrence*, Kennedy wrote for the majority. He was joined by the four justices in the liberal bloc: Ginsburg, Breyer, Sotomayor and Kagan. Though the ruling didn't overturn state laws that prohibited same-sex marriages, it did say the federal government couldn't deny federal benefits to gay couples who were legally married. *Windsor*'s verdict was clear, but the rationale was confused—a hodgepodge of federalism, equality and liberty. It was as if Kennedy figured that sticking with one item on the doctrinal menu couldn't possibly be as good as going with a medley of three.

The equal protection and due process aspects had been spelled out in the Court's prior rulings. In saying that DOMA was both too broad and too narrow, *Windsor* had a little of *Romer* and a little of *Lawrence*. Each strand had its flaws. Had Kennedy relied solely on either, there would have been an inexorable logic for declaring all state bans on same-sex marriage unconstitutional. But he wasn't ready to do that yet. Nor was it clear to Kennedy that he had four other votes. So he had to mix in references to federalism—that somehow the states' "traditional" control over domestic relations law was sufficient to block Congress from interfering in the form of DOMA.

There was a time-bomb problem with that approach. What was Kennedy going to do when the issue of gay marriage was squarely before the Court? If he was ultimately inclined to decide gay marriages were constitutionally protected—overriding many state laws in doing so—then preaching federalism now was just setting himself up for howls about hypocrisy later. The only difference, perhaps, was that it wouldn't be Congress overriding state prerogatives in that situation. It would be the Court. For Kennedy, that rarely was a concern.

The dissenters in *Windsor*—Scalia, Thomas, Alito and Roberts—saw the problem. Unless in the end the Court allowed "the people of each state" to define marriage, Alito warned, "the whiffs of federalism in today's opinion . . . will soon be scattered to the wind." Roberts was similarly suspicious that Kennedy's opinion could be confined to the rights of gay couples against the federal government. That was especially so because he realized from the conference after oral argument that Kennedy was itching to soon take the last step and proclaim same-sex marriage a constitutional right. If states, rather than Congress, were masters of "the marital relation" and Congress had no place in interfering with its definition, the chief justice wrote, then state autonomy had to "come into play on the other side of the board in future cases" when the Court would be asked to second-guess definitions of marriage.

And then there was Scalia. "By formally declaring anyone opposed to same-sex marriage an enemy of human decency, the majority arms well every challenger to a state law restricting marriage to its traditional definition," he wrote. A Court that "finds it so horrific that Congress ir-rationally and hatefully robbed same-sex couples of the 'personhood and dignity' which state legislatures conferred upon them, will of a certitude be similarly appalled by state legislatures' irrational and hateful failure to acknowledge that 'personhood and dignity' in the first place." Any distinction between objections to federal law and state counterparts took "real cheek," as he put it.

According to Scalia, "whatever disappearing trail of its legalistic argle-bargle one chooses to follow," the true rationale behind *Windsor* was to lay the last stonework for constitutionalizing same-sex marriage down the road. He openly accused Kennedy of the duplicity that Alito and Roberts had only implied. "No one should be fooled," he wrote. "It is just a matter of listening and waiting for the other shoe." The "enthroned" Court's overreaching, he said, sprang forth "from the same diseased root: an exalted conception of the role of this institution in America." That description might have been insightful, except that the day before, Scalia and other *Windsor* dissenters (along with Kennedy) had in *Shelby County* gutted the Voting Rights Act.

Even with "argle-bargle" and "diseased root," Scalia's language was more temperate than his "homosexual agenda" harangue 10 years earlier in *Lawrence*. At least on the Scalia-o-Meter, he sounded like the kind of serene middle-of-the-roader he couldn't stand. "In the majority's tell-ing, this story is black-and-white: Hate your neighbor or come along with us," he wrote. "The truth is more complicated. It is hard to admit that one's political opponents are not monsters. . . . A reminder that disagreement over something so fundamental as marriage can still be politically legitimate would have been a fit task for what in earlier times was called the judicial temperament. We might have covered ourselves with honor today, by promising all sides of this debate that it was theirs to settle." The reason for Scalia's civil tone wasn't that he'd moderated his true political and religious views. This time, he just happened to have a counter-clerk in chambers that term who coaxed him to control his vituperative pen.

IT TOOK ONLY TWO YEARS for the other shoe prophesied by Scalia to drop. Any judicial caution urged by *Windsor* had evaporated. Reading Kennedy's *Windsor* majority opinion as a signal, but citing Scalia's dissent as well, same-sex couples around the country filed dozens of lawsuits in 2013 and 2014 challenging state bans on same-sex marriage. All of them cited equal protection and due process. *Windsor* might have counseled deference to state regulation of domestic relations, but that was yesterday. Having dispatched congressional interference with the right to marry, lawyers for gay rights now argued that individual state judgments had to succumb to a national standard set by the Fourteenth Amendment. The logic wasn't exactly consistent. "It takes inexplicable contortions of the mind," observed one lower-court judge, "to interpret *Windsor*'s endorsement of the state control of marriage as eliminating the state control of marriage."

Over the next 16 months, the four federal appeals courts (out of the nation's 13) that considered same-sex marriage ruled it was a constitutional right. Twenty-eight federal trial courts and three state supreme courts reached the same outcome. Presumably because of all the judicial activity, only three state legislatures themselves took the step of legalizing gay marriage, though public opinion was moving toward its acceptance. Back in 2003, right after *Lawrence v. Texas*, 39 percent of the country supported same-sex marriage, according to Gallup. Right after *Windsor*, approval had risen to 54 percent, hitting 60 percent two years later right before *Obergefell*. By that point, primarily because of judicial decisions, gay marriage was legal in 37 states and D.C.

Although the Court had chances to get involved after the federal appellate rulings, it didn't grant cert. The justices saw the wisdom in staying above the fray. In late 2014, the calculus changed when the Sixth Circuit, based in Cincinnati, became the first federal appeals court to say gay marriage had no constitutional basis. "When the courts do not let the people resolve new social issues like this one, they perpetuate the idea that the heroes in these change events are judges and lawyers," wrote Judge Jeffrey Sutton. "Better, in this instance, we think, to allow change through the customary political processes, in which the people, gay and straight alike, [meet] each other not as adversaries in a court system but as fellow citizens seeking to resolve a new social issue." (This was the same Sutton deemed "spineless" by Donald Trump because Sutton had voted to uphold the congressional statute creating Obamacare.)

Now there was a split in the lower federal courts, which frequently triggered Supreme Court review. It did so, in early January 2015, in *Obergefell v. Hodges* (consisting of four consolidated cases, concerning same-sex marriage bans in Kentucky, Michigan, Ohio and Tennessee). The questions in the appeal would be controversial, but taking it was not. In the conference, no justice objected to granting cert. Three months later, the Court heard two and a half hours of argument—an unusually long session. Court watchers knew it would be historic: They started camping out in front of the building four days beforehand, as if it were a Grateful Dead concert—or paying a service $50 an hour to hold a spot in line. (When the main act took the stage, the audience included the Roberts, Kennedy and Breyer spouses—who didn't have to wait in line.)

The oral argument was the logical continuation of *Romer, Lawrence* and *Windsor*. The script included all the highlights—with references to historical persecution, ancient Greece, social science, biology, children, polygamy, incest, public opinion, state autonomy, the meaning of the Fourteenth Amendment, and the virtue of democracy. The justices aligned along familiar liberal-conservative lines, with Kennedy in the middle.

Roberts wanted to dwell on the "quick change" in public thinking toward social acceptance. "If you prevail," he told one of the lawyers for the gay couples, "there will be no more debate." Closing a debate "can

for those convinced the Court had become just another political branch of the government.

As a matter of constitutional law, Kennedy's opinion tried to root itself in the "synergistic" and "interlocking nature" of equal protection and due process. The clauses of the Fourteenth Amendment, he wrote, were "connected in a profound way, though they set forth independent principles" in advancing "our understanding of what freedom is and must become." In short, the right to same-sex marriage was about "equal dignity." (It was a term he loved, having used it in a completely different context—presidential ballots in *Bush v. Gore* 15 years before.) As in *Windsor*, it all sounded good, but "synergistic" was just a fancier word for "everything but the kitchen sink." If anyone cared about doctrine, *Obergefell* was less than satisfying. Kennedy was much better at rhapsodizing about marriage. "Since the dawn of history, marriage has transformed strangers into relatives, binding families and societies together," he said. "No longer may this liberty be denied" to gay couples. When he read those words from the bench, many in the capacity audience wept. Minutes later, when word reached the plaza in front of the Court, jubilant gay activists chanted, "Love has won!"

Although *Obergefell* concerned same-sex marriage, the ruling was also just as much the Court's latest justification of its own centrality. But it was hardly obvious that the Court's place was to intercede—all the more so at this moment. The dissenters devoted most of their 63 collective pages to that theme, even though the four of them had shown no reluctance to trample democratic choices in other cases.

Scalia, in one of his last opinions, was in top form. "The substance of today's decree is not of immense personal importance to me," he wrote (rather disingenuously if one looked at all that he had written over the years about gay rights). Instead, he said he was duty-bound "to call attention to this Court's threat to American democracy." In his view, *Obergefell* amounted to a "judicial Putsch" carried out by "nine men and women, all of them successful lawyers who studied at Harvard or Yale Law School." Four of the nine were "natives of New York City"; eight "grew up in East- and West-coast states"; "only one hails from the vast expanse in-between"; and "not a single evangelical Christian" or "even a Protestant of any denomination."

It was the best rendition yet of Scalia's indictment of those anti-democratic elites infesting the Court and seizing "super-legislative" power. "The five justices who compose today's majority are entirely comfortable concluding that every state violated the Constitution for all of the 135 years between the Fourteenth Amendment's ratification and Massachusetts' permitting of same-sex marriages in 2003," Scalia wrote. "They have discovered in the Fourteenth Amendment a 'fundamental right' overlooked by every person alive at the time of ratification, and almost everyone else in the time since"—from "John Marshall Harlan, Oliver Wendell Holmes, Jr., Learned Hand, Louis Brandeis, [and] William Howard Taft," to "Benjamin Cardozo, Hugo Black, Felix Frankfurter, Robert Jackson, and Henry Friendly." The justices of the *Obergefell* majority "know that limiting marriage to one man and one woman is contrary to reason" and "cannot possibly be supported by anything other than ignorance or bigotry."

Kennedy came in for a special tongue-lashing. His opinion, according to Scalia, was "couched in a style that is as pretentious as its content is egotistic." He would know. Scalia then declared, "If, even as the price to be paid for a fifth vote, I ever joined an opinion for the Court that began: 'The Constitution promises liberty to all within its reach, a liberty that includes certain specific rights that allow persons, within a lawful realm, to define and express their identity,' I would hide my head in a bag. The Supreme Court of the United States has descended from the disciplined legal reasoning of John Marshall and Joseph Story to the mystical aphorisms of the fortune cookie." (And yet, despite being enraged, Scalia had shown characteristic grace in private. A former clerk who was a prominent married gay man in corporate America—Paul Cappuccio, the longtime general counsel of Time Warner—wanted to be in the courtroom when *Obergefell* was announced. He surmised it might be on June 26. Scalia arranged for Cappuccio to be in one of the justice's VIP seats.)

Chief Justice Roberts expressed his displeasure more coolly—about judicial lawlessness and its effect on self-rule. "However heartened the proponents of same-sex marriage might be on this day," he wrote, "it is worth acknowledging what they have lost, and lost forever: the opportunity to win the true acceptance that comes from persuading their fellow citizens of the justice of their cause. And they lose this just when the winds of change were freshening at their backs." The chief repeated those words in the courtroom, the first and only time he'd issued a dissent from the bench. (His aim, successful as it turned out, was to preempt another dissenter from speaking up in a way that might be more divisive.) Roberts scolded Kennedy in particular for hypocrisy. Here Kennedy was disregarding the judgments of voters in different states. But just the prior year, Roberts observed, in the *Schuette* affirmative action case, Kennedy bemoaned that it was "demeaning to the democratic process to presume that the voters are not capable of deciding an issue of this sensitivity on decent and rational grounds."

Many Americans, the chief wrote, "will rejoice at this decision, and I begrudge none their celebration." He meant it. He had no animus toward gay rights—he just didn't believe courts should be the principal source of them. "Celebrate the achievement of a desired goal," he went on. "Celebrate the opportunity for a new expression of commitment to a partner. Celebrate the availability of new benefits. But do not celebrate the Constitution. It had nothing to do with it." Because, he said, what Kennedy and the others had done was "an act of will, not legal judgment," resulting in "the transformation of a social institution that has formed the basis of human society for millennia, for the Kalahari Bushmen and the Han Chinese, the Carthaginians and the Aztecs."

"Just who do we think we are?" the chief demanded.

Leaving aside that they weren't the Kalahari or the Han Chinese or the Carthaginians or the Aztecs, that was an easy question: "We" were the ones who wrote *Heller*, *Citizens United* and *Shelby County*—and *Bush v. Gore* before that. During the Court's march to the fore of American society, the conservative emperors on the Court had shown they had no clothes. Scalia's "judicial Putsch" and Roberts's "act of will" could just as well have been ascribed to the majorities in those earlier rulings.

THEN ROBERTS TURNED his sights on *Roe*. Much of the conservatives' frustration over *Obergefell* was that they saw it as *Roe* by any other name. For them, that 1973 ruling—creating a limited right to abortion, based on substantive due process—remained the archetype of liberal overreach by the Court. Roberts first invoked *Dred Scott* and *Lochner*, the worst discredited rulings of yesteryear (he referred to *Lochner* 21 times), to show what could happen when justices submitted to the temptation "to confuse our own preferences with the requirements of the law." The "need for restraint in administering the strong medicine of substantive due process is a lesson this Court has learned the hard way," he warned.

Next, Roberts threw back at Ginsburg her own words, written eight years before she joined the Court. Ginsburg had criticized the "heavy-handed judicial intervention" of *Roe*, which may have "provoked, not resolved, conflict." In Roberts's telling, she was a "thoughtful commentator" on "another issue"; only in a formal citation did he name her.

Alito's and Thomas's references were even more veiled. "Today's decision shows that decades of attempts to restrain this Court's abuse of its authority have failed," Alito wrote. "Substantive due process exalts judges at the expense of the people from whom they derive their authority," added Thomas. But the subtext of both justices was unmistakable. For the conservatives, *Obergefell* was another *Roe*—and they had lost this round.

It wasn't an airtight analogy. Whereas *Roe v. Wade* seemed to emerge from the constitutional ether, the seeds of *Obergefell* had been planted as far back as *Lawrence* a decade earlier. And from a purely practical perspective, *Obergefell* didn't present the same stakes as *Roe*. For abortion opponents, *Roe* sanctioned homicide. *Obergefell* had no such consequences. A marriage license for gay couples in no way affected any other couple, notwithstanding religious outcries to the contrary. At the Court itself, at least among the conservative clerks, *Obergefell* pressed few buttons. That was mostly due to their coming of age at elite colleges and law schools, where gays and lesbians were accepted members of the community. But from where the older conservative justices themselves sat, it felt like they were now enduring *Roe* in their own time.

Purely on the doctrinal merits, Kennedy probably had the better of the argument. The three prior cases had nicely teed *Obergefell* up. As a matter of equal protection, he surely had been correct in *Romer*—the Fourteenth Amendment didn't allow a state to create a class of pariahs. So, too, in *Lawrence*, though the added elements of prosecution, as well as governmental intrusion into the bedroom, made the ruling reasonable on grounds of due process as well—the right to privacy indeed. *Windsor*, despite its detour into federalism, was a variation on *Romer*.

As a result, the country—even Scalia, and particularly him—could see *Obergefell* coming. Ginsburg's oft-stated lament about *Roe*—"too far, too fast," with the Court "biting off more than it could chew"— therefore didn't apply as compellingly to same-sex marriage. She had even remarked so to allies, noting, as Kennedy had, both the run of time since *Romer* and rapidly shifting public opinion in favor of same-sex marriage. *Windsor*, for example, produced none of the backlash that followed the Hawaii Supreme Court ruling in 1993.

Moreover, the Court's vigilance on gay rights fit well into its modern concern for the "discrete and insular minorities" described in Footnote Four of *Carolene Products*. It was true enough that gays and lesbians didn't resemble the paradigm in U.S. history: blacks in the Jim Crow South. Even so, gays and lesbians had been historically maltreated and were un-likely in many jurisdictions to make headway through regular electoral processes—hardly the dominating political force in Scalia's reckoning. That made them very different from those disadvantaged, say, by abor-tion or contraception policies. Of the 38 U.S. jurisdictions where same-sex marriage was legal at the time of *Obergefell*, only a dozen had reached that result democratically, either in legislatures or at the ballot box.

On the whole, the history made for a solid argument why *Obergefell*, once on the docket, was correctly decided. But *Romer*, *Lawrence* and *Windsor* all were about protecting gays and lesbians *from* government. It was a far bigger move to mandate—at that moment—their affirma-tive right to marry. That was where the Court got it wrong, deciding to leap in. Good judging benefited from "the marvelous mystery of time," Bickel had said. "Justice is not to be taken by storm," Ginsburg had wisely observed at her confirmation hearings. "She is to be wooed by slow advance." Twenty years later, referring specifically to *Roe*, she said it was individuals, not the courts, who "initiated" change. "If people don't care, the Court will not save this society," she told law students. "The Court can put its stamp of approval on the side of change and let that change develop in the political process."

In three gay rights cases over the course of two decades, the justices had already put their imprimatur on change. By then allowing other governmental actors to take charge, any potential backlash could best be minimized. The Court could've continued that approach, declining to take the appeals from the Sixth Circuit, staying its hand until another day. The tremendous upside would have been that the justices, even riding the crest of favorable public opinion, would have displayed institutional humility: *Just because we can doesn't mean we will.* Sometimes, as the scholar Cass Sunstein has written, "the best decision is to leave things undecided." There was no urgency. It would have been a moment of bravery to alter the narrative of a triumphal Court, all the more when it was lining up so differently from, say, the 9-to-0 vote of *Brown v. Board of Education.*

Lower courts would have continued to issue opinions, reacting perhaps to other courts and perhaps to unusual facts in particular jurisdictions. Popular attitudes would have continued to evolve, likely in the direction of tolerance—that had been the trend. In turn, legislatures and referendums presumably would have reflected shifts in those attitudes, fully legalizing same-sex marriage or moving in that direction—though of course in some states voters might have chosen otherwise. It would have been representative democracy in bloom, which by most lights was superior to intervention by the Court. In this alternate scenario, such new laws (or lower-court decisions) surely would have ended up before the justices, eventually giving them the opportunity they passed up in *Obergefell.*

The imperfect result for the moment would have been that gay marriage was legal in most, but not all, states. In the four midwestern states composing the Sixth Circuit—which had ruled against James Obergefell and other plaintiffs before the Supreme Court granted cert—same-sex marriage would have remained illegal. Several other states, in the heart-lands and in the South, would have retained bans on gay marriage. The country would have had different laws in different states—just as it had on myriad policy matters, especially in the area of domestic relations (divorce, child custody, adoption). Not all rights got vindicated at the same time, not every solution needed to be immediately nationalized. While gay and lesbian couples would not have been able to marry in some states, there was a greater corresponding good for the Court as an institution.

And the developing law itself actually might have improved. Some-times a split in the lower courts was beneficial, prodding judges over time to sharpen their positions when confronted with alternative rea-soning. Indeed, if the circuits were in disagreement, it suggested that an obvious answer wasn't so clear. "Wise adjudication," Felix Frankfurter once observed, "has its own time for ripening." Though the Court often heard appeals to resolve state conflicts on constitutional issues—when they occurred because of splits in federal appellate rulings—there was no rule to do so. And there were plenty of instances in which the justices stood aside, in spite of Kennedy's assertion that the Court had a "duty to address" Obergefell's claims now.

It is altogether consistent to believe that same-sex marriage warranted constitutional status at some point, but at the same time to conclude the Court should not have said so in 2015, even if little backlash wound up resulting. There were larger goals. Ends matter, but so do means. It is a distinction long lost on the public—understandably so, given how accustomed it has become to Court intervention. But the justices them-selves know better. They know their institution's history. They know that triumphalism hasn't always been the way. They just choose to step in anyway. They do because they can. It is what has made the Supreme Court the most dangerous branch.

A LESS DANGEROUS BRANCH

AMONG THE MANY TALENTS OF JOHN ROBERTS WAS AN ABILITY TO MASK his ambitions. Though conversational in chambers, about the day's head-lines or what he did over the weekend, he was by nature reticent. Law clerks around the building, both his own and others, didn't feel they got to know him as well as, say, Clarence Thomas or Steve Breyer. So when the chief justice a few years ago let his guard down—unprompted—it astonished his listeners. And it revealed a hunger for greatness that went along with an abiding affection for the institution he led.

Several clerks were taking Roberts to lunch a few blocks from the Court. On the walk, one innocently asked him, "How do you like the job?" Instead of something like "It's the privilege of a lifetime," he of-fered a telling response. Roberts began by reminding the clerks that there had been only 16 before him who had occupied the center seat. In that sense, he was delighted to be No. 17. But Roberts understood the history of the Court and of the nation. Even among the chiefs, he observed, there had been only one John Marshall, who served for 34 years at the beginning of the 19th century and wrote the seminal *Marbury v. Madison*, which solidified the Court's place in the constitutional blueprint. Marshall "had the opportunity to decide the great questions because the Constitution was undeveloped," Roberts told the clerks.

"It's not like that anymore," he said. "I was born in the wrong era."

Perhaps not quite so. The chief might yet have the chance to be great. In his early 60s, he was still the third-youngest member of the Court. If he served until he was 80, he wouldn't even reach the halfway point of his tenure until 2020.

Consider the near-term future of the Court. Trump's newest nominee would veer it further to the right, joining conservative stalwarts Gorsuch, Thomas and Alito. With Ginsburg, Breyer, Sotomayor and Kagan on the left, that means the new swing justice would be the chief. The newly constituted Court will truly be the Roberts Court.

ROBERTS SEEMED TO APPRECIATE what greatness in his own time looked like. His votes on gun control, campaign finance and voting rights were indeed injudicious intrusions on democracy and ran counter to his exhortations about how same-sex marriage ought to be left to the political process. But in 2012, in the signal case of Roberts's time on the Court and the most important appeal since *Bush v. Gore*—on the fate of Obamacare—the chief justice might have proven himself a worthy descendant of Marshall.

As the decisive vote in *NFIB v. Sebelius*, the 5-to-4 ruling that upheld the Affordable Care Act (ACA), Roberts kept the Court out of the political maelstrom. The law in question was the signature policy achievement of Barack Obama's presidency. Lower courts had disagreed on the constitutionality of the law's so-called individual mandate, which required most Americans to have health insurance or to pay a penalty based on income and what basic insurance would have cost them. (Congress ultimately repealed the mandate in late 2017, with Trump's rabid support.) The justices agreed to resolve the conflict. Had the justices invalidated the law, the Court could well have become the overriding issue in the November 2012 presidential election between Obama and

Mitt Romney. Roberts understood the institutional toll that might take on the Court.

The individual mandate aimed to address a dilemma: Millions of people participated in the health care market, yet failed to have health insurance. They were able to obtain health care, for example, because hospitals, legally and ethically, couldn't turn away emergencies. Some of those uninsured people paid their bills. Most did not—those consumers received services for nothing. The costs wound up being absorbed by others, which wound up raising the price for those who did have insurance. The mandate made almost everybody pay, one way or another, for their participation in a market that involved trillions of dollars and more than 15 percent of the U.S. gross domestic product. Opponents of the ACA—those who had lost the legislative debate, in the arena of democracy—went to court to undo the law. The constitutionality of the mandate turned on two questions: Did Congress have power under the Commerce Clause to coerce individuals to engage in a specific activity? And could the ACA's penalty qualify as a "tax," which therefore could be levied under the Constitution's Taxing Clause (which stated "Congress shall have power to lay and collect taxes")?

Most constitutional experts thought the first answer was easy: yes. That rendered a second answer unnecessary. But the oral arguments at the Court in March 2012, over the course of three days, showed otherwise on both questions. If people chose not to buy insurance, different justices asked, how could those people be participating in the health care marketplace? By that logic—inaction amounts to action—there were few bounds to government regulation. Scalia pushed the point with an analogy that seemed specious, but then was invoked three more times during the arguments. "Everybody has to buy food sooner or later," he said. "Therefore, everybody is in the market. Therefore, you can make people buy broccoli." The bit wasn't Scalia's spontaneous invention. He was echoing political conservatives who had been making the broccoli argument for three years. Justices borrowed ideas from the academy and beyond all the time. But to the extent it looked like a member of the Court was doing the bidding of Rush Limbaugh and the *Wall Street Journal* editorial page, it was unseemly.

The broccoli analogy was far-fetched, even if Kennedy wound up steaming about it in chambers in the weeks after the arguments. The failure of some people to buy a vegetable hardly had an impact on the overall food market; and for broccoli itself, reduced demand might drive down the price. But health care spending was a very different market. As the government lawyer defending the ACA, Solicitor General Donald Verrilli, explained: "Virtually everybody" is "either in that market or will be in that market," and its "distinguishing feature" is that "people cannot generally control when they enter that market or what they need when they enter."

But the simpler response might have been, sure, it would be theoretically fine for Congress to require people to buy broccoli (or be penalized for not doing so)—if legislators rationally concluded that diet affected health, health affected interstate commerce, and trying to foster intake of green veggies would improve health. A National Eat-Your-Broccoli Act would be silly, but not unconstitutional.

The penalty-qua-tax question was even less complicated, despite the penalty being a tool to affect conduct rather than to raise revenue. Obama and various lawmakers strained to say the penalty wasn't a tax, but that scarcely meant it couldn't be construed as an exercise of Congress's taxing power. (Opponents of the ACA *did* call the mandate a tax.) Nor did it matter that the ACA itself failed to designate the penalty a tax. Judges routinely cut through labels to get at what a statute or executive order really meant. Word games by politicians didn't dictate constitutional law. A rose was still a rose.

The biggest problem for the mandate was that the Obama administration had to contradict itself legally. Before insisting on Day 2 of the arguments that the penalty for refusing to buy health insurance *was* a tax, the administration on Day 1 claimed the penalty was *not* a tax. That's because the obscure 19th-century federal Tax Anti-Injunction Act prohibited litigants from challenging a tax before they actually paid it. Since the ACA penalty hadn't yet taken effect, the Tax Anti-Injunction Act barred a current lawsuit if the penalty was a tax. The administration wanted the uncertainty resolved, so for purposes of the Tax Anti-Injunction Act, it had to argue the penalty wasn't a tax.

Justice Alito was quick to point out the incongruity. "Today, you are arguing that the penalty is not a tax," he told the SG. "Tomorrow, you are going to be back and you will be arguing that the penalty *is* a tax?"

Alito knew better. Legal interpretation, both constitutional and statutory, often required semantics—otherwise called judging. It was the only sensible way to deal with text and subtext. The legal battleground in *NFIB v. Sebelius* was just another chapter in the debate between the literalism championed by Scalia and the pragmatism advocated by Breyer. The debate was always a bit bogus. All judges engaged in interpretation—the only issue was what they called it and the degree to which they conceded it.

Roberts himself, no fan of either constricted literalism or unbounded pragmatism, seemed to admit as much when he pressed one of the lawyers challenging the ACA. "The idea that the mandate is something separate from whether you want to call it a penalty or tax just doesn't seem to make much sense," he said. The chief was foreshadowing how he would come out in the case—and with much accompanying drama.

At the justices' conference on March 30, two days after arguments, Roberts took his seat at the head of the oblong walnut table, under three crystal chandeliers. In this private setting, within the suite of rooms that made up the chief's chambers, neither he nor his colleagues wore their robes. At the far end of the baize-topped table, opposite the chief, was the most senior associate justice, Scalia. Seated to the chief's right were the next three most senior: Kennedy, Thomas and Ginsburg. To the chief's left were the four most junior: Breyer, Alito, Sotomayor and Kagan.

Right behind Scalia was the room's black marble fireplace, with a matching clock on the mantel. Above the mantel, directly facing Roberts, hung a circa-1834 portrait of Chief Justice Marshall. Roberts himself had selected the various portraits in the room, which also included those of Justices Robert Jackson, Benjamin Cardozo and the first John Harlan. (Cardozo, for example, got wall space because he was a

New Yorker, just like three current justices: Ginsburg, Sotomayor and Kagan. Roberts chose Jackson because he so revered his writing.) The chief particularly liked the idea of the venerable Marshall gazing down at the conference, perhaps a muse for the current members of the Court. As always, the conference after *NFIB v. Sebelius* began with handshakes all around—a tradition that dates to the late 19th century. The custom was a reminder that the justices all had the same goals in mind, though Justice James F. Byrnes described it as more like nine boxers about to go to their corners before coming out punching.

Even though the chief owned but one vote, he had an important role at conference. He summarized each case, getting a chance to frame the issues. He went first in the discussion and had the opportunity to cast the opening vote. And when he was in the majority, he determined who wrote the opinion, even though longer-tenured associate justices might be part of the majority.

Roberts outlined the difficult questions raised in the arguments. He carefully acknowledged competing positions on the tax question. But he was certain the mandate was impermissible under the Commerce Clause, so he voted to strike down at least that part of Obamacare, concluding as well that the Taxing Clause couldn't save the mandate. (Whether the rest of the law could survive in the absence of the mandate was left unresolved for now.) Scalia went next—another vote against the mandate (and with it the entire law). Kennedy and Thomas agreed with Scalia's position—two more against. One more vote was needed. While Ginsburg and Breyer then voted to uphold the mandate, Alito sided with Scalia, and the conservatives had their majority, even with Sotomayor and Kagan joining Ginsburg and Breyer. The Court was split 4–4. The chief assigned himself the opinion.

However, that's where the storyline got fuzzier. Based on Roberts's vote, the other justices, immediately after the conference, walked back to their respective chambers and reported to their clerks that the Court was throwing out the most important piece of social legislation in two generations. Clerks reacted predictably—with elation or despair. But Roberts had doubts on the Taxing Clause question, even if he didn't identify them that way in the conference. Votes there are tentative.

Justices aren't locked in. They may re-evaluate based on what someone else's opinion looks like, or if they're writing for the Court themselves, they may discover "the opinion doesn't write."

That's what happened to Roberts during the next two months. He instructed different clerks in his chambers to write alternative drafts of an opinion, the different outcomes turning on the tax question. He finally decided that the mandate could be considered a tax and therefore represented a legitimate congressional exercise of the taxing power. The Commerce Clause aspect became irrelevant. He revealed his new position to the other justices during a subsequent conference. Much as Roberts didn't like how the ACA became law, he thought it was constitutional. On June 28, 2012, the Court announced its decision.

It was the first time the chief had joined the four liberals in a 5-to-4 vote, let alone a ruling that big. (One scholar said it was more like a 4–1–4 decision.) "The text of a statute can sometimes have more than one possible meaning," Roberts wrote. "And it is well established that if a statute has two possible meanings, one of which violates the Constitution, courts should adopt the meaning that does not do so." Bearing in mind that principle of interpretation, he said the mandate "may reasonably be characterized as a tax. Because the Constitution permits such a tax, it is not our role to forbid it, or to pass upon its wisdom or fairness." Even as he granted Congress its due, his opinion scorned congressional ineptitude, suggesting, as one scholar observed, "the fools couldn't even figure out how to structure [the ACA] to render it constitutional."

Roberts viewed what he had done as diligent judging. The other four conservatives thought otherwise. Had Roberts voted initially with the liberals, the conservatives obviously would have been disappointed. But to them, Roberts had caved. Scalia vented about it in a way that surprised even those at the Court who were used to his eruptions. In private, some of Roberts's defenders suggested he didn't actually reverse his position because he hadn't committed in the first place. But internal Court correspondence and draft opinions themselves make clear he indeed had reconsidered. It wasn't that Roberts had decided his initial view was wrong—only that an alternate view was permissible. Because that alternate view deferred to Congress—and in favor of constitutionality—the chief concluded he was required to adopt the alternative view.

Conservatives were so livid that they wrote Roberts off as another David Souter—disloyal to the president and the party who gave him a lifetime seat. According to that narrative, in 1992, only two years after President George H.W. Bush put Souter on the Court, Souter had voted the "wrong" way in *Casey*, the abortion ruling that mostly upheld *Roe v. Wade*; Justices Kennedy and O'Connor also stood convicted of a double-cross on *Roe*. And it was Kennedy who Scalia, Thomas and Alito thought was most likely to stray in *NFIB v. Sebelius*. In fact, it was Kennedy who devoted the most energy to trying to win Roberts back, even as Roberts tried to convince Kennedy to join *him*.

Doctrinally speaking, Roberts's reasoning wasn't the most persuasive—any more, for example, than Earl Warren's had been in *Brown v. Board of Education*. If one tried to diagram Roberts's Obamacare opinion, it might resemble a pretzel. But his logic was good enough, and it kept the Court out of a political quagmire that could do it grave injury. What the Court did, and what it did not do, weren't robotic commands. Decisions required judgment, prudence, timing. In that sense, writing an opinion was akin to doing what the best *umpires* did. Stephen Jay Gould, the evolutionary biologist, once famously explained why it had been right for the umpire Babe Pinelli to call a pitch—quite outside—a strike to finish off Don Larsen's perfect game in the 1956 World Series. "Context matters," Gould wrote. "Truth is a circumstance, not a spot."

Roberts's point that the Court wasn't opining on the ACA's "wisdom or fairness" was a sop to the right, which he repeated when he announced the decision in the courtroom. He emphasized the ruling "is not in any way based on our judgment about whether the Affordable Care Act is good policy." Instead, as he wrote in his opinion, that judgment, "under the Constitution," was "reserved to the people."

To his conservative critics, that naturally wasn't enough. The chief justice hadn't only voted wrong. He'd committed the sin of changing his mind—the second "switch in time that saved nine" at the Court.

(The first had been in 1937 when another Roberts on the Court, Owen Roberts, reversed sides on the constitutionality of New Deal legislation.) Ever since, conservatives have smoldered over what they saw as John Roberts's betrayal. These resentments were what led to Trump's fulminations against Roberts during the 2016 campaign.

The day after the Obamacare ruling, Roberts exhibited his usual sense of humor. Attending a conference of lower-court judges, arriving early, he found himself alone at the head table. "It's lonely here, all by myself," he sardonically remarked to a friend. Later, playing to a big audience, Roberts mentioned he was headed off to Malta to teach a two-week course on American law. "Malta, as you know, is an impregnable island fortress," he explained. "It seemed like a good idea."

The conservative justices and their clerks knew Roberts had switched and someone let word slip out. Such finger-pointing leaks—reported a month before the ruling, by the conservative columnist George Will and others—were unprecedented. The Court simply didn't let anything about pending decisions get out. But the fact of the leaks reflected how much the conservative justices felt they had been duped. It may also have been a clumsy attempt to intimidate Roberts back into the fold.

Conservatives spun such efforts as merely a response to shameful political pressure from lefty law professors, senators and Obama himself. "Taunting" and "get[ting] under Roberts's skin"—"politics at its filthiest"—was "beneath the dignity of the Court," a conservative *Washington Post* columnist called it weeks before the ruling. Never mind that the widely read piece by Kathleen Parker itself could fairly be called an attempt at working the ref. All of it, on both sides of the aisle, was just more evidence that smart people now saw the Supreme Court as a political body susceptible to lobbying that extended beyond the legal briefs.

Four days after the Obamacare ruling, the most dramatic leak of all happened. Citing "two sources with specific knowledge of the deliberations," Jan Crawford of CBS News reported that Roberts had changed his mind. If those sources were the conservative justices or clerks, the leak no longer could serve to win Roberts back. Now, it was just about trying to embarrass him.

At any rate, Roberts hardly had cast his lot fully with the Court's liberal bloc. Much of his opinion focused on the Commerce Clause, which he found proscribed the mandate. That finding didn't alter the outcome of the appeal because Roberts held that Congress still had authority under the Taxing Clause to enact the mandate. But his forceful views on the limits of the Commerce Clause had the faraway potential to radically shrink the power of the federal government to regulate the workplace, promote social welfare, set education policy, and more. Since the New Deal, the Court had almost always upheld legislation against Commerce Clause challenges. Roberts's opinion questioned nearly eight decades of constitutional law. The mandate "does not regulate existing commercial activity," he wrote. "It instead compels individuals to *become* active in commerce by purchasing a product, on the ground that their failure to do so affects interstate commerce. Construing the Commerce Clause to permit Congress to regulate individuals precisely *because* they are doing nothing would open a new and potentially vast domain to congressional authority." That, he said, was not what the Framers had in mind.

Although the four other conservatives declined to join that part of his opinion—or even acknowledge Roberts had written on the Commerce Clause—their views on the subject coincided with his. He was with them more than he was against them. Theirs was a counterrevolutionary view of the Commerce Clause. Many scholars pointed out there weren't a lot of federal laws attempting to compel activity. The "broccoli horrible," as Ginsburg mocked it, was less an actual possibility than a caricature of Big Government—Alice Waters meets George Orwell.

Even so, Roberts's opinion on the Commerce Clause was significant for two reasons. First, he chose to write it at all. There was no need to do so, since the appeal was resolved on the ground of the taxing power. After all, this was the chief who had often said the Court should be in the business of deciding no more than it had to. "Our usual practice," he had counseled in *Northwest Austin*, the 2009 case on the Voting Rights Act, "is to avoid the unnecessary resolution of constitutional questions." Three years before, in a commencement speech at Georgetown, he stressed, "If it's not necessary to decide more to dispose of a case, in my view it is necessary *not* to decide more." Whatever ruminations he'd had about the Commerce Clause were superfluous. Second, he was providing a dog whistle to both libertarians and conservatives that a majority of the justices might be receptive to fresh attempts to curtail federal regulatory authority. By giving Congress and the president what they sought at that instant—but laying down a long-term marker on federal power—Roberts was imitating what John Marshall had deftly executed in *Marbury v. Madison* 209 years earlier.

Marshall's middle-ground ruling found the new administration of President Jefferson had wrongly acted under the federal law at issue. But a constitutional provision on jurisdiction deprived the Court of the power to do anything about it. Jefferson, a political adversary, thus had no incentive to object, even as Marshall, unconstrained, established the authority of the Court to strike down acts of Congress that the justices said violated the Constitution. Marshall put himself "in the delightful position . . . of rejecting and assuming power in a single breath," as a leading historian of the Court extolled it. *Marbury* was "a masterwork of misdirection, a brilliant example of Marshall's capacity to sidestep danger while seeming to court it."

Similarly, in *NFIB v. Sebelius*, Roberts, avoiding a confrontation with a sitting president, was able to rein in Commerce Clause doctrine on the sly—"to advance in one direction while his opponents are looking in another," as Bickel had praised Marshall. A few conservative politicians appreciated what Roberts had pulled off. Most did not. And whatever points he had registered on the constitutional scoreboard would appear only in the distant future.

At the White House, Obama was ecstatic the ACA had survived, even if part of the ruling limited the law's expansion of Medicaid. (Seven justices agreed that Congress had overstepped its authority by trying to coerce states into joining the expansion; if states had refused, they risked losing even their existing funding.) The president was relieved as well. But privately, he professed intellectual admiration for the chief's masterstroke, as much as he disagreed with half of it. "He's clearly playing the long game," Obama told Vice President Biden as they and several aides in the Oval Office pored over the 187 pages of opinions.

Obama had always thought the institutionally minded Roberts was more likely than Kennedy to provide a fifth vote to uphold the ACA. And Obama himself, early on in the litigation in various federal courts, had signed off on the Justice Department's request to argue the mandate was a tax, even though he'd gone on *Good Morning America* to assert it was not. Obama understood that Roberts was more likely than Kennedy to buy into the tax argument. But Obama had not anticipated Roberts's next beat, on the Commerce Clause. Of the various presidential speeches that had been prepared in advance of the rulings, none contemplated exactly what the chief ended up doing.

It MAY WELL BE that Roberts voted to uphold Obamacare chiefly as a way to disguise remaking the Commerce Clause. But such a ploy has yet to pay dividends in any new rulings, and it won him few new admirers on the right. On the Court itself, his conservative colleagues gave him no credit for threading a needle. Moreover, if Roberts really believed the ACA was suspect, he had the chance in another appeal three years later, *King v. Burwell*, to kill it. But with Kennedy also joining the majority this time, Roberts declined to do so.

There's a more basic, less Machiavellian explanation for what motivated him. He thought *NFIB v. Sebelius* was a close case. On the one hand, he believed that Commerce Clause doctrine was not so boundless as to justify regulation based on inactivity—and given the attention that issue had received in the lower courts, he had to address it. But on the other hand, the Taxing Clause was probably broad enough to allow the mandate. In a close case, Congress deserved the benefit of the doubt. Seeing himself as the steward of the Court's legitimacy, Roberts chose to keep the Court out of harm's way. He had failed to do so in *Shelby County*, in *Citizens United* and in *Heller*, but now perhaps, at least in this one case, four months before a presidential election, he had rethought his role and become a judicial statesman—an advocate not for one or another issue, but for the Court itself.

What Roberts actually wrote offered no hint of his motivation, and he of course didn't confess he had switched sides. During oral arguments, he had already indicated that mere labels didn't end the inquiry. Nor was it conclusive that the Obama administration claimed the mandate wasn't a tax under the Tax Anti-Injunction Act. After the conference, he simply rethought the legal issues, deciding the appeal on the merits.

But yes, in a close case, more than the particular issues, he made the Court's institutional needs paramount. Roberts hadn't been on the Court for *Bush v. Gore*, but he had seen the price the Court paid for the ruling. Maybe the chief was acting with the judicial humility he had counseled for others—judicial "politics" in the best sense. If so, in an age when the Court has become ascendant, Roberts's destiny might be, as he told clerks, to do great things.

Maybe.

With a Republican in the White House through at least January 2021, conservatives saw the Court as their best way to accomplish policy ends. (Liberals no doubt would've done the same thing if Hillary Clinton had won and Democrats had taken back the Senate.) Even as Donald Trump floundered, members of his party repeatedly touted Justice Neil Gorsuch as the greatest achievement of the Trump administration. Now, with another appointment to the Court, following Kennedy's retirement, Republicans saw the opportunity, finally, to lock down conservative control of the third branch.

As that possibility increased, much of the legal right discarded talk of merely returning the Court to its more minimalist roots or merely undoing such rulings as *Roe*. With five votes, such changes were too modest. Now the goal would be to get the justices to recognize new constitutional rights—to do precisely what conservatives had denounced liberals for doing for decades. Conservatives of course didn't admit it would be just more judicial activism. Instead, many rebranded their aim as "judicial engagement."

Judicial engagement, a phrase that went back only to 2011, dismissed the idea that the democratic branches deserved any overweening deference if they infringed on freedoms. "The rightful liberties of the people are so capacious they cannot all be enumerated or listed," explained Randy Barnett, a leading libertarian at Georgetown law school. Among other things, judicial engagement adored the open-ended Ninth Amendment, which stated that the existence of certain rights spelled out in the Constitution (like freedom of expression or freedom of religion) didn't preclude other, unlisted ones that were "retained by the people." Judges should be the ones to protect those natural rights, according to the theory.

The chief proponent of judicial engagement was the Institute for Justice, the libertarian public interest shop and "merry band of litigators" that had been behind *Heller*. In establishing its Center for Judicial Engagement, the institute said its mission was to "reinvigorate the courts' role as bulwarks of liberty." It urged the appointment of avenging judges who would "fully enforce the limits our Constitution places on the government's exercise of power over our lives," rather than "abdicate" their duties by showing "misguided deference to other branches." Deference, the institute explained, was "fake judging." In the age of Trump, it has been especially active in trying to seed lower courts with test cases that someday the Supreme Court might use to undo accepted doctrine on federal authority.

The problem with judicial engagement was determining how a conservative justice's view of "rightful liberties" could properly be distinguished from a liberal justice's view of "rightful liberties." As Justice William Brennan had taught, with five votes, you could do anything. To its credit, the institute was consistent. It supported the gay couples in *Obergefell* and took on free speech causes dear to liberals. But in the hands of judicial engagers, the relevant liberties usually centered on the chains of economic regulation—like minimum-wage and maximum-hour laws, rules on health and safety in the workplace, environmental statutes, a government directive to buy health insurance, zoning restrictions on land, and mandatory participation in Social Security. Judicial engagement sounded a lot like restoration of the *Lochner* era, when the Court, in the name of capitalism, struck down New Deal legislation. In justices like Gorsuch, Thomas and Alito, judicial engagement had friends.

Roberts had his complaints about federal regulatory power. He made that much clear when he said the ACA violated the Commerce Clause. He, too, might yet side with radicals on the Court who want to scupper the Voting Rights Act entirely, to topple what was left of campaign finance regulation, and to protect carrying guns in public. But at the end of the day, the chief's instinct for preserving the Court's prestige had prevailed in the Obamacare ruling. And it might also occur to him that repositioning judicial aggrandizement as judicial engagement ought to be resisted, in defense of the Court.

If so, then Roberts might well be hesitant to overturn *Roe*—despite his disapproval of the ruling. Whatever grief he suffered by alienating himself further from conservatives wasn't worth the cost to the Court of looking like the handmaid of radicals. In short, the conventional wisdom about the pending demise of *Roe* in a post-Kennedy Court was hardly obvious.

IN THE 2017–18 TERM OF the Court, Roberts, as well as other justices, sent mixed signals on any embrace of humility. *We're modest, except when we're not.* On the one hand, several rulings seemed to indicate the Court was willing to defer to other branches of government: to Trump on his travel ban and congressional indifference about it; to states that engaged in bald-faced partisan gerrymandering, as well as gerrymandering based on race; to states that wanted out-of-state Internet merchants to collect sales taxes; and to states that wanted to aggressively purge their voting rolls of nonvoters. But on the other hand, the Court was perfectly happy to ignore choices by other governmental actors—most notably at the state level, about discrimination based on sexual orientation and about what medical information had to be provided to pregnant women—as well as, on one major occasion, its own 41-year-old precedent concerning public unions.

Pollyanna would say the rulings merely reflected nine conscientious jurists grappling with the imprecision of constitutional law. The more accurate assessment, though, would acknowledge that the 2017–18 term was a pageant of hypocrisy, driven less by an honest reckoning of hard cases than by conforming to a conservative political agenda. So, the Court gave the thumbs-up to:

- the exercise of vast power over immigration by a Republican in the White House;
- established political parties, which typically meant keeping in office more Republicans than Democrats;
- claims of religious freedom prevailing over discrimination laws protecting gays (in the closely watched case involving a Colorado baker of wedding cakes); and
- claims of pro-life free speech prevailing over the medical interests of pregnant women.

And it was thumbs-down to:

- the idea that President Trump might have been motivated by anti-Muslim bias in enacting his travel ban;
- Democratic votes that had been diluted by reapportionment maneuvering;
- minorities inhibited from voting or whose voting power was diluted by reapportionment; and
- organized labor (which leans toward Democrats and generously funds them).

That last decision—the precedent-busting *Janus v. AFSCME*—typified the conservative majority's goals. The issue was whether government employees who opted not to join unions could still be compelled to help pay for collective bargaining and grievance procedures that benefited them. More than 20 states have laws requiring such "agency fees," which restrict freeloaders. In 1977, the Court unanimously blessed such laws. The Roberts Court reached out to say otherwise. Writing for a 5–4 majority, Justice Alito said agency fees violated the First Amendment: The nonmembers of a union were being forced to subsidize the speech of others.

But that wasn't exactly true. The 1977 ruling already barred agency fees going to overt political activities. Negotiating a collective bargaining agreement hardly sounded like the same thing. It's a question of degree. If government mandates that all lunch counters and hotels must be desegregated, are the First Amendment freedoms of association and speech of business owners violated purely because those individuals don't like the *idea* of integration? Are the rights of a candy bar manufacturer infringed when it has to include a calorie count on the label? Few would see constitutional violations in either situation. Besides, government employees already give up some First Amendment rights because there are some things they're not allowed to say on the job. Nonetheless, the Court in *Janus* found a First Amendment violation. No longer was the First Amendment a shield for the powerless—it was now a sword to be wielded by big business, just as it had been used in *Citizens United* by big money.

Why was it that, according to Alito, the 1977 decision had to be abandoned? It "was poorly reasoned," he alleged, as if poor reasoning didn't live in a whole lot of precedents. No, the transparent explanation for *Janus* was that the conservatives didn't like unions and had the votes to weaken them.

"Don't like a decision?" Justice Kagan taunted in dissent. "Just throw some gratuitous criticisms into a couple of opinions and a few years later point to them as 'special justifications'" for dispensing with stare decisis.

The two rulings, in late June, that best exposed the Court's hypocrisy involved partisan gerrymandering and Trump's travel ban. In each unusual case, in which the justices most assuredly should have intervened to rein in others in government who had overstepped constitutional bounds, they shrunk from their duty—the equivalent of a judicial shrug. Neither ruling would likely have gone the same way if President Obama's nominee—Merrick Garland—rather than Gorsuch, had been on the Court.

The reapportionment cases, *Gill v. Whitford* (about Republican-controlled Wisconsin) and *Benisek v. Lamone* (about Democratic-controlled Maryland), constituted the Court's best chance in a generation to finally fix the worst structural defect in our politics. Indeed, the two cases could have been the Court's most important rulings in years and showed the justices at their best—not picking ideological winners and losers, but enforcing rules of the game.

In the age of supercomputers and hyperpartisanship, legislators in some states had become especially adept at gerrymandering. The party in power drew up congressional districts and state legislative districts that entrenched its power. The mapmakers' technique was to "pack" and "crack." Packing meant concentrating supermajorities of one party in districts so it won overwhelmingly, but in only a few districts. Cracking entailed spreading the disfavored party among districts so it won nothing in the cracked districts. Packing and cracking worked exquisitely well to "waste" votes of the party out of power. What benefit the practices had for democracy was far less apparent. In Wisconsin, for example, in 2012 Republicans won 48.6 percent of the statewide vote for state assembly, but 60 of the 99 seats. Two years later, Republicans got 63 of the seats with 52 percent of the statewide vote.

Such numbers illustrated what the scholar John Hart Ely was talking about when he explained that elected legislatures alone, Republican or Democratic, couldn't be trusted with reapportionment. They just had too much interest vested in maintaining the status quo—in keeping themselves in office. In this instance, democracy didn't foster democracy. In order to "clear the channels of political change," it was obvious that "representative government cannot be trusted." Under those circumstances, as Kagan wrote in *Gill*, it was up to the Court to play its hand. "Here," she said, "politicians' incentives conflict with voters' interests, leaving citizens without any political remedy for their constitutional harms."

Kagan, along with the three other liberals, joined a unanimous Court in *Gill* to reject the challenge on technical grounds—that the particular plaintiffs challenging Wisconsin's districts lacked "standing" to bring the case. That was because those voters didn't actually live in a gerrymandered district, which meant they didn't have sufficient skin in the game. (The Court sent *Gill* back to a lower court to reconsider; the two dissenters wanted the case dismissed entirely. In *Benisek*, the

Maryland case, the Court also ducked the main issue, finding that the challengers had waited too long to file a lawsuit.)

The Court's objection in *Gill* wasn't ridiculous, but the justices could easily have concluded that the plaintiffs' injuries were statewide in nature. Instead, they preferred to skirt the issues, in large part because Kennedy was on the fence—and certainly not prepared to join Kagan's four-justice concurrence. Kennedy had been straddling the problem of partisan gerrymandering for more than a decade, but still wasn't ready—even as he was retiring—to take a side. A flimsy declaration by the Court didn't do anybody much good, and with Kennedy departing, there remained the possibility of an eventual resolution on the constitutional merits. Kagan's opinion—by laying out how challengers next time could solve the standing problem by presenting a First Amendment right-of-association claim—offered a road map on how to win a Court majority. Whether the newest justice, taking Kennedy's seat, might provide the decisive fifth vote was another story.

Gill was all the more galling given that the Court, on the same day, did intervene in another dispute—supposedly governed by the First Amendment—that involved the political process. In a case from Minnesota, the justices struck down a state law that prohibited individuals in a polling place from wearing hats, T-shirts, badges, and other gear that expressed a political message. So, evidently, the Court knew that some constitutional rights in the context of elections needed vindication.

While the decision on Trump's travel ban may not have long-term significance, it demonstrated that the Court seemed content to look the other way when doing so dovetailed with a partisan agenda. The five justices who upheld Trump's executive order in *Trump v. Hawaii* were associated with the GOP (just as the four dissenters were connected to Democrats). This wasn't a reprise of *Bush v. Gore*, but one would be forgiven for believing political preferences might have had something to do with the outcome. If, say, a President Hillary Clinton had issued an executive order that appeared to be animated by bias, would the same five justices have approved? As in the reapportionment cases, the Court could have distinguished itself by checking another branch of the government that had exceeded constitutional limits.

The travel ban had its origins in Trump's presidential campaign, when he unrelentingly advocated a "Muslim ban." He read on TV a "Statement on Preventing Muslim Immigration" that called for a "total and complete shutdown of Muslims entering the United States until our country's representatives can figure out what's going on." As a candidate, he also declared that "Islam hates us" and the United States was "having problems with Muslims coming into the country." Shortly after Election Day, when Trump was asked whether violence in Europe had affected his plans to "ban Muslim immigration," he replied, "You know my plans."

A week after Trump was sworn in, he issued his first executive order banning foreign travelers from several mainly Muslim countries; according to an adviser, the president called it a "Muslim ban" since "we can't allow people coming into the country who have this hatred of the United States." After lower courts blocked the first order, Trump issued another version, insisting that it was "much tougher." It was a third order, in effect since December 2017 and imposing indefinite restrictions on travel, that the Supreme Court considered.

Trump's orders on foreign travel might have been unremarkable under other circumstances. The president has extraordinary discretion over border policy, because Congress had delegated that authority. But Trump's anti-Muslim enmity, though expressed chiefly during his campaign, raised the question of whether he was discriminating on the basis of religion. According to Roberts, in a 5-to-4 decision, the travel ban was legal because it was neutral on its face and justified by national security—Trump's other, noxious statements were beside the point. To blunt Trump's words, Roberts explained that "we must consider not only the statements of a particular president, but also the authority of the presidency itself."

Sotomayor would have none of it. In a vehement dissent from the bench, she recounted a litany of Trump's words. "Let the gravity of those statements sink in," she said. They "were spoken or written by the current president of the United States." In her written opinion, she concluded with a defense of judicial action: "Our Constitution demands, and our country deserves, a judiciary willing to hold the coordinate branches to account when they defy our most sacred legal commitments." In this case, she was right.

Trump v. Hawaii was especially infuriating, Sotomayor said, because the Court used it to officially repudiate *Korematsu*, the 1944 ruling that upheld the wartime detention of Japanese Americans. Trump's travel ban, according to Sotomayor, was little different. The parallels, she said, were manifest: "an ill-defined national-security threat to justify an exclusionary policy of sweeping proportion"; "an exclusion rooted in dangerous stereotypes about . . . a particular group's supposed inability to assimilate and desire to harm the United States"; and "strong evidence that impermissible hostility and animus motivated the government's policy." In redeploying "the same dangerous logic underlying *Korematsu*, the Court "replaces one gravely wrong decision with another."

Anthony Kennedy remained an essential fifth vote in close cases like *Gill* and *Trump v. Hawaii*, as well as *Janus*. But the 2017–18 term was the first time in more than a decade in which he didn't vote with the liberals in at least one 5-to-4 ruling. (The year before, he was with the liberals in those cases half the time.) There were 18 decisions in 2017–18 that split 5–4 on ideological issues—and Kennedy sided with the conservative justices every time. It was the most riven Court in years: Only 34 percent of its rulings were unanimous, down 23 percentage points from the prior term. When Kennedy had the opportunity to act as a brake on the conservative onslaught, he was in the back seat. He had relished his time in the center of the storm. But he decided he was done.

The liberal justices couldn't miss Kennedy's vanishing act. Combined with Gorsuch's arrival the year before, it conspired to produce a term of abject misery (even if Gorsuch in his first full year didn't prove to be quite as conservative as Thomas or Alito). And with Kennedy's replacement—the 53-year-old Brett Kavanaugh—looming, the liberals knew the future looked grim. What they feared most was that an energetically retrograde Court would suffer in the eyes of a public that no longer respected it. The justices always faced that risk if their anti-democratic ways diverged too far from the body politic. But it was hardly clear that the emboldened conservative majority, unshackled by Donald Trump, appreciated the peril.

VARIOUS STRUCTURAL REFORMS have been suggested to restrain an arrogant Court, to depoliticize the appointments process, and to lower
the stakes for filling its vacancies. The best of these ideas was to eliminate life tenure and to phase in staggered, non-renewable terms—say, for
18 years, which eventually would result in a vacancy every two years. In
such a system, presidents would no longer have disproportionate incentive to name youthful justices—Trump's advisers call age 55 the "sell-by
date" for Court candidates—and no single justice could have protracted
influence. The last six justices to leave the Court served, on average, for
29 years. One well-known judge called the federal judiciary "the nation's
premier geriatric occupation." When the Framers created the Court,
Americans who survived childhood had a life expectancy of around
60 years. When he was a lawyer in the Reagan administration, Roberts
himself endorsed a 15-year term limit for federal judges. But that kind
of change would require a constitutional amendment, and the political
party in power at the Court would never support it.

Likewise, a statute requiring justices to move to lower federal courts
after a period of years—they'd retain their life tenure—would be politically unrealistic. So, too, would be the idea of staffing the Supreme
Court sequentially with nine experienced judges chosen at random from
the federal appellate courts, who would serve for a limited time before
returning to their original posts. Nor was it likely, back in the real world,
that any president would unilaterally begin nominating moderates, the
better to create a nonideological Court whose rulings wouldn't be seen
as extensions of partisan agendas. Obama might have come closest to
that ideal in naming Merrick Garland, but Obama did so only because
of political calculation.

No, the best chance for the Court to reclaim its stature is from
within, and it is John Roberts who provides the Court's best hope. If the
Court is to become a less dangerous branch, he has the opportunity, the
temperament and maybe the skill to help to make it so.

In recent decades, most conservatives deplored the Court for *Roe* and

Obergefell, while their liberal counterparts saluted those decisions. Just as predictably, liberals denounced *Bush v. Gore*, *Heller*, *Citizens United* and *Shelby County*, while conservatives applauded. If mere outcomes are the lodestar for evaluating the work of the justices, that altogether makes sense. But the modern history of the Court shows that the real institutional problem isn't this or that unwise ruling. It's that the justices simply are involving themselves too often and with too much certitude.

Other branches surely can do grievous harm, and have: tolerance of slavery for decades; failing to head off the Great Depression; 58,000 American deaths in the Vietnam War; and countless missteps on taxation, education, debt, infrastructure and other vast swaths of policy. But the Supreme Court's accretion of power—steady, subtle, unstated—produces its own danger. We have come to expect from the Court what it should not deliver. And in turn we demand even less from our democratically chosen representatives.

Once upon a time, the exemplar of judicial deference—Oliver Wendell Holmes Jr., who served on the Court from 1902 to 1932—wrote to his British friend, Harold Laski, and quipped: "If my fellow citizens want to go to hell, I will help them. It's my job." Holmes was right, even if hell wasn't the optimal destination. Roberts said much the same thing, more forgivingly, in the first Obamacare ruling: "It is not our job to protect the people from the consequences of their political choices."

Impatiently, myopically, with deep distrust in our elected representatives, we have come to believe that democracy is broken. And we have come to see the justices as our saviors. With so much dysfunction elsewhere in government, the justices see themselves that way, too. But we need more politics, not less politics. It is a sign of weakness that we countenance an almighty Court to resolve so many of our hardest choices. We do not need, nor should we want, the Court to save us from ourselves.

THE COURT IN THE AGE OF TRUMP

THE TRUMP COURT ALMOST NEVER HAPPENED. AND IF IT HADN'T, THE Trump presidency might have been sunk as well.

At least that's what key GOP senators and strategists feared might be the denouement of Brett Kavanaugh's confirmation hearings during the first week of October 2018, after Christine Blasey Ford, under oath, accused him of sexually assaulting her during their time in high school. Ford's testimony before the Senate Judiciary Committee was credible, and her demeanor was unassailable. If Senator Susan Collins, the Republican moderate from Maine, hadn't voted to confirm Kavanaugh, his nomination likely would've been rejected. Not only would the Trump administration have sustained a pivotal political loss, it would have gone into the midterm congressional elections without having secured conservative control over the Court at last. Trump would not have been able to parade Kavanaugh before his base as his greatest accomplishment. Now the Democrats would be the ones smelling electoral blood. The Democrats might have been able to take back the Senate, and Republicans wouldn't have had enough time after Election Day to rush in another nominee.

The end result: virtual certainty that no subsequent Trump nominee to the Supreme Court could be confirmed before the 2020 presidential election. Facing such an apocalyptic political defeat, Trump's prospects for a second term would be dim.

So went the terrified GOP narrative on Capitol Hill as Collins deliberated how to vote. In the end, perhaps foolishly, she bought into Kavanaugh's private reassurances that he would respect the doctrine of stare decisis, rule incrementally, and defer to other decision-makers in government when appropriate, and that he wasn't really the Trump toady he sounded like when he testified. Bellicose and indignant, Kavanaugh had labeled the hearings a "circus" and a "national disgrace"—the identical words Clarence Thomas had chosen during his hearings 27 years earlier—and accused his accusers of participating in a conspiracy driven by "pent-up anger about President Trump" and "revenge on behalf of the Clintons" to "destroy my good name." Because of the "bias" reflected in that "performance," former Justice John Paul Stevens soon thereafter called Kavanaugh unqualified for the Court. No problem, said Collins. And because of her, Kavanaugh was confirmed, then sworn in almost immediately. Two days later, he was over at the White House for a political pep rally led by the president, at whose side stood Anthony Kennedy, the justice that Kavanaugh replaced.

Thus was born a new Court, and a decidedly different Court.

BY THE LATE FALL OF 2018, the chief justice finally had enough.

For the first two years of the Trump administration, John Roberts had watched and listened to the president's attacks on the motives of federal judges. Intentionally or unwittingly, Trump stoked public confusion over the proper role of the judiciary, continually saying he viewed the Supreme Court itself as no more than a political accessory. Roberts didn't do press interviews and made fewer public appearances than, say, Justice Stephen Breyer. At a personal level, the chief didn't particularly enjoy being a spokesperson for the Court. Institutionally, he felt the less said, the better: The Court's imprimatur rested in part on the nine justices' remove from the spotlight. In their black robes, residing in the marble temple, the justices spoke through their opinions; and that, Roberts thought, ought to be enough most of the time.

But he concluded that Trump's barrage against the judiciary—unheard of in modern presidencies—at long last needed to be countered. And Roberts believed only the chief justice of the United States could do it. The last straw came in November when Trump railed against a lower-court judge who had ordered the administration to resume accepting asylum claims from migrants no matter how they entered the United States or where they were from. "An Obama judge!" Trump complained to reporters. (The judge had in fact been appointed by Obama.)

Responding to an Associated Press request for comment—the kind of thing justices invariably ignore—Roberts issued a statement. "We do not have Obama judges or Trump judges, Bush judges or Clinton judges," he wrote. "What we have is an extraordinary group of dedicated judges doing their level best to do equal right to those appearing before them. That independent judiciary is something we should all be thankful for."

To educate the public and more so to assure the judges of the lower federal judiciary that he had their backs, Roberts had been itching to say something in defense of the branch of government that he led. Trump seemed to behave as if the federal judiciary, including the Court, was a wholly owned subsidiary of the White House. And it hadn't escaped the chief justice's notice that some of the shots—dating to the 2016 presidential campaign—were aimed at him.

Several other justices had already decried the politicization of the Court recently. For example, a month earlier, during a talk at Princeton, Elena Kagan said it was "an incredibly important thing for the Court to guard its reputation . . . of being neutral, of not being simply an extension of the terribly polarized political process and environment that we live in." She made her comments eight days after Kavanaugh's tumultuous hearings ended. As much as Trump's attacks on federal judges, those hearings made the Court look like another political, and hyperpartisan, branch of government.

It was against that backdrop that Roberts had to decide when, and if, to say something publicly. Rather than issue a comment on his own—he most assuredly didn't own a Twitter account—or wait until he was scheduled to speak at a legal conference or a law school, the chief jumped at the chance the AP request offered. Within the hour, and without running it by the other justices, he issued his statement about "Trump judges" and "Obama judges." This was the idealized Roberts in full measure: self-possessed, tactical, careful, media-savvy, and unfaltering when it came to judicial autonomy.

With Kennedy's retirement, Roberts now served not only as chief but also as what passed for the ideological center of the Court. On many key cases, for the first time since his arrival in 2005, it was his vote that would be decisive between the equally divided liberal and conservative wings. Even as he had to adjust to the new dynamic, he reveled in his new role. A few weeks after the 2018–19 term ended, Kagan offered this crack about Roberts: "The chief justice is very clear that the associate justices are *not* leaders of the Supreme Court." She said it playfully to law students at Georgetown, but with an edge. They laughed; she chortled. (For his part, ex-Justice Kennedy had to adjust as well. He stayed in D.C., kept a small chambers at the Court, and, unlike other retired justices, often could be seen puttering around the place. He wanted to remain useful, and it was left to the chief justice to find legal committees on which he was still eligible to serve. Kennedy had gone from being the most powerful individual in the building—and sometimes the country—to being a relic.)

Roberts's statement (and the inevitable presidential tweet of defiance in response) came out the day before Thanksgiving—one of the slowest news days of the year. Although it might be that fewer Americans checked the headlines that day, at the same time, in the absence of other news, Roberts's rebuke of the president dominated the holiday news cycle through the weekend.

STILL, WHILE THE CHIEF'S LOFTY declarations about judicial neutrality sounded all well and good, some of the Court's rulings that ensued over the next eight months belied them. Much of the 2018–19 term was quiet, perhaps because the justices aimed to lay low for a time. By far, the year's most consequential decision was about partisan gerrymandering—an issue the Court had dodged just a year earlier. The case was *Rucho v. Common Cause*, announced on the last day of the term, in June 2019. Over the last two decades, the justices have gravely erred in various cases—like *Heller* in 2008 (guns), *Citizens United* in 2010 (campaign spending) and *Shelby County* in 2013 (voting rights). But *Rucho* took the prize as the Court's worst decision since *Bush v. Gore* in 2000. Though *Bush v. Gore*'s mistake was about the Court fundamentally overstepping its constitutional bounds, the ruling affected just one election. *Rucho* stands to subvert countless legislative races across the national map for generations.

And more than a ruling on any specific social issue—like abortion or same-sex marriage or immigration or gun control—*Rucho* goes to the heart of how we structure our entire political system and whether we protect the sanctity of every vote. An unfair electoral system undermines citizens' ability to influence any particular social policy. The right to vote preserves all other rights. Without it, citizens have no voice in determining any other rights. Yet in *Rucho*, the Court concluded it was incapable of curbing even extreme partisan gerrymandering. The justices thereby abdicated their constitutional responsibility to guarantee that every voter in every state is able to participate equally in the political process.

The vote in *Rucho* was 5–4. The majority consisted of the five justices appointed by Republican presidents, including Trump's two appointees, Kavanaugh and Neil Gorsuch. Roberts wrote the emphatic majority opinion. The minority consisted of the four justices appointed by Democratic presidents, including Barack Obama's two appointees, Kagan and Sonia Sotomayor. So much for the chief justice's insistence that there were no "Trump judges" or "Obama judges." And so much for claims that it was unreasonable to predict outcomes in crucial cases based on the political leanings of justices, long before briefs in the cases were filed and arguments were heard. The fault line in *Rucho* suggested otherwise—that most members of the Court got there because they'd be reliable votes rather than because they had independent minds.

Both Republicans and Democrats have engaged in partisan gerrymandering. The justices chose the two cases in *Rucho*—one challenging North Carolina districting maps drawn by Republicans, the other challenging Maryland districting maps drawn by Democrats—because they involved election-rigging by each party. But the effectiveness of grotesque partisan gerrymanders—enabled by big data and advances in computing technology—is a phenomenon that benefits the GOP more. In part that's because Republicans control the most state legislatures these days, and entrenching legislative majorities helps Republicans more. It's also because Republicans simply are better at hardball. Senator Mitch McConnell's obstruction of Obama's nomination of Merrick Garland to the Supreme Court in 2016 was Exhibit A of that unfortunate prowess. Whatever Roberts's protestations, the likely devastating result of *Rucho* was to cement overall GOP dominance in statehouses and many congressional districts.

Even so, the most remarkable aspect of the ruling was its unmitigated hypocrisy. Here was the Court thrusting its juridical arms in the air, feigning helplessness to remedy partisan gerrymandering, even as Roberts conceded the practice was "incompatible with democratic principles." Yet in recent years the Court had cast the deciding vote in a presidential election; invented a personal right to own a gun under the Second Amendment; crippled the Voting Rights Act of 1965; eviscerated campaign finance limits; mortally wounded unions; and created a constitutional right for same-sex couples to marry. And on occasion, the justices did the most aggressive judicial thing of all—they expressed contempt for precedent.

Such cases demanded the justices to make close calls; to balance interests; to weigh competing constitutional values, the vast open spaces left by constitutional text, and conflicting historical evidence—in short, *to judge*. Most of the rulings in those cases forced the Court to second-guess what other branches of government had done. For example, on the same day as *Rucho*, the Court, 5–4 and with Roberts writing the opinion, rejected (correctly so) the Trump administration's "contrived" basis for adding a question on citizenship to the 2020 census. In *Rucho*, Roberts himself acknowledged the Court's self-confidence that more modest jurists might call arrogant: "No one can accuse this Court of having a crabbed view of the reach of its own competence," he wrote. No one indeed.

But lo and behold, when it came to partisan gerrymandering, the Court's view suddenly turned humble. In the North Carolina case, map-makers hardly hid their intent to maintain the state congressional delegation's division into 10 Republicans and three Democrats, even though state voting patterns did not divide along those lines. "I think electing Republicans is better than electing Democrats," explained David Lewis, one of the Republican legislators in charge of redistricting. He proposed bizarrely shaped maps to keep the 10-to-3 split, he said, helpfully, only "because I do not believe it's possible to draw a map with *11 Republicans* and two Democrats." The lower court threw out the maps as a violation of equal protection under the Fourteenth Amendment.

Roberts and the conservatives disagreed. "Federal judges," he wrote, "have no license to reallocate political power between the two major political parties, with no plausible grant of authority in the Constitution, and no legal standards to limit and direct their decisions." Yet the Constitution's Equal Protection Clause offered exactly that "plausible grant of authority." Roberts's caveat about the need for "legal standards" was stronger. But the Court drew lines all the time—including on gun control, campaign spending and the Voting Rights Act, as well as abortion. Moreover, when it came to gerrymanders, the Court had been perfectly comfortable for years weighing in on, and outlawing, racial gerrymandering that diluted African-American voting power and departures from the principle of "one person, one vote." Evaluating electoral districts gerrymandered on the basis of politics wasn't any harder than evaluating them when they were gerrymandered based on race. Contrary to the chief's bemoaning a lack of limiting principles, experts in *Rucho* had presented a range of manageable standards that judges could use to identify extreme gerrymanders.

One can reasonably differ with legislative choices that restrict gun ownership, abortion, campaign expenditures and the scope of the Voting Rights Act. The Constitution gives us the remedy for disagreements: Throw the rascals out of office and vote for better representatives. But the Supreme Court has often short-circuited that route, substituting its own judgment under the cloak of constitutional law. The justices have done so even though the ordinary machinery of democracy was well-suited to the job—if the people in fact wanted change, they could vote for it. Gerrymandering is different, because legislators can distort and corrupt the electoral process that might otherwise send them packing. Voters are supposed to pick their representatives—not the other way around. It is in precisely such circumstances—when the "channels of political change" are clogged by gerrymanders—that "majority tyranny" sets in and democracy can't be trusted. It is in those circumstances that the Court *ought* to flex its muscle. In *Rucho*, and in other cases, the modern Court got it exactly backwards—inserting itself when it should not have, abstaining when it should have intervened.

In her finest dissent since joining the Court, Kagan warned that "the practices challenged in these cases imperil our system of government." Writing for the four liberals, Kagan pointed out that "part of the Court's role in that system" is "to defend its foundations. None is more important than free and fair elections." "For the first time in this nation's history," she said, what the Roberts-led majority had done was to find "an acknowledged constitutional violation" and then "declare that it can do nothing." Writing with the kind of passion more often seen in the opinions of Sonia Sotomayor, Kagan said, "Of all times to abandon the Court's duty to declare the law, this was not the one." She had hoped to pick off Kavanaugh as a fifth vote to command a majority. As dean at Harvard Law School, Kagan had hired Judge Kavanaugh to be a visiting professor, and the two were friends. But Kavanaugh wasn't on the fence, and she never had a chance.

Roberts answered that the solution to partisan gerrymandering rested not with the Court, but with state constitutional amendments, state courts, independent state redistricting commissions, Congress, and state legislatures themselves. Really? It was state legislatures that created the very problem. Asking them to police themselves was like asking Yogi Bear to guard the picnic baskets. And the chief's suggestion about independent commissions smacked of absurdity, since he had told Arizona in a dissent four years earlier that its commission was, wouldn't you know it, unconstitutional.

THERE WERE OTHER NOTEWORTHY RULINGS in the 2018–19 term. On First Amendment grounds, the Court struck down a federal statute barring registration of vulgar trademarks. It allowed a 32-foot cross honoring World War I soldiers to remain on government land in Maryland, despite the Constitution's ban on "establishment" of religion. In criminal law, the justices declined to overrule precedents permitting two prosecutions—one federal, one state—for the same criminal offense, even though the Fifth Amendment bars "double jeopardy." And the justices decided that a massive antitrust class action against Apple could proceed. The rulings were neither self-aggrandizing nor especially controversial. The liberal and conservative wings didn't vote in lockstep; Kavanaugh voted with Gorsuch only 53 percent of the time in non-unanimous cases, nearly as often as Kavanaugh voted with Kagan or Breyer. (Kavanaugh voted most frequently with Roberts and Samuel Alito.)

But that small set of statistics didn't prove a whole lot, though the justices themselves liked to cite them as evidence the Court was a neutral institution resistant to politics. *Rucho* was the lone blockbuster of the term—and it split right down the ideological divide. The census ruling only went against Trump because the chief justice—apparently late in the game—sided with the liberals, on extremely narrow statutory grounds (and even that ruling permitted a do-over). Kavanaugh, Gorsuch, Thomas and Alito had no qualms about the administration lying to the Court. The ruling incensed Trump, and he momentarily considered disobeying it by issuing an executive order.

It's fair to suppose that the justices in 2018–19 were biding their time. To the extent the chief had an agenda, and to the extent he could engineer the Court's discretionary docket, the motivation would be understandable. After the Kavanaugh hearings, and with Democratic presidential candidates looking to make the Court an issue in 2020, Roberts might've much preferred to keep the Court out of the political crossfire. That's the most charitable way to explain *Rucho*.

However, the Court in the 2018–19 term did throw down markers for rulings that would leave in the dust any claim to judicial minimalism. The battle cry of sophisticated conservatives has long been "deconstructing the administrative state"—which is fancy-pants lingo for reducing the modern authority of federal agencies. Pro-life activists didn't care about that crusade, and Trump didn't get the constitutional niceties, but successfully attacking the legal basis for the federal bureaucracy going back to the New Deal would change American life. In *Kisor v. Wilkie*, the Court appeared to be just one vote short of discarding that 75-year-old legal footing, stopping short only because Roberts wouldn't go that far just yet. Merely "a stay of execution," Gorsuch called it. He, and at least Kavanaugh, Thomas and Alito, preferred trusting themselves—judges—rather than the agencies to which Congress had delegated the responsibility of implementing statutes and regulations.

Abortion, of course, remained on the horizon. Energized by Kavanaugh's replacement of Kennedy, nine state legislatures in 2019 passed bills restricting abortion rights. Several amounted to virtual bans and were geared to test the continued viability of *Roe v. Wade* all the way to the Supremes. While only Thomas has voted explicitly to overturn *Roe*, it's a smart bet that Alito and Gorsuch will someday join him. The fate of *Roe* would then be in the hands of Kavanaugh and Roberts, both of whom would be needed to undo the precedent. Twice in 2018–19, the Court avoided dealing with *Roe*. In one case, the justices declined to determine if a state could forbid abortions based on the sex, race, or disability of a fetus, but in the same case upheld a requirement that abortion providers bury or cremate fetal remains. In the other case, with Roberts casting the deciding vote, the Court temporarily blocked a Louisiana law that might have left just one physician in the state authorized to provide abortions.

The latter case could easily arrive back at the Court during the 2019–20 term (as will cases on gun rights, transgender discrimination, and the Trump administration's attempt to end DACA, the program that shields young undocumented immigrants). Whether the conservative justices will directly confront *Roe*—and with it the merits of precedent in a landmark ruling that's been constitutional law for nearly half a century—will represent John Roberts's greatest test so far, even more than his 2012 vote on Obamacare. The conservatives would relish the ensuing storm. Whether the chief has the sea legs for it could define his tenure.

His colleagues have warned of the peril ahead. In May 2019, the Roberts Court decided a jurisdictional issue about sovereign immunity— whether private parties could sue a state in the courts of a different state. In 1979, the justices had said yes. This time, the Court said no, 5–4, overturning a 40-year-old precedent. The right wing of the Court constituted the majority. Granted, not many such state lawsuits arise and the ruling itself doesn't have broad implications. But the dissent called out the conservatives' evident scorn for stare decisis. Breyer spoke for the four liberal justices. "It is one thing to overrule a case when it 'defies practical workability,' when 'related principles of law have so far developed as to have left the old rule no more than a remnant of abandoned doctrine,' or when 'facts have so changed . . . as to have robbed the old rule of significant application,'" he wrote, citing the Court's own previous pronouncements. Those factors did not exist in the case before the Court. "It is far more dangerous to overrule a decision only because five members of a later Court come to agree with earlier dissenters on a difficult legal question," Breyer said.

He didn't have to mention *Roe v. Wade*. Anybody reading the dissent knew what he was alluding to: He quoted extensively from *Planned Parenthood v. Casey*, the 1992 decision that upheld *Roe*. Then, in his last line, the amiable (and cautious) Breyer uncharacteristically seemed to goad the conservatives: "Today's decision can only cause one to wonder which cases the Court will overrule next."

For all its profound doctrinal flaws, if *Roe* were reversed, it would mark the first time in American history that a constitutional right was revoked. It's one thing for the Court to have stayed out of the abortion morass in the first place, as even some of the current liberal justices might have preferred to do had they been on the Court at the time. But taking back a right risked enormous cost to the institution. The chief justice, and maybe Kavanaugh, may opt to chip away at *Roe* without administering the coup de grâce. They could do so by voting to uphold

any regulation short of an outright ban. But at a certain point that kind
of finesse will be seen for what it is. On abortion, as well as on remaking
the rules of federal power, this was a Court on the brink.

In the background of the term loomed the 2020 presidential campaign. Politics is never far from the Court, regardless of what the chief
justice might wish. With Breyer and Ruth Bader Ginsburg into their
80s, the winner in the 2020 race will probably get the opportunity to
nominate at least one justice. With the Garland episode and Trump's
two appointments fresh in memory, Democratic rage abides—and with
it the first serious discussion of Court-packing in eight decades.

The Constitution itself, by omission, contemplates packing the
Court (or as proponents call it, "changing the number of seats based on
changed circumstances"). All that Article III says—its *text*, as Neil Gorsuch, Brett Kavanaugh, Clarence Thomas and others could tell you—is
that there shall be a Supreme Court, whose members shall "hold their
offices during good behavior," which has been taken to mean for life.
That's why there's agreement it would take a constitutional amendment
to institute term limits for justices. (It's an excellent idea—justices nowadays serve for ever-longer periods—and it will never happen.) However,
the Court's size is up to Congress and there's nothing magical about the
number nine. In the first century of the Republic, Congress changed the
number of justices seven times, from six to five to six to seven to nine
to 10 to seven and then, in 1869, the bench returned to nine, and there
it has remained. The presidents supporting such changes included John
Adams, Thomas Jefferson, Andrew Jackson and Abraham Lincoln—not
a radical among them.

So Congress is entirely free to pass legislation that increases the size
of the Court (or decreases it by attrition). Anybody who intimates differently is disingenuous at best. Given the current Court's activism, and
given the effective theft by Senator McConnell of Antonin Scalia's seat,
is it time for Democrats to pack the Court if they gain control of both
houses of Congress and the presidency? Mainstream Democrats, in-

cluding those running for president, have raised the possibility and new groups with that mission have been founded.

There are plenty of good arguments against Court-packing. Some were made back in 1937, when Franklin Roosevelt first proposed it as a way to get around rulings he disliked that kept undercutting the New Deal. Undeniably, Court-packing would politicize the institution even more; it would extinguish any notion about the "rule of law"; and it would confirm that the Court is little different than the other branches of government. Court-packing would also raise the specter of an endless arms race between successive Democratic and Republican administrations. The Court would become subject to ongoing manipulation, a seesaw based solely on its roster—"not unlike Argentina under Juan Perón or Venezuela under Hugo Chávez," as two Harvard political scientists declared in their 2018 bestseller, *How Democracies Die*.

But then there was Merrick Garland. Though Court-packing would demolish a norm that's lasted 150 years, what the Republican Senate did to Garland, too, was norm-shattering. So, too, were the musings of GOP senators that they would try to block any Court nominee by a Democratic president, no matter when a vacancy occurred—the Garland blockade carried to the nth degree. Democrats could respond to the Garland episode—and the loss of liberal control of the Court that accompanied it—in kind, by obstructing when the tables are turned someday. Under a Republican president and a Senate controlled by Democrats, that day could come soon enough if a conservative justice unexpectedly left the Court. But with the oldest conservative only in his early 70s (Thomas), and two conservatives not yet 55 (Kavanaugh and Gorsuch)—and with many recent justices serving well into their 80s—the odds of having an opportunity to reciprocate the treatment of Garland are slim.

No, the best retaliatory gambit for Democrats is Court-packing (along with elimination of the filibuster for legislation, which it would require). If Democrats were to add a seat, it presumably would be filled with a reliable liberal. The Court would then be split 5–5. If Democrats were to add *two* liberals—even numbers on appellate courts are disfavored, lest ties result—the conservative tilt of the current Court would vanish. That outcome would compensate for the stolen Garland seat, and Republicans would be powerless to stop it. They might bellyache about the power play—with absolutely no appreciation of irony—but for Democrats such whining would just be a bonus. Of course, down the road, when Republicans retook power, they probably would add two seats of their own, for a 7-to-6 majority. At some point, the vicious arms race might require justices to double up in their chambers and trade in their custom chairs on the bench for Southwest Airlines seats—or to beg Congress for a larger building.

No matter how sweet the taste, retribution isn't sustainable as a governing MO. But if one side persists in escalating bad behavior, the other side has little option other than to respond in the same way, fighting fire with fire until each side recognizes that the flames are about to consume them all. The seemingly sensible alternative—behaving well when the other side isn't, and thereby rewarding impunity—is a death sentence. It's the classic prisoner's dilemma, in which noncooperation looks like the best strategy in the short term. Eventually, though, the combatants come to realize that bilateral disarmament is the only way to endure. In the case of the Supreme Court, maybe both sides would figure it out in a few years, or maybe in 50. In the interim, the prestige of the Court would surely suffer. Do you have to burn down the house to save it? If so, that's not a pro-liberal scheme or an anti-conservative scheme—it's an imperfect plan to ultimately reclaim the Court from the clutches of politics gone awry.

ACKNOWLEDGMENTS

Each time I write a book, I learn again it's hard. It's slow, long and solitary. Each time, I've come to rely on a range of friends, as well as individuals particular to the project. I want to thank them all.

The justices and law clerks who spoke to me recognized they were doing the unusual. I appreciate their time and trust.

My editor at Crown, Roger Scholl, championed this book from the beginning. Without his guidance, patience and editing skills, there would be no book. As always, my nonpareil agent, Esther Newberg, has been there when I needed her. I'm grateful to both of them.

This is my first book at Crown and I want to thank the entire publishing team: Molly Stern, Annsley Rosner, Craig Adams, Sarah Breivogel, Lisa Erickson, Eliana Seochand and Erin Little. It is a brilliant group. Thanks, too, to Zoe Sandler, Alexandra Heimann and Colin Graham at ICM.

The manuscript benefited from the thoughtful suggestions of Audrey Feinberg, Barbara Kaplan, Joshua Kaplan, Larry Kramer, Martin Sklar and three readers who asked that I not use their names. Barbara's laborious line editing saved me from umpteen blunders; had she seen this page, she would have crossed out *umpteen*. Thanks to all.

Thanks as well to Kathy Arberg and Patricia McCabe Estrada at the Supreme Court's Public Information Office; and Ryan Reft at the Library of Congress's Manuscript Division. And for kindnesses large and small along the way, my thanks to Paul Aiken, Jonathan Alter, Cage Ames, Randall Balmer, Philip Bobbitt, Mia Diehl, the late Norman Dorsen, Andrew Duchnycz, Fred Frawley, Richard Gilbert, Stephen Gillers, Hank Gilman, Jerry Goldman, Boyden Gray, Linda Greenhouse, Mike Isikoff, Danielle Lermer, Tony Mauro, Dan McGinn, Dick Polenberg, Mary Quigley, Marcia Schiff, John Sexton, Steve Solomon, Nina Totenberg, Larry Tribe, Eugene Volokh and Steve Wermiel. Five lower-court federal judges also provided valuable counsel to me, much as they disagreed with the premise of the book; because they still do business with the Supreme Court, I'm omitting their names.

In the late 1980s, almost a decade after I attended NYU law school, the late Gerry Gunther of Stanford challenged me to think anew about constitutional law. Gerry was politically progressive but judicially cautious. For four decades, he was a model for how to think about the Court. My writing at *Newsweek* (including about *Roe v. Wade* and *Bush v. Gore*) owes much to his wisdom and to his friendship. While working on this book, I was asked on occasion who I thought might have made a good justice. One answer is Gerry Gunther.

For some reason, my family tolerates my book-writing immersions. I would be lost without them. My love to Nathaniel, Joshua and Audrey.

NOTE ON SOURCES

MUCH OF *THE MOST DANGEROUS BRANCH* IS BASED ON MY INTERVIEWS with a majority of the justices on the Supreme Court during the 2017–18 term; past justices; 65 law clerks who worked at the Court; other individuals with direct knowledge of the justices, on and off the bench; White House, congressional and Justice Department officials dating to the Reagan administration; senators; and 25 federal and state judges, some of whom were considered for nomination to the Court. The condition for obtaining virtually all of these 165 interviews was that they be "on background." We agreed that meant I could publish what I was told, but identify neither its source nor, more generally, who talked to me at all. Such lack of attribution isn't ideal, but it is the only practicable way to write about life inside the current or recent Court. Where possible, I have tried to have more than one source for controversial details about justices or cases. In addition, those justices to whom I didn't speak were given an opportunity to comment on what would be written about them.

This book also relies on an array of journalism and scholarship, as well as the papers of various justices at the Library of Congress. These sources are detailed in the endnotes.

For Supreme Court opinions, I mostly used the well-organized Cornell Legal Information Institute, though the website of the Court itself also posts opinions. For recordings of the Court's oral arguments (which date to 1955), as well as transcripts of oral arguments, I used the online Oyez Project, the best trove of such material; these materials are also available at the physical locations of the National Archives (transcripts at the branch in D.C., recordings at the branch in College Park, Maryland). Oyez also includes recordings and transcripts of announcements from the bench.

SCOTUSblog has become the preeminent website for news of the Court beyond the excellent daily coverage by the *New York Times*, *Washington Post*, *Wall Street Journal*, *Los Angeles Times*, *USA Today*, NPR, and *Slate*; in one place, *SCOTUSblog* includes filings, argument calendars, orders, briefs and analyses. *ScotusMap* nicely tracks the travel of the justices; the Court website does not. These are all indispensable resources.

NOTES

INTRODUCTION: THE END OF THE WORLD
AS THEY KNEW IT

xiii   **The president asked:** Erik Wemple, " 'That's a Shocker': Trump Ribs Press on Visit by Retiring Justice Anthony Kennedy," *Washington Post*, June 27, 2018, washingtonpost.com/blogs/erik-wemple/wp/2018/06/27 /thats-a-shocker-trump-ribs-press-on-visit-by-retiring-justice-anthony -kennedy/?noredirect=on&utm_term=.f5dd19d3bf0d.

xiii   **Kennedy's retirement:** Jack Goldsmith, "Justice Kennedy's Retirement Leaves the Future of U.S. Constitutional Law Entirely Up for Grabs," *Washington Post*, June 27, 2018, washingtonpost.com/opinions/justice -kennedys-retirement-is-the-biggest-event-in-us-jurisprudence-in-at-least -15-years/2018/06/27/746db704-585d-11e7-b38e-35fd8e0c288f_story.html.

PROLOGUE: DEATH AT THE RANCH

1   **"where the rainbows":** Harvey H. Jackson III, *The New Encyclopedia of Southern Culture* (Chapel Hill: UNC Press Books, 2014), 16:5.

2   **"that's not really":** "Justice Elena Kagan at the Aspen Ideas Festival," *Aspen Ideas Festival*, June 29, 2013, aspenideas.org/session/justice-elena -kagan-aspen-ideas-festival.

3   **"My uncle Frank":** Jennifer Senior, "In Conversation: Antonin Scalia," *New York*, Oct. 6, 2013, 22.

3   **With nearly 900 members**: "Honoring God by Honoring His Creatures," *International Order of St. Hubertus*, iosh-usa.com.

3   **"Scalia spent his last hours"**: Amy Brittain & Sari Horwitz, "Scalia
Spent Final Hours with Men from Society of Hunters," *Washington Post*,
Feb. 25, 2016, A8.

4   **"why I am the way I am"**: Jeffrey S. Sutton, "Antonin Scalia—A Justice
in Full," *National Review*, Feb. 29, 2016, nationalreview.com/article/
432005/antonin-scalia-justice-full. Sutton's comments are part of a collection of reminiscences.

6   **county officials:** The sheriff's report in Case #16-066 can be read at
assets.documentcloud.org/documents/2719258/Scaliareport.pdf.

6   **Recent presidents:** Art Caplan & Jonathan D. Moreno, "We Need Un-
biased Medical Exams for Presidential Candidates," *Chicago Tribune*,
May 17, 2016, chicagotribune.com/news/opinion/commentary/ct-health
-medical-exam-trump-clinton-president-perspec-0518-20160517-story
.html. See also, for example, Linda Greenhouse, "Chief Justice Is Admitted to Hospital After Seizure," *New York Times*, July 31, 2007, A11.

6   **"Tony . . . this is my last big trip"**: Josh Blackman, *Unraveled: Obamacare, Religious Liberty, and Executive Power* (New York: Cambridge University Press, 2016), 478.

6   **"shrouded in mystery"**: "Scalia's Death Is Par for the Course," *Donald-
Jeffries*, Feb. 17, 2016, donaldjeffries.wordpress.com/2016/02/17/scalias
-death-is-par-for-the-course/.

6   **"founded by the Bohemian"**: Kit Daniels, "Scalia's Death Linked to Bohemian Grove, Illuminati," *InfoWars*, Feb. 25, 2016, infowars.com/scalias
-death-linked-to-bohemian-grove-illuminati/.

7   **"My friends, it's Saturday"**: Alex Jones, "Breaking: Justice Scalia Murdered?" *Facebook*, Feb. 13, 2016, facebook.com/alexanderemerickjones/
videos/10153919891063459/.

7   **"I wonder if"**: Donald J. Trump, *Twitter*, Feb. 20, 2016, twitter.com/
realDonaldTrump/status/701084443889381377?lang=en.

7   **Few D.C. pundits:** See Chloe Nurik, "Obama's Funeral Attendance,"
FactCheck, Mar. 17, 2016, factcheck.org/2016/03/obamas-funeral
-attendance/.

8   **"the most important"**: "Exit Poll: Future Supreme Court Appointments
Important Factor in Presidential Voting," *NBC News*, Nov. 6, 2016,
nbcnews.com/card/nbc-news-exit-poll-future-supreme-court-appointments
-important-factor-n680381.

10   **The usually less excitable:** Adam Liptak, "Supreme Court Appointment Could Reshape American Life," *New York Times*, Feb. 19, 2016,
A1. The language got hotter when Justice Kennedy retired in June 2018.
See Charlie Savage, "Trump Gets Chance to Influence American Life for
Generations Through Supreme Court Pick," *New York Times*, June 27,
2018, nytimes.com/2018/06/27/us/politics/trump-supreme-court-legacy
.html. The anchor Brian Williams one-upped him on MSNBC by saying
Kennedy's replacement "could shape American life for half of a century or
more."

10   **On abortion:** *Roe v. Wade*, 410 U.S. 113 (1973).

11   **And of course that:** "National Vital Statistics Reports," *U.S. Department of Health and Human Services*, Nov. 6, 2014, cdc.gov/nchs/data/nvsr/ nvsr63/nvsr63_07.pdf.

11   **In Congress:** "The Fifteenth Congress by the Numbers," *Legistorm*, legistorm.com/congress_by_numbers/index/by/house.html.

13   **"A word is not a crystal":** *Towne v. Eisner*, 245 U.S. 418, 419 (1918).

13   **"abstract and dimly":** Alexander M. Bickel, *The Least Dangerous Branch: The Supreme Court at the Bar of Politics*, 2d ed. (New Haven, Conn.: Yale University Press, 1962), 26.

14   **"The Constitution is":** Ibid., 98.

15   **The best jurists:** Stephen Breyer, *Active Liberty: Interpreting Our Democratic Constitution* (New York: Knopf, 2005), 19.

15   **It is a style:** Justice Harlan didn't have "II" at the end of his name, but because his grandfather—also a justice, who wrote the famous dissent in *Plessy v. Ferguson*—had the same name, he's often referred to with the "II." So, too, the first Harlan is sometimes referred to as John Marshall Harlan I.

16   **"The only good Constitution":** Bruce Allen Murphy, "Scalia and the 'Dead' Constitution," *New York Times*, Feb. 15, 2016, A19; Tasha Tsiaperas, "Constitution a 'Dead, Dead, Dead' Document, Scalia Tells SMU Audience," *Dallas Morning News*, Jan. 28, 2013, dallasnews.com/news/ highland-park/2013/01/28/constitution-a-dead-dead-dead-document -scalia-tells-smu-audience.

17   **"A gift to America":** "Supreme Court Justice Sotomayor," *C-SPAN*, Sept. 16, 2009, c-span.org/video/?286080-1/supreme-court-justice-sotomayor.

17   **"If [the people] don't like":** "Supreme Court Chief Justice Roberts," *C-SPAN*, June 19, 2009, c-span.org/video/?286078-1/supreme-court-chief -justice-roberts&start=268.

17   **"objective":** "Supreme Court Justice Alito," *C-SPAN*, Sept. 2, 2009, c-span.org/video/?286073-1/supreme-court-justice-alito.

17   **"paradox":** Martin H. Redish, "Trump Is Not Above the Courts," *New York Times*, Mar. 16, 2017, nytimes.com/2017/03/16/opinion/trump-is -not-above-the-courts.html.

18   **Apart from a presidential tweet:** "Court-bashing," at least at the state level, is increasingly in vogue in the age of Trump. Various politicians have proposed to punish judges who issue rulings the politicians don't like—for example, on partisan gerrymandering. The proposals have ranged from cutting salaries to impeachment. See, for example, "Legislative Assaults on State Courts," *Brennan Center for Justice* (2018), brennancenter.org/analysis/legislative-assaults-state-courts-2018. But these proposals have not been directed at the Supreme Court.

18   **"Courts stand against":** *Chambers v. Florida*, 309 U.S. 227 (1940).

18   **"The job is to decide":** See, for example, Brian Lamb, Susan Swain & Mark Farkas, eds., *The Supreme Court: A C-SPAN Book Featuring the Justices in Their Own Words* (New York: PublicAffairs, 2010), 124.

18   **"The most important thing":** Alexander M. Bickel, *The Unpublished Opinions of Mr. Justice Brandeis* (Cambridge, Mass.: Harvard University Press, 1957), 17.

19   **Though the Court:** Memo to technicalists: Yes, there are some cases the Court must accept—for example, disputes between states. But in this book, *appeals* refers to the overwhelming majority of cases that arrive at the Court, over which the justices have complete discretion.

20   **"We need more":** Donald J. Trump, *Twitter*, Mar. 28, 2018, twitter.com/realDonaldTrump/status/978932860307505153?lang=en.

20   **Those critics:** Ilya Shapiro, "Courts Shouldn't Join the #Resistance," *Cato at Liberty*, May 29, 2017, cato.org/blog/courts-shouldnt-join-resistance. See also, for example, Josh Blackman, "The Legal Resistance to Donald Trump," *National Review*, Oct. 11, 2017, nationalreview.com/article/452506/donald-trump-courts-lawyers-legal-resistance.

20   **Trump himself:** Donald J. Trump, *Twitter*, Feb. 4, 2016, twitter.com/realDonaldTrump/status/827867311054974976?lang=en.

20   **"immutable principles":** Richard A. Posner, "The Rise and Fall of Judicial Self-Restraint," 100 *California Law Review* 519, 520 (2012).

20   **"morphed into rule by":** Ibid.

20   **Not surprisingly:** Lincoln Caplan, "A Workable Democracy," *Harvard Magazine*, Mar.–Apr. 2017, 50, harvardmagazine.com/2017/03/a-workable-democracy. See "Supreme Court," 2000–2017, *Gallup News*, news.gallup.com/poll/4732/supreme-court.aspx.

CHAPTER 1: THE MARBLE TEMPLE

26   **most powerful:** Bickel made this point, with irony, in the first sentence of his famous book: "The least dangerous branch of the American government is the most extraordinarily powerful court of law the world has ever known." Bickel, *Least Dangerous Branch*, 1.

27   **They're "gifts to you":** *Guide for Counsel*, Oct. Term 2015, supremecourt.gov/casehand/guideforcounsel.pdf, 4.

27   **"I am the *chief* justice!":** See oral argument in *United States v. Gaubert*, 499 U.S. 315 (1991), oyez.org/cases/1990/89-179. See also oral argument in *Teague v. Lane*, 489 U.S. 288 (1989), oyez.org/cases/1988/87-5259, in which a lawyer committed the sin of calling Rehnquist "Judge."

27   **"something different is":** "Supreme Court Chief Justice Roberts," *C-SPAN*, June 19, 2009, c-span.org/video/?286078-1/supreme-court-chief-justice-roberts.

28   **"You're fired":** There are many versions of the story—for example, Eli Savit, *Twitter*, Sept. 18, 2017, twitter.com/EliNSavit/status/909817701950001152. Savit had clerked for O'Connor.

28   **"I'm sure we could do":** "*The Supreme Court: Home to America's Highest Court*, 2010 Edition," *C-SPAN*, Dec. 20, 2010, c-span.org/video/?297213-1/supreme-court-home-americas-highest-court-2010-edition.

29   **"Congressmen and Diplomats":** For example, see William O. Douglas
      to the Marshal of the Court, Oct. 30, 1972, *Harry A. Blackmun Papers*,
      Manuscript Division, Library of Congress, Washington, D.C. (hereafter
      "*HAB-LOC*"), Box 1404, Folder 8. Douglas wrote "it is inconceivable
      to me that the Congressmen and Senators would decline the very small,
      minute request" of allowing "occasional use of not more than 9 cars by
      Justices of the Court." Much to-and-fro follows.

30   **"our job is not to":** "A Conversation with Chief Justice John G. Roberts
      Jr.," *YouTube*, Apr. 12, 2017, youtube.com/watch?v=TuZEKlRgDEg. The
      conversation was at RPI.

30   **"We might end up talking":** Ibid.

31   **most recently in a Trump travel ban case:** *Trump v. Hawaii*, No. 17-965
      (argued Apr. 25, 2018).

32   **"Who do you hear":** "Homes of the Court," *Supreme Court Historical
      Society*, supremecourthistory.org/history-of-the-court/home-of-the-court/.

33   **"of dignity and importance":** Ibid.

33   **"the place is almost":** Harlan Fiske Stone to his sons, May 24, 1935,
      quoted in Clare Cushman, *Courtwatchers: Eyewitness Accounts in Supreme
      Court History* (Lanham, Md.: Rowman & Littlefield, 2011), 110.

33   **"the greatest show on earth":** Nan Rehnquist to William Brennan,
      William J. Brennan Papers, Manuscript Division, Library of Congress,
      Washington, D.C. (hereafter "*WJB-LOC*"), Part II: Correspondence
      File, 1946-1998, Box II: 114, Folder 2 (under "Members of the Court—
      Rehnquist")(access by permission), n.d.

33   **clanking pipes and fickle phones:** For example, in the 1980s, Justice
      Thurgood Marshall complained to the chief justice about the "heavy drill-
      ing and hammering and pounding" just underneath his chambers. Later,
      Marshall wanted "to know why we can't get a telephone that works,"
      to which the chief answered (by letter), "So do I!" Marshall to Warren
      Burger, Sept. 18, 1980, *Thurgood Marshall Papers*, Manuscript Division,
      Library of Congress, Washington, D.C. (hereafter "*TM-LOC*"), Box 33;
      Marshall to Burger, May 30, 1985, *TM-LOC*, Box 34.

35   **search-and-seizure:** *Utah v. Strieff*, 136 S. Ct. 2056 (2016).

38   **"They are independent":** "Brutus," perhaps Robert Yates, was an anti-
      Federalist. See Brutus, No. 15, Mar. 20, 1788, quoted in Sanford Levin-
      son, *Framed: America's 51 Constitutions and the Crisis of Governance* (New
      York: Oxford University Press, 2012), 273.

38   **"While some of the tales":** John M. Broder & Carolyn Marshall, "White
      House Memos Offer Opinions on Supreme Court," *New York Times*, July
      30, 2005, A11.

CHAPTER 2: NO. 9

41   **"*Chevron* deference":** *Chevron v. Natural Resources Defense Council*, 467
      U.S. 837 (1984).

42 **"Executive bureaucracies":** *Gutierrez-Brizuela v. Lynch*, 834 F.3d 1142, 1149 (10th Cir. 2016).

43 **"poses a grave threat":** Neil M. Gorsuch, "2016 Sumner Canary Memorial Lecture: Of Lions and Bears, Judges and Legislators, and the Legacy of Justice Scalia," 66 *Case Western Reserve Law Review* 905 (2016).

43 **"robbed Americans":** See, for example, Christopher Caldwell, "What Does Steve Bannon Want?" *New York Times*, Feb. 26, 2017, SR1:

43 **the justices made no secret:** For an excellent survey of such disdain in one term, 2011–12, see Pamela S. Karlan, "The Supreme Court, 2011 Term—Foreword: Democracy and Disdain," 126 *Harvard Law Review* 1 (2012).

43 **"Who wrote this statute?":** *Perry v. Merit Systems Protection Board*, 137 S. Ct. 1975 (2017).

43 **Alito has such strong dislike:** David G. Savage, "Obama and Biden Meet with Supreme Court Justices," *Los Angeles Times*, Jan. 15, 2009, articles.latimes.com/2009/jan/15/nation/na-obama-roberts15.

44 **That fabled phrase:** *Marbury v. Madison*, 5 U.S. 137 (1803).

44 **accepted wisdom since:** See *Cooper v. Aaron*, 358 U.S. 1 (1958), a unanimous landmark ruling on the Court's supremacy.

44 **"accumulation" of federal power:** *Garco Construction v. Speer*, No. 17-225 (2018) (dissenting from the denial of cert).

45 **doctoral dissertation at Oxford:** Neil M. Gorsuch, *The Future of Assisted Suicide and Euthanasia* (Princeton, N.J.: Princeton University Press, 2009).

47 **approaching the extremism of Thomas:** See Lee Epstein, Andrew D. Martin & Kevin Quinn, "President-Elect Trump and His Possible Justices," Dec. 15, 2016, pdfserver.amlaw.com/nlj/PresNominees2.pdf.

47 **"simply things you might":** The correspondent was Jan Crawford. "Trump's Supreme Court Nomination," *Charlie Rose*, Feb. 1, 2017, charlierose.com/videos/29789.

49 **"best-organized, best-funded":** Jerry Landay, "The Federalist Society: The Conservative Cabal That's Transforming American Law," *Washington Monthly*, Mar. 2000, 19.

52 **So he expressed:** *Seven-Sky v. Holder*, 661 F.3d 1 (D.C. Cir. 2011), *cert denied*, 133 S. Ct. 63 (2012).

55 **"Who would the Donald":** Justice Don Willett, *Twitter*, June 16, 2015, twitter.com/justicewillett/status/610856791291916290?lang=en; and Apr. 7, 2016, twitter.com/justicewillett/status/718280241752510465?lang=en.

57 **stockpiled:** Melodi Erdogan & Jennifer Blake, "Elderly Nun Sentenced to Nearly Three Years for Tennessee Nuclear Break-in," *Reuters*, Feb. 18, 2014, reuters.com/article/us-usa-security-nuclear/elderly-nun-sentenced-to-nearly-three-years-for-tennessee-nuclear-break-in-idUSBREA1H0SS20140219.

56 **"Sherlock or Oliver Wendell":** *United States v. Takhalov*, 827 F.3d 1307 (11th Cir. 2016).

CHAPTER 3: CONFIRMATION WORLD

59 **"how Roberts got his":** "Legacy of Henry Friendly," *C-SPAN*, Mar. 10, 2017, c-span.org/video/?424016-1/justice-john-roberts-judge-merrick -garland-discuss-legacy-judge-henry-friendly&start=1263.

60 **"I wondered if":** Barack Obama, *The Audacity of Hope: Thoughts on Reclaiming the American Dream* (New York: Three Rivers Press, 2006), 83.

61 **"For a variety of":** Obama to Brennan, Dec. 7, 1990, and Brennan to Obama, Dec. 13, 1990, *WJB-LOC*, Part II: Correspondence File, 1946–1998, Box II: 94, Folder 4 (under "'O' miscellaneous")(access by permission).

68 **a video of his 2013 memorial service:** "Celebration of the Life of Robert H. Bork, 1927–2012," *Federalist Society*, archive.fed-soc.org/aboutus/page/ celebration-of-the-life-of-robert-h-bork-1927-2012.

70 **"Seldom, if ever":** "Cardozo Is Named to Supreme Court; Nomination Hailed," *New York Times*, Feb. 16, 1932, 1.

71 **a little-known 45-year-old:** Victor H. Kramer, "The Case of Justice Stevens: How to Select, Nominate and Confirm a Justice of the United States Supreme Court," 7 *Constitutional Commentary* 325, 329, 331 (1990), citing memos in the Ford White House.

74 **"vapid and hollow":** Elena Kagan, "Confirmation Messes, Old and New," 62 *University of Chicago Law Review* 919 (1995).

75 **The ruling about which nominees:** *Bush v. Gore*, 531 U.S. 98 (2000).

75 **the worst example:** *Dred Scott v. Sandford*, 60 U.S. 393 (1857).

CHAPTER 4: DEPLOYING THE WARHEAD

78 **"I remember muffling":** Obama, *Audacity of Hope*, 82–83.

79 **"Republicans have subscribed":** David Leonhardt, "Democrats Had a Knife, and the GOP Had a Gun," *New York Times*, Dec. 20, 2016, A27. See also Carl Hulse, "New Group Hopes to Lure Democrats to Judicial Fight," *New York Times*, May 4, 2018, A15.

82 **But couldn't Leahy have pressed:** Neil Gorsuch, "Justice White and Judicial Excellence," *United Press International*, May 4, 2002, upi.com/ Justice-White-and-judicial-excellence/72651020510343/.

84 **"'No vehicles in the park'":** *Federal Communications Commission v. Next-wave Personal Communications*, 537 U.S. 293 (2003).

85 **"merely more than de minimis":** *Endrew F. v. Douglas County School District*, 137 S. Ct. 988 (2017).

89 **"the single most significant":** "Remarks by President Trump and Senate Majority Leader Mitch McConnell in Joint Press Conference," *White House*, Oct. 16, 2017, whitehouse.gov/the-press-office/2017/10/16 /remarks-president-trump-and-senate-majority-leader-mitch-mcconnell -joint.

89   **they circulated:** "But Gorsuch Meme," me.me/i/but-gorsuch -18005076.

89   **misrepresented Gorsuch's words:** Donald J. Trump, *Twitter*, Feb. 9, 2017, twitter.com/realDonaldTrump/status/829660612452036608.

89   **"loyal":** First to report Trump's private reaction was Ashley Parker et al., "Trump Talked About Rescinding Gorsuch's Nomination," *Washington Post*, Dec. 19, 2017, A1. In a tweet, Trump denied he reacted that way to Blumenthal's disclosure, calling his supposed reaction "FAKE NEWS." Donald J. Trump, *Twitter*, twitter.com/realDonaldTrump/status/943135588496093190.

89   **should have nominated Rudy Giuliani:** Michael Wolff, *Fire and Fury: Inside the Trump White House* (New York: Henry Holt, 2018), 86.

91   **Gorsuch's first dissent:** *Perry v. Merit Systems Protection Board*, 137 S. Ct. 1975 (2017).

92   **Although a handful:** *Trump v. International Refugee Assistance Project*, 137 S. Ct. 2210 (2017) (travel ban); *Peruta v. California*, 137 S. Ct. 1995 (2017) (concealed guns); and *Pavan v. Smith*, No. 137 S. Ct. 2075 (2017) (gay rights).

92   **"If a statute needs":** *Perry v. Merit Systems Protection Board*.

92   **"general principles":** *Trinity Lutheran Church v. Comer*, 137 S. Ct. 2012 (2017).

92   **In a highly technical case:** *Artis v. District of Columbia*, No. 16-460, 1, 18 (2018)(dissent).

92   **In her majority opinion:** Ibid., 10, 16 n.12.

94   **insignificant criminal case:** *Hicks v. United States*, 137 S. Ct. 2000 (2017).

95   **Only once before:** *Pacific Bell Telephone Co. v. linkLine Communications*, 555 U.S. 438 (2009).

95   **"I was frightened":** Linda Greenhouse, "Court Veteran Remembers a Scary Start," *New York Times*, Feb. 16, 2006, A31.

96   **"Dude, pick your spots!":** The professor, Daniel Epps, made the remark on his podcast *First Monday*, co-hosted with Ian Samuel. The quote is also recounted in Adam Liptak, "Confident and Assertive, Gorsuch Hurries to Make His Mark," *New York Times*, July 4, 2017, A13.

97   **Days after the term ended:** Karen Antonacci, "Supreme Court Justice Neil Gorsuch Rides in Niwot Parade," *Denver Post*, July 4, 2017, denverpost.com/2017/07/04/neil-gorsuch-july-4-homecoming-niwot -parade/.

97   **By contrast:** John P. Gregg, "Videos: Supreme Court Justice Stephen Breyer Reads Declaration in Plainfield," *Valley News* [N.H.], July 5, 2017, vnews.com/Justice-Breyer-Reads-Declaration-of-Independence-in-N-H -Town-11111260.

98   **"Well, Clarence":** Cushman, *Courtwatchers*, 95.

CHAPTER 5: THE INSTITUTIONALIST
AND THE NOTORIOUS

99   **ambassador of the law:** "Cardigan's Commencement Address by Chief
        Justice John G. Roberts Jr.," *YouTube*, June 6, 2017, youtube.com/
        watch?v=Gzu9S5FL-Ug.

100   **"The odd historical":** Robert Barnes & Del Quentin Wilbur, "High
        Court Speculation: Did Roberts Switch Vote?" *Washington Post*, June 30,
        2012, A1.

102   **"the subtle and unfortunate":** John Paul Stevens, *Five Chiefs: A Supreme
        Court Memoir* (New York: Back Bay Books, 2012), 212–14.

102   **When he was a child:** Anne E. Kornblut, "In Re Grammar, Roberts's
        Stance Is Crystal Clear," *New York Times*, Aug. 29, 2005, A1.

103   **Roberts's artistry:** See, for example, Tony Mauro, "Courtside: Katyal's
        Path to Hogan Lovells," *National Law Journal Supreme Court Insider*,
        Sept. 7, 2011.

104   **"What's shakin', Chiefy baby?":** Bob Woodward & Scott Armstrong,
        The Brethren: Inside the Supreme Court (New York: Avon Books, 1979), 64.

105   **"The conference today":** *HAB-LOC*, Blackmun Notes, Box 116, Feb.
        15, 1980, and Mar. 28, 1980. For a sympathetic view generally of Burger's
        tenure, see "Life and Legacy of Chief Justice Warren Burger" (John Sex-
        ton), *C-SPAN*, June 5, 2017, c-span.org/video/?429437-2/life-legacy-chief
        -justice-warren-burger.

105   **It was even worse:** Bernard Schwartz, *Decision: How the Supreme Court
        Decides Cases* (New York: Oxford University Press, 1996), 43.

105   **"Bambi":** Andrew Hamm, "Ginsburg and Sotomayor Talk Food at the
        Court," *SCOTUSblog* (June 2, 2016), scotusblog.com/2016/06/ginsburg
        -and-sotomayor-talk-food-at-the-court/.

106   **"the strike zone is":** Bruce Weber, "Umpires v. Judges," *New York Times*,
        July 11, 2009, WK1. Or as an earlier umpire, the Hall of Famer Bill
        Klem, said: "It ain't nothin' till I call it." Fred R. Shapiro, ed., "Bill Klem
        Quotes," *The Yale Book of Quotations* (New Haven, Conn.: Yale University
        Press, 2006), 433.

106   **Balls and strikes:** See Jon O. Newman, "Judging's a Lot More Than Balls
        and Strikes," *Hartford Courant*, Sept. 8, 2009, articles.courant.com/2009
        -09-08/news/newman-sotomayor-supreme_1_strike-zone-individual-judge
        -judge-s-role. See also Aaron Zelinsky, "The Justice as Commissioner:
        Benching the Judge-Umpire Analogy," 119 *Yale Law Journal Online* 113
        (2010).

106   **"I just want you to know":** Jon O. Newman, *Benched: Abortion, Terror-
        ists, Drones, Crooks, the Supreme Court, Kennedy, Nixon, Demi Moore, and
        Other Tales from the Life of a Federal Judge* (Getzville, N.Y.: William S.
        Hein, 2017), 1.

107   **"the Thurgood Marshall":** Antonin Scalia, "Ruth Bader Ginsburg,"
        Time, Apr. 15, 2015, time.com/3823889/ruth-bader-ginsburg-2015
        -time-100/.

108   **"All they wanted to do":** The secretary, Alice Stovall, is quoted in Gilbert
        King, *Devil in the Grove: Thurgood Marshall, the Groveland Boys, and the
        Dawn of a New America* (New York: Harper Perennial, 2013), 5.

108   **"No wonder that across":** Ibid.

108   **"On and off the bench":** Dahlia Lithwick, "Justice LOLZ Grumpycat
        Notorious R.B.G.," *Slate*, Mar. 16, 2015, slate.com/articles/double_x/
        doublex/2015/03/notorious_r_b_g_history_the_origins_and_meaning_
        of_ruth_bader_ginsburg_s.html.

109   **even if the colorful:** The video, from "everybody's favorite guessing
        game"—"brought to you by Helene Curtis"—is at "Justice William O.
        Douglas—'What's My Line?'" *YouTube*, May 6, 1956, youtube.com/
        watch?v=0u_DgK-TIDA. Douglas failed to stump the panel.

109   **best-selling mash-up:** Irin Carmon & Shana Knizhnik, *Notorious RBG:
        The Life and Times of Ruth Bader Ginsburg* (New York: HarperCollins,
        2015), 116, 100.

109   **There's also the recent:** Tom F. O'Leary, *The Ruth Bader Ginsburg Color-
        ing Book: A Tribute to the Always Colorful and Often Inspiring Life of the
        Supreme Court Justice Known as RBG* (Silver Spring, Md.: Gumdrop Press,
        2016); Debbie Levy & Elizabeth Baddeley, *I Dissent: Ruth Bader Ginsburg
        Makes Her Mark* (New York: Simon & Schuster, 2016).

110   **Ben & Jerry's has been:** "Create 'Ruth Bader Ginger' Ice Cream!"
        Change.org, change.org/p/please-benandjerrys-create-a-ruthbaderginger
        -ice-cream-flavor.

110   **"I'm not queen":** William G. Gilroy, "A Conversation with Justice Ruth
        Bader Ginsburg," *Notre Dame News*, Sept. 13, 2016, nd.edu/news/ruth
        -bader-ginsburg/.

111   **"If you were stranded":** Ruth Bader Ginsburg, "Antonin Scalia—A
        Justice in Full," *National Review*, Feb. 29, 2016, nationalreview.com/
        article/432005/antonin-scalia-justice-full.

111   **"too far, too fast":** Ruth Bader Ginsburg, "Speaking in a Judicial Voice,"
        67 *New York University Law Review* 1185, 1204 (1992). See also Ruth
        Bader Ginsburg, "Some Thoughts on Autonomy and Equality," 63 *North
        Carolina Law Review* 375 (1985). Later, after becoming a justice, she used
        the "too far, too fast" idea several times. See, for example, Adam Liptak,
        "Shadow of Roe v. Wade Looms over Ruling on Gay Marriage," *New York
        Times*, Mar. 24, 2013, A1.

112   **"earned acclaim":** Robert Barnes, "Ginsburg Gives No Hint of Giving
        Up the Bench," *Washington Post*, Apr. 12, 2009, A1.

112   **"Both are unlikely to":** Randall Kennedy, "The Case for Early Retire-
        ment," *New Republic*, Apr. 28, 2011, newrepublic.com/article/87543/
        ginsburg-breyer-resign-supereme-court.

113   **But in crucial cases:** *Obergefell v. Hodges*, 135 S. Ct. 2584 (2015).

CHAPTER 6: THE LEFT FLANK

115   **"First Ruth, and now":** Cass Sunstein recounted the story in "In Memoriam: Justice Antonin Scalia," 130 *Harvard Law Review* 1 (2016).

116   **And finally, though:** *Shelby County v. Holder,* 133 S. Ct. 2612 (2013).

116   **Scalia's originalist-textualist:** Antonin Scalia, *A Matter of Interpretation: Federal Courts and the Law* (Princeton, N.J.: Princeton University Press, 1997).

117   **"democratically determined":** Breyer, *Active Liberty*, 134. See also Stephen Breyer, *Making Our Democracy Work: A Judge's View* (New York: Vintage Books, 2010).

117   **"there's only two people":** David Margolick, "Scholarly Consensus Builder: Stephen Gerald Breyer," *New York Times*, May 14, 1994, 11.

118   **"You know, he grows":** *Gonzales v. Raich*, 545 U.S. 1 (2005).

120   **Although she let on little:** Sonia Sotomayor, *My Beloved World* (New York: Vintage Books, 2014).

120   **With more than 300,000:** Clarence Thomas, *My Grandfather's Son: A Memoir* (New York: Harper, 2007); Sandra Day O'Connor, *Lazy B.: Growing Up on a Cattle Ranch in the American Southwest* (New York: Random House, 2002).

120   **credit card debt:** Compare *Financial Disclosure Report*, "Liabilities," CY2014, *OpenSecrets.org*, 4, pfds.opensecrets.org/N99999915_2014.pdf, with *Financial Disclosure Report*, "Liabilities," CY2013, *OpenSecrets.org*, 4, pfds.opensecrets.org/N99999915_2013.pdf, and *Financial Disclosure Report*, "Liabilities," CY2012, *OpenSecrets.org*, 4, pfds.opensecrets.org/N99999915_2012.pdf.

120   **"not one, but two":** Sonia Sotomayor, *Mi mundo adorado* (New York: Vintage Spanish, 2013).

121   **She was the only justice:** Emily Smith, "The Clooneys Dine with Supreme Court Justice Sotomayor," *New York Post*, Apr. 9, 2015, pagesix.com/2015/04/09/the-clooneys-dine-with-supreme-court-justice-sotomayor/.

123   **"demographic appeal":** The letter appears, without explanation, on the website of the Ethics & Public Policy Center, which describes itself as "Washington, D.C.'s premier institute dedicated to applying the Judeo-Christian moral tradition to critical issues of public policy." Laurence H. Tribe to Barack Obama, *Ethics & Public Policy Center*, May 4, 2009. eppc.org/docLib/20101028_tribeletter.pdf.

123   **"I have no illusions":** David Axelrod, "A Surprising Request from Justice Scalia," *CNN Online*, Mar. 9, 2016, cnn.com/2016/02/14/opinions/david-axelrod-surprise-request-from-justice-scalia/.

123   **Obama already knew:** *Silverman v. Major League Baseball Player Relations Committee*, 880 F. Supp. 246 (S.D.N.Y. 1995).

124   **the mutters that she wasn't:** Philip Sean Curran, "Supreme Court Justice Sonia Sotomayor Reveals She Almost Ended Her Bid for High Court,"

Apr. 3, 2017, *CentralJersey.com*, centraljersey.com/news/supreme-court
-justice-sonia-sotomayor-reveals-she-almost-ended-her/article_5d81a3a0
-1877-11e7-9da8-ab30bd6867ca.html.

126 **During the pendency:** *Ricci v. DeStefano*, 557 U.S. 557 (2009).

127 **"All-purpose brain":** Dana Milbank, "Wonderwonk," *New Republic*,
May 18, 1998, newrepublic.com/article/74863/wonderwonk.

128 **"true reflection":** Frank Michelman to Thurgood Marshall, June 5, 1986,
TM-LOC, Box 571.

128 **"first openly gay":** Howard Kurtz, "White House Slams CBS on Blog
Post About Kagan's Sexuality," *Washington Post*, Apr. 16, 2010, C1.

128 **published a large photo:** "Court Nominee Comes to the Plate," *Wall
Street Journal*, May 11, 2010, A1.

129 **gall to ask:** Jennifer Fermino, "Does a Picture of Elena Kagan Playing
Softball Suggest She's a Lesbian?" *New York Post*, May 13, 2010, nypost
.com/2010/05/13/does-a-picture-of-elena-kagan-playing-softball-suggest
-shes-a-lesbian/.

129 **close enough:** "Justices Share Devotion to Baseball," *New York Times*,
nytimes.com/slideshow/2010/05/31/us/20100601-BAR.html?_r=0, Slide 1,
May 31, 2010.

129 **extended the story further:** Maureen Dowd, "Supremely Girly Girl,"
New York Times, May 16, 2010, WK11.

129 **"I've known her for most":** Ben Smith, "Kagan's Friends: She's Not
Gay," *Politico*, May 11, 2010, politico.com/story/2010/05/kagans-friends
-shes-not-gay-037114.

131 **"the food should be unconstitutional":** Becky Krystal, "How Federal
Government Cafeterias Stack Up," *Washington Post*, July 14, 2010, E2.

131 **Replacing her:** "At College Speech, Gorsuch Stresses Need for Civil Discourse," *CBS Philly*, Jan. 23, 2018, philadelphia.cbslocal.com/2018/01/23/
neil-gorsuch-stockton/.

131 **"master pool shark":** Nina Totenberg, "At Harvard, Kagan Won More
Fans Than Foes," *NPR*, May 18, 2010, npr.org/templates/story/story
.php?storyId=126826571.

132 **"I can't say that":** Souter to Brennan (postcard), July 12, 1994, *WJB-
LOC*, Box II: 114; Souter to Brennan (postcard), Aug. 30, 1994, ibid.;
Brennan to Souter (letter), Sept. 6, 1994, ibid.

CHAPTER 7: THE RIGHT FLANK

134 **He was with:** *District of Columbia v. Heller*, 554 U.S. 570 (2008); *Citizens United v. Federal Election Commission*, 558 U.S. 310 (2010). The first
Obamacare ruling was *National Federation of Independent Business v. Sebelius*, 567 U.S. 519 (2012). The second was *King v. Burwell*, 135 S. Ct. 475
(2015). Both upheld President Obama's defining piece of legislation, the
Affordable Care Act, passed by Congress in 2010.

134   **"I am a textualist":** Nina Totenberg, "Scalia Vigorously Defends a 'Dead' Constitution," *NPR*, Apr. 28, 2008, npr.org/templates/story/story .php?storyId=90011526.

135   **violate the Eighth Amendment:** See, for example, Antonin Scalia, "Originalism: The Lesser Evil," 57 *University of Cincinnati Law Review* 849, 864 (1989).

135   **By one count:** Emma Green, "The Clarence Thomas Effect," *Atlantic,* July 10, 2019, theatlantic.com/politics/archive/2019/07/clarence-thomas -trump/593596/.

136   **without asking a question:** Adam Liptak, "Thomas Ends 10-Year Silence on the Bench," *New York Times*, Mar. 1, 2016, A1.

136   **"prop me up on the bench":** Various versions of this story appear. I heard one version from Marshall's son, Goody, as far back as 1987. See also, for example, David Savage, " 'Thurgood' Play Captures Justice Thurgood Marshall," *Los Angeles Times*, July 13, 2010, latimes.com/2010/jul/13/ entertainment/la-et-thurgood-savage-20100713.

137   **Their interview:** The story was recounted by Jon Meacham, the biographer of George H.W. Bush, speaking at Vanderbilt University, May 4, 2016, vanderbilt.edu/2016/05/04/politics-front-and-center-in-fight-for -next-supreme-court-justice-panel-says/.

137   **"chicken-shit operation":** Jon Meacham, *Destiny and Power* (New York: Random House, 2015), 490.

138   **Never mind that Thomas:** Jill Abramson, "Do You Believe Her Now?" *New York*, Feb. 5, 2018, nymag.com/daily/intelligencer/2018/02/the-case -for-impeaching-clarence-thomas.html.

138   **"He shrugged at the news":** Roxanne Roberts, "He Said v. She Said," *Washington Post*, Apr. 10, 2016, E10.

139   **"Whoop-de-damn-do":** Robert Barnes, "At Conservatives' Gathering, Clarence Thomas Puts Any Gloominess Aside," *Washington Post*, Nov. 16, 2013, A3.

139   **"victimization":** "Liberty University Commencement Address," *C-SPAN*, May 11, 1996, c-span.org/video/?71900-1/liberty-university -commencement-address.

139   **"the worst things":** Ruben Navarrette, "Clarence Thomas Is Right About Race," *CNN Online*, Feb. 14, 2014, cnn.com/2014/02/14/opinion/ navarrette-clarence-thomas-race.

140   **"we simply annihilate":** "Justice Thomas Remarks at the Heritage Foundation," *C-SPAN*, Oct. 26, 2016, c-span.org/video/?417506-1/supreme -court-justice-clarence-thomas-delivers-remarks-heritage-foundation.

140   **"universally untrustworthy":** Diane Brady, "Online Extra: Justice Thomas Speaks," *BusinessWeek*, Mar. 12, 2007, bloomberg.com/news/ articles/2007-03-11/online-extra-supreme-court-justice-clarence-thomas -speaks.

140   **"lots of eggs and butter":** Malveaux, an economist with a PhD from MIT, went on to become president of Bennett College. An audio of

Thomas's remarks can be heard at "The DisHonor Awards," *Media Research Center*, Dec. 9, 1999, archive.mrc.org/notablequotables/dishonor1999/welcome.asp.

140 **Her L.A. law firm's:** Laurie Winer, "The Avenger," *New York Times*, June 20, 2010, ST1.

141 **"to experience what Lincoln said":** "Justice Thomas Remarks at the Heritage Foundation," *C-SPAN*, Oct. 26, 2016.

141 **"the meanness you see":** "Clarence Thomas: The Justice Nobody Knows," *60 Minutes*, Sept. 27, 2007, cbsnews.com/news/clarence-thomas -the-justice-nobody-knows/.

142 **calling the claim:** Marcia Coyle, "Young Scholar, Now Lawyer, Says Clarence Thomas Groped Her in 1999," *National Law Journal*, Oct. 27, 2016, law.com/nationallawjournal/almID/1202770918142/Young -Scholar-Now-Lawyer-Says-Clarence-Thomas-Groped-Her-in-1999/ ?et=editorial&bu=National%20Law%20Journal&cn=20161027&src= EMC-Email&pt=Daily%20Headlines.

142 **Likewise:** Abramson, "Do You Believe Her Now?" *New York*, Feb. 5, 2018.

142 **"I won't hire clerks who":** Adam Liptak, "In Clerks' Careers, Signs of Polarization on the Supreme Court Bench," *New York Times*, Sept. 6, 2010, A16.

142 **"nine scorpions in a bottle":** The scorpions quotation is usually attributed to Oliver Wendell Holmes Jr. A recent book makes the convincing case it belongs to Alexander Bickel. See Noah Feldman, *Scorpions: The Battles and Triumphs of FDR's Great Supreme Court Justices* (New York: Twelve, 2010), 437.

143 **"Well, he should have":** David Lat, "Justice Alito Turned Away from Sunday Brunch," *Above the Law* blog, Oct. 26, 2014, abovethelaw .com/2014/10/justice-alito-turned-away-from-sunday-brunch/.

144 **"It is not often":** The quote is from Breyer's remarks from the bench when he announced his dissent in *Parents Involved in Community Schools v. Seattle School District No. 1*, 551 U.S. 701 (2007).

144 **"most consistent":** Michael Stokes Paulsen, "2014 Supreme Court Roundup," *First Things*, Nov. 2014, firstthings.com/article/2014/11 /2014-supreme-court-roundup. While a summer intern in the Reagan Justice Department, Paulsen played on the same softball team as Alito.

145 **"quick smile":** George W. Bush, *Decision Points* (New York: Crown, 2010), 98.

146 **"was fabulous":** Elisabeth Bumiller, "An Interview by, Not with, the President," *New York Times*, July 21, 2005, A1.

147 **"He's good in every way":** Rich Landers, "O'Connor: Roberts 'Good in Every Way, Except He's Not a Woman,'" *Spokesman-Review*, July 20, 2005, spokesman.com/stories/2005/jul/20/oconnor-roberts-good-in-every -way-except-hes-not/.

147 **"If I had it to do over":** Bush, *Decision Points*, 101.

149   **"best pick on the draft":** Ibid., 102.

150   **"Sam, you ought to thank":** Ibid.

150   **Bickel died of cancer:** Lawrence Van Gelder, "Alexander M. Bickel Dies: Constitutional Law Expert," *New York Times*, Nov. 8, 1974, 42.

150   **"the countermajoritarian difficulty":** Bickel, *Least Dangerous Branch*, 16.

151   **In such mostly forgotten:** Alexander M. Bickel, *The Supreme Court and the Idea of Progress* (New York: Harper & Row, 1970).

151   **"Stare decisis is like wine":** David M. O'Brien, ed., *Judges on Judging: Views from the Bench*, 5th ed. (Washington, D.C.: CQ Press, 2016), 139, quoting Josh Blackman, "Justice Alito Reflects on His 10th Anniversary on SCOTUS," joshblackman.com/blog/2015/09/21/justice-alito-reflects -on-his-tenth-anniversary-on-scotus/.

151   **"The judiciary is indisputably":** "The Path to the U.S. Supreme Court," Sept. 2, 2016, *NYU Shanghai*, shanghai.nyu.edu/news/path-us-supreme -court.

152   **"Having eight":** Jess Bravin, "With Court at Full Strength, Alito Foresees Less Conservative Compromise with Liberal Bloc," *Wall Street Journal*, Apr. 21, 2017, blogs.wsj.com/washwire/2017/04/21/with-court-at-full -strength-alito-foresees-more-aggressive-conservative-majority/.

CHAPTER 8: DEUS EX MACHINA

154   **a majority of one:** Jeffrey Rosen, "A Majority of One," *New York Times Magazine*, June 3, 2001, 32.

154   **"Cases swing—I don't!":** The video is embedded at "U.S. Supreme Court Associate Justice Anthony Kennedy Visits HLS," *Harvard Law Today*, Oct. 23, 2015, today.law.harvard.edu/u-s-supreme-court-associate-justice -anthony-kennedy-visits-hls/.

155   **He was thoroughly pleased:** See Massimo Calabresi & David Von Drehle, "What Will Justice Kennedy Do?" *Time*, June 18, 2012.

156   **Few clerks:** The case was *Planned Parenthood v. Casey*, 505 U.S. 833 (1992), which reaffirmed that abortion was a limited constitutional right but upheld regulations that did not place an "undue burden" on the right. Nearly a quarter-century later, the Court said regulation had to confer "medical benefits sufficient to justify the burden upon access" to an abortion. *Whole Woman's Health v. Hellerstedt*, 136 S. Ct. 2292 (2016).

156   **"Sometimes you don't":** Terry Carter, "Crossing the Rubicon," *California Lawyer*, Oct. 1992, 39.

156   **"I need to brood":** Ibid., 103.

157   **"The spirit of liberty":** Learned Hand, "The Faith We Fight For," *New York Times Magazine*, July 2, 1944, 26.

157   **In 1996 he wrote the majority:** *Romer v. Evans,* 517 U.S. 620 (1996).

157   **"Monday's decision":** Blackmun to Kennedy, May 23, 1996, *HAB-LOC*, Box 1405.

157   **"No one told us":** Kennedy to Blackmun, May 28, 1996, ibid.

157   **In opinions, in speeches:** See, for example, Jeffrey Rosen, "The Ago-
        nizer," *New Yorker*, Nov. 11, 1996, 82.

157   **Hamlet of the Supreme Court:** See, for example, Dahlia Lithwick, "Will
        He or Won't He?" *Slate*, May 26, 2017, slate.com/articles/news_and_
        politics/jurisprudence/2017/05/how_anthony_kennedy_s_retirement_
        decision_became_a_battle_over_the_trump.html; and Jeffrey Rosen,
        "Supreme Leader: On the Arrogance of Anthony Kennedy," *New Repub-
        lic*, June 16, 2007, newrepublic.com/article/60925/supreme-leader-the
        -arrogance-anthony-kennedy.

157   **"You know Hamlet better":** Kennedy made the remarks in an ad-
        dress, "The Essential Right to Human Dignity," on June 3, 2005, to the
        Academy of Achievement in New York City, achievement.org/achiever/
        anthony-m-kennedy/#interview.

158   **"I thought if he wrote":** Adam Liptak, "As Justices Get Back to Business,
        Old Pro Reveals Tricks of the Trade," *New York Times*, Oct. 3, 2011, A12;
        see also Stevens, *Five Chiefs*, 237–38.

159   **"a very exclusive organization":** Blackmun to Kennedy, Nov. 12, 1987,
        HAB-LOC, Box 1405.

159   **"You now qualify for":** Ibid.

160   **Joseph Story:** Kennedy to Blackmun, Nov. 16, 1987, *HAB-LOC*, Box 1405.

161   **His views on immigrants:** *Trump v. Hawaii*, No. 17-965 (2018).

CHAPTER 9: SLEEPING GIANT

165   **some state courts:** See, for example, Saikrishna B. Prakash & John C.
        Yoo, "The Origins of Judicial Review," 70 *University of Chicago Law Re-
        view* 887 (2003).

165   **It is there that the rhetoric:** Recent historical scholarship has found that
        the arguments for judicial supremacy actually emerged in the mid-1790s
        and were well known before *Marbury*. The concept was a pivotal part of
        the arguments around the Virginia and Kentucky Resolutions, as well
        as during debate over repeal of the Judiciary Act of 1801 (the so-called
        Midnight Judges Act). Endorsed by Federalists, judicial supremacy was
        strongly rejected by Republicans, who accepted the idea of judicial review
        but not the notion of supremacy. The dominance of Republicans when
        Marbury was decided led Marshall to write an opinion that carefully
        avoided the arguments commonly used by supporters of judicial suprem-
        acy, instead borrowing language from Jeffersonian judges that supported
        only the narrower case for judicial review. In context, then, *Marbury* was
        seen as a retreat from judicial supremacy, making the modern Court's reli-
        ance on it for the principle deeply ironic. This also explains why President
        Jefferson never pushed back—not because Marshall had outmaneuvered
        him, but because Marshall had acceded to Jefferson's own views about the
        role of the Court. See Larry D. Kramer, "Marbury and the Retreat from
        Judicial Supremacy," 20 *Constitutional Commentary* 205 (2003).

166 **In 1810:** *Fletcher v. Peck,* 10 U.S. 87 (1810).

166 **Six years later:** *Martin v. Hunter's Lessee,* 14 U.S. 304 (1816).

166 **"Let the end be":** *McCulloch v. Maryland,* 17 U.S. 316 (1819).

168 **"sort of like green pastel":** John Hart Ely, *Democracy and Distrust: A Theory of Judicial Review* (Cambridge, Mass.: Harvard University Press, 1980), 18.

168 **"liberty of contract":** *Lochner v. New York,* 198 U.S. 45 (1905).

169 **"the most influential":** Stevens, *Five Chiefs,* 25.

169 **While some commentators:** An example of the effort to pardon *Lochner* is David E. Bernstein, *Rehabilitating Lochner: Defending Individual Rights Against Progressive Reform* (Chicago: University of Chicago Press, 2011). See also, for example, George F. Will, "Why Liberals Fear 'Lochner,' " *Washington Post,* Sept. 8, 2011, A19.

169 **"capitulation to big business":** See Morton J. Horowitz, "Foreword, The Constitution of Change: Legal Fundamentality Without Fundamentalism," 107 *Harvard Law Review* 30, 77 (1993).

169 **"the symbol, indeed":** Robert H. Bork, *The Tempting of America* (New York: Free Press, 1990), 44.

169 **For the next three decades:** The first landmark case in this era of substantive due process was really *Allgeyer v. Louisiana,* 165 U.S. 578 (1897), eight years before *Lochner.* The Court found that a constitutional right of contract—supposedly derived from Fourteenth Amendment "liberty"— meant Louisiana couldn't forbid local entities from doing business with out-of-state marine insurance companies. But that ruling took place five years before Holmes joined the Court—and it was his commanding dissent in *Lochner* that gave the ruling its infamy.

169 **The most prominent examples:** *Meyer v. Nebraska,* 262 U.S. 390 (1923) and *Pierce v. Society of Sisters,* 268 U.S. 510 (1925).

169 **In 1935:** *A.L.A. Schechter Poultry Corp. v. United States,* 295 U.S. 495 (1935).

170 **In *West Coast Hotel:*** *West Coast Hotel Co. v. Parrish,* 300 U.S. 379 (1937).

170 **was coincidental:** Roberts himself denied it, and Frankfurter called the charge false. Felix Frankfurter, "Mr. Justice Roberts," 104 *University of Pennsylvania Law Review* 311, 313 (1955). For good discussions of the episode, see Jeff Shesol, *Supreme Power: Franklin Roosevelt vs. the Supreme Court* (New York: W.W. Norton, 2010), 412–15 and 590 n.434; and Edward L. Carter & Edward E. Adams, "Justice Owen J. Roberts on 1937," 15 *Green Bag* 2d 375, 40–41 (2012).

170 **But ultimately:** *Skinner v. Oklahoma,* 316 U.S. 535 (1942).

171 **"is a job for the nation's":** *Youngstown Sheet & Tube Co. v. Sawyer,* 343 U.S. 579 (1952) (known as the Steel Seizure Case).

171 **In an analogous case:** *United States v. Nixon,* 418 U.S. 683 (1974) (known as the Nixon Tapes Case).

172 **Two years after:** *Brown v. Board of Education,* 347 U.S 483 (1954).

172   **"equal but separate":** *Plessy v. Ferguson*, 163 U.S. 537 (1896).

173   **"You're whittling it":** Mark V. Tushnet, ed., *Thurgood Marshall: His Speeches, Writings, Arguments, Opinions, and Reminiscences* (Chicago: Lawrence Hill Books, 2001), 463.

174   **"Why, this is a social":** The anecdote was recounted in 2003 by Abner Mikva, a law clerk for Justice Sherman Minton who was at the luncheon, to Nina Totenberg of NPR, in a series on the 50th anniversary of *Brown*. See Nina Totenberg, "The Supreme Court and 'Brown v. Board of Ed.': The Deliberations Behind the Landmark 1954 Ruling," *NPR*, Dec. 8, 2003, npr.org/templates/story/story.php?storyId=1537409. Mikva later was a judge on the D.C. Circuit and White House counsel to Bill Clinton.

174   **"Are you one of those":** John David Fassett et al., "Supreme Court Law Clerks' Recollections of Brown v. Board of Education," 78 *St. John's Law Review* 515, 528 (2004).

175   **"Stan, you're all by yourself":** Richard Kluger, *Simple Justice* (New York: Vintage Books, 1977), 698.

175   **empathy for a colleague:** See Stephen Ellmann, "The Rule of Law and the Achievement of Unanimity in Brown," 49 *New York Law School Review* 741, 763 (2004).

176   **"was looking me right":** The Marshall quote comes from John Egerton, *Speak Now Against the Day: The Generation Before the Civil Rights Movement in the South* (New York: Knopf, 1994), 608.

176   **One of Reed's:** Ibid.

176   **"with all deliberate speed":** *Brown v. Board of Education*, 349 U.S. 294 (1955)("*Brown II*").

176   **Over the decades:** See the controversial Gerald N. Rosenberg, *The Hollow Hope: Can Courts Bring About Social Change?* 2d ed. (Chicago: University of Chicago Press, 2008).

177   **The Southern backlash:** See Michael J. Klarman, "How Brown Changed Race Relations: The Backlash Thesis," 81 *Journal of American History* 81 (1994), and Michael J. Klarman, *From Jim Crow to Civil Rights: The Supreme Court and the Struggle for Racial Equality* (New York: Oxford University Press, 2004).

177   **"Like poetry":** Bickel, *Least Dangerous Branch*, 245.

177   **"For African-Americans":** Adam Cohen, "The Supreme Struggle," *New York Times*, Jan. 18, 2004, WK24. The lawyer was Theodore Shaw, associate director-counsel of the NAACP Legal Defense Fund.

177   **"third legislative chamber":** Gerald Gunther, *Learned Hand: The Man and the Judge* (New York: Knopf, 1994), 652–57; see also 118–19.

177   **A medley:** See, for example, Herbert Wechsler, "Toward Neutral Principles of Constitutional Law," 73 *Harvard Law Review* 1 (1959).

178   **Bickel himself:** See, for example, Bickel, *Least Dangerous Branch*, 56–63.

178   **"on an assumption":** The quote is from a concurring opinion by Justice Thomas in *Missouri v. Jenkins*, 515 U.S. 70, 114 (1995).

179 **"one person, one vote":** An observant historian noted that the language of "one person, one vote" quickly turned into "one *man*, one vote." Rosenberg, *Hollow Hope*, 295 n.29. Rosenberg said his research revealed that only Alexander Bickel "repeatedly used the correct language."

179 **"political thicket":** The phrase comes from his opinion in *Colegrove v. Green*, 328 U.S. 549, 556 (1946).

179 **"a massive repudiation":** *Baker v. Carr*, 369 U.S. 186, 267 (1962).

179 **"The Constitution is not a panacea":** *Reynolds v. Sims*, 377 U.S. 533, 624 (1964).

180 **It's equally hard:** Ely, *Democracy and Distrust*, 117, 120.

180 **"clear the channels":** Ibid., 105, 183.

180 **"when one team is gaining":** Ibid., 102–3.

180 **In theory:** *Gill v. Whitford*, No. 16-1161 (2018); *Benisek v. Lamone*, No. 17-333 (2018).

180 **published falsehoods:** *New York Times v. Sullivan*, 376 U.S. 254 (1964).

180 **The same year:** *Miranda v. Arizona*, 384 U.S. 436 (1964).

181 **Frankfurter wrote the opinion:** *Poe v. Ullman*, 367 U.S. 497 (1961).

182 **In *Griswold*:** *Griswold v. Connecticut*, 381 U.S. 479 (1965).

182 **"specific guarantees":** Ibid., at 484.

182 **"zones of privacy":** Douglas said even the Third Amendment was relevant, because it prohibits the quartering of soldiers "in any house" in times of peace without the consent of the owner.

183 **"Don't emanate in my penumbras!":** "John Yoo on Scalia and the Future of the Supreme Court," *FrontPage Mag*, Apr. 22, 2016, frontpagemag.com/fpm/262578/john-yoo-scalia-and-future-supreme-court-frontpagemagcom.

183 **"rational basis":** *Eisenstadt v. Baird*, 405 U.S. 438 (1972).

183 **"If the right of privacy":** The italics are mine.

184 **"case histories":** "Opinions of William J, Brennan Jr." (usually referred to as the "Case Histories"), Oct. Term 1971, *WJB-LOC*, Part II, Box 6, Folder 14, XI.

184 **Even if Brennan:** One lower federal court picked up the scent early on, declaring Connecticut's abortion statute unconstitutional months before *Roe*. In *Abele v. Markle*, 351 F. Supp. 224 (D. Conn. 1972), the court cited *Eisenstadt*'s discussion of an individual's decision "whether to bear or beget a child."

184 **In 1938:** *United States v. Carolene Products Co.*, 304 U.S. 144 (1938).

184 **"the Court's first":** David A. Strauss, "Is Carolene Products Obsolete?" 2010 *University of Illinois Law Review* 1251, 1254 (2010).

185 **"*Carolene Products* Court":** John Hart Ely, "Foreword: On Discovering Fundamental Values," 92 *Harvard Law Review* 5, 5–6 (1978).

185   **"a welfare check"**: *Lynch v. Household Finance*, 405 U.S. 538, 552
       (1972).

185   **"Our power"**: *West Virginia State Board of Education v. Barnette*, 319 U.S.
       624, 648 (1943).

185   **opportunistic double standard:** There is much scholarship on the
       "double standard." See, for example, Barry Friedman, "The Birth of an
       Academic Obsession: The History of the Countermajoritarian Diffi-
       culty, Part Five," 112 *Yale Law Journal* 153 (2002), and Gerald Gunther,
       Constitutional Law, 12th ed. (Westbury, N.Y.: Foundation Press, 1991),
       505–6.

186   **"That the transition"**: J. Harvie Wilkinson III, *Cosmic Constitu-
       tional Theory: Why Americans Are Losing Their Inalienable Right to Self-
       Governance* (New York: Oxford University Press, 2012), 28.

186   **"sacred precincts"**: The words are those of Justice Douglas from *Gris-
       wold*, 381 U.S. at 485.

186   **"historical traditions"**: The language comes from a dissent in *Planned
       Parenthood v. Casey*, 505 U.S. at 952, which upheld a limited constitu-
       tional right to an abortion.

186   **"freedom to do with"**: The phrase is Brennan's, used in a letter to Doug-
       las on Dec. 30, 1971, on the pending *Roe* and *Doe* abortion cases. *WJB-
       LOC*, Part I, Box 285.

186   **"not nothing"**: John Hart Ely, "The Wages of Crying Wolf: A Comment
       on Roe v. Wade," 82 *Yale Law Journal* 920, 931 (1973).

186   **"Dogs are not 'persons'"**: Ibid., 926.

CHAPTER 10: THE RUNAWAY COURT

188   **"serious defect"**: *Doe v. Bolton*, 410 U.S. 179 (1973).

188   **But with two:** For discussions of the internal debates, see Seth Stern &
       Stephen Wermiel, *Justice Brennan: Liberal Champion* (Boston: Houghton
       Mifflin Harcourt, 2010), 370–73; and Linda Greenhouse, *Becoming Justice
       Blackmun: Harry Blackmun's Supreme Court Journey* (New York: Times
       Books, 2007), 80–86.

188   **"concerned about the impact"**: "Opinions of William J. Brennan Jr.,"
       Oct. Term 1971, *WJB-LOC*, Part II, Box 6, Folder 14, LI.

189   **In early 1971**: *United States v. Vuitch*, 402 U.S. 62 (1971).

189   **"Here we go"**: Blackmun memo, n.d., *HAB-LOC*, Box 123, Folder 8.

190   **"excoriated"**: Blackmun notation, Oct. 13, 1972, *HAB-LOC*, Box 151,
       Folder 8.

190   **His intention:** Stern & Wermiel, *Justice Brennan*, 374–75. See also Black-
       mun notation, Oct. 13, 1972, *HAB-LOC*, Box 151, Folder 3 (Blackmun
       to Conference, Jan. 16, 1973; Brennan to Conference, Jan. 17, 1973); and
       "Opinions of William J. Brennan Jr.," Oct. Term 1972, *WJB-LOC*, Part
       II, Box 6, Folder 14, LXVIII–IX.

190 **"right to be let alone":** *Olmstead v. United States*, 277 U.S. 438 (1928), which recalled Brandeis's article "The Right to Privacy," 4 *Harvard Law Review* 193 (1890).

191 **"odious" and "invidious":** *Loving v. Virginia*, 388 U.S. 1, 8, 10 (1967).

192 **hospital administrator:** See Archibald Cox, *The Role of the Supreme Court in American Government* (New York: Oxford University Press, 1976), 113–14.

192 **"clearly on a collision":** O'Connor was dissenting, in *Akron v. Akron Center for Reproductive Health*, 462 U.S. 416, 458 (1983), which, among other things, struck down an ordinance requiring a 24-hour waiting period and parental consent before an unmarried minor could have an abortion.

192 **One could imagine:** Some of this analysis of *Roe*, here and below, first appeared in an earlier book I wrote: David A. Kaplan, *The Accidental President: How 413 Lawyers, 9 Supreme Court Justices, and 5,963,110 Floridians (Give or Take a Few) Landed George W. Bush in the White House* (New York: William Morrow, 2001).

193 **Why was viability:** "Magic moment" has been used by many scholars, including John Hart Ely, in *On Constitutional Ground* (Princeton, N.J.: Princeton University Press, 1996), 284.

193 **"The fetus then":** *Roe v. Wade*, 410 U.S. at 163.

193 **"to mistake a definition":** Ely, "Wages of Crying Wolf," 924.

193 **"arbitrary":** Blackmun to his colleagues (memo), Nov. 21, 1972, *HAB-LOC*, Box 151, Folder 8.

194 **Early in his *Roe* opinion:** *Roe v. Wade*, 410 U.S. at 117.

194 **"an improvident and":** The quote is from the dissent of White and Rehnquist, in *Doe v. Bolton*, 410 U.S. at 221, the companion case to *Roe* that involved Georgia's more lenient abortion statute, also struck down by the Court by a 7-to-2 vote.

194 **"so long as some care":** Ely, "Wages of Crying Wolf," 929.

194 **The "problem with":** Ibid., 943.

195 **"a very bad decision":** Ibid., 947.

195 **"Would there have been":** Ginsburg, "Speaking in a Judicial Voice," 67 *New York University Law Review* at 1199. The Texas and Georgia litigations that led to *Roe* might have been preempted in importance by litigation in New York, but a lawsuit there ended because the state changed its law. For an alternative look at how a federal court might have ruled on abortion, see A. Raymond Randolph, "Before Roe v. Wade: Judge Friendly's Draft Abortion Opinion," 29 *Harvard Journal of Law & Public Policy* 1035 (2006). That draft, written in 1970 by the judge for whom John Roberts first clerked, found no constitutional right to abortion.

195 **"no grand philosophy":** Ginsburg, "Speaking in a Judicial Voice," 67 *New York University Law Review* at 1204, 1186.

195 **"disadvantageous treatment":** Ibid., 1202.

196   **A group of 11:** Jack M. Balkin, ed., *What Roe v. Wade Should Have Said: The Nation's Top Legal Experts Rewrite America's Most Controversial Decision* (New York: New York University Press, 2005); the analogous exercise played out earlier in Jack M. Balkin, ed., *What Brown v. Board Should Have Said: The Nation's Top Legal Experts Rewrite America's Landmark Civil Rights Decision* (New York: New York University Press, 2002).

196   **"Wandering Jew of constitutional law":** Richard A. Posner, "Legal Reasoning from the Top Down and from the Bottom Up: The Question of Unenumerated Constitutional Rights," 59 *University of Chicago Law Review* 433, 441–42 (1992).

196   **"It will be an unsettled":** Blackmun, notation on outline, Oct. 13, 1972, *HAB-LOC*, Box 151, Folder 8.

197   **"I am getting anniversary":** Greenhouse, *Becoming Justice Blackmun*, 137.

197   **"Hogwash":** Blackmun, notation on Post-it, *HAB-LOC*, Box 152, Folder 2 ("Miscellany"). Some articles are marked "pro" and others "con," though the *Washingtonian* piece isn't labeled; Kim Isaac Eisler, "The Real Story Behind Roe v. Wade," *Washingtonian*, Oct. 1993.

198   **"By relying on the courts":** "The Unborn and the Born Again," *New Republic*, July 2, 1977, 5.

198   **"tragically premature":** Barbara Ehrenreich, "Mothers Unite," *New Republic*, July 10, 1989, 30.

198   **"Juricentric":** See Linda Greenhouse & Reva B. Siegel, *Before Roe v. Wade: Voices That Shaped the Abortion Debate Before the Supreme Court's Ruling* (New York: Kaplan Publishing, 2010), 33–34; Linda Greenhouse & Reva B. Siegel, "Before (and After) Roe v. Wade: New Questions About Backlash," 120 *Yale Law Journal* 2028 (2011); and Linda Greenhouse & Reva B. Siegel, "Backlash to the Future: From Roe to Perry," 60 *UCLA Law Review* 240 (2013). Greenhouse is the former longtime Supreme Court correspondent for the *New York Times*. (Full disclosure and small-world bit: I went to Sunday school with Reva Siegel in the 1960s.)

199   **If nothing more:** For the most part, I use *pro-choice* and *pro-life* rather than *pro-abortion* and *anti-abortion*. It's easier, though the former phrases, too often, are as much cant as description.

199   **Thayer's disciples:** Philip B. Kurland, *Felix Frankfurter on the Supreme Court: Extrajudicial Essays on the Court and the Constitution* (Cambridge, Mass.: Harvard University Press, 1970), 252.

200   **"dwarf the political":** James Bradley Thayer, *John Marshall* (Boston: Houghton Mifflin, 1901), 107.

200   **"the thunderbolt of":** Ibid., 109.

200   **"fly paper":** See Rosenberg, *Hollow Hope*, 339, 341.

200   **"Under no system":** James B. Thayer, "The Origin and Scope of the American Doctrine of Constitutional Law," 7 *Harvard Law Review* 129, 156 (1893).

200   **As a former Brennan clerk:** See Larry D. Kramer, "Judicial Supremacy and
       the End of Judicial Restraint," 100 *California Law Review* 621, 629 (2012).

201   **"I don't understand":** Linda Greenhouse, "Misconceptions," *New York
       Times*, Jan. 23, 2013, opinionator.blogs.nytimes.com/2013/01/23/
       misconceptions/?_r=0.

201   **"Pro-choice people went":** Laurie Johnston, "Abortion Foes Gain Sup-
       port as They Intensify Campaign," *New York Times*, Oct. 23, 1977, 1.

201   **"The political organization":** Rosenberg, *Hollow Hope*, 339.

201   **"a single target":** Adam Liptak, "Court Is 'One of Most Activist,' Gins-
       burg Says, Vowing to Stay," *New York Times*, Aug. 24, 2013, A1.

202   **historical overkill:** See also Randall Balmer, "The Real Origins of
       the Religious Right," *Politico*, May 27, 2014, politico.com/magazine/
       story/2014/05/religious-right-real-origins-107133.

202   **"grassroots pro-life organization":** "Statement of the Administrative
       Committee, National Conference of Catholic Bishops on the Anti-
       Abortion Amendment," *U.S. Conference of Catholic Bishops*, Sept. 18,
       1973, usccb.org/csupload/85741.pdf.

202   **various versions:** David J. Garrow, *Liberty and Sexuality: The Right to
       Privacy and the Making of Roe v. Wade* (Berkeley: University of California
       Press, 1998), 618–19.

203   **68 versions:** Jeffrey Rosen, *The Most Democratic Branch: How the Courts
       Serve America* (New York: Oxford University Press, 2006), 96.

203   **"a middle ground between":** The resolution was in June 1974. Mary
       Ziegler, *After Roe: The History of the Abortion Debate* (Cambridge, Mass.:
       Harvard University Press, 2015), 14.

203   **During the 1975:** Michael J. Gerhardt, "How Jimmy Carter Imperiled
       Roe v. Wade," *Salon*, Mar. 30, 2013, salon.com/2013/03/30/how_jimmy_
       carter_imperiled_roe_v_wade/.

203   **"when you have a black":** Charlie Savage, "On Nixon Tapes, Ambiva-
       lence over Abortion, Not Watergate," *New York Times*, June 23, 2009, A1.

203   **"consistently opposed":** Gerald R. Ford to Joseph L. Bernardin, Sept. 10,
       1976, *American Presidency Project*, University of California, Santa Barbara,
       www.presidency.ucsb.edu/ws/print.php?pid=6320. More than two decades
       later, Ford identified himself as "strongly pro-choice." Richard L. Berke,
       "Ford Urges GOP to Drop Abortion Issue and Shift Center," *New York
       Times*, Jan. 20, 1998, A15.

203   **Never mind that:** Lou Cannon, "How Church and State Made Their
       Match," *New York Times*, May 20, 2007, WK12.

203   **Before the first:** "1976's Sleeper Issue," *Newsweek*, Feb. 9, 1976, 21.

203   **"the darling":** Laurence H. Tribe, *Abortion: The Clash of Absolutes* (New
       York: W.W. Norton, 1990), 148.

203   **"a continuance of":** *Republican Party Platform of 1976*, Aug. 18, 1976,
       American Presidency Project, presidency.ucsb.edu/ws/index.php?pid=25843.

204   **Pro-lifers "are a very significant force":** Martin Tolchin, "Senators Elu-
       cidate Shift on Abortions," *New York Times*, July 1, 1977, A24.

NOTES

412   NOTES

204   **"Too narrow":** Randall Balmer, *Thy Kingdom Come: How the Religious Right Distorts Faith and Threatens America* (New York: Basic Books, 2006), xvii.

204   **According to Gallup:** "Abortion," 1975–present, *Gallup News*, news .gallup.com/poll/1576/abortion.aspx. For a nuanced view of the range of polls since *Roe*, see, for example, David Leonhardt, "In Public Opinion on Abortion, Few Absolutes," *New York Times*, July 7, 2013, fivethirtyeight .blogs.nytimes.com/2013/07/17/in-public-opinion-on-abortion-few -absolutes/?_r=0.

205   **Whereas in 1976:** Polling about evangelicals is a bit of a mess. Balmer states the "nearly" 50 percent for 1976, but offers no corresponding figure for 1980. Randall Balmer, "Jimmy Carter's Evangelical Downfall: Reagan, Religion and the 1980 Presidential Election," *Salon*, May 25, 2014, salon .com/2014/05/25/jimmy_carters_evangelical_downfall_reagan_religion_ and_the_1980_presidential_election/. Various press accounts described a significant drop-off for Carter. For example, the *New York Times* reported exit polls among "born-again or evangelical Christians" at 56 percent to 40 percent for Reagan over Carter. "Religion—National Exit Polls Table," *New York Times*, Nov. 5, 2008, nytimes.com/elections/2008/results/ president/national-exit-polls.html. The Associated Press right after Election Day in 1980 reported the split at 56–39 for Reagan, compared with 50–37 percent for Carter four years earlier.

205   **One pollster suggested:** Balmer, *Thy Kingdom Come*, xvii.

205   **It also helped:** "Abortion Surveillance—United States, 2005," *Centers for Disease Control and Prevention*, Nov. 28, 2008, Figure 1, cdc.gov/mmwr/ preview/mmwrhtml/ss5713a1.htm.

205   **on the Sunday before:** John Herbers, "Sweeping Right-to-Life Goals Set as Movement Gains New Power," *New York Times*, Nov. 27, 1978, A1; Douglas E. Kneeland, "Clark Defeat in Iowa Laid to Abortion Issue," *New York Times*, Nov. 13, 1978, A18.

206   **It's a chicken-and-egg problem:** See Balmer, "Real Origins of the Religious Right," *Politico*; and Randall Balmer, *Redeemer: The Life of Jimmy Carter* (New York: Basic Books, 2014).

206   **"awakening" of "Religious":** Howell Raines, "Reagan Backs Evangelicals in Their Political Activities," *New York Times*, Aug. 23, 1980, A8.

206   **"I know you can't":** "God in America: Of God and Caesar" (2010), *PBS*, pbs.org/godinamerica/view/.

206   **"sins of America":** See Jerry Falwell, *Listen America!: The Conservative Blueprint for America's Moral Rebirth* (New York: Bantam, 1980).

206   **"Many of you have been":** "Remarks at a White House Briefing for Right to Life Activists," July 30, 1987, *American Presidency Project*, University of California, Santa Barbara, presidency.ucsb.edu/ws/?pid=34624.

207   **"unborn babies can feel":** *Republican Platform 2016*, 14, prod-cdn-static .gop.com/media/documents/DRAFT_12_FINAL[1]-ben_1468872234 .pdf.

207   **"unconstitutionally usurp":** Ibid., 10.

207   **The party's nominee:** See, for example, Philip Bump, "Donald Trump Took Five Different Positions on Abortion in Three Days," *Washington Post*, Apr. 3, 2016, washingtonpost.com/news/the-fix/wp/2016/04/03/ Donald-trumps-ever-shifting-positions-on-abortion/?utm_term= .e231737a3392.

207   **Hyde Amendment:** *Harris v. McRae*, 448 U.S. 297 (1980).

208   **gag rule:** *Rust v. Sullivan*, 500 U.S. 173 (1991).

208   **In a bitterly fragmented:** *Planned Parenthood v. Casey*, 505 U.S. at 833.

208   **Now, with only:** The earlier cases were *Akron v. Akron Center for Reproductive Health*, 462 U.S. 416 (1983), and *Thornburgh v. American College of Obstetricians and Gynecologists*, 476 U.S. 747 (1986).

208   **"the central holding of":** *Planned Parenthood v. Casey*, 505 U.S. at 867.

209   **"the distance between the":** Ibid., 505 U.S. at 922–23, 943.

209   **Back and forth:** *Stenberg v. Carhart*, 530 U.S. 914 (2000).

209   **seven years later:** *Gonzales v. Carhart*, 550 U.S. 124 (2007).

210   **In late June:** *Whole Woman's Health v. Hellerstedt*, 136 S. Ct. 2292 (2016).

211   **"the *Dred Scott* of our time":** This quote has been attributed to Kennedy multiple times, and never challenged. See, for example, "Anthony M. Kennedy," *Almanac of the Federal Judiciary* (Austin, Tex.: Aspen Publishers, 2011), 2:17.

211   **Judges aren't algorithms:** In the days before computers, the iconoclastic Yale law professor Fred Rodell used a different analogy, belittling those who believed the Court was like "a nine-headed calculating machine, intricately adjusted to the words of the Constitution and of lesser laws, and ready to give automatic answers to any attorneys who drop their briefs in the proper slot and push the button." Fred Rodell, *Nine Men: A Political History of the Supreme Court from 1790 to 1955* (New York: Random House, 1955), 7.

211   **"accelerated the movement":** Posner, "Rise and Fall of Judicial Self-Restraint," 532 n.50.

212   **"passive virtues":** Bickel, *Least Dangerous Branch*, 111–98. See also Alexander M. Bickel, "The Supreme Court, 1960 Term—Foreword: The Passive Virtues," 75 *Harvard Law Review* 40 (1961).

212   **"staying its hand":** Ibid., 70–71.

212   **He understood:** Bickel's ends-means distinction was well articulated in the context of post-9/11 national security cases in Steve Vladek, "Online Alexander Bickel Symposium: The Passive Virtues as Means, Not Ends," *SCOTUSblog*, Aug. 21, 2012, scotusblog.com/2012/08/online-alexander-bickel-symposium-the-passive-virtues-as-means-not-ends/.

212   **Sometimes the inconsistencies:** Professor Gerald Gunther derided Bickel's belief in the "passive virtues" as an argument for courts that were "100 percent principled" but only "20 percent of the time." Gerald Gunther, "The Subtle Vices of the 'Passive Virtues'—A Comment on Principle and Expediency in Judicial Review," 64 *Columbia Law Review* 1, 3 (1964).

But Gunther undervalued the Court preserving its institutional reserves, and he seemed unrealistic in believing the Court typically was able to extricate political expediency from principled adjudicating.

213   **school violence and interstate commerce:** *United States v. Lopez*, 514 U.S. 549 (1995).

213   **reasonable policy makers:** *United States v. Morrison*, 529 U.S. 598 (2000).

CHAPTER 11: REVENGE OF THE RIGHT

215   **the Cherokee Nation:** *Worcester v. Georgia*, 31 U.S. 515 (1832).

216   **The question was:** For a superb historical account challenging conventional wisdom that the Court's word has always been supreme—or should be—see Larry D. Kramer, *The People Themselves: Popular Constitutionalism and Judicial Review* (New York: Oxford University Press, 2004).

216   **In drafting:** For the history, see Larry D. Kramer, "The Supreme Court, 2000 Term—Foreword: We the Court," 115 *Harvard Law Review* 4, 156 n.688 (2001).

217   **The official tally:** The official margin of 537 votes was debatable. It could have been 930, as I suggested in Kaplan, *Accidental President*, based on what the Court ruled. The real margin, of course, is even more hotly contested, ranging from 154 to 165 to 193 to 204 in Bush's favor, based on abbreviated recounts that were halted by the Court; to various numbers indicating a Gore victory, based on later recounts conducted by the media, as well as mathematical models by political scientists. Mercifully, I won't here recount the respective bases for the figures.

218   **The *New York Times* ran off:** Much of this reporting and analysis first appeared in my earlier book, Kaplan, *Accidental President*.

219   **Once lawsuits began:** See Jeffrey Toobin, *The Nine: Inside the Secret World of the Supreme Court* (New York: Anchor Books, 2008), 171–73.

221   **"Federal judges":** *Siegel v. LePore*, 120 F. Supp. 2d 1041, 1050–52 (S.D. Fla. 2000).

222   **To the horror of:** *Bush v. Palm Beach County Canvassing Board*, 531 U.S. 70 (2000).

222   **Pentagon Papers:** *New York Times v. United States*, 403 U.S. 713 (1971).

222   **Nixon Tapes:** *United States v. Nixon*, 418 U.S. 683 (1974).

223   **"any clearly ascertainable":** *Texas Election Code*, Section 127.130(d)(4) and (e).

225   **"Judicial restraint":** Laurence H. Tribe, *American Constitutional Law*, 2d ed. (Mineola, N.Y.: Foundation Press, 1978), viii.

228   **"I guess we'll have to meet":** "Supreme Court Justice John Paul Stevens Opens Up," *60 Minutes*, Nov. 23, 2010, cbsnews.com/news/supreme -court-justice-john-paul-stevens-opens-up/.

230   **internment of Japanese Americans:** *Korematsu v. United States*, 323 U.S. 214 (1944). *Korematsu* was overruled in 2018 in *Trump v. Hawaii*, when the Court called it "morally repugnant," "objectively unlawful," "gravely wrong the day it was decided," and "overruled in the court of history."

232   **"was terrible":** See, for example, Michael Isikoff, "The Truth Behind the Pillars," *Newsweek*, Dec. 24, 2000, newsweek.com/truth-behind -pillars-155985.

233   **The post-O'Connor Court:** Karlan, *Democracy and Disdain*, 5.

233   **"legal arguments":** Adam Liptak, "Judging a Court with Ex-Judges Only," *New York Times*, Feb. 17, 2009, A14.

233   **"one more day":** This scene was first reported in my *Accidental President*, 284, which was also excerpted at David A. Kaplan, "The Secret Vote That Made Bush President," *Newsweek*, Sept. 17, 2001, 28. Much effort at Choate was devoted to refuting the account, including letters from partici-pants to various publications, writing that they hadn't heard Souter speak those words. Three years later, an article in *Vanity Fair* purported to dis-prove the account, stating it "appeared inconsistent with the facts." David Margolick et al., "The Path to Florida," *Vanity Fair*, Oct. 2004, 358. The only "fact" offered was the "belief" of clerks that "Souter had spent most of the last few crucial days in chambers brooding over the case rather than working any back channels." The *Vanity Fair* article was silly. My book didn't state Souter attempted to win Kennedy over. All it did was recount Souter's state of mind—that if he'd had "one more day," which he didn't have, then perhaps *Bush v. Gore* would have come out differently. Never mind that if Souter had wanted to work back channels, he had a phone in chambers to call anybody while he was "brooding." The "one more day" scene—widely cited since, without contradiction—is accurate and Souter has never denied it.

233   **"I might have persuaded":** Jan Crawford Greenburg, *Supreme Conflict: The Inside Story of the Struggle for Control of the United States Supreme Court* (New York: Penguin Books, 2007), 177.

236   **"Surely Bill Clinton would":** Stephen Gillers, "Who Says the Election Has a Dec. 12 Deadline?" *New York Times*, Dec. 2, 2000, A19.

237   **By a 6-to-1 vote:** *Palm Beach County Canvassing Board v. Harris*, 772 So.2d 1273, 1291–92 (Fla. 2000).

237   **Thomas said:** Neil A. Lewis, "Justice Thomas Speaks Out on a Timely Topic, Several of Them, in Fact," *New York Times*, Dec. 14, 2000, A23.

241   **Moreover, the Florida court:** See *Jacobs v. Seminole County Canvassing Board*, 773 So.2d 519 (Fla. 2000); *Taylor v. Martin County Canvassing Board*, 773 So.2d 517 (Fla. 2000).

241   **"*this* change in Florida law":** Balkin, "Bush v. Gore and the Boundary Between Law and Politics," 110 *Yale Law Journal* 1407, 1435 n.90 (2001).

241   **And indeed:** *Arizona v. Inter Tribal Council of Arizona*, 133 S. Ct. 2247 (2013).

242   **"the same class as":** The justice was Owen Roberts in *Smith v. Allright*, 321 U.S. 649, 699 (1944).

242   **"does not sit to"**: *United States v. Virginia*, 518 U.S. 515 (1996).

243   **"almost a parody"**: Balkin, "Bush v. Gore and the Boundary Between Law and Politics," 1433, quoting Mark A. Graber, "The Passive-Aggressive Virtues: Cohen v. Virginia and the Problematic Establishment of Judicial Power," 12 *Constitutional Comment* 67 (1995). See also "Online Alexander Bickel Symposium: The Passive Virtues as Means, Not Ends," *SCOTUSblog*.

244   **"A question which involved"**: Maurice Finkelstein, "Further Notes on Judicial Self-Limitation," 39 *Harvard Law Review* 221, 243 (1925), quoted in Bickel, *Least Dangerous Branch*, 185.

244   **"We will have to decide"**: *Gill v. Whitford*, No. 16-1161 (argued Oct. 3, 2017).

245   **But if only undervotes:** For those scoring at home and wanting to determine who-really-won, see a good summary of independent post hoc recounts in Wade Payson-Denney, "So Who Really Won?" *CNN Online*, Oct. 31, 2015, cnn.com/2015/10/31/politics/bush-gore-2000-election -results-studies/index.html. See also Ford Fessenden & John M. Broder, "Examining the Vote: The Overview," *New York Times*, Nov. 12, 2001, A1. The underlying data of the most comprehensive study, by the National Opinion Research Center, is at "2000 Florida Ballots Project," electionstudies.org/florida2000/data/data_files.htm. Good luck sorting through the innumerable permutations.

246   **"zero"**: "Justice Thomas Speaks Out on a Timely Topic," *New York Times*, A23.

246   **"the last political act"**: Linda Greenhouse, "Another Kind of Bitter Split," *New York Times*, Dec. 14, 2000, A23.

246   **"believed in Santa Claus"**: Balkin, "Bush v. Gore and the Boundary Between Law and Politics," 1407.

246   **"a piece of shit"**: David Margolick, "The Path to Florida," *Vanity Fair*, Oct. 2004, 358.

246   **"an easy case"**: "Scalia on Healthcare Ruling," *YouTube*, Nov. 28, 2012, youtube.com/watch?v=zAt1GcxTA8Y.

246   **"We were the laughingstock"**: "Antonin Scalia," *Charlie Rose*, June 20, 2008, charlierose.com/videos/15555.

246   **"Some court was going"**: "Scalia on Healthcare Ruling," *YouTube*, Nov. 28, 2012, youtube.com/watch?v=zAt1GcxTA8Y.

246   **"Get over it!"**: See, for example, "Justice Scalia on the Record," *60 Minutes*, Apr. 27, 2008, cbsnews.com/news/justice-scalia-on-the-record/; and Jim Salemi, "Supreme Court Justice Antonin Scalia Speaks at Wesleyan," *Middletown Press*, Mar. 8, 2012, middletownpress.com/ general-news/20120308/supreme-court-justice-antonin-scalia-speaks-at -wesleyan-with-video-2?viewmode=fullstory.

247   **"lingering bitterness"**: Joan Biskupic, "Election Decision Still Splits Court," *USA Today*, Jan. 22, 2001, usatoday30.usatoday.com/news/ court/2001-01-21-election.htm.

247   **"it wasn't the end":** "Insight and Ideas," *Aspen Ideas Festival*, June 30,
      2011, aspenideas.org/session/insights-and-ideas-money-politics-and
      -judicial-elections.

247   **"Maybe the court":** Emily Bazelon, "Sandra Day Late," *Slate*, May
      1, 2013, slate.com/articles/news_and_politics/jurisprudence/2013/05/
      justice_sandra_day_o_connor_s_bush_v_gore_regrets_she_shouldn_t_
      have_retired.html.

CHAPTER 12: JAMES MADISON MADE US DO IT

249   **The percentage has been:** "Supreme Court," 2000–2017, *Gallup News*,
      news.gallup.com/poll/4732/supreme-court.aspx.

250   **"A well regulated militia":** For the sake of readability, I've not capi-
      talized words such as *militia* and *arms*, even though the Constitution
      does.

251   **It was this right:** For a first-rate history of the Second Amendment, see
      Michael Waldman, *The Second Amendment: A Biography* (New York:
      Simon & Schuster, 2014).

251   **even if the idea:** See Garry Wills, "To Keep and Bear Arms," *New York
      Review of Books*, Sept. 21, 1995, nybooks.com/articles/1995/09/21/to-keep
      -and-bear-arms/.

251   **In the 1700s:** Adam Winkler, *Gunfight: The Battle over the Right to Bear
      Arms in America* (New York: W.W. Norton, 2011), 13.

252   **"the most famous machine-gun":** Ibid., 191.

252   **There wasn't widespread:** Brian L. Frye, "The Peculiar Story of United
      States v. Miller," 3 *NYU Journal of Law & Liberty* 48, 63 (2008). The ar-
      ticle, cited by Scalia in his majority opinion in *Heller*, has more fun retell-
      ing the Miller tale than Miller probably had living it.

252   **By the time:** Ibid., 52–58.

253   **When he found:** Ibid., 82–83.

253   **"an impenetrable mess":** *United States v. Miller*, 307 U.S. 174 (1939).

253   **In keeping:** Frye, "The Peculiar Story of United States v. Miller," 68.

253   **It wasn't until:** For the broader history, see Franklin E. Zimring, "Fire-
      arms and Federal Law: The Gun Control Act of 1968," 4 *Journal of Legal
      Studies* 133 (1975), scholarship.law.berkeley.edu/cgi/viewcontent.cgi?article
      =2114&context=facpubs.

254   **"the automobile is":** Ronald Reagan, "Ronald Reagan Champions Gun
      Ownership," *Guns & Ammo*, Sept. 1975, *Patriot Post*, patriotpost.us/
      pages/171.

255   **"What the Subcommittee":** "The Right to Keep and Bear Arms," *Report
      of the Subcommittee on the Constitution of the Committee on the Judiciary*
      (preface), Jan. 20, 1982, constitution.org/mil/rkba82.pdf.

255   **"The Constitution in the Year 2000":** "The Constitution in the Year
      2000: Choices Ahead in Constitutional Interpretation," *Office of Legal*

Policy, Department of Justice, Oct. 11, 1988, babel.hathitrust.org/cgi/pt?id=mdp.39015014943511;view=1up;seq=3.

255   **The report didn't say a thing:** Waldman, *Second Amendment*, 118.

255   **"like a rifle and powder horn":** Warren E. Burger, "The Right to Bear Arms: A Distinguished Citizen Takes a Stand," *Parade*, Jan. 4, 1990, 4.

256   **"If the militia":** "PBS NewsHour," *YouTube*, Dec. 16, 1991, youtube.com/watch?v=Eya_k4P-iEo.

256   **"If liberals interpreted":** Michael Kinsley, "Slicing Up the Second Amendment," *Washington Post*, Feb. 8, 1990, A25.

256   **After Scalia's death:** "$1 Million Endows Professorship at George Mason University," *George Mason University Media and Public Relations*, Jan. 28, 2003, eagle.gmu.edu/newsroom/399/; Nicholas Fandos, "Law School Renamed for Antonin Scalia, Again. Blame Acronym," *New York Times*, Apr. 5, 2016, nytimes.com/2016/04/06/us/politics/antonin-scalia-george-mason-law-school-acronym.html?_r=0.

257   **the NRA bankrolled:** Waldman, *Second Amendment*, 98.

257   **"For too long":** Sanford Levinson, "The Embarrassing Second Amendment," 99 *Yale Law Journal*, 637, 658 (1989).

257   **"the perhaps subconscious fear":** Ibid., 642.

257   **It was not until 1977:** Waldman, *Second Amendment*, 88–91.

257   **The group's radicalization:** David Frum, *How We Got Here: The 70s, the Decade That Brought You Modern Life—for Better or Worse* (New York: Basic Books, 2000), 19.

258   **At NRA headquarters:** Waldman, *Second Amendment*, 88, 96.

258   **energetically opposed the Democrat:** The NRA didn't endorse George H.W. Bush in 1992 or Bob Dole in 1996.

258   **"The text and the original intent":** The full letter can be read on the website of the NRA's lobbying arm, the NRA-ILA Institute for Legislative Action, nraila.org/media/2421928/Ashcroft.pdf (May 17, 2001).

258   **"whole areas":** *Printz v. United States*, 521 U.S. 898, 938–39 (1997).

258   **Thomas had shown:** See generally Kramer, *People Themselves*.

259   **Public opinion, too:** "Guns," *Gallup News*, Feb. 8–10, 2008, news.gallup.com/poll/1645/guns.asp.

259   **a new constitutional right:** *United States v. Emerson*, 270 F.3d 203 (5th Cir. 2001), *cert denied*, 536 U.S. 907 (2002).

260   **he became an author:** For a detailed account of the Levy-Neily-Simpson backstory, see Marcia Coyle, *The Roberts Court: The Struggle for the Constitution* (New York: Simon & Schuster, 2014), 124–35.

260   **Because *Heller*:** Sam Skolnik, "Heller Attorneys Awarded $1.1M in Fees, One-Third of Their Request," *Legal Times*, Dec. 29, 2011, legaltimes.typepad.com/blt/2011/12/heller-attorneys-awarded-11m-in-fees-one-third-of-their-request.html.

261 **they would be far from:** Adam Liptak, "Carefully Plotted Course Propels Gun Case to Top," *New York Times*, Dec. 3, 2007, A16.

261 **"years of unchanged":** *Parker v. District of Columbia*, 311 F. Supp. 2d 101, 109–10 (D.D.C. 2004). Parker was the name of an initial plaintiff who was dismissed from the case.

261 **"dead letter":** *Parker v. District of Columbia*, 478 F.3d 370, 378 (D.C. Cir. 2007).

262 **Scottish highlanders:** See Reva B. Siegel, "Dead or Alive: Originalism as Popular Constitutionalism in Heller," 122 *Harvard Law Review* 191, 192 (2008), for a fine discussion of this and other "temporal oddities" of the majority's analysis of "original meaning." See also Laurence Tribe & Joshua Matz, *Uncertain Justice: The Roberts Court and the Constitution* (New York: Henry Holt, 2014), 172.

262 **The court was flooded:** The 19 friend-of-the-court briefs for D.C. can be read at scotusblog.com/2008/01/amicus-briefs-for-dc-available-in -guns-case/. The 47 briefs on Heller's behalf can be read at scotusblog .com/2008/02/amicus-briefs-for-heller-available-in-guns-case/.

263 **"were just as 'causey' ":** Coyle, *Roberts Court*, 181.

263 **"aware of the problem":** *District of Columbia v. Heller*, 554 U.S. at 636.

263 **"The range":** Richard A. Posner, "In Defense of Looseness," *New Republic*, Aug. 27, 2008, newrepublic.com/article/62124/defense-looseness.

264 **In the spring of 2018:** John Paul Stevens: "Repeal the Second Amendment," *New York Times*, Mar. 28, 2018, A23.

265 **"As time passes":** Bickel, *Least Dangerous Branch*, 39.

265 **"vindication of originalism":** Coyle, *Roberts Court*, 163.

266 **"has taken sides":** *Lawrence v. Texas*, 539 U.S. 558 (2003).

266 **"fidelity to law":** Siegel, "Dead or Alive," 237–38.

266 **"If the policy of the":** *Planned Parenthood v. Casey*, 505 U.S. at 996, 997.

267 **"arrogance cloaked as humility":** William J. Brennan Jr., "The Constitution of the United States: Contemporary Ratification," 27 *South Texas Law Review* 433, 435 (1986).

267 **"The *Roe* and *Heller* Courts":** J. Harvie Wilkinson III, "Of Guns, Abortions, and the Unraveling Rule of Law," 95 *Virginia Law Review* 253, 254 (2009). See also Wilkinson, *Cosmic Constitutional Theory*, 57–58.

267 **"just as easily be seen":** Wilkinson, "Of Guns, Abortions," 256, 265.

268 **"the Constitution's text":** Ibid., 273.

268 **"obviously":** "Gun Control—Supreme Court Justice Scalia," *Fox News Sunday*, July 29, 2012, video.foxnews.com/v/1760716797001.

268 **"nationalizing":** Posner, "In Defense of Looseness."

268 **The title:** Richard A. Posner, "The Incoherence of Antonin Scalia," *New Republic*, Aug. 24, 2012, newrepublic.com/article/106441/scalia-garner -reading-the-law-textual-originalism.

268   **"I did not":** Terry Baynes, "Fanning Furor, Justice Scalia Says Appeals
Court Judge Lied," *Reuters*, Sept. 17, 2012, reuters.com/article/us-usa
-court-scalia-idUSBRE88H06X20120918; "The Benchslap Dispatches:
Justice Scalia on Judge Posner's 'Hatchet Job,'" Sept. 10, 2012, *Above the
Law* blog, abovethelaw.com/2012/09/the-benchslap-dispatches-justice
-scalia-on-judge-posners-hatchet-job/#more-190407; Richard A. Posner,
"Richard Posner Responds to Antonin Scalia's Accusation of Lying," *New
Republic*, Sept. 20, 2012, newrepublic.com/article/107549/richard-posner
-responds-antonin-scalias-accusation-lying.

269   **"dangerous and unusual":** *McDonald v. Chicago*, 561 U.S. 742 (2010).
The ruling involved Chicago's handgun ban that was similar to Washington's.

269   **"a disfavored right":** *Peruta v. California*, 137 S. Ct. 1995 (2017).

269   **Despite the Thomas-Gorsuch cry:** *Silvester v. Becerra*, No. 17-342 (2018)
(dissenting from the denial of cert).

270   **five years after *Heller*:** The 2013 case involved the Defense of Marriage
Act (DOMA).

CHAPTER 13: FOR THE LOVE OF MONEY

271   **"criminalizing a movie":** Adam Liptak, "Supreme Court to Revisit 'Hillary' Documentary," *New York Times*, Aug. 29, 2009, A1.

272   **"a hogshead and a barrel":** See references at "Beer," *George Washington's
Mount Vernon*, mountvernon.org/digital-encyclopedia/article/beer/.

272   **"Virtually every means":** *Buckley v. Valeo*, 424 U.S. 1 (1976).

274   **"reams of disquieting":** *McConnell v. Federal Election Commission*, 540
U.S. 93 (2003).

275   **"Where the First":** *Federal Election Commission v. Wisconsin Right to Life,
Inc.*, 551 U.S. 449 (2007).

275   **"Gosh":** "Justice Sandra Day O'Connor Remarks on Choosing
Judges" (Georgetown University), *C-SPAN*, Jan. 26, 2010, c-span.org/
video/?291663-3/justice-sandra-day-oconnor-remarks-choosing-judges;
Jeffrey Rosen, "Why I Miss Sandra Day O'Connor," *New Republic*, July 1,
2011, newrepublic.com/article/91146/sandra-day-o-connor-supreme
-court-alito.

276   **"the founding fathers' vision":** "Who We Are," *Citizens United*,
citizensunited.org/who-we-are.aspx.

276   **All they had to do:** Stephanie Mencimer, "Hillary's Hero: Judge Royce
Lamberth," *Mother Jones*, Jan. 2008, motherjones.com/politics/2008/01/
hillarys-hero-judge-royce-lamberth/.

278   **According to multiple:** See Jeffrey Toobin, *The Oath: The Obama White
House and the Supreme Court* (New York: Doubleday, 2012), 167–69, and
Coyle, *Roberts Court*, 249–52. Stevens confirms some of these accounts
in Adam Liptak, "Justice Stevens Suggests Solution for 'Giant Step in the
Wrong Direction,'" *New York Times*, Apr. 22, 2014, A14.

279   **He was ready:** The earlier case was *Austin v. Michigan Chamber of Commerce*, 494 U.S. 652 (1990), which upheld a ban on corporations making expenditures to support or oppose candidates, even if the expenditures were independent of a campaign.

280   **and a related lower-court ruling:** The case was *SpeechNow.org v. Federal Election Commission*, 599 F.3d 686 (D.C. Cir. 2010).

280   **In that year, 83 Super PACs:** The numbers come from customizable graphs and tables put together by the Center for Responsive Politics. See "Financial Activity by Super PACs," *OpenSecrets.org*, opensecrets.org/outsidespending/summ.php?chrt=V&type=S.

281   **But politicians and pundits:** For a good early analysis, only days after the ruling, see Nathaniel Persily, "The Floodgates Were Already Open," *Slate*, Jan. 25, 2010, slate.com/articles/news_and_politics/jurisprudence /2010/01/the_floodgates_were_already_open.html.

284   **"Not true":** "Alito Mouths 'Not True,'" *YouTube*, Jan. 27, 2010, youtube .com/watch?v=4pB5uR3zgsA.

284   **"the image":** "Chief Justice John Roberts Remarks," *C-SPAN*, Mar. 9, 2010, c-span.org/video/?292439-1/chief-justice-john-roberts-remarks.

285   **"rude":** Robert Barnes, "In the Court of Public Opinion, No Clear Ruling," *Washington Post*, Jan. 29, 2010, A1.

287   **"Why is it easier":** "'Hillary: The Movie' Gets New Airing at High Court," *CNBC*, Aug. 2, 2010, cnbc.com/id/32754702.

288   **Having a First Amendment:** The idea that the First Amendment was being dangerously "weaponized" was nicely expressed by Elena Kagan in another context in 2018. See *Janus v. AFSCME*, No. 16-1466 (2018). The conservative justices, she wrote in dissent, were "weaponizing" the First Amendment "in a way that unleashes judges . . . to intervene in economic and regulatory policy."

288   **"The losers in *Heller*":** Wilkinson, "Of Guns, Abortions," 323.

CHAPTER 14: A DISDAIN FOR DEMOCRACY

289   **A Disdain for Democracy:** Apologies on the title to Professor Pam Karlan of Stanford. See Karlan, "Democracy and Disdain," which itself was a play on Professor John Hart Ely's *Democracy and Distrust*.

289   **In particular, rulings:** See, for example, *Hamdi v. Rumsfeld*, 542 U.S. 507 (2004), along with two other cases, upholding the right of enemy combatants, even foreigners, to challenge their detentions in federal courts: *Hamdan v. Rumsfeld*, 548 U.S. 557 (2006), invalidating military commissions established by the Bush administration to try detainees at Guantanamo Bay; and *Boumediene v. Bush*, 553 U.S. 723 (2008), declaring Congress lacked the power to strip federal courts of jurisdiction to hear challenges by foreigners detained at Guantanamo.

291   **Its singular moment:** Robert A. Caro, "When LBJ Said, 'We Shall Overcome,'" *International Herald Tribune*, Aug. 29, 2008, 8.

292   **The case was called:** *Parents Involved in Community Schools v. Seattle School District No. 1*, 551 U.S. 701 (2007).

293   **the school districts cited:** See *Grutter v. Bollinger*, 539 U.S. 306 (2003), and *Gratz v. Bollinger*, 539 U.S. 244 (2003).

293   **The Court was confirming:** *Regents of the University of California v. Bakke*, 438 U.S. 265 (1978).

294   **Never mind that he lifted:** See *Parents Involved in Community Schools v. Seattle School District No. 1*, 426 F.3d 1162, 1222 (9th Cir. 2005) (Judge Carlos Bea dissenting). Breyer's dissent, in criticizing Roberts's "slogan," quoted Bea's line—"the way to end racial discrimination is to stop discriminating by race"—and cited it as the origin for the slogan. Linda Greenhouse also discussed the "benign plagiarism" in "A Tale of Two Justices," 11 *Green Bag* 2d 37, 40–41 (2008).

294   **Oral dissents:** See, for example, Christopher W. Schmidt & Carolyn Shapiro, "Oral Dissenting on the Supreme Court," 19 *William & Mary Bill of Rights Journal* 75 (2010).

296   **Six years later:** *Fisher v. University of Texas*, 133 S. Ct. 2411 (2013).

296   **But when she:** *Schuette v. Coalition to Defend Affirmative Action*, 134 S. Ct. 1623 (2014).

296   **"To doubt":** Sotomayor, *My Beloved World*, 245.

298   **"proves our unbending":** Ronald Reagan, "Remarks on Signing the Voting Rights Act Amendments of 1982," *Reagan Library Archives*, June 29, 1982, reaganlibrary.archives.gov/archives/speeches/1982/62982b.htm.

298   **Congress heard:** See *Shelby County v. Holder*, 679 F.3d 848, 865 (D.C. Cir. 2012).

299   **Between 1965:** "Total Section 5 Changes Received by the Attorney General, 1965 Through 2013," *U.S. Department of Justice* (2013), justice.gov/crt/section-5-changes-type-and-year-2.

299   **For example:** "New Voting Restrictions in America," *Brennan Center for Justice* (2017), brennancenter.org/new-voting-restrictions-america.

299   **"Congress is declaring":** Remarks of Lynn Westmoreland, *Congressional Record—House*, vol. 152, pt. 11, July 13, 2006, 14327.

299   **"unremitting and ingenious":** *South Carolina v. Katzenbach*, 303 U.S. 301 (1966).

299   **in 2009 the Roberts Court:** *Northwest Austin Municipal Utility District No. 1 v. Holder*, 557 U.S. 193 (2009).

300   **"racial and ethnic":** "About Us," *Project on Fair Representation*, projectonfairrepresentation.org/about/.

300   **"I find the plaintiff":** Morgan Smith, "One Man Standing Against Race-Based Laws," *New York Times*, Feb. 24, 2012, A21.

301   **Was this the same justice:** *United States v. Windsor*, 133 S. Ct. 2675 (2013).

302   **"on the narrowest possible":** "Georgetown University Law Center Commencement Address," *C-SPAN*, May 21, 2006, c-span.org/video/?192685 -1/georgetown-university-law-center-commencement-address.

303   **"Roberts blinked"**: Richard L. Hasen, "Initial Thoughts on NAMUDNO: Chief Justice Roberts Blinked," *Election Law Blog*, June 22, 2009, electionlawblog.org/archives/cat_vra_renewal_guest_blogging .html.

303   **"It is a sordid business"**: *League of United Latin American Citizens v. Perry*, 548 U.S. 399 (2006).

303   **"we were burned"**: Richard L. Hasen, "Roberts' Iffy Support for Voting Rights," *Los Angeles Times*, Aug. 3, 2005, citing administration documents released by the National Archives, articles.latimes.com/2005/aug/03/ opinion/oe-hasen3.

303   **Roberts was suggesting:** See Reva B. Siegel, "The Supreme Court, 2012 Term—Foreword: Equality Divided," 127 *Harvard Law Review* 1, 72–73 (2013).

303   **As various commentators:** Ibid., 52 n.254 and 75 n.382.

304   **"doctrine of one last"**: Richard M. Re, "The Doctrine of One Last Chance," 17 *Green Bag* 2d 173 (2014).

305   **"moonshining-est"**: Robert H. Brown, "One of Biggest Moonshin- ing Districts in the Nation," *Herald-Journal* (Spartanburg, S.C.), Apr. 9, 1935, reprinted in Donna R. Causey, *Alabama Pioneers*, vol. 1 (2011), alabamapioneers.com/shelby-county-once-had-the-reputation-as-being -the-moonshingest-county-in-the-state-of-alabama/.

305   **As it turned out:** The $250,000 was an interesting figure. It represented what Blum's organization said it paid the lawyers. But the lawyers later asked for $2 million in reimbursement from the federal government. A court denied any reimbursement. See *Shelby County v. Lynch*, No. 14-5138 (D.C. Cir. 2015). The two figures represented the difference between how lawyers valued their time and what they were actually paid.

307   **"using phony statistics"**: Akilah Johnson, "Massachusetts Official Chal- lenges Chief Justice Roberts' Claim About Voting," *Boston Globe*, Feb. 28, 2013, boston.com/news/local-news/2013/02/28/massachusetts-official -challenges-chief-justice-roberts-claim-about-voting. For examples of how the Court sometimes gets its facts wrong, see also Ryan Gabrielson, "It's a Fact: Supreme Court Errors Aren't Hard to Find," *ProPublica*, Oct. 17, 2017, propublica.org/article/supreme-court-errors-are-not-hard-to-find.

310   **"equality of states"**: *South Carolina v. Katzenbach*, 383 U.S. 301, 328–29 (1966). The assertion of equal terms for admission wasn't quite so. Utah was granted statehood in 1896 only on the condition that a ban on po- lygamy be put in the state constitution. See Article III of the Utah State Constitution and Justice Scalia's dissent in *Romer v. Evans,* 517 U.S. at 648, for a discussion of the conditions for Utah statehood.

310   **"of which I had never"**: Richard A. Posner, "Supreme Court 2013: The Year in Review," *Slate*, June 26, 2013, slate.com/articles/news_ and_politics/the_breakfast_table/features/2013/supreme_court_2013/ the_supreme_court_and_the_voting_rights_act_striking_down_the_ law_is_all.html.

311   **If Alabama still:** See Eric Posner, "Supreme Court 2013: The Year in Review," *Slate*, June 26, 2013, slate.com/articles/news_and_politics/

the_breakfast_table/features/2013/supreme_court_2013/supreme_court_ on_the_voting_rights_act_chief_justice_john_roberts_struck.html. Eric Posner is the son of Richard Posner.

312 **"like throwing away your":** See Ellen D. Katz, "Justice Ginsburg's Umbrella," in Samuel R. Bagenstos, ed., *A Nation of Widening Opportunities: The Civil Rights Act at 50* (Ann Arbor: Michigan Publishing, 2015).

313 **"target African Americans":** *North Carolina State Conference of the NAACP v. McCrory,* 831 F.3d 204 (4th Cir. 2016).

314 **"It's a serious problem":** "Justice Anthony Kennedy Notes Power Shift," *Associated Press,* Mar. 7, 2013, sfgate.com/politics/article/Justice-Anthony -Kennedy-notes-power-shift-4337821.php.

314 **"This is Anthony Kennedy's country":** Richard H. Fallon Jr., *The Dynamic Constitution: An Introduction to American Constitutional Law and Practice,* 2d ed. (New York: Cambridge University Press, 2013), xxv. See also, for example, Michael Brendan Dougherty, "Anthony Kennedy Can't Be Allowed to Die," *National Review,* Jan. 23, 2018, nationalreview.com /article/455683/anthony-kennedy-swing-vote-supreme-court-we-need-him -alive?utm_source=newsletter&utm_medium=email&utm_campaign =politics-daily-newsletter&utm_content=20180123&silverid=MzEwMT kwMTU5MTQxS0.

CHAPTER 15: ROE BY ANY OTHER NAME?

315 **"Well, Harry, I didn't learn":** Woodward & Armstrong, *The Brethren,* 235.

315 **"You don't say":** Fred Barbash, "Blackmun's Papers Shine Light into Court," *Washington Post,* Mar. 5, 2005, A1.

316 **When the Warren Court:** *Poe v. Ullman,* 367 U.S. 497 (1961).

316 **Ten years later:** *Doe v. Commonwealth's Attorney of Richmond,* 425 U.S. 901 (1976).

316 **Another decade passed:** *Bowers v. Hardwick,* 478 U.S. 186 (1986).

317 ***Bowers* involved:** Joyce Murdoch & Deb Price, *Courting Justice: Gay Men and Lesbians v. the Supreme Court* (New York: Basic Books, 2002), 284; Stern & Wermiel, *Justice Brennan,* 497–98.

317 **"Sexual activity":** John C. Jeffries Jr., *Lewis F. Powell Jr.: A Biography* (New York: Fordham University Press, 2001), 521.

318 **"Yes":** Ibid.

318 **"I don't believe":** Ibid.

318 **Powell had as clerks 18:** Murdoch & Price, *Courting Justice,* 23.

318 **"4½ to 4½":** Jeffries, *Lewis Powell Jr.,* 524, quoting Powell's notes in the margin of a memo Stevens had sent him.

318 **So it:** Many scholars observed it was White's opinion that was facetious. Among other things, they said, he got even the basic history of sodomy wrong by suggesting that homosexuality had long been associated with it.

See, for example, Richard A. Posner, *Sex and Reason* (Cambridge, Mass.: Harvard University Press, 1992), 343.

318   **"dispatched the issue"**: Jeffries, *Lewis Powell Jr.*, 525.

319   **He slyly took that quote:** The case was *Paris Adult Theatre I v. Slaton*, 413 U.S. 49, 63 (1973).

319   **Gay rights groups:** For a list of some, see Earl M. Matz, "The Prospects for a Revival of Conservative Activism in Constitutional Jurisprudence," 24 *Georgia Law Review* 629, 645 (1990).

319   **"preposterous and contradictory"**: "The Right to Be Left Alone" (editorial), *Boston Globe*, July 1, 1986, 18.

319   **"stunningly harsh and dismissive"**: Garrow, *Liberty and Sexuality*, 666.

319   **As time went by:** See William N. Eskridge Jr., *Dishonorable Passions: Sodomy Laws in America, 1861–2003* (New York: Penguin, 2008), 263.

319   **"I think I probably"**: Anand Agneshwar, "Ex-Justice Says He May Have Been Wrong," *National Law Journal*, Nov. 5, 1990, 3.

319   **That set the stage:** On the bench, Kennedy's views were hardly enlightened. Eight months after becoming a lower-court judge, Kennedy participated in a little-noticed gay rights case, involving a federal employee in Seattle who claimed he was fired because he was gay. Though Kennedy didn't write the opinion, he did sign on to it. In dismissing the employee's claim, the opinion discussed the employee's "immoral and notoriously disgraceful conduct," and that he "openly and publicly flaunted his homosexual way of life." Kennedy and the other judges said they were following precedent. *Singer v. U.S. Civil Service Commission*, 530 F.2d 247 (9th Cir. 1976).

320   **Popular culture:** Opinion polls showed widespread disapproval of laws that criminalized homosexual sodomy. Eskridge, *Dishonorable Passions*, 268–69.

320   **"Ellen effect"**: The phrase was coined by Kris Franklin in "The Rhetorics of Legal Authority: Constructing Authoritativeness, the 'Ellen Effect,' and the Example of Sodomy Law," 33 *Rutgers Law Journal* 49 (2001).

321   **"fundamental right to participate"**: *Evans v. Romer*, 854 P.2d 1270, 1282 (Colo. 1993).

323   **"one-way ratchet"**: See, for example, Akhil Reed Amar, "Attainder and Amendment 2: Romer's Rightness," 95 *Michigan Law Review* 203, 206 (1996).

324   **"everyone else"**: Akhil Reed Amar, *The Law of the Land: A Grand Tour of Our Constitutional Republic* (New York: Basic Books, 2015), 93.

325   **Both details:** Dale Carpenter, *Flagrant Conduct: The Story of Lawrence v. Texas* (New York: W.W. Norton, 2012), 63, 114.

325   **"pharmacological impairment"**: See Brian Rogers & Peggy O'Hare, "Rosenthal Cites Prescription Drugs in Resignation as DA," *Houston Chronicle*, Feb. 15, 2008, chron.com/news/houston-texas/article/Rosenthal-cites-prescription-drugs-in-resignation-1600712.php, and Monica Rhor, "Ex–Houston Prosecutor Avoids Charges over Emails,"

Associated Press, Dec. 2, 2008, sandiegouniontribune.com/sdut-texas
-prosecutors-downfall-120208-2008dec02-story,amp.html.

325   **The visitors' pews:** Eskridge, *Dishonorable Passions*, 323.

325   **The lawyer for the two men:** Carpenter, *Flagrant Conduct*, 212.

327   **"straight answer":** Eskridge, *Dishonorable Passions*, 324.

330   **"counter-clerk":** Gil Seinfeld, "The Good, the Bad, and the Ugly: Reflections of a Counter-Clerk," 114 *Michigan Law Review First Impressions* 111 (2016).

330   **"What would have happened":** Ian Samuel, "The Counter-Clerks of Justice Scalia," 10 *New York University Journal of Law & Liberty* 1 (2016).

331   **In 1971:** *Baker v. Nelson*, 291 Minn. 310 (1971).

331   **Phyllis Schlafly:** "ERA and Homosexual 'Marriages,'" *Phyllis Schlafly Report*, Sept. 1974, eagleforum.org/publications/psr/sept1974.html#
.WbiVI6Pamng.mailto.

331   **"Legalizing gay":** Andrew Sullivan, "Here Comes the Groom: A (Conservative) Case for Gay Marriage," *New Republic*, Aug. 28, 1989, newrepublic.com/article/79054/here-comes-the-groom.

331   **"compelling state interest":** *Baehr v. Lewin*, 74 Haw. 645 (1993). See also Garrow, *Liberty and Sexuality*, 725–26.

331   **39 states:** See, for example, Jill Pellettieri, "Explainer: FAQ: Gay Marriage," *Slate*, Feb. 27, 2004, slate.com/articles/news_and_politics/
explainer/2004/02/faq_gay_marriage.html.

332   **"Whether and whom to marry":** *Goodridge v. Department of Public Health*, 440 Mass. 309 (2003).

332   **Massachusetts thus became:** The other jurisdictions were British Columbia and Ontario in Canada, as well as Belgium and the Netherlands. See Michael J. Klarman, *From the Closet to the Altar: Courts, Backlash, and the Struggle for Same-Sex Marriage* (New York: Oxford University Press, 2013), 90.

332   **The ruling was a watershed:** Ibid., 91.

332   **Public opinion yo-yoed:** Tribe & Matz, *Uncertain Justice*, 46.

333   **Windsor sued:** See Ariel Levy, "The Perfect Wife: How Edith Windsor Fell in Love, Got Married, and Won a Landmark Case for Gay Marriage," *New Yorker*, Sept. 30, 2013, 54; Robert D. McFadden, "Edith Windsor, 88, Marriage Equality Plaintiff, Dies," *New York Times*, Sept. 13, 2017, A1; Jo Becker, *Forcing the Spring: Inside the Fight for Marriage Equality* (New York: Penguin Press, 2014), 253–55; and "Brief on the Merits for Respondent Edith Schlain Windsor," *Supreme Court of the United States*, Feb. 26, 2013, americanbar.org/content/dam/aba/publications/supreme
_court_preview/briefs-v2/12-307_resp_merits.authcheckdam.pdf.

333   **They said their lawsuit:** Jesse McKinley, "Bush v. Gore Foes Join to Fight California Gay Marriage Ban," *New York Times*, May 27, 2009, A1.

333   **The U.S. Supreme Court:** *Hollingsworth v. Perry*, 133 S. Ct. 2652 (2013).

335   ***Windsor*'s verdict:** Some scholars think otherwise. See, for example, Heather K. Gerken, "Windsor's Mad Genius: The Interlocking Gears of Rights and Structure," *Yale Faculty Scholarship Series*, Paper 4892 (2015), digitalcommons.law.yale.edu/fss_papers/4892.

337   **"It takes inexplicable":** *Conde-Vidal v. Garcia-Padilla*, 54 F. Supp. 3d 157, 166 (2014). The judge in the case upheld Puerto Rico's ban on same-sex marriage. Later, after *Obergefell*, he refused to reverse himself, leading a federal appeals court to remove him from the case. But his insubordination didn't render his initial observation invalid.

337   **right after *Lawrence*:** "Marriage," 1996–present, *Gallup News*, news.gallup.com/poll/117328/marriage.aspx.

338   **"When the courts do not":** *DeBoer v. Snyder*, 772 F.3d 388, 421 (2014).

338   **They started camping out:** Dahlia Lithwick & Mark Joseph Stern, "Not All Must Rise," *Slate*, Apr. 27, 2015, slate.com/articles/news_and_politics/jurisprudence/2015/04/standing_in_line_for_supreme_court_gay_marriage_arguments_draw_crowd_days.html.

338   **the audience included:** Mark A. Walsh, "A View from the Courtroom: Same-Sex Marriage Edition," *SCOTUSblog*, Apr. 28, 2015, scotusblog.com/2015/04/a-view-from-the-courtroom-same-sex-marriage-edition/.

339   **But the justices could have:** *Naim v. Naim*, 197 Va. 734, *appeal dismissed*, 350 U.S. 985 (1956).

339   **"one bombshell":** Rosenberg, *Hollow Hope*, 81. Other sources attribute the quote to Justice Tom C. Clark. See also Klarman, *From Jim Crow to Civil Rights*, 321–23.

340   **Judges should be:** See, for example, "Principles of Judicial Engagement," *Institute for Justice*, ij.org/center-for-judicial-engagement/programs/principles-of-judicial-engagement/.

342   **"However heartened":** Roberts's legal position seemed unrelated to his personal views. In 1996, he donated his time to assist lawyers for gay activists preparing to argue *Romer v. Evans*. In a moot court session, he played the part of Justice Scalia. Roberts's name doesn't appear on any of the legal papers. His work came to light in a newspaper article when he was nominated to the Court. Such pro bono work is voluntary. Richard A. Serrano, "Roberts Donated Help to Gay Rights Case," *Los Angeles Times*, Aug. 4, 2005, A1.

345   **"biting off more than":** Ginsburg made the "more than it could chew" comment in 2009 at Princeton. Adam Liptak, "In Battle over Marriage, the Timing May Be Key," *New York Times*, Oct. 27, 2009, A14.

345   **"the marvelous mystery":** Bickel, *Least Dangerous Branch*, 26.

345   **"Justice is not":** She was quoting Justice Benjamin Cardozo, who made the remark in 1923, when he was serving on New York's highest court.

346   **"If people don't care":** Ginsburg was at the University of Chicago. "Justice Ruth Bader Ginsburg and Geoffrey Stone: *Roe* at 40," *YouTube*, May 11, 2013, youtube.com/watch?v=xw3CMRyvkq4.

346   **"the best decision":** Cass R. Sunstein, *One Case at a Time: Judicial Mini-malism on the Supreme Court* (Cambridge, Mass.: Harvard University Press, 1999), 263.

346   **In the four:** For a state-by-state map of pre-*Obergefell* law, see "The Changing Landscape of Same-Sex Marriage," *Washington Post*, June 26, 2015, washingtonpost.com/wp-srv/special/politics/same-sex-marriage/.

347   **Sometimes a split:** See, for example, Diane P. Wood, "Is It Time to Abolish the Federal Circuit's Exclusive Jurisdiction in Patent Cases?" 13 *Chicago-Kent Journal of Intellectual Property* 1, 5–6 (2013).

347   **"Wise adjudication":** *Maryland v. Baltimore Radio Show*, 338 U.S. 912, 918 (1950).

EPILOGUE: A LESS DANGEROUS BRANCH

349   **As the decisive vote:** *National Federation of Independent Business v. Sebelius*, 567 U.S. 519 (2012).

350   **"Everybody has to buy":** For enriching histories of the broccoli analogy, see Mark D. Rosen & Christopher W. Schmidt, "Why Broccoli? Limiting Principles and Popular Constitutionalism in the Health Care Case," 61 *UCLA Law Review* 66, 100–10 (2013), and James B. Stewart, "How Broccoli Landed on Supreme Court Menu," *New York Times*, June 14, 2012, A1.

353   **The custom:** Del Dickson, ed., *The Supreme Court in Conference (1940–1985): The Private Discussions Behind Nearly 300 Supreme Court Decisions* (New York: Oxford University Press, 2001), 5.

354   **One scholar:** The scholar was Akhil Reed Amar, quoted in Ezra Klein, "The Political Genius of John Roberts," *Washington Post*, June 28, 2012, washingtonpost.com/news/wonk/wp/2012/06/28/the-political-genius-of-john-roberts/. See also Karlan, *Democracy and Disdain*, 50.

355   **"Context matters":** Stephen Jay Gould, "The Strike That Was Low and Outside," *New York Times*, Nov. 10, 1984, 23.

356   **These resentments:** Roberts's switch was first reported by CBS News days after the ruling. Jan Crawford, "Roberts Switched Views to Uphold Health Care Law," *CBS News*, July 2, 2012, cbsnews.com/news/roberts-switched-views-to-uphold-health-care-law/. See also Paul Campos, "Roberts Wrote Both Obamacare Opinions," *Salon*, July 3, 2012, salon.com/2012/07/03/roberts_wrote_both_obamacare_opinions/.

356   **"Malta, as you know":** Adam Liptak, "After Ruling, Roberts Makes a Getaway from the Scorn," *New York Times*, July 2, 2012, A10.

356   **Such finger-pointing:** George F. Will, "A Liberal Squeeze Play," *Washington Post*, May 27, 2012, A27. See also, for example, Orin Kerr, "More on the Supreme Court Leak," *Volokh Conspiracy*, July 3, 2012, volokh.com/2012/07/03/more-on-the-supreme-court-leak/, and the remarks quoted there from Ramesh Ponnuru, which are available in full in a podcast at *Princeton Alumni Weekly*, June 2, 2012, princeton.edu/paw/ROXEN/av_files/pawlitics_podcast.mp3. For a discussion of Court leaks

generally and the guessing game associated with the putative leaks on the Obamacare ruling, see Sam Baker, "Supreme Court Healthcare Ruling Leaks Have D.C. Buzzing: Who Is the Culprit?" *The Hill*, July 4, 2012, thehill.com/policy/healthcare/236197-supreme-court-talk-has-dc-buzzing -who-is-the-leaker.

356   **working the ref:** Kathleen Parker, "Democrats Put John Roberts on Trial," *Washington Post*, May 23, 2012, A21. See also Mark Tushnet, "Reasons for Thinking That Law Mattered," *Balkinization*, July 3, 2012, balkin.blogspot.com/2012/07/reasons-for-thinking-that-law-mattered.html.

357   **"broccoli horrible":** One New York writer spoke up in broccoli's defense: Adam Gopnik, " 'The Broccoli Horrible': A Culinary-Legal Dissent," *New Yorker*, June 28, 2012, newyorker.com/news/news-desk/the-broccoli -horrible-a-culinary-legal-dissent.

357   **"If it's not necessary":** "Georgetown University Law Center Commence-1ment Address," *C-SPAN*, May 21, 2006.

358   **"in the delightful position":** Robert G. McCloskey, *The American Supreme Court* (Chicago: University of Chicago Press, 1960), 42.

358   **"a masterwork of misdirection":** Ibid., 40. See also, for example, Daniel Epps, "In Health Care Ruling, Roberts Steals a Move from John Marshall's Playbook," *Atlantic*, June 28, 2012, theatlantic.com/national/ archive/2012/06/in-health-care-ruling-roberts-steals-a-move-from-john -marshalls-playbook/259121/.

359   **Roberts declined:** In *King v. Burwell*, 135 S. Ct. 475 (2015), the Court upheld Obamacare on statutory rather than constitutional grounds. The issue involved sloppy wording in the ACA that opponents claimed had to be interpreted literally, even if the result was ridiculous. Roberts, for a 6-to-3 majority, found that the statute's overall "context and structure" took precedence. "Congress passed the Affordable Care Act to improve health insurance markets, not to destroy them," he wrote.

360   **"The rightful liberties":** Randy Barnett, " 'Judicial Engagement' Is Not the Same as 'Judicial Activism,' " *Washington Post*, Jan. 28, 2014, washingtonpost.com/news/volokh-conspiracy/wp/2014/01/28/judicial -engagement-is-not-the-same-as-judicial-activism/. See also George F. Will, "Why Conservatives Need Judicial Activism," *Washington Post*, Jan. 23, 2014, A17. For an earlier variant of these themes, not mentioning judicial engagement, see Randy Barnett, "Restoring the Lost Constitution, Not the Constitution in Exile," 75 *Fordham Law Review* 669 (2006).

361   **The chief proponent:** "Merry Band of Litigators Celebrates 20 Years," *Institute for Justice*, ij.org/news/merry-band-of-litigators-celebrates-20-years/.

361   **"fully enforce":** "A Brief History of Fake Judging," *Institute for Justice*, ij.org/center-for-judicial-engagement/programs/a-brief-history-of-fake -judging/.

361   **In the age:** See, for example, "Economic Liberty," *Institute for Justice*, ij.org/pillar/first-amendment/?post_type=case; "Private Property," *Institute for Justice*, ij.org/pillar/private-property/?post_type=case; and "First Amendment," *Institute for Justice*, ij.org/pillar/first-amendment/?post_ type=case.

362 **the chief's instinct:** Roberts's scrupulous concern for the Court's prestige—and authority—was fully voiced in a little-noticed dissent in early 2018. The chief believed that Congress had overstepped its bounds in effectively dismissing a lawsuit brought by a litigant. While Congress does control much of the jurisdiction of the federal courts, Roberts argued that Congress wasn't allowed to be choosing winners and losers in individual cases. *Patchak v. Zinke*, No. 16-498 (2018).

362 **On the one hand:** *Trump v. Hawaii*, No. 17-965 (2018) (travel ban); *Gill v. Whitford*, No. 16-1161 (2018) and *Benisek v. Lamone*, No. 17-333 (2018) (partisan gerrymandering); *Abbott v. Perez*, No. 17-586 and 17-626 (2018) (racial gerrymandering in Texas); *South Dakota v. Wayfair*, No. 17-494 (2018) (Internet sales tax); and *Husted v. A. Philip Randolph Institute*, No. 16-980 (2018) (purging voting rolls).

362 **on the other hand:** *Masterpiece Cakeshop v. Colorado Civil Rights Commission*, No. 16-111 (2018) (discrimination based on sexual orientation); *National Institute of Family and Life Advocates v. Becerra*, No. 16-1140 (2018) (information about abortion); and *Janus v. AFSCME*, No. 16-1466 (2018) (public labor unions), overruling *Abood v. Detroit Board of Education*, 431 U.S. 209 (1977). See also *Arlene's Flowers v. Washington*, No. 17-108 (2018), in which the Court mystifyingly declined to face exactly the question presented in *Masterpiece Cakeshop* but in which the odd facts of *Masterpiece Cakeshop* didn't exist.

363 **thumbs-up:** *Trump v. Hawaii*, No. 17-965 (2018) (travel ban); *Gill v. Whitford*, No. 16-1161 (2018) and *Benisek v. Lamone*, No. 17-333 (2018) (political parties); *Masterpiece Cakeshop v. Colorado Civil Rights Commission*, No. 16-111 (2018) (religious freedom); and *National Institute of Family and Life Advocates v. Becerra*, No. 16-1140 (2018) (medical interests of pregnant women).

363 **thumbs-down:** *Trump v. Hawaii*, No. 17-965 (2018) (travel ban); *Gill v. Whitford*, No. 16-1161 (2018) and *Benisek v. Lamone*, No. 17-333 (2018) (reapportionment); *Husted v. A. Philip Randolph Institute*, No. 16-980 (2018) (minority voting); *Abbott v. Perez*, No. 17-586 and 17-626 (2018) (racial gerrymandering); and *Janus v. AFSCME*, No. 16-1466 (2018) (public labor unions).

363 **That last decision:** *Janus v. AFSCME*, overruling *Abood v. Detroit Board of Education*, 431 U.S. 209 (1977).

364 **not allowed to say:** See, for example, *Garcetti v. Ceballos*, 547 U.S. 410 (2006).

366 **straddling the problem:** In *Vieth v. Jubelirer*, 541 U.S. 267 (2004), a case declining to curb partisan gerrymandering in Pennsylvania, Kennedy wrote a lone concurrence that held out the alternative possibility if a workable judicial standard could be found.

366 **In a case from:** *Minnesota Voters Alliance v. Mansky*, No. 16-1435 (2018).

368 **Only 34 percent of its rulings:** Adam Liptak & Alicia Parlapiano, "Conservatives in Charge, the Supreme Court Moved Right," *New York Times,* June 28, 2018, nytimes.com/interactive/2018/06/28/us/politics/supreme-court-2017-term-moved-right.html.

369   **The best of these ideas:** See, for example, Lee Drutman, "The Case for Supreme Court Term Limits Has Never Been Stronger," *Vox*, Jan. 21, 2017, vox.com/policy-and-politics/2017/1/31/14463724/case-for-supreme-court-term-limits; Norm Ornstein, "Why the Supreme Court Needs Term Limits," *Atlantic*, May 22, 2014, theatlantic.com/politics/archive/2014/05/its-time-for-term-limits-for-the-supreme-court/371415/; Stuart Taylor Jr., "Life Tenure Is Too Long for Supreme Court Justices," *Atlantic*, June 2005, theatlantic.com/magazine/archive/2005/06/life-tenure-is-too-long-for-supreme-court-justices/304134/; and "Term Limits," *Fix the Court*, fixthecourt.com/fix/term-limits/.

369   **"the nation's premier":** Richard A. Posner, *Aging and Old Age* (Chicago: University of Chicago Press, 1995), 180.

369   **When the Framers:** See, for example, Steven G. Calabresi & James Lindgren, "Term Limits for the Supreme Court: Life Tenure Reconsidered," 29 *Harvard Journal of Law & Public Policy* 769, 788 (2006).

369   **When he was a lawyer:** John M. Broder & Carolyn Marshall, "White House Memos Offer Opinions on Supreme Court," *New York Times*, July 30, 2005, A11.

369   **So, too, would be:** See Joshua D. Hawley, "The Most Dangerous Branch," *National Affairs*, Fall 2012, nationalaffairs.com/publications/detail/the-most-dangerous-branch. Hawley clerked for Chief Justice Roberts and later was elected attorney general of Missouri.

370   **"If my fellow citizens":** Holmes to Harold Laski, Mar. 4, 1920, quoted in Richard A. Posner, *The Problems of Jurisprudence* (Cambridge, Mass.: Harvard University Press, 1993), 222.

AFTERWORD TO THE PAPERBACK EDITION:
THE COURT IN THE AGE OF TRUMP

371   **his nomination likely would've been rejected:** The vote to confirm Kavanaugh turned out to be 50–48. Republican Lisa Murkowski abstained, as a courtesy to Republican senator Steve Daines, who was attending his oldest daughter's wedding. Otherwise Murkowski would have voted no and Daines would have voted yes. Net result: 51–49, for Kavanaugh. Had Collins gone the other way, the vote would've been 50–50, and Vice President Mike Pence would have cast the tie-breaker for Kavanaugh. But if Collins had gone the other way, Democrat Joe Manchin no longer would have voted no. He had voted yes only because his vote didn't matter at that point, and he sought cover in his close reelection campaign in conservative West Virginia.

372   **Stevens soon thereafter:** "Retired Justice John Paul Stevens on Judge Kavanaugh," *C-SPAN*, Oct. 4, 2018, youtube.com/watch?v=PkgR50q5-L0&feature=youtu.be. (Stevens died the following July, at 99.)

372   **Two days later:** Other successful nominees have gone to the White House after being confirmed. Like Kavanaugh, Neil Gorsuch had his unofficial

swearing-in there. Sonia Sotomayor and Elena Kagan were present for brief presidential speeches and receptions—Sotomayor after she was sworn in, and Kagan before. But none of the events for Gorsuch, Sotomayor, or Kagan took on the air of a campaign event. Kavanaugh's participation thrilled the president, but did no favor for the Court's image.

374 **A few weeks after:** "Justice Kagan Remarks at Georgetown University Law Center," *C-SPAN*, July 18, 2019, c-span.org/video/?462748-1/justice -kagan-remarks-georgetown-university-law-center&start=2556.

375 **The case was:** *Rucho v. Common Cause*, No. 18-422 (2019), decided with *Lamone v.Benisek*, No. 18-726 (2019).

376 **on the same day:** *Department of Commerce v. New York*, No. 18-966 (2019).

377 **when it came to:** The best of the experts explained such standards in an amicus curiae brief filed by Eric Lander, a mathematician and geneticist at MIT. An expert on analyzing large datasets (and merci-fully not a lawyer), he was a principal mapper on the Human Genome Project. The Lander brief is available at supremecourt.gov/DocketPDF/ 18/18-422/91120/20190307163214118_18-422%20Brief%20for%20 Amicus%20Curiae%20Eric%20S.%20Lander.pdf.

378 **The chief's suggestion:** The case on independent commissions was *Arizona State Legislature v. Arizona Independent Redistricting Commission*, 135 S. Ct. 2652 (2015).

379 **On First Amendment grounds:** *Iancu v. Brunetti*, No. 18-302 (2019).

379 **It allowed a 32-foot cross:** *American Legion v. American Humanist Asso-ciation*, No. 17-1717 (2019).

379 **In criminal law:** *Gamble v. United States*, No. 17-646 (2019).

379 **And the justices decided:** *Apple v. Pepper*, No. 17-204 (2019).

379 **Kavanaugh voted with Gorsuch:** Adam Liptak & Alicia Parlapiano, "A Term Marked by Shifting Alliances and Surprise Votes," *New York Times*, June 30, 2019, A26.

380 **just one vote:** *Kisor v. Wilkie*, No. 18-15 (2019). The two cases the Court declined to overrule were *Auer v. Robbins*, 519 U.S. 452 (1997) and *Bowles v. Seminole Rock & Sand Co.*, 325 U.S. 410 (1945). *Chevron v. Natural Resources Defense Council*, 467 U.S. 837 (1984), also long on the conser-vatives' hit list as a ruling that gave too much power to federal agencies, was mentioned only briefly in *Kisor*—its demise, like that of *Auer* and *Seminole Rock*, awaits another day. See Chapter 2, 41–44. See also *Gundy v. United States*, No. 17-6086 (2019), declining, in the context of the Sex Offender Registration and Notification Act, to address just how much au-thority Congress can delegate to the executive branch.

380 **Energized by Kavanaugh's replacement:** K. K. Rebecca Lai, "Abortion Bans: 9 States Have Passed Bills to Limit the Procedure This Year," *New York Times*, May 29, 2019, nytimes.com/interactive/2019/us/abortion -laws-states.html.

380 **In one case:** *Box v. Planned Parenthood*, No. 18-483 (2019).

380 **In the other case:** *June Medical Services v. Gee*, No. 18A774 (2019).

380 **Whether the conservative justices:** The Louisiana case could also spell the end of *Whole Woman's Health v. Hellerstedt*, decided in 2016. That unexpected ruling struck down a Texas statute, H.B. 2, which placed two strict limitations on abortion providers. Kennedy joined the majority, the first time in 24 years he had voted to invalidate an abortion restriction. Kavanaugh could go the other way.

381 **"It is one thing":** *Franchise Tax Board of California v. Hyatt*, No. 17-1299 (2019), overruling *Nevada v. Hall*, 440 U.S. 410 (1979).

382 **Mainstream Democrats:** See, for example, Carl Hulse, "A Modest Proposal Not All Are Swift to Embrace," *New York Times*, March 28, 2019, A19; Burgess Everett & Marianne Levine, "2020 Dems Warm to Expanding Supreme Court," *Politico*, March 18, 2019, politico.com/story/2019/03/18/2020-democrats-supreme-court-1223625; and Russell Wheeler, "Pack the Court? Putting a Popular Imprint on the Federal Judiciary," *Brookings*, Apr. 3, 2019, brookings.edu/blog/fixgov/2019/04/03/pack-the-court-putting-a-popular-imprint-on-the-federal-judiciary/. See also the websites of Take Back the Court and Demand Justice, organizations urging Democrats to add seats to the Court: takebackthecourt.today/ and actionnetwork.org/groups/demandjustice.

383 **"not unlike Argentina":** Steven Levitsky & Daniel Ziblatt, *How Democracies Die* (New York: Crown, 2018), 118–19 and 130–33.

384 **It's the classic prisoner's dilemma:** See, for example, Samarth Desai, "The Senator's Dilemma: Game Theory, Gorsuch, and the Nuclear Option," *Harvard Political Review*, April 8, 2017, harvardpolitics.com/united-states/senators-dilemma-game-theory-gorsuch-nuclear-option/.

CASES

Gill v. Whitford, No. 16-1161 (2018)

Gonzales v. Carhart, 550 U.S. 124 (2007)

Gonzales v. Raich, 545 U.S. 1 (2005)

Goodridge v. Department of Public Health, 440 Mass. 309 (2003)

Gratz v. Bollinger, 539 U.S. 244 (2003)

Griswold v. Connecticut, 381 U.S. 479 (1965)

Grutter v. Bollinger, 539 U.S. 306 (2003)

Gundy v. United States, No. 17-6086 (2019)

Gutierrez-Brizuela v. Lynch, 834 F.3d 1142 (10th Cir. 2016)

Hamdan v. Rumsfeld, 548 U.S. 557 (2006)

Hamdi v. Rumsfeld, 542 U.S. 507 (2004)

Harris v. McRae, 448 U.S. 297 (1980)

Hicks v. United States, 137 S. Ct. 2000 (2017)

Hollingsworth v. Perry, 133 S. Ct. 2652 (2013)

Husted v. A. Philip Randolph Institute, No. 16-980 (2018)

Iancu v. Brunetti, No. 18-302 (2019)

Jacobs v. Seminole County Canvassing Board, 773 So.2d 519 (Fla. 2000)

Janus v. AFSCME, No. 16-1466 (2018)

June Medical Services v. Gee, No. 18A774 (2019)

King v. Burwell, 135 S. Ct. 475 (2015)

Kisor v. Wilkie, No. 18-15 (2019)

Korematsu v. United States, 323 U.S. 214 (1944)

Lamone v. Benisek, No. 18-726 (2019)

Lawrence v. Texas, 539 U.S. 558 (2003)

League of United Latin American Citizens v. Perry, 548 U.S. 399 (2006)

Lochner v. New York, 198 U.S. 45 (1905)

Loving v. Virginia, 388 U.S. 1 (1967)

Lynch v. Household Finance, 405 U.S. 538 (1972)

Marbury v. Madison, 5 U.S. 137 (1803)

Martin v. Hunter's Lessee, 14 U.S. 304 (1816)

Maryland v. Baltimore Radio Show, 338 U.S. 912 (1950)

Masterpiece Cakeshop v. Colorado Civil Rights Commission, No. 16-111 (2018)

McConnell v. Federal Election Commission, 540 U.S. 93 (2003)

McCulloch v. Maryland, 17 U.S. 316 (1819)

McDonald v. Chicago, 561 U.S. 742 (2010)

Meyer v. Nebraska, 262 U.S. 390 (1923)

Minnesota Voters Alliance v. Mansky, No. 16-1435 (2018)

Miranda v. Arizona, 384 U.S. 436 (1964)

Missouri v. Jenkins, 515 U.S. 70 (1995)

Naim v. Naim, 197 Va. 734, *appeal dismissed,* 350 U.S. 985 (1956)

National Federation of Independent Business v. Sebelius, 567 U.S. 519 (2012)

National Institute of Family and Life Advocates v. Becerra, No. 16-1140 (2018)

Nevada v. Hall, 440 U.S. 410 (1979)

New York Times v. Sullivan, 376 U.S. 254 (1964)

New York Times v. United States, 403 U.S. 713 (1971)

North Carolina State Conference of the NAACP v. McCrory, 831 F.3d 204 (4th Cir. 2016)

Northwest Austin Municipal Utility District No. 1 v. Holder, 557 U.S. 193 (2009)

Obergefell v. Hodges, 135 S. Ct. 2584 (2015)

Olmstead v. United States, 277 U.S. 438 (1928)

Pacific Bell Telephone Co. v. linkLine Communications, 555 U.S. 438 (2009)

Palm Beach County Canvassing Board v. Harris, 772 So.2d 1273 (Fla. 2000)

Parents Involved in Community Schools v. Seattle School District No. 1, 551 U.S. 701 (2007)

Parents Involved in Community Schools v. Seattle School District No. 1, 426 F.3d 1162 (9th Cir. 2005)

Paris Adult Theatre I v. Slaton, 413 U.S. 49 (1973)

Parker v. District of Columbia, 311 F. Supp. 2d 101 (D.D.C. 2004)

Parker v. District of Columbia, 478 F.3d 370, 378 (D.C. Cir. 2007)

Patchak v. Zinke, No. 16-498 (2018)

Pavan v. Smith, 137 S. Ct. 2075 (2017)

Perry v. Merit Systems Protection Board, 137 S. Ct. 1975 (2017)

Peruta v. California, 137 S. Ct. 1995 (2017)

Pierce v. Society of Sisters, 268 U.S. 510 (1925)

Trump v. Hawaii, No. 17-965 (2018)

Trump v. International Refugee Assistance Project, 137 S. Ct. 2210 (2017)

United States v. Carolene Products Co., 304 U.S. 144 (1938)

United States v. Emerson, 270 F.3d 203 (5th Cir. 2001), *cert denied*, 536 U.S. 907 (2002)

United States v. Gaubert, 499 U.S. 315 (1991)

United States v. Lopez, 514 U.S. 549 (1995)

United States v. Miller, 307 U.S. 174 (1939)

United States v. Morrison, 529 U.S. 598 (2000)

United States v. Nixon, 418 U.S. 683 (1974)

United States v. Takhalov, 827 F.3d 1307 (11th Cir. 2016)

United States v. Virginia, 518 U.S. 515 (1996)

United States v. Vuitch, 402 U.S. 62 (1971)

United States v. Windsor, 133 S. Ct. 2675 (2013)

Utah v. Strieff, 136 S. Ct. 2056 (2016)

Vieth v. Jubelirer, 541 U.S. 267 (2004)

West Coast Hotel Co. v. Parrish, 300 U.S. 379 (1937)

West Virginia State Board of Education v. Barnette, 319 U.S. 624 (1943)

Whole Woman's Health v. Hellerstedt, 136 S. Ct. 2292 (2016)

Worcester v. Georgia, 31 U.S. 515 (1832)

Youngstown Sheet & Tube Co. v. Sawyer, 343 U.S. 579 (1952)

For a complete bibliography, see davidakaplan.com.

PHOTO CREDITS

INDEX

Sessions, Jefferson B., III ("Jeff"),
49–50, 53
sexual harassment, 137–142
sexual orientation, 128–130, 255,
315, 320, 323–324. *See also*
homosexuality
Shelby County v. Holder (2013), 10–11,
109, 116, 130, 134, 143, 153, 155,
180, 200, 290, 292, 299–300,
303–314, 322, 329, 336, 339, 343,
359, 370, 375
Simpson, Steve, 260–261
Sims, Reynolds v. (1964), 179–180, 238,
291
Sixth Amendment, 18
"60 Minutes" (TV program), 141
Skinner v. Oklahoma (1942), 170, 182,
190–191
Slate, 310, 388
slavery, 166–168, 178, 290, 306–307,
370. *See also Dred Scott v. Sandford;
Plessy v. Ferguson*
Smith, Emmitt, 161
Smith, Paul, 325–327
Smithsonian Institution, 135
socialism, 10
Society of Sisters, Pierce v. (1925), 169
sodomy, 266, 316–318, 325–326,
328–329
Soros, Charles, 281
Sotomayor, Sonia, 10, 17, 19, 32–37,
60–62, 67, 97, 100–101, 106,
119–127, 132–133, 143, 150, 210,
279–280, 296–297, 306–308, 334,
349, 352–353, 367–368, 375, 378
Souter, David H., xii, xiii, 15, 19, 50–51,
54–55, 63, 101, 122–124, 130–132,
137, 143–147, 156, 159, 208–209,
222, 230, 233, 239, 246, 262–263,
279–280, 283, 321, 355
Spanish-American War, 251
special interest groups, 21, 256–262,
271–284, 287–288, 305, 320–321

Specter, Arlen, 69
Sporck, Franz Anton von, 3
Spyer, Thea, 332
Srinivasan, Sri, 63–64
Stanford Law School, 194, 200, 262
Stanton, Elizabeth Cady, 109
stare decisis (precedent), 15, 46, 75–76, 82,
85, 86, 91, 126, 134–135, 151, 159,
174–175, 242, 261–264, 277, 279,
283, 293, 321, 328, 376, 379–381
Starr, Kenneth, 52, 55
state autonomy, 12n, 306, 335, 338
state sovereignty, 49, 166, 258, 301–302,
307, 310–311
states' rights, 206, 220, 299
Steel Seizure Case (*Youngstown Sheet &
Tube Co. v. Sawyer*), 172, 177
Stevens, John Paul, 70–71, 101–102,
124–126, 143, 158, 168–169, 203,
222–224, 228–230, 239–241,
263–264, 278, 280–283, 295, 321,
372
Stevenson, Bryan, 127
Stewart, Jimmy, 78
Stewart, Malcolm, 278, 280
Stewart, Potter, 72
Stone, Harlan Fiske, 33, 156, 184
Story, Joseph, 160
Strauss, David, 127
strict construction, 12
Strieff, Edward, 35–36
Strieff, Utah v. (2016), 35–37, 122
Sullivan, Andrew, 331
Sullivan, New York Times v. (1964),
180–181
Sunstein, Cass, 124, 127
Sununu, John, 55
Super PACs, 280–282
*The Supreme Court and the Idea of
Progress* (Bickel), 151
Sutton, Jeffrey, 53, 338
Sykes, Diane, 54
Syria, U.S. involvement, 88

ABOUT THE AUTHOR

DAVID A. KAPLAN is the former legal affairs editor of *Newsweek*, where his coverage of the Supreme Court won many prizes. His other books include *The Silicon Boys* (a *New York Times* bestseller that has been translated into six languages); *The Accidental President* (an account of the 2000 election on which the HBO film "Recount" was partially based); and *Mine's Bigger* (a biography of the largest private sailboat in history that won the Loeb Award for Best Business Book of 2008). A graduate of Cornell and the New York University School of Law, Kaplan currently teaches courses in journalism and ethics at NYU. He lives in Irvington-on-Hudson, New York, with his wife, Audrey Feinberg. They have two sons, Joshua and Nathaniel.